White Rose Maths Edition

Year 4C
A Guide to Teaching for Mastery

Series Editor: Tony Staneff
Lead author: Josh Lury

Contents

Introduction to the author team	4
What is *Power Maths*?	5
What's different in the new edition?	6
Your *Power Maths* resources	7
The *Power Maths* teaching model	10
The *Power Maths* lesson sequence	12
Using the *Power Maths* Teacher Guide	15
Power Maths Year 4, yearly overview	16
Mindset: an introduction	20
The *Power Maths* characters	21
Mathematical language	22
The role of talk and discussion	23
Assessment strategies	24
Keeping the class together	26
Same-day intervention	27
The role of practice	28
Structures and representations	29
Variation helps visualisation	30
Practical aspects of *Power Maths*	31
Working with children below age-related expectation	33
Providing extra depth and challenge with *Power Maths*	35
Using *Power Maths* with mixed age classes	37
List of practical resources	38
Getting started with *Power Maths*	39

Unit 11 – Decimals (2) — 40
Make a whole	42
Partition decimals	46
Flexibly partition decimals	50
Compare decimals	54
Order decimals	58
Round to the nearest whole	62
Halves and quarters as decimals	66
End of unit check	70

Unit 12 – Money — 72
Write money using decimals	74
Convert between pounds and pence	78
Compare amounts of money	82
Estimate with money	86
Calculate with money	90
Solve problems with money	94
End of unit check	98

Unit 13 – Time — 100

Years, months, weeks and days	102
Hours, minutes and seconds	106
Convert between analogue and digital times	110
Convert to the 24 hour clock	114
Problem solving – convert units of time	118
End of unit check	122

Unit 14 – Geometry and 3D shapes — 124

Identify angles	126
Compare and order angles	130
Triangles	134
Quadrilaterals	138
Polygons	142
Reason about polygons	146
Lines of symmetry	150
Complete a symmetric figure	154
End of unit check	158

Unit 15 – Statistics — 160

Interpret charts	162
Solve problems with charts (1)	166
Solve problems with charts (2)	170
Interpret line graphs (1)	174
Interpret line graphs (2)	178
Draw line graphs	182
End of unit check	186

Unit 16 – Geometry – position and direction — 188

Describe position	190
Describe position using coordinates	194
Plot coordinates	198
Draw 2D shapes on a grid	202
Translate on a grid	206
Describe translation on a grid	210
End of unit check	214

Introduction to the author team

Power Maths arises from the work of maths mastery experts who are committed to proving that, given the right mastery mindset and approach, **everyone can do maths**. Based on robust research and best practice from around the world, *Power Maths* was developed in partnership with a group of UK teachers to make sure that it not only meets our children's wide-ranging needs but also aligns with the National Curriculum in England.

Power Maths – White Rose Maths edition

This edition of *Power Maths* has been developed and updated by:

Tony Staneff, Series Editor and Author

Vice Principal at Trinity Academy, Halifax, Tony also leads a team of mastery experts who help schools across the UK to develop teaching for mastery via nationally recognised CPD courses, problem-solving and reasoning resources, schemes of work, assessment materials and other tools.

Josh Lury, Lead Author

Josh is a specialist maths teacher, author and maths consultant with a passion for innovative and effective maths education.

The first edition of *Power Maths* was developed by a team of experienced authors, including:

- **Tony Staneff and Josh Lury**
- **Trinity Academy Halifax** (Michael Gosling CEO, Emily Fox, Kate Henshall, Rebecca Holland, Stephanie Kirk, Stephen Monaghan and Rachel Webster)
- **David Board, Belle Cottingham, Jonathan East, Tim Handley, Derek Huby, Neil Jarrett, Stephen Monaghan, Beth Smith, Tim Weal, Paul Wrangles** – skilled maths teachers and mastery experts
- **Cherri Moseley** – a maths author, former teacher and professional development provider
- **Professors Liu Jian and Zhang Dan**, Series Consultants and authors, and their team of mastery expert authors: **Wei Huinv, Huang Lihua, Zhu Dejiang, Zhu Yuhong, Hou Huiying, Yin Lili, Zhang Jing, Zhou Da and Liu Qimeng**

  Used by over 20 million children, Professor Liu Jian's textbook programme is one of the most popular in China. He and his author team are highly experienced in intelligent practice and in embedding key maths concepts using a C-P-A approach.

- **A group of 15 teachers and maths co-ordinators**

  We consulted our teacher group throughout the development of *Power Maths* to ensure we are meeting their real needs in the classroom.

What is *Power Maths*?

Created especially for UK primary schools, and aligned with the new National Curriculum, *Power Maths* is a whole-class, textbook-based mastery resource that empowers every child to understand and succeed. *Power Maths* rejects the notion that some people simply 'can't do' maths. Instead, it develops growth mindsets and encourages hard work, practice and a willingness to see mistakes as learning tools.

Best practice consistently shows that mastery of small, cumulative steps builds a solid foundation of deep mathematical understanding. *Power Maths* combines interactive teaching tools, high-quality textbooks and continuing professional development (CPD) to help you equip children with a deep and long-lasting understanding. Based on extensive evidence, and developed in partnership with practising teachers, *Power Maths* ensures that it meets the needs of children in the UK.

Power Maths and Mastery

Power Maths makes mastery practical and achievable by providing the structures, pathways, content, tools and support you need to make it happen in your classroom.

To develop mastery in maths, children must be enabled to acquire a deep understanding of maths concepts, structures and procedures, step by step. Complex mathematical concepts are built on simpler conceptual components and when children understand every step in the learning sequence, maths becomes transparent and makes logical sense. Interactive lessons establish deep understanding in small steps, as well as effortless fluency in key facts such as tables and number bonds. The whole class works on the same content and no child is left behind.

Power Maths

- Builds every concept in small, progressive steps
- Is built with interactive, whole-class teaching in mind
- Provides the tools you need to develop growth mindsets
- Helps you check understanding and ensure that every child is keeping up
- Establishes core elements such as intelligent practice and reflection

The *Power Maths* approach

Everyone can!
Founded on the conviction that every child can achieve, *Power Maths* enables children to build number fluency, confidence and understanding, step by step.

Child-centred learning
Children master concepts one step at a time in lessons that embrace a concrete-pictorial-abstract (C-P-A) approach, avoid overload, build on prior learning and help them see patterns and connections. Same-day intervention ensures sustained progress.

Continuing professional development
Embedded teacher support and development offer every teacher the opportunity to continually improve their subject knowledge and manage whole-class teaching for mastery.

Whole-class teaching
An interactive, whole-class teaching model encourages thinking and precise mathematical language and allows children to deepen their understanding as far as they can.

What's different in the new edition?

If you have previously used the first editions of *Power Maths*, you might be interested to know how this edition is different. All of the improvements described below are based on feedback from *Power Maths* customers.

Changes to units and the progression

- The order of units has been slightly adjusted, creating closer alignment between adjacent year groups, which will be useful for mixed age teaching.
- The flow of lessons has been improved within units to optimise the pace of the progression and build in more recap where needed. For key topics, the sequence of lessons gives more opportunities to build up a solid base of understanding. Other units have fewer lessons than before, where appropriate, making it possible to fit in all the content.
- Overall, the lessons put more focus on the most essential content for that year, with less time given to non-statutory content.
- The progression of lessons matches the steps in the new White Rose Maths schemes of learning.

Lesson resources

- There is a Quick recap for each lesson in the Teacher Guide, which offers an alternative lesson starter to the Power Up for cases where you feel it would be more beneficial to surface prerequisite learning than general number fluency.
- In the **Discover** and **Share** sections there is now more of a progression from 1 a) to 1 b). Whereas before, 1 b) was mainly designed as a separate question, now 1 a) leads directly into 1 b). This means that there is an improved whole-class flow, and also an opportunity to focus on the logic and skills in more detail. As a teacher, you will be using 1 a) to lead the class into the thinking, then 1 b) to mould that thinking into the core new learning of the lesson.
- In the **Share** section, for KS1 in particular, the number of different models and representations has been reduced, to support the clarity of thinking prompted by the flow from 1 a) into 1 b).
- More fluency questions have been built into the guided and independent practice.
- Pupil pages are as easy as possible for children to access independently. The pages are less full where this supports greater focus on key ideas and instructions. Also, more freedom is offered around answer format, with fewer boxes scaffolding children's responses; squared paper backgrounds are used in the Practice Books where appropriate. Artwork has also been revisited to ensure the highest standards of accessibility.

New components

480 Individual Practice Games are available in *ActiveLearn* for practising key facts and skills in Years 1 to 6. These are designed in an arcade style, to feel like fun games that children would choose to play outside school. They can be accessed via the Pupil World for homework or additional practice in school – and children can earn rewards. There are Support, Core and Extend levels to allocate, with Activity Reporting available for the teacher. There is a Quick Guide on *ActiveLearn* and you can use the Help area for support in setting up child accounts.

There is also a new set of lesson video resources on the Professional Development tile, designed for in-school training in 10- to 20-minute bursts. For each part of the *Power Maths* lesson sequence, there is a slide deck with embedded video, which will facilitate discussions about how you can take your *Power Maths* teaching to the next level.

Your *Power Maths* resources

Pupil Textbooks

Discover, **Share** and **Think together** sections promote discussion and introduce mathematical ideas logically, so that children understand more easily.

Using a Concrete-Pictorial-Abstract approach, clear mathematical models help children to make connections and grasp concepts.

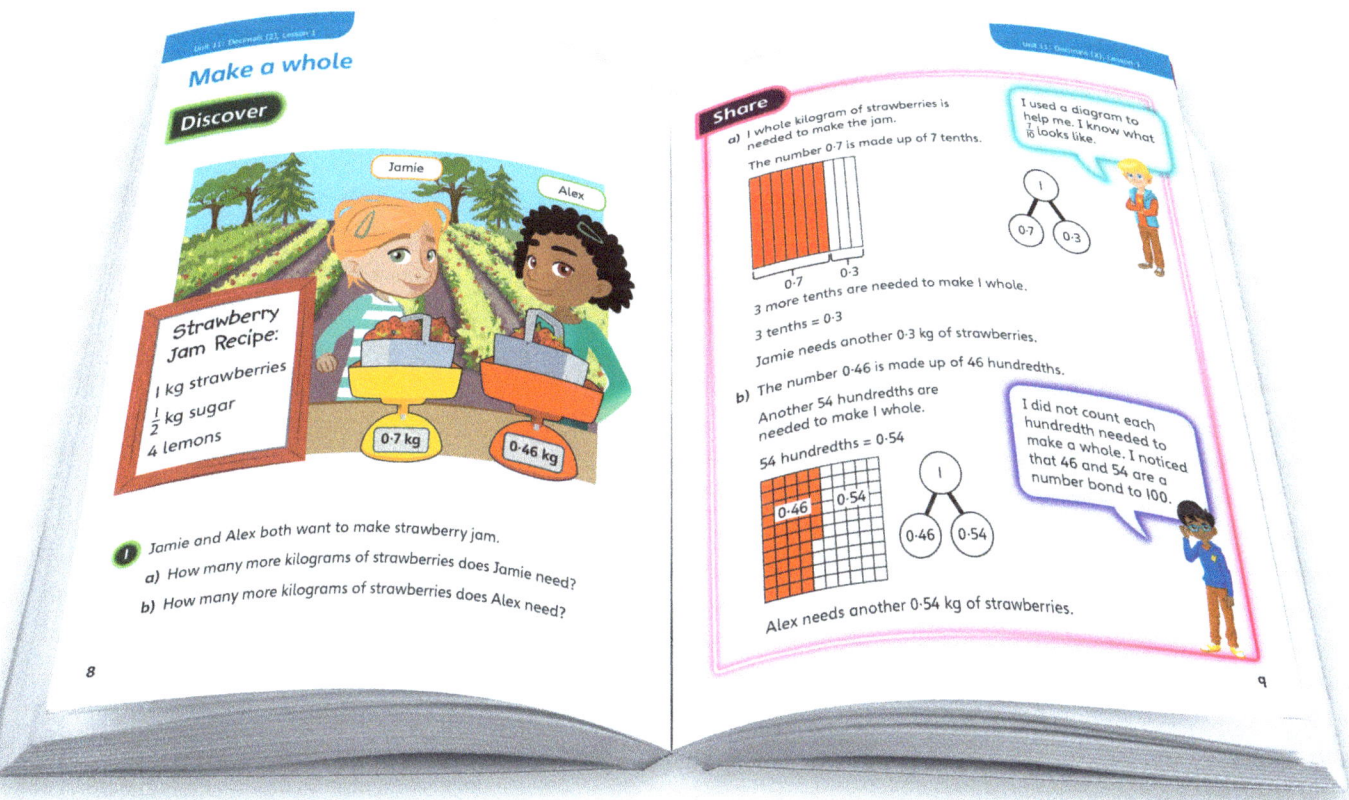

Appealing scenarios stimulate curiosity, helping children to identify the maths problem and discover patterns and relationships for themselves.

Friendly, supportive characters help children develop a growth mindset by prompting them to think, reason and reflect.

To help you teach for mastery, *Power Maths* comprises a variety of high-quality resources.

The coherent *Power Maths* lesson structure carries through into the vibrant, high-quality textbooks. Setting out the core learning objectives for each class, the lesson structure follows a carefully mapped journey through the curriculum and supports children on their journey to deeper understanding.

Pupil Practice Books

The Practice Books offer just the right amount of intelligent practice for children to complete independently in the final section of each lesson.

Practice questions are finely tuned to move children forward in their thinking and to reveal misconceptions.

The practice questions are for everyone – each question varies one small element to move children on in their thinking.

Calculations are connected so that children think about the underlying concept.

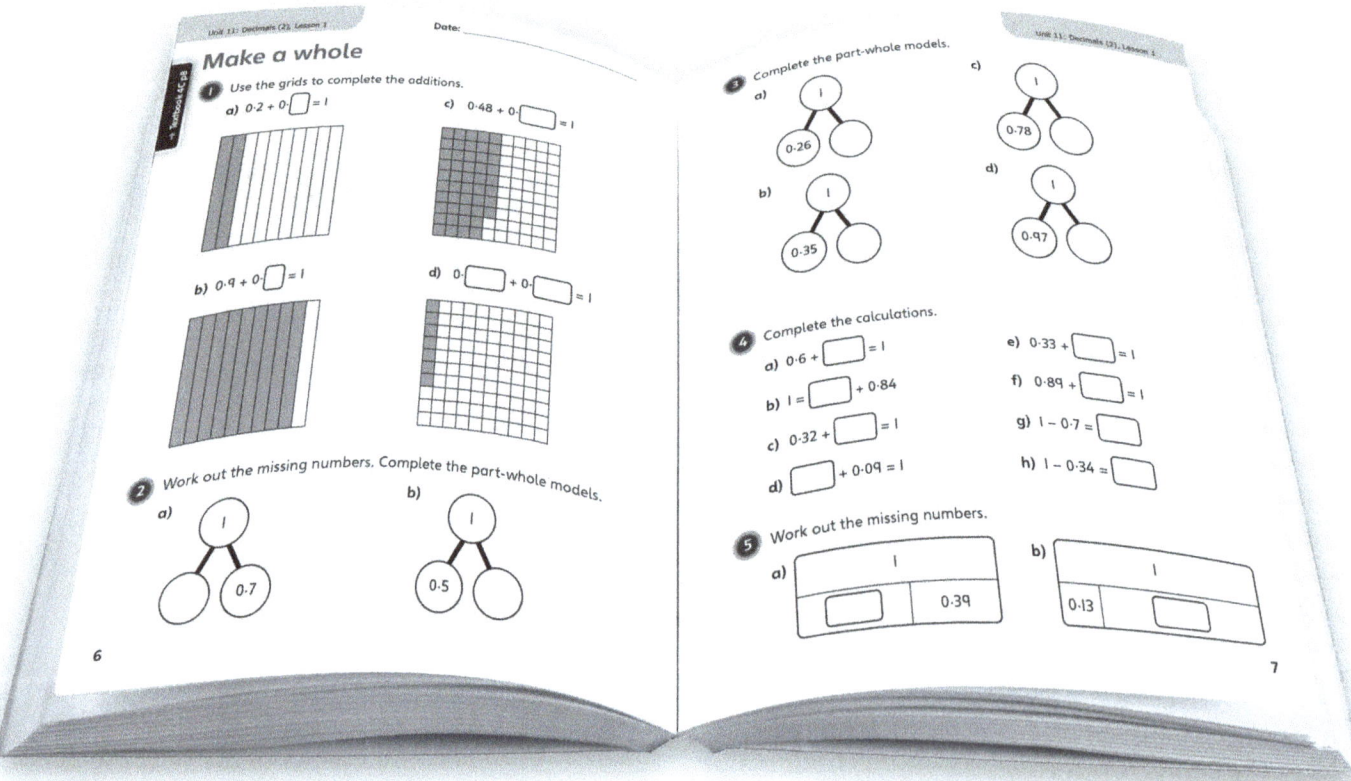

Challenge questions allow children to delve deeper into a concept.

The *Power Maths* characters support and encourage children to think and work in different ways.

Think differently questions encourage children to use reasoning as well as their mathematical knowledge to reach a solution.

Reflect questions reveal the depth of each child's understanding before they move on.

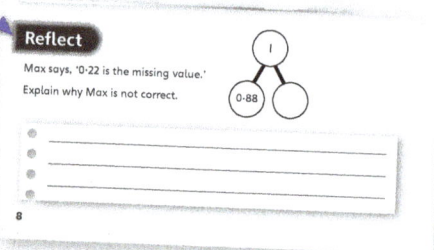

Online subscription

The online subscription will give you access to additional resources and answers from the Textbook and Practice Book.

eTextbooks

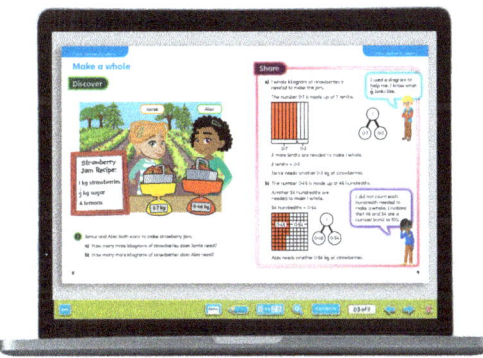

Digital versions of *Power Maths* Textbooks allow class groups to share and discuss questions, solutions and strategies. They allow you to project key structures and representations at the front of the class, to ensure all children are focusing on the same concept.

Teaching tools

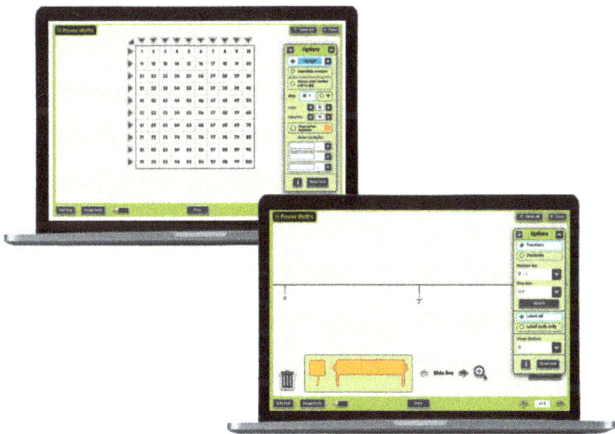

Here you will find interactive versions of key *Power Maths* structures and representations.

Power Ups

Use this series of daily activities to promote and check number fluency.

Online versions of Teacher Guide pages

PDF pages give support at both unit and lesson levels. You will also find help with key strategies and templates for tracking progress.

Unit videos

Watch the professional development videos at the start of each unit to help you teach with confidence. The videos explore common misconceptions in the unit, and include intervention suggestions as well as suggestions on what to look out for when assessing mastery in your students.

End of unit Strengthen and Deepen materials

The Strengthen activity at the end of every unit addresses a key misconception and can be used to support children who need it. The Deepen activities are designed to be low ceiling/high threshold and will challenge those children who can understand more deeply. These resources will help you ensure that every child understands and will help you keep the class moving forward together. These printable activities provide an optional resource bank for use after the assessment stage.

Individual Practice Games

These enjoyable games can be used at home or at school to embed key number skills (see page 6).

Professional Development videos and slides

These slides and videos of *Power Maths* lessons can be used for ongoing training in short bursts or to support new staff.

The *Power Maths* teaching model

At the heart of *Power Maths* is a clearly structured teaching and learning process that helps you make certain that every child masters each maths concept securely and deeply. For each year group, the curriculum is broken down into core concepts, taught in units. A unit divides into smaller learning steps – lessons. Step by step, strong foundations of cumulative knowledge and understanding are built.

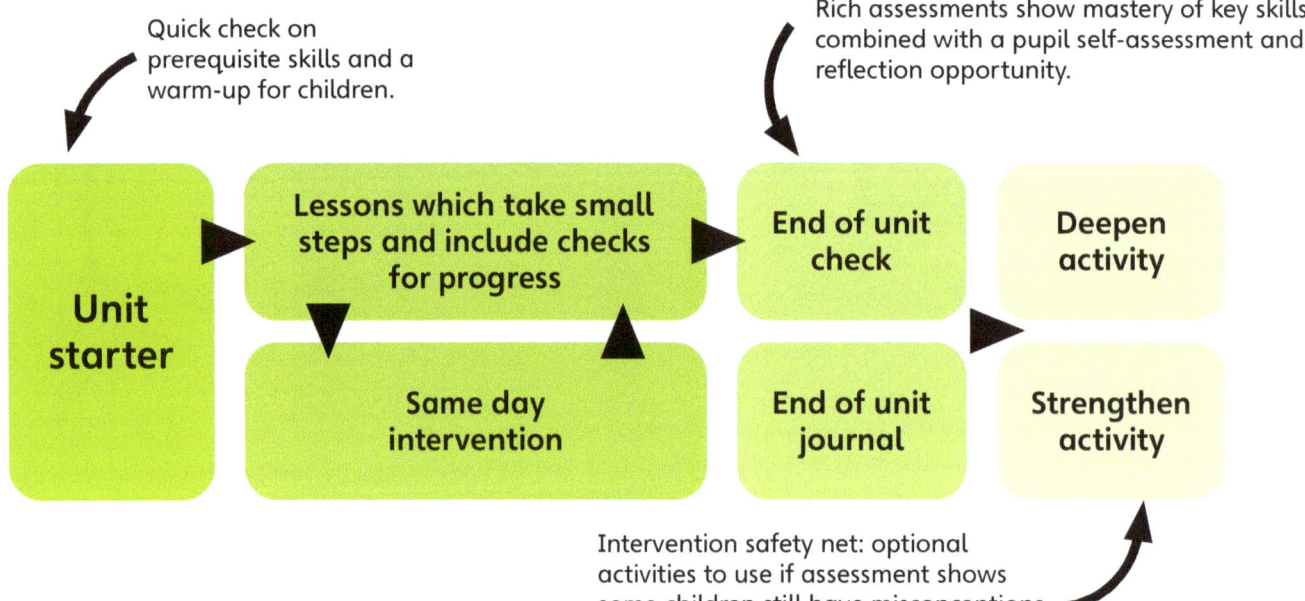

Unit starter

Each unit begins with a unit starter, which introduces the learning context along with key mathematical vocabulary and structures and representations.

- The Textbooks include a check on readiness and a warm-up task for children to complete.
- Your Teacher Guide gives support right from the start on important structures and representations, mathematical language, common misconceptions and intervention strategies.
- Unit-specific videos develop your subject knowledge and insights so you feel confident and fully equipped to teach each new unit. These are available via the online subscription.

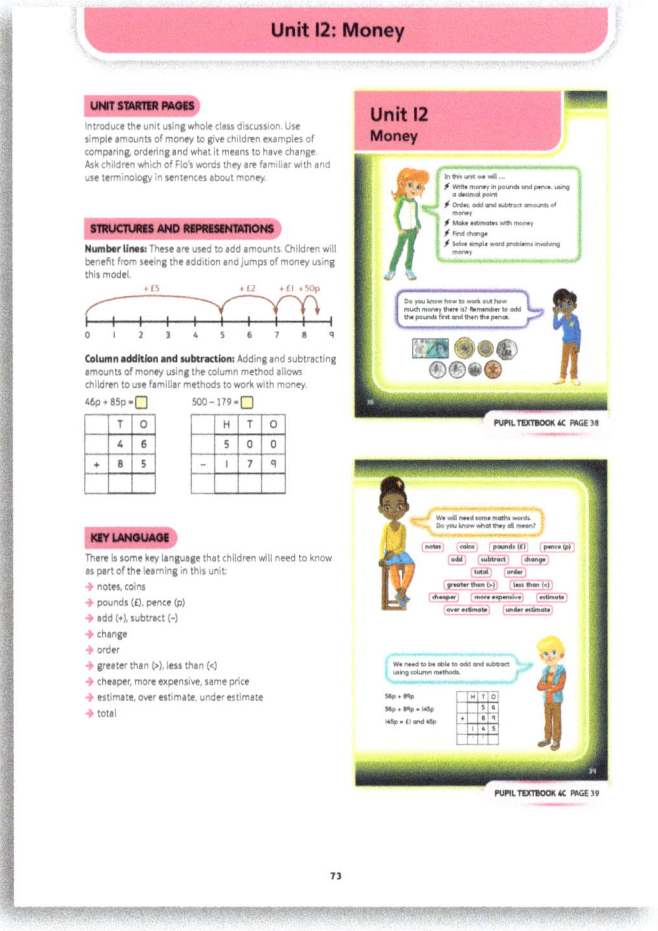

Lesson

Once a unit has been introduced, it is time to start teaching the series of lessons.

- Each lesson is scaffolded with Textbook and Practice Book activities and begins with a Power Up activity (available via online subscription) or the Quick recap activity in the Teacher Guide (see page 15).
- *Power Maths* identifies lesson by lesson what concepts are to be taught.
- Your Teacher Guide offers lots of support for you to get the most from every child in every lesson. As well as highlighting key points, tricky areas and how to handle them, you will also find question prompts to check on understanding and clarification on why particular activities and questions are used.

Same-day intervention

Same-day interventions are vital in order to keep the class progressing together. This can be during the lesson as well as afterwards (see page 27). Therefore, *Power Maths* provides plenty of support throughout the journey.

- Intervention is focused on keeping up now, not catching up later, so interventions should happen as soon as they are needed.
- Practice section questions are designed to bring misconceptions to the surface, allowing you to identify these easily as you circulate during independent practice time.
- Child-friendly assessment questions in the Teacher Guide help you identify easily which children need to strengthen their understanding.

End of unit check and journal

For each unit, the End of unit check in the Textbook lets you see which children have mastered the key concepts, which children have not and where their misconceptions lie. The Practice Books also include an End of unit journal in which children can reflect on what they have learned. Each unit also offers Strengthen and Deepen activities, available via the online subscription.

The Teacher Guide offers different ways of managing the End of unit assessments as well as giving support with handling misconceptions.

The End of unit check presents multiple-choice questions. Children think about their answer, decide on a solution and explain their choice.

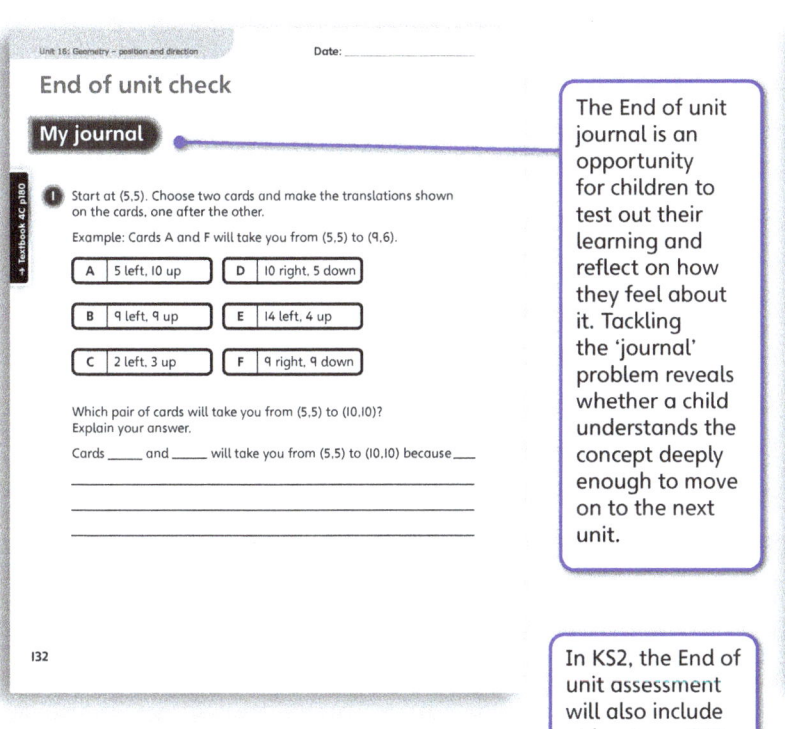

The End of unit journal is an opportunity for children to test out their learning and reflect on how they feel about it. Tackling the 'journal' problem reveals whether a child understands the concept deeply enough to move on to the next unit.

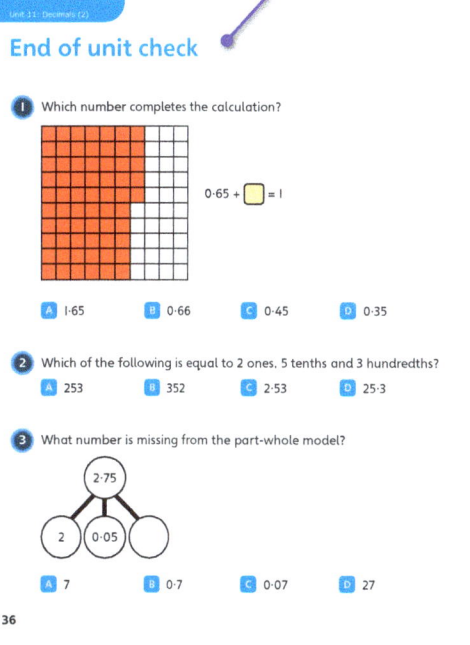

In KS2, the End of unit assessment will also include at least one SATs-style question.

The *Power Maths* lesson sequence

At the heart of *Power Maths* is a unique lesson sequence designed to empower children to understand core concepts and grow in confidence. Embracing the National Centre for Excellence in the Teaching of Mathematics' (NCETM's) definition of mastery, the sequence guides and shapes every *Power Maths* lesson you teach.

Flexibility is built into the *Power Maths* programme so there is no one-to-one mapping of lessons and concepts and you can pace your teaching according to your class. While some children will need to spend longer on a particular concept (through interventions or additional lessons), others will reach deeper levels of understanding. However, it is important that the class moves forward together through the termly schedules.

Power Up  5 minutes

Each lesson begins with a Power Up activity (available via the online subscription) which supports fluency in key number facts.

The whole-class approach depends on fluency, so the Power Up is a powerful and essential activity.

The Quick recap is an alternative starter, for when you think some or all children would benefit more from revisiting pre-requisite work (see page 15).

TOP TIP
If the class is struggling with the task, revisit it later and check understanding.

Power Ups reinforce the two key things that are essential for success: times-tables and number bonds.

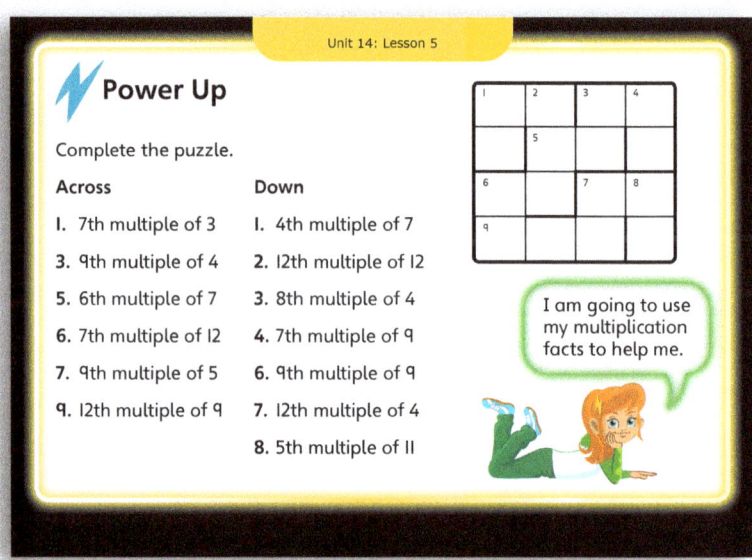

Discover 10 minutes

A practical, real-life problem arouses curiosity. Children find the maths through story telling.

A real-life scenario is provided for the **Discover** section but feel free to build upon these with your own examples that are more relevant to your class, or get creative with the context.

TOP TIP
Discover works best when run at tables, in pairs with concrete objects.

Question ❶ a) tackles the key concept and question ❶ b) digs a little deeper. Children have time to explore, play and discuss possible strategies.

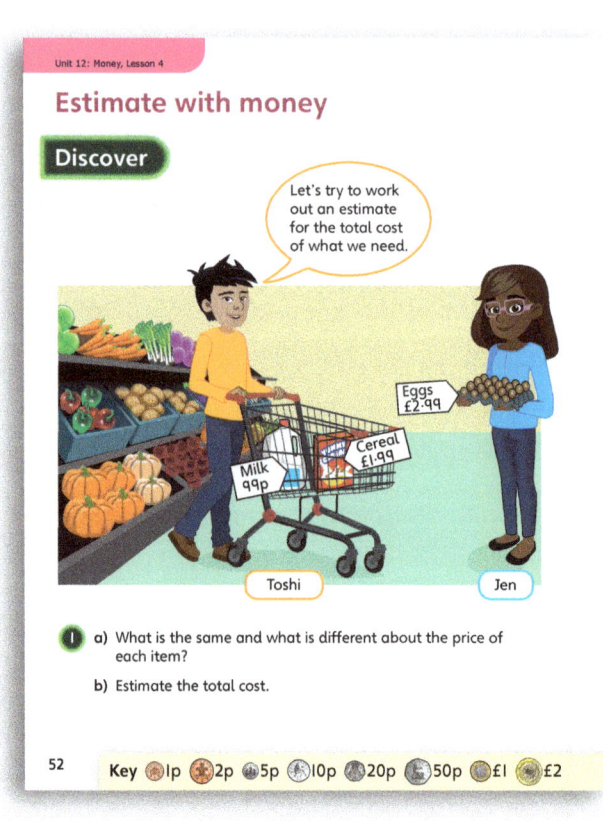

Share ⏲ 10 minutes

Teacher-led, this interactive section follows the **Discover** activity and highlights the variety of methods that can be used to solve a single problem.

TOP TIP
Pairs sharing a textbook is a great format for **Share**!

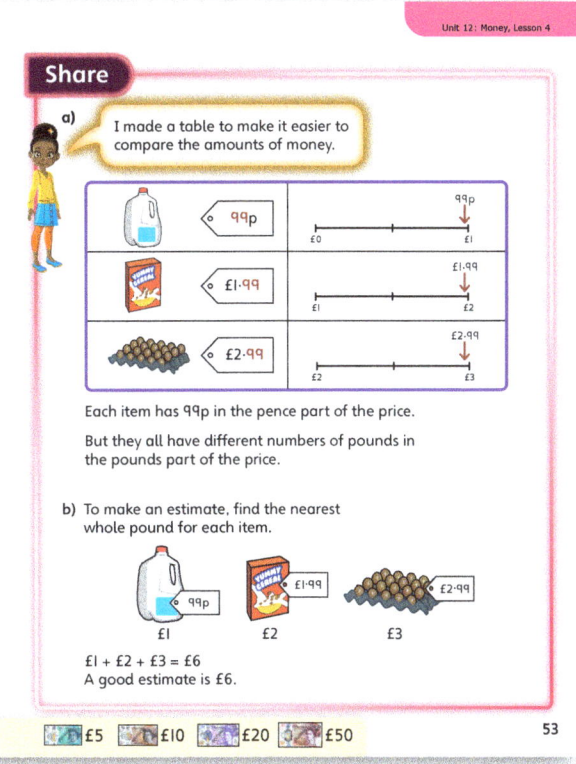

Your Teacher Guide gives target questions for children. The online toolkit provides interactive structures and representations to link concrete and pictorial to abstract concepts.

Bring children to the front to share and celebrate their solutions and strategies.

Think together

⏲ 10 minutes

Children work in groups on the carpet or at tables, using their textbooks or eBooks.

TOP TIP
Make sure children have mini whiteboards or pads to write on if they are not at their tables.

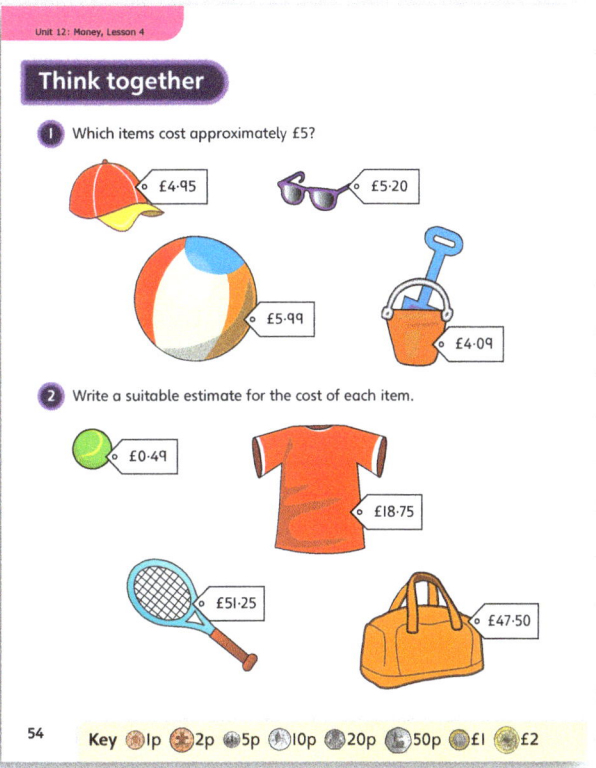

Using the Teacher Guide, model question ❶ for your class.

Question ❷ is less structured. Children will need to think together in their groups, then discuss their methods and solutions as a class.

In question ❸ children try working out the answer independently. The openness of the **Challenge** question helps to check depth of understanding.

Practice ⏱ 15 minutes

Using their Practice Books, children work independently while you circulate and check on progress.

Questions follow small steps of progression to deepen learning.

TOP TIP
Some children could work separately with a teacher or assistant.

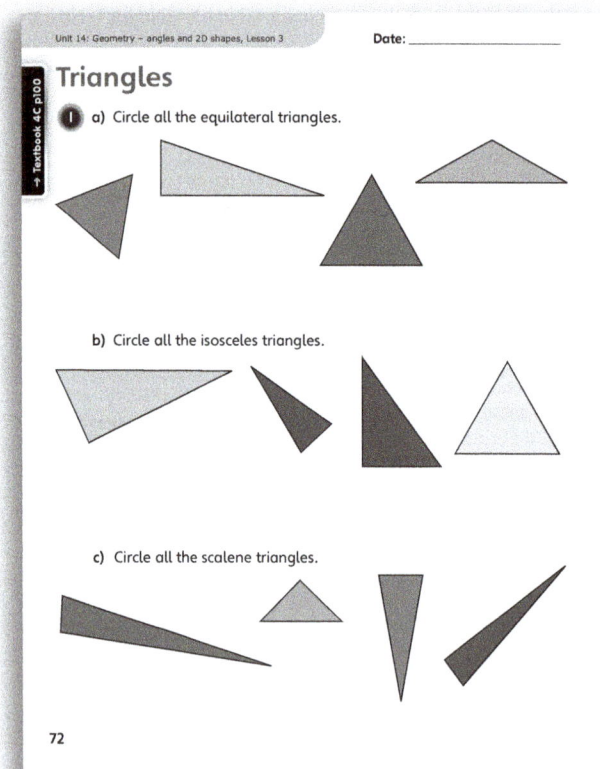

Are some children struggling? If so, work with them as a group, using mathematical structures and representations to support understanding as necessary.

There are no set routines: for real understanding, children need to think about the problem in different ways.

Reflect ⏱ 5 minutes

'Spot the mistake' questions are great for checking misconceptions.

The **Reflect** section is your opportunity to check how deeply children understand the target concept.

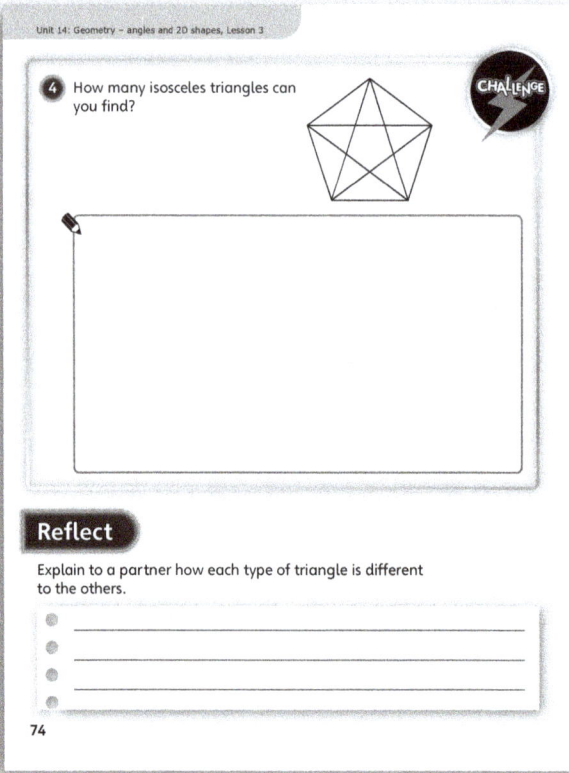

The Practice Books use various approaches to check that children have fully understood each concept.

Looking like they understand is not enough! It is essential that children can show they have grasped the concept.

Using the *Power Maths* Teacher Guide

Think of your Teacher Guides as *Power Maths* handbooks that will guide, support and inspire your day-to-day teaching. Clear and concise, and illustrated with helpful examples, your Teacher Guides will help you make the best possible use of every individual lesson. They also provide wrap-around professional development, enhancing your own subject knowledge and helping you to grow in confidence about moving your children forward together.

There is a Teacher Guide per year group for every term, with unit and lesson level guidance and support.

Never feel stuck! You will find ideas for introducing every unit and lesson and questions to encourage teacher reflection before and after each lesson.

Tips and advice on key elements such as C-P-A approaches, misconceptions, language, modelling growth mindsets and same day intervention.

Annotations for every Textbook and Practice Book page, providing prompts for key questions to ask to expose understanding and explanations as to why key questions have been chosen.

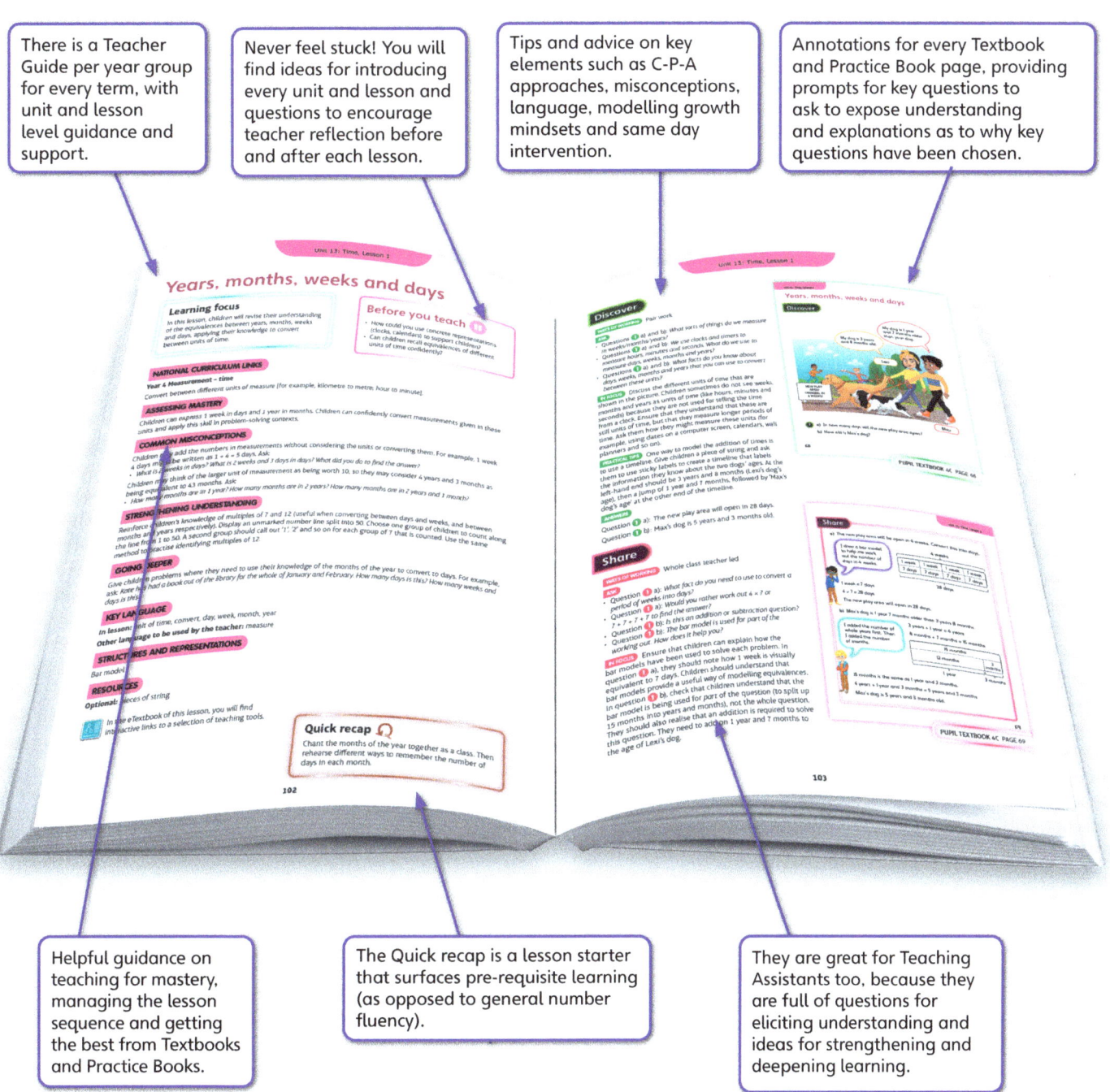

Helpful guidance on teaching for mastery, managing the lesson sequence and getting the best from Textbooks and Practice Books.

The Quick recap is a lesson starter that surfaces pre-requisite learning (as opposed to general number fluency).

They are great for Teaching Assistants too, because they are full of questions for eliciting understanding and ideas for strengthening and deepening learning.

At the end of each unit, your Teacher Guide helps you identify who has fully grasped the concept, who has not and how to move every child forward. This is covered later in the Assessment strategies section.

Power Maths Year 4, yearly overview

Textbook	Strand	Unit		Number of lessons
Textbook A / Practice Workbook A (Term 1)	Number – number and place value	1	Place value – 4-digit numbers (1)	8
	Number – number and place value	2	Place value – 4-digit numbers (2)	8
	Number – addition and subtraction	3	Addition and subtraction	16
	Measurement	4	Measure – area	5
	Number – multiplication and division	5	Multiplication and division (1)	12
Textbook B / Practice Workbook B (Term 2)	Number – multiplication and division	6	Multiplication and division (2)	16
	Measurement	7	Length and perimeter	6
	Number – fractions	8	Fractions (1)	9
	Number – fractions	9	Fractions (2)	8
	Number – fractions (including decimals and percentages	10	Decimals (1)	12
Textbook C / Practice Workbook C (Term 3)	Number – fractions (including decimals and percentages	11	Decimals (2)	7
	Measurement	12	Money	6
	Measurement	13	Time	5
	Geometry – properties of shapes	14	Geometry – angles and 2D shapes	8
	Statistics	15	Statistics	6
	Geometry – position and direction	16	Geometry – position and direction	6

Power Maths Year 4, Textbook 4C (Term 3) overview

Strand	Unit		Lesson number	Lesson title	NC Objective 1	NC Objective 2
Number – fractions (including decimals and percentages)	11	Decimals (2)	1	Make a whole	Recognise and write decimal equivalents of any number of tenths or hundredths	
Number – fractions (including decimals and percentages)	11	Decimals (2)	2	Partition decimals	Recognise and write decimal equivalents of any number of tenths or hundredths	
Number – fractions (including decimals and percentages)	11	Decimals (2)	3	Flexibly partition decimals	Recognise and write decimal equivalents of any number of tenths or hundredths	
Number – fractions (including decimals and percentages)	11	Decimals (2)	4	Compare decimals	Compare numbers with the same number of decimal places up to two decimal places	
Number – fractions (including decimals and percentages)	11	Decimals (2)	5	Order decimals	Compare numbers with the same number of decimal places up to two decimal places	
Number – fractions (including decimals and percentages)	11	Decimals (2)	6	Round to the nearest whole	Round decimals with one decimal place to the nearest whole number	
Number – fractions (including decimals and percentages)	11	Decimals (2)	7	Halves and quarters as decimals	Recognise and write decimal equivalents to $\frac{1}{4}, \frac{1}{2}, \frac{3}{4}$	
Measurement	12	Money	1	Write money using decimals	Estimate, compare and calculate different measures, including money in pounds and pence	
Measurement	12	Money	2	Convert between pounds and pence	Estimate, compare and calculate different measures, including money in pounds and pence	
Measurement	12	Money	3	Compare amounts of money	Estimate, compare and calculate different measures, including money in pounds and pence	
Measurement	12	Money	4	Estimate with money	Estimate, compare and calculate different measures, including money in pounds and pence	
Measurement	12	Money	5	Calculate with money	Estimate, compare and calculate different measures, including money in pounds and pence	
Measurement	12	Money	6	Solve problems with money	Estimate, compare and calculate different measures, including money in pounds and pence	
Measurement	13	Time	1	Years, months, weeks and days	Convert between different units of measure [for example, kilometre to metre; hour to minute]	
Measurement	13	Time	2	Hours, minutes and seconds	Convert between different units of measure [for example, kilometre to metre; hour to minute]	

Strand	Unit		Lesson number	Lesson title	NC Objective 1	NC Objective 2
Measurement	13	Time	3	Convert between analogue and digital times	Convert between different units of measure [for example, kilometre to metre; hour to minute]	
Measurement	13	Time	4	Convert to the 24 hour clock	Convert between different units of measure [for example, kilometre to metre; hour to minute]	
Measurement	13	Time	5	Problem solving – convert units of time	Convert between different units of measure [for example, kilometre to metre; hour to minute]	
Geometry – properties of shapes	14	Geometry – angles and 2D shapes	1	Identify angles	Identify acute and obtuse angles and compare and order angles up to two right angles by size	
Geometry – properties of shapes	14	Geometry – angles and 2D shapes	2	Compare and order angles	Identify acute and obtuse angles and compare and order angles up to two right angles by size	
Geometry – properties of shapes	14	Geometry – angles and 2D shapes	3	Triangles	Compare and classify geometric shapes, including quadrilaterals and triangles, based on their properties and sizes	
Geometry – properties of shapes	14	Geometry – angles and 2D shapes	4	Quadrilaterals	Compare and classify geometric shapes, including quadrilaterals and triangles, based on their properties and sizes	
Geometry – properties of shapes	14	Geometry – angles and 2D shapes	5	Polygons	Compare and classify geometric shapes, including quadrilaterals and triangles, based on their properties and sizes	
Geometry – properties of shapes	14	Geometry – angles and 2D shapes	6	Reason about polygons	Compare and classify geometric shapes, including quadrilaterals and triangles, based on their properties and sizes	
Geometry – properties of shapes	14	Geometry – angles and 2D shapes	7	Lines of symmetry	Identify lines of symmetry in 2D shapes presented in different orientations	
Geometry – properties of shapes	14	Geometry – angles and 2D shapes	8	Complete a symmetric figure	Complete a simple symmetric figure with respect to a specific line of symmetry	
Statistics	15	Statistics	1	Interpret charts	Interpret and present discrete and continuous data using appropriate graphical methods, including bar charts and time graphs	
Statistics	15	Statistics	2	Solve problems with charts (1)	Solve comparison, sum and difference problems using information presented in bar charts, pictograms, tables and other graphs	
Statistics	15	Statistics	3	Solve problems with charts (2)	Interpret and present discrete and continuous data using appropriate graphical methods, including bar charts and time graphs	
Statistics	15	Statistics	4	Interpret line graphs (1)	Interpret and present discrete and continuous data using appropriate graphical methods, including bar charts and time graphs	
Statistics	15	Statistics	5	Interpret line graphs (2)	Solve comparison, sum and difference problems using information presented in bar charts, pictograms, tables and other graphs	
Statistics	15	Statistics	6	Draw line graphs	Interpret and present discrete and continuous data using appropriate graphical methods, including bar charts and time graphs	

Strand	Unit		Lesson number	Lesson title	NC Objective 1	NC Objective 2
Geometry – position and direction	16	Geometry – position and direction	1	Describe position	Describe positions on a 2D grid as coordinates in the first quadrant	
Geometry – position and direction	16	Geometry – position and direction	2	Describe position using coordinates	Describe positions on a 2D grid as coordinates in the first quadrant	
Geometry – position and direction	16	Geometry – position and direction	3	Plot coordinates	Plot specified points and draw sides to complete a given polygon	Describe positions on a 2D grid as coordinates in the first quadrant
Geometry – position and direction	16	Geometry – position and direction	4	Draw 2D shapes on a grid	Plot specified points and draw sides to complete a given polygon	
Geometry – position and direction	16	Geometry – position and direction	5	Translate on a grid	Describe movements between positions as translations of a given unit to the left/right and up/down	
Geometry – position and direction	16	Geometry – position and direction	6	Describe translation on a grid	Describe movements between positions as translations of a given unit to the left/right and up/down	

Mindset: an introduction

Global research and best practice deliver the same message: learning is greatly affected by what learners perceive they can or cannot do. What is more, it is also shaped by what their parents, carers and teachers perceive they can do. Mindset – the thinking that determines our beliefs and behaviours – therefore has a fundamental impact on teaching and learning.

Everyone can!

Power Maths and mastery methods focus on the distinction between 'fixed' and 'growth' mindsets (Dweck, 2007).[1] Those with a fixed mindset believe that their basic qualities (for example, intelligence, talent and ability to learn) are pre-wired or fixed: 'If you have a talent for maths, you will succeed at it. If not, too bad!' By contrast, those with a growth mindset believe that hard work, effort and commitment drive success and that 'smart' is not something you are or are not, but something you become. In short, everyone can do maths!

Key mindset strategies

A growth mindset needs to be actively nurtured and developed. *Power Maths* offers some key strategies for fostering healthy growth mindsets in your classroom.

It is okay to get it wrong

Mistakes are valuable opportunities to re-think and understand more deeply. Learning is richer when children and teachers alike focus on spotting and sharing mistakes as well as solutions.

Praise hard work

Praise is a great motivator, and by focusing on praising effort and learning rather than success, children will be more willing to try harder, take risks and persist for longer.

Mind your language!

The language we use around learners has a profound effect on their mindsets. Make a habit of using growth phrases, such as, 'Everyone can!', 'Mistakes can help you learn' and 'Just try for a little longer'. The king of them all is one little word, 'yet'… I can't solve this…yet!' Encourage parents and carers to use the right language too.

Build in opportunities for success

The step-by-small-step approach enables children to enjoy the experience of success. In addition, avoid ability grouping and encourage every child to answer questions and explain or demonstrate their methods to others.

The *Power Maths* characters

The *Power Maths* characters model the traits of growth mindset learners and encourage resilience by prompting and questioning children as they work. Appearing frequently in the Textbooks and Practice Books, they are your allies in teaching and discussion, helping to model methods, alternatives and misconceptions, and to pose questions. They encourage and support your children, too: they are all hardworking, enthusiastic and unafraid of making and talking about mistakes.

Meet the team!

Creative Flo is open-minded and sometimes indecisive. She likes to think differently and come up with a variety of methods or ideas.

Determined Dexter is resolute, resilient and systematic. He concentrates hard, always tries his best and he'll never give up – even though he doesn't always choose the most efficient methods!

'Let's try again.'

'Mistakes are cool!'

'Have I found all of the solutions?'

'Let's try it this way…'

'Can we do it differently?'

'I've got another way of doing this!'

'I'm going to try this!'

'I know how to do that!'

'Want to share my ideas?'

Curious Ash is eager, interested and inquisitive, and he loves solving puzzles and problems. Ash asks lots of questions but sometimes gets distracted.

'What if we tried this…?'

'I wonder…'

'Is there a pattern here?'

Miaow!

Sparks the Cat

Brave Astrid is confident, willing to take risks and unafraid of failure. She's never scared to jump straight into a problem or question, and although she often makes simple mistakes, she's happy to talk them through with others.

Mathematical language

Traditionally, we in the UK have tended to try simplifying mathematical language to make it easier for young children to understand. By contrast, evidence and experience show that by diluting the correct language, we actually mask concepts and meanings for children. We then wonder why they are confused by new and different terminology later down the line! *Power Maths* is not afraid of 'hard' words and avoids placing any barriers between children and their understanding of mathematical concepts. As a result, we need to be deliberate, precise and thorough in building every child's understanding of the language of maths. Throughout the Teacher Guides you will find support and guidance on how to deliver this, as well as individual explanations throughout the pupil Textbooks.

Use the following key strategies to build children's mathematical vocabulary, understanding and confidence.

Precise and consistent

Everyone in the classroom should use the correct mathematical terms in full, every time. For example, refer to 'equal parts', not 'parts'. Used consistently, precise maths language will be a familiar and non-threatening part of children's everyday experience.

Full sentences

Teachers and children alike need to use full sentences to explain or respond. When children use complete sentences, it both reveals their understanding and embeds their knowledge.

Stem sentences

These important sentences help children express mathematical concepts accurately, and are used throughout the *Power Maths* books. Encourage children to repeat them frequently, whether working independently or with others. Examples of stem sentences are:

'4 is a part, 5 is a part, 9 is the whole.'

'There are .... groups. There are .... in each group.'

Key vocabulary

The unit starters highlight essential vocabulary for every lesson. In the pupil books, characters flag new terminology and the Teacher Guide lists important mathematical language for every unit and lesson. New terms are never introduced without a clear explanation.

Mathematical signs

Mathematical signs are used early on so that children quickly become familiar with them and their meaning. Often, the *Power Maths* characters will highlight the connection between language and particular signs.

The role of talk and discussion

When children learn to talk purposefully together about maths, barriers of fear and anxiety are broken down and they grow in confidence, skills and understanding. Building a healthy culture of 'maths talk' empowers their learning from day one.

Explanation and discussion are integral to the *Power Maths* structure, so by simply following the books your lessons will stimulate structured talk. The following key 'maths talk' strategies will help you strengthen that culture and ensure that every child is included.

Sentences, not words

Encourage children to use full sentences when reasoning, explaining or discussing maths. This helps both speaker and listeners to clarify their own understanding. It also reveals whether or not the speaker truly understands, enabling you to address misconceptions as they arise.

Working together

Working with others in pairs, groups or as a whole class is a great way to support maths talk and discussion. Use different group structures to add variety and challenge. For example, children could take timed turns for talking, work independently alongside a 'discussion buddy', or perhaps play different *Power Maths* character roles within their group.

Think first – then talk

Provide clear opportunities within each lesson for children to think and reflect, so that their talk is purposeful, relevant and focused.

Give every child a voice

Where the 'hands up' model allows only the more confident child to shine, *Power Maths* involves everyone. Make sure that no child dominates and that even the shyest child is encouraged to contribute – and praised when they do.

Assessment strategies

Teaching for mastery demands that you are confident about what each child knows and where their misconceptions lie; therefore, practical and effective assessment is vitally important.

Formative assessment within lessons

The **Think together** section will often reveal any confusions or insecurities; try ironing these out by doing the first **Think together** question as a class. For children who continue to struggle, you or your Teaching Assistant should provide support and enable them to move on.

Performance in practice can be very revealing: check Practice Books and listen out both during and after practice to identify misconceptions.

The **Reflect** section is designed to check on the all-important depth of understanding. Be sure to review how the children performed in this final stage before you teach the next lesson.

End of unit check – Textbook

Each unit concludes with a summative check to help you assess quickly and clearly each child's understanding, fluency, reasoning and problem solving skills. Your Teacher Guide will suggest ideal ways of organising a given activity and offer advice and commentary on what children's responses mean. For example, 'What misconception does this reveal?'; 'How can you reinforce this particular concept?'

Assessment with young children should always be an enjoyable activity, so avoid one-to-one individual assessments, which they may find threatening or scary. If you prefer, the End of unit check can be carried out as a whole-class group using whiteboards and Practice Books.

End of unit check – Practice Book

The Practice Book contains further opportunities for assessment, and can be completed by children independently whilst you are carrying out diagnostic assessment with small groups. Your Teacher Guide will advise you on what to do if children struggle to articulate an explanation – or perhaps encourage you to write down something they have explained well. It will also offer insights into children's answers and their implications for next learning steps. It is split into three main sections, outlined below.

My journal is designed to allow children to show their depth of understanding of the unit. It can also serve as a way of checking that children have grasped key mathematical vocabulary. The question children should answer is first presented in the Textbook in the Think! section. This provides an opportunity for you to discuss the question first as a class to ensure children have understood their task. Children should have some time to think about how they want to answer the question, and you could ask them to talk to a partner about their ideas. Then children should write their answer in their Practice Book, using the word bank provided to help them with vocabulary.

The **Power check** allows pupils to self-assess their level of confidence on the topic by colouring in different smiley faces. You may want to introduce the faces as follows:

Each unit ends with either a Power play or a Power puzzle. This is an activity, puzzle or game that allows children to use their new knowledge in a fun, informal way.

Progress Tests

There are *Power Maths* Progress Tests for each half term and at the end of the year, including an Arithmetic test and Reasoning test in each case. You can enter results in the online markbook to track and analyse results and see the average for all schools' results. The tests use a 6-step scale to show results against age-related expectation.

How to ask diagnostic questions

The diagnostic questions provided in children's Practice Books are carefully structured to identify both understanding and misconceptions (if children answer in a particular way, you will know why). The simple procedure below may be helpful:

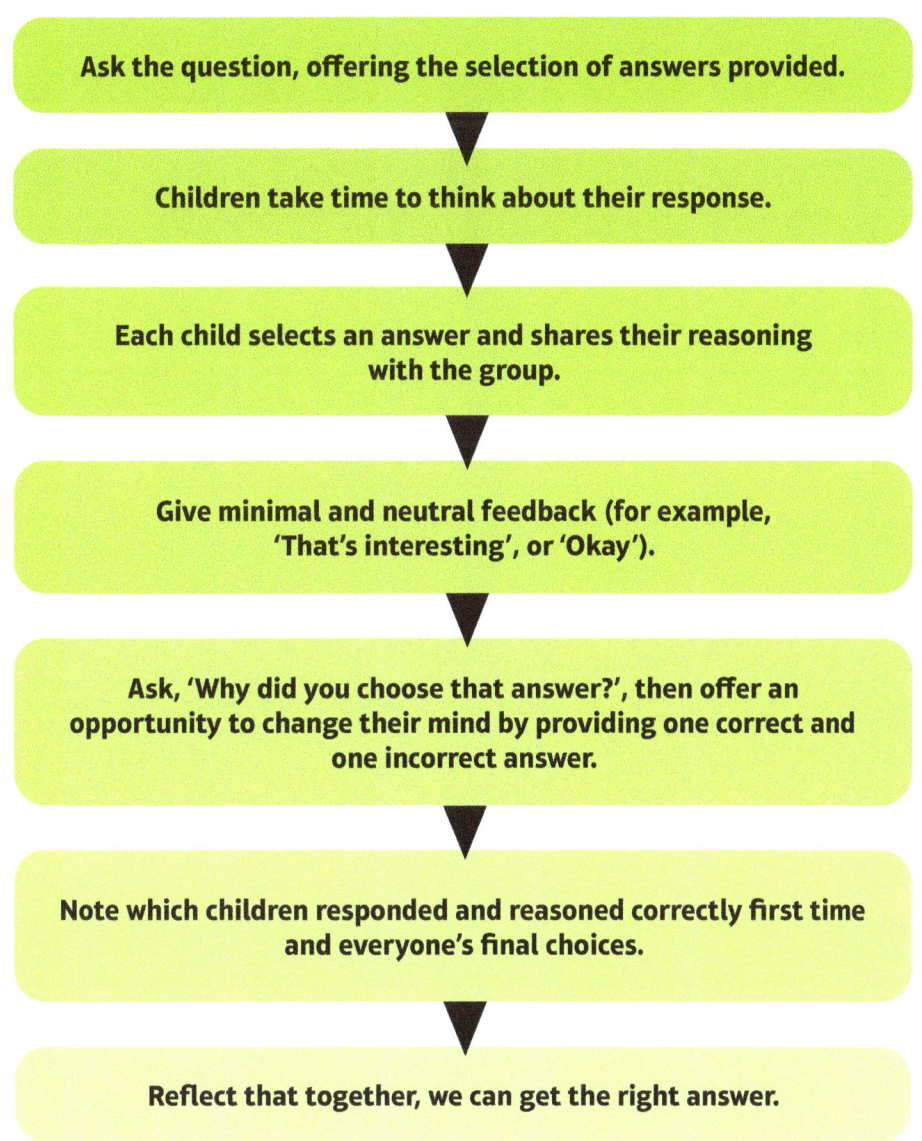

Keeping the class together

Traditionally, children who learn quickly have been accelerated through the curriculum. As a consequence, their learning may be superficial and will lack the many benefits of enabling children to learn with and from each other.

By contrast, *Power Maths'* mastery approach values real understanding and richer, deeper learning above speed. It sees all children learning the same concept in small, cumulative steps, each finding and mastering challenge at their own level. Remember that when you teach for mastery, EVERYONE can do maths! Those who grasp a concept easily have time to explore and understand that concept at a deeper level. The whole class therefore moves through the curriculum at broadly the same pace via individual learning journeys.

For some teachers, the idea that a whole class can move forward together is revolutionary and challenging. However, the evidence of global good practice clearly shows that this approach drives engagement, confidence, motivation and success for all learners, and not just the high flyers. The strategies below will help you keep your class together on their maths journey.

Mix it up

Do not stick to set groups at each table. Every child should be working on the same concept, and mixing up the groupings widens children's opportunities for exploring, discussing and sharing their understanding with others.

Recycling questions

Reuse the Textbook and Practice Book questions with concrete materials to allow children to explore concepts and relationships and deepen their understanding. This strategy is especially useful for reinforcing learning in same-day interventions.

Strengthen at every opportunity

The next lesson in a *Power Maths* sequence always revises and builds on the previous step to help embed learning. These activities provide golden opportunities for individual children to strengthen their learning with the support of Teaching Assistants.

Prepare to be surprised!

Children may grasp a concept quickly or more slowly. The 'fast graspers' won't always be the same individuals, nor does the speed at which a child understands a concept predict their success in maths. Are they struggling or just working more slowly?

Same-day intervention

Since maths competence depends on mastering concepts one by one in a logical progression, it is important that no gaps in understanding are ever left unfilled. Same-day interventions – either within or after a lesson – are a crucial safety net for any child who has not fully made the small step covered that day. In other words, intervention is always about keeping up, not catching up, so that every child has the skills and understanding they need to tackle the next lesson. That means presenting the same problems used in the lesson, with a variety of concrete materials to help children model their solutions.

We offer two intervention strategies below, but you should feel free to choose others if they work better for your class.

Within-lesson intervention

The **Think together** activity will reveal those who are struggling, so when it is time for practice, bring these children together to work with you on the first practice questions. Observe these children carefully, ask questions, encourage them to use concrete models and check that they reach and can demonstrate their understanding.

After-lesson intervention

You might like to use the **Think together** questions to recap the lesson with children who are working behind expectations during assembly time. Teaching Assistants could also work with these children at other convenient points in the school day. Some children may benefit from revisiting work from the same topic in the previous year group. Note also the suggestion for recycling questions from the Textbook and Practice Book with concrete materials on page 26.

The role of practice

Practice plays a pivotal role in the *Power Maths* approach. It takes place in class groups, smaller groups, pairs, and independently, so that children always have the opportunities for thinking as well as the models and support they need to practise meaningfully and with understanding.

Intelligent practice

In *Power Maths*, practice never equates to the simple repetition of a process. Instead we embrace the concept of intelligent practice, in which all children become fluent in maths through varied, frequent and thoughtful practice that deepens and embeds conceptual understanding in a logical, planned sequence. To see the difference, take a look at the following examples.

Traditional practice

- Repetition can be rote – no need for a child to think hard about what they are doing
- Praise may be misplaced
- Does this prove understanding?

Intelligent practice

- Varied methods – concrete, pictorial and abstract
- Equation expressed in different ways, requiring thought and understanding
- Constructive feedback

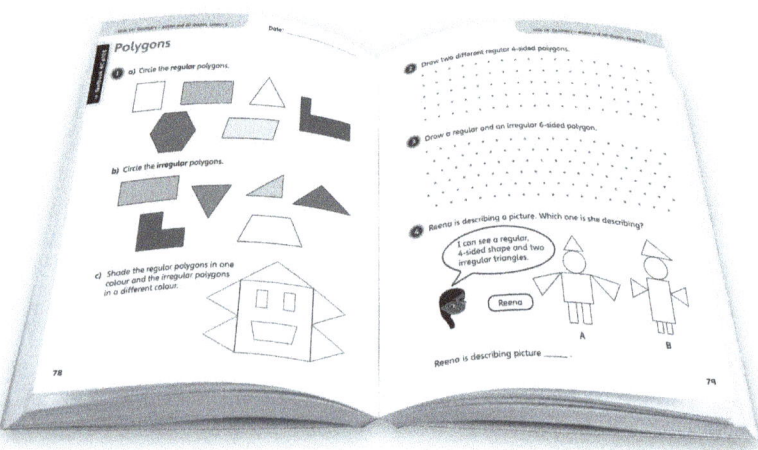

All practice questions are designed to move children on and reveal misconceptions.

Simple, logical steps build onto earlier learning.

C-P-A runs throughout – different ways of modelling and understanding the same concept.

Conceptual variation – children work on different representations of the same maths concept.

Friendly characters offer support and encourage children to try different approaches.

A carefully designed progression

The Practice Books provide just the right amount of intelligent practice for children to complete independently in the final sections of each lesson. It is really important that all children are exposed to the practice questions, and that children are not directed to complete different sections. That is because each question is different and has been designed to challenge children to think about the maths they are doing. The questions become more challenging so children grasping concepts more quickly will start to slow down as they progress. Meanwhile, you have the chance to circulate and spot any misconceptions before they become barriers to further learning.

Homework and the role of parents and carers

While *Power Maths* does not prescribe any particular homework structure, we acknowledge the potential value of practice at home. For example, practising fluency in key facts, such as number bonds and times-tables, is an ideal homework task. You can share the Individual Practice Games for homework (see page 6), or parents and carers could work through uncompleted Practice Book questions with children at either primary stage.

However, it is important to recognise that many parents and carers may themselves lack confidence in maths, and few, if any, will be familiar with mastery methods. A Parents' and Carers' evening that helps them understand the basics of mindsets, mastery and mathematical language is a great way to ensure that children benefit from their homework. It could be a fun opportunity for children to teach their families that everyone can do maths!

Structures and representations

Unlike most other subjects, maths comprises a wide array of abstract concepts – and that is why children and adults so often find it difficult. By taking a concrete-pictorial-abstract (C-P-A) approach, *Power Maths* allows children to tackle concepts in a tangible and more comfortable way.

Non-linear stages

Concrete

Replacing the traditional approach of a teacher working through a problem in front of the class, the concrete stage introduces real objects that children can use to 'do' the maths – any familiar object that a child can manipulate and move to help bring the maths to life. It is important to appreciate, however, that children must always understand the link between models and the objects they represent. For example, children need to first understand that three cakes could be represented by three pretend cakes, and then by three counters or bricks. Frequent practice helps consolidate this essential insight. Although they can be used at any time, good concrete models are an essential first step in understanding.

Pictorial

This stage uses pictorial representations of objects to let children 'see' what particular maths problems look like. It helps them make connections between the concrete and pictorial representations and the abstract maths concept. Children can also create or view a pictorial representation together, enabling discussion and comparisons. The *Power Maths* teaching tools are fantastic for this learning stage, and bar modelling is invaluable for problem solving throughout the primary curriculum.

Abstract

Our ultimate goal is for children to understand abstract mathematical concepts, symbols and notation and of course, some children will reach this stage far more quickly than others. To work with abstract concepts, a child must be comfortable with the meaning of and relationships between concrete, pictorial and abstract models and representations. The C-P-A approach is not linear, and children may need different types of models at different times. However, when a child demonstrates with concrete models and pictorial representations that they have grasped a concept, we can be confident that they are ready to explore or model it with abstract symbols such as numbers and notation.

Use at any time and with any age to support understanding

Variation helps visualisation

Children find it much easier to visualise and grasp concepts if they see them presented in a number of ways, so be prepared to offer and encourage many different representations.

For example, the number six could be represented in various ways:

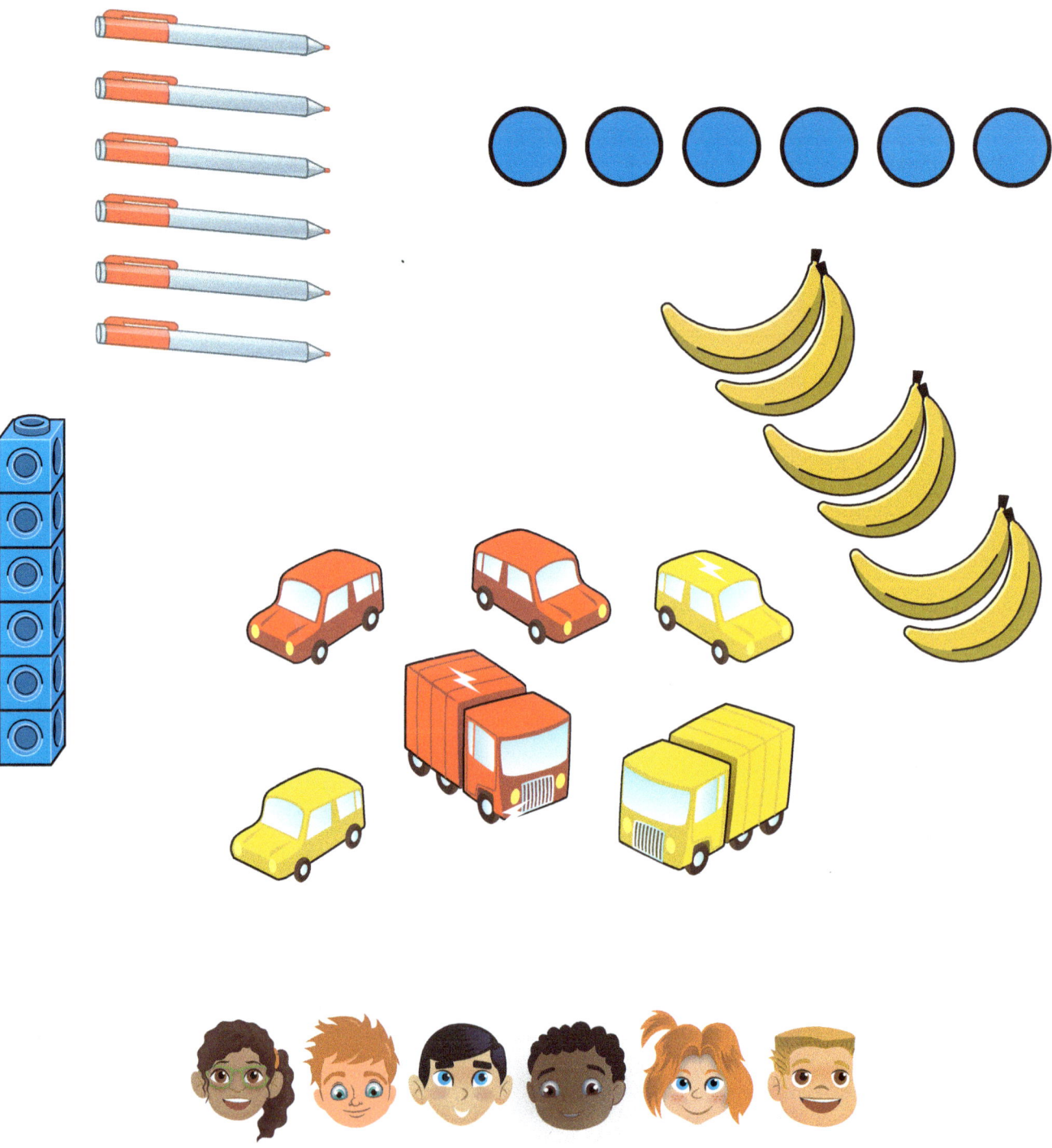

Practical aspects of *Power Maths*

One of the key underlying elements of *Power Maths* is its practical approach, allowing you to make maths real and relevant to your children, no matter their age.

Manipulatives are essential resources for both key stages and *Power Maths* encourages teachers to use these at every opportunity, and to continue the Concrete-Pictorial-Abstract approach right through to Year 6.

The Textbooks and Teacher Guides include lots of opportunities for teaching in a practical way to show children what maths means in real life.

Discover and Share

The **Discover** and **Share** sections of the Textbook give you scope to turn a real-life scenario into a practical and hands-on section of the lesson. Use these sections as inspiration to get active in the classroom. Where appropriate, use the **Discover** contexts as a springboard for your own examples that have particular resonance for your children – and allow them to get their hands dirty trying out the mathematics for themselves.

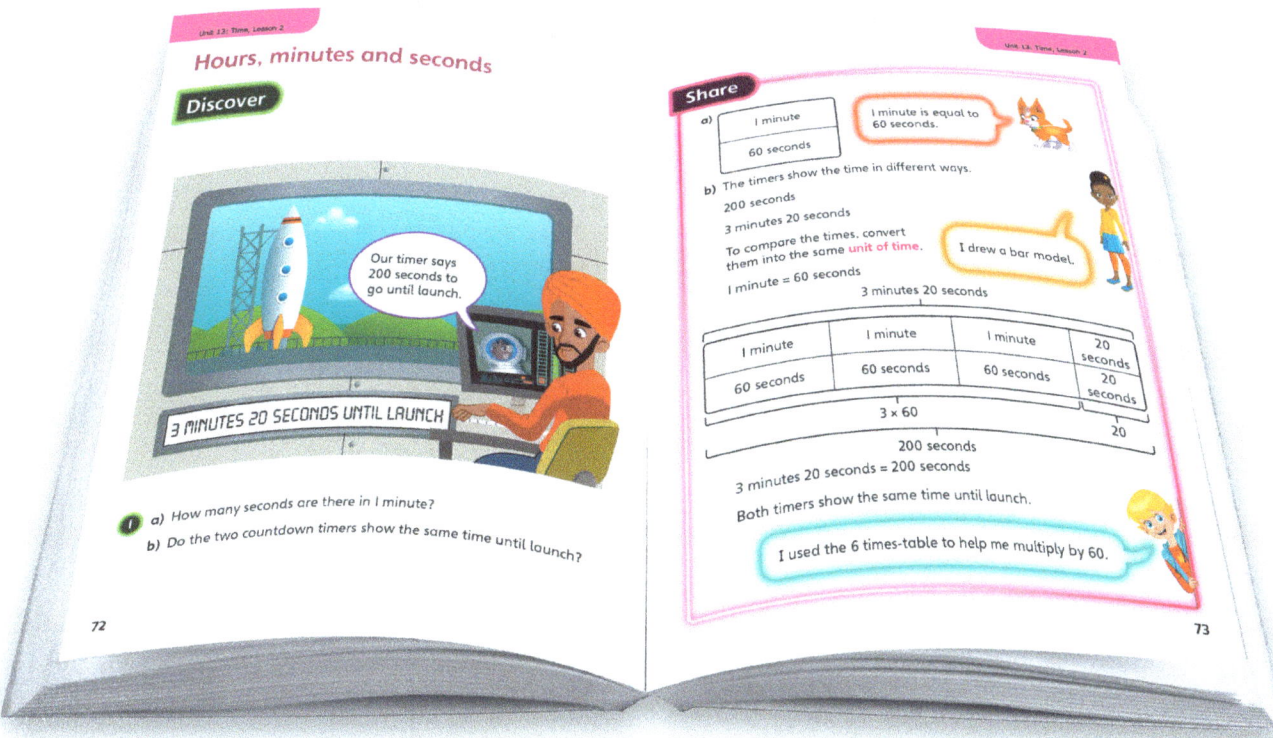

Unit videos

Every term has one unit video which incorporates real-life classroom sequences.

These videos show you how the reasoning behind mathematics can be carried out in a practical manner by showing real children using various concrete and pictorial methods to come to the solution. You can see how using these practical models, such as part-whole and bar models, helps them to find and articulate their answer.

Mastery tips

Mastery Experts give anecdotal advice on where they have used hands-on and real-life elements to inspire their children.

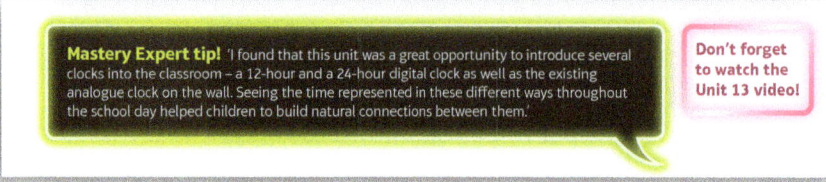

Concrete-Pictorial-Abstract (C-P-A) approach

Each **Share** section uses various methods to explain an answer, helping children to access abstract concepts by using concrete tools, such as counters. Remember, this isn't a linear process, so even children who appear confident using the more abstract method can deepen their knowledge by exploring the concrete representations. Encourage children to use all three methods to really solidify their understanding of a concept.

Pictorial representation – drawing the problem in a logical way that helps children visualise the maths

Concrete representation – using manipulatives to represent the problem. Encourage children to physically use resources to explore the maths.

Abstract representation – using words and calculations to represent the problem.

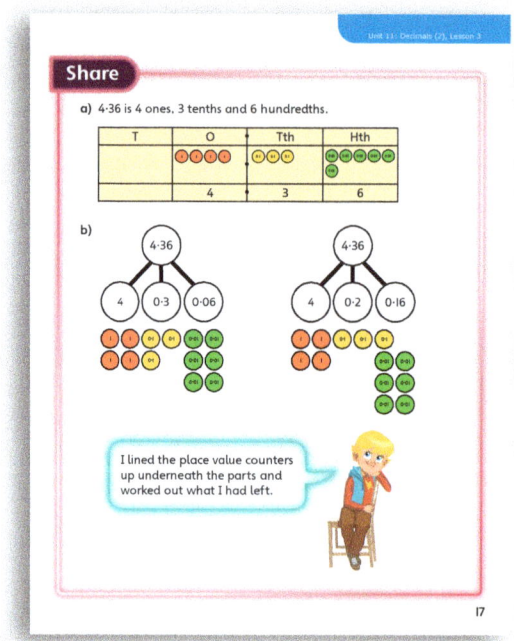

Practical tips

Every lesson suggests how to draw out the practical side of the **Discover** context.

You'll find these in the **Discover** section of the Teacher Guide for each lesson.

> **PRACTICAL TIPS** Begin without a calendar. Ask children to 'guess' the number of days in one year. Talk about any general knowledge that they may have about the number of days in a week, month and year.

Resources

Every lesson lists the practical resources you will need or might want to use. There is also a summary of all of the resources used throughout the term on page 38 to help you be prepared.

> **RESOURCES**
> **Mandatory:** base 10 equipment
> **Optional:** place value counters, specifically numbered number lines

Working with children below age-related expectation

This section offers advice on using *Power Maths* with children who are significantly behind age-related expectation. Teacher judgement will be crucial in terms of where and why children are struggling, and in choosing the right approach. The suggestions can of course be adapted for children with special educational needs, depending on the specific details of those needs.

General approaches to support children who are struggling

Keeping the pace manageable
Remember, you have more teaching days than *Power Maths* lessons so you can cover a lesson over more than one day, and revisit key learning, to ensure all children are ready to move on. You can use the + and − buttons to adjust the time for each unit in the online planning. The NCETM's Ready-to-Progress criteria can be used to help determine what should be highest priority.

Same-day intervention
You could go over the Textbook pages or revisit the previous year's work if necessary (see Addressing gaps). Remember that same-day intervention can be within the lesson, as well as afterwards (see page 27). As children start their independent practice, you can work with those who found the first part of the lesson difficult, checking understanding using manipulatives.

Fluency sessions
Fit in as much practice as you can for number bonds and times-tables, etc., at other times of the day. If you can, plan a short 'maths meeting' for this in the afternoon. You might choose to use a Power Up you haven't used already.

Addressing gaps
Use material from the same topic in the previous year to consolidate or address gaps in learning, e.g. Textbook pages and Strengthen activities. The End of unit check will help gauge children's understanding.

Pre-teaching
Find a 5- to 10-minute slot before the lesson to work with the children you feel would benefit. The afternoon before the lesson can work well, because it gives children time to think in between. Recap previous work on the topic (addressing any gaps you're aware of) and do some fluency practice, targeting number facts etc. that will help children access the learning.

Focusing on the key concepts
If children are a long way behind, it can be helpful to take a step back and think about the key concepts for children to engage with, not just the fine detail of the objective for that year group (e.g. addition with a specific number of columns). Bearing that in mind, how could children advance their understanding of the topic?

Providing extra support within the lesson

Support in the Teacher Guide
First of all, use the Strengthen support in the Teacher Guide for guided and independent work in each lesson, and share this with Teaching Assistants, where relevant. As you read through the lesson content and corresponding Teacher Guide pages before the lesson, ask yourself what key idea or nugget of understanding is at the heart of the lesson. If children are struggling, this should help you decide what's essential for all children before they move on.

Annotating pages
You can annotate questions to provide extra scaffolding or hints if you need to, but aim to build up children's ability to access questions independently wherever you can. Children tend to get used to the style of the *Power Maths* questions over time.

Quick recap as lesson starter
The Quick recap for each lesson in the Teacher Guide is an alternative starter activity to the Power Up. You might choose to use this with some or all children if you feel they will need support accessing the main lesson.

Consolidation questions
If you think some children would benefit from additional questions at the same level before moving on, write one or two similar questions on the board. (This shouldn't be at the expense of reasoning and problem-solving opportunities: take longer over the lesson if you need to.)

Hard copy Textbooks
The Textbooks help children focus in more easily on the mathematical representations, read the text more comfortably, and revisit work from a previous lesson that you are building on, as well as giving children ownership of their learning journey. In main lessons, it can work well to use the e-Textbook for **Discover** and give out the books when discussing the methods in the **Share** section.

Reading support
It's important that all children are exposed to problem solving and reasoning questions, which often involve reading. For whole-class work you can read questions together. For independent practice you could consider annotating pages to help children see what the question is asking, and stem sentences to help structure their answer. A general focus on specific mathematical language and vocabulary will help children access the questions. You could consider pairing weaker readers with stronger readers, or read questions as a group if those who need support are on the same table.

Providing extra depth and challenge with *Power Maths*

Just as prescribed in the National Curriculum, the goal of *Power Maths* is never to accelerate through a topic but rather to gain a clear, deep and broad understanding. Here are some suggestions to help ensure all children are appropriately challenged as you work with the resources.

Overall approaches

First of all, remember that the materials are designed to help you keep the class together, allowing all children to master a concept while those who grasp it quickly have time to explore it in more depth. Use the Deepen support in the Teacher Guide (see below) to challenge children who work through the questions quickly. Here are some questions and ideas to encourage breadth and depth during specific parts of the lesson, or at any time (where no part of the lesson sequence is specified):

- **Discover**: 'Can you demonstrate your solution another way?'
- **Share**: Make sure every child is encouraged to give answers and engage with the discussion, not just the most confident.
- **Think together**: 'Can you model your answers using concrete materials? Can you explain your solution to a partner?'
- Practice: Allow all children to work through the full set of questions, so that they benefit from the logical sequence.
- **Reflect**: 'Is there another way of working out the answer? And another way?'
  'Have you found all the solutions?'
  'Is that always true?'
  'What's different between this question and that question? And what's the same?'

Note that the **Challenge** questions are designed so that all children can access and attempt them, if they have worked through the steps leading up to them. There may be some children in a given lesson who don't manage to do the **Challenge**, but it is not supposed to be a distinct task for a subset of the class. When you look through the lesson materials before teaching, think about what each question is specifically asking, and compare this with the key learning point for the lesson. This will help you decide which questions you feel it's essential for all children to answer, before moving on. You can at least aim for all children to try the **Challenge**!

Deepen activities and support

The Teacher Guide provides valuable support for each stage of the lesson. This includes Deepen tips for the guided and independent practice sections, which will help you provide extra stretch and challenge within your lesson, without having to organise additional tasks. If you have a Teaching Assistant, they can also make use of this advice. There are also suggestions for the lesson as a whole in the 'Going Deeper' section on the first page of the Teacher Guide section for that lesson. Every class is different, so you can always go a bit further in the direction indicated, if appropriate, and build on the suggestions given.

There is a Deepen activity for each unit. These are designed to follow on from the End of unit check, stretching children who have a firm understanding of the key learning from the unit. Children can work on them independently, which makes it easier for the teacher to facilitate the Strengthen activity for children who need extra support. Deepen activities could also be introduced earlier in the unit if the necessary work has been covered. The Deepen activities are on *ActiveLearn* on the Planning page for each unit, and also on the Resources page).

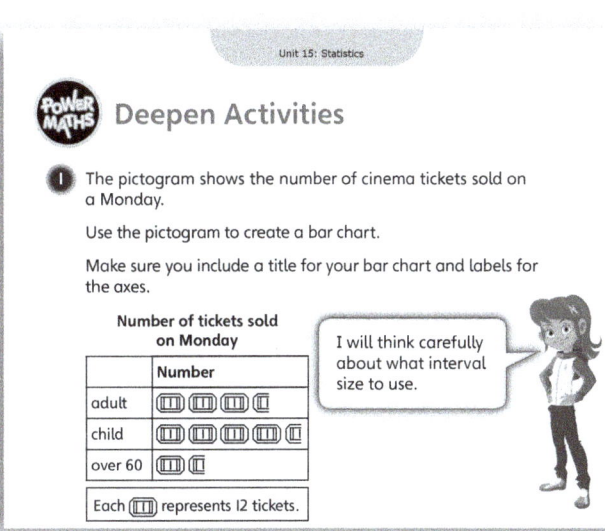

Using the questions flexibly to provide extra challenge

Sometimes you may want to write an extra question on the board or provide this on paper. You can usually do this by tweaking the lesson materials. The questions are designed to form a carefully structured sequence that builds understanding step by step, but, with careful thought about the purpose of each question, you can use the materials flexibly where you need to. Sometimes you might feel that children would benefit from another similar question for consolidation before moving on to the next one, or you might feel that they would benefit from a harder example in the same style. It should be quick and easy to generate 'more of the same' type questions where this is the case.

For this example (from Unit 3, Lesson 6), you could ask children to make up their own question(s) for a partner to solve. If you blot out more than four digits, does that make it easier or harder? Can children still devise questions with one exchange? (For any of the examples on this page you could ask early finishers to create their own question for a partner. 'Guess my number' questions are also good for this, e.g. Practice Book 4A page 20.).

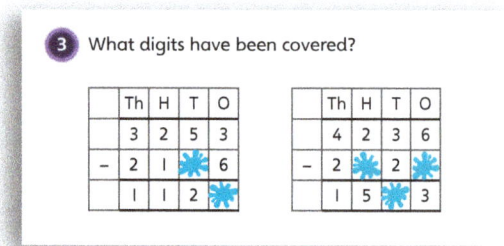

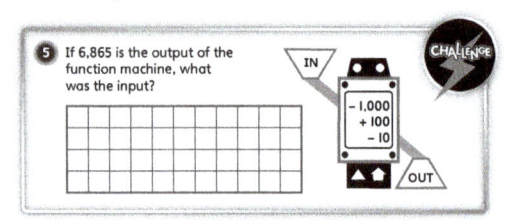

When you see a question like this one (from Unit 1, Lesson 7), it's easy to make extra examples to do afterwards if you need them. You could choose any 4-digit number, or choose tricky examples designed to cross 1000s (e.g. 1967 or 9909).

Here's an example (from Unit 3, Lesson 16) where some of the information in the picture is used for questions in the lesson, but not all. Clearly there are extra questions you could ask using the same information. For example, what's the biggest and smallest difference between two camps? Or, how much climbing is it to go from Camp 4 down to Camp 1 and then back up to Camp 3?

Besides creating additional questions, you should be able to find a question in the lesson that you can adapt into a game or open-ended investigation, if this helps to keep everyone engaged. It could simply be that, instead of answering 5 × 5 etc. on the page, they could build a robot with 5 lots of 5 cubes. Many lessons introduce a game anyway (e.g. Textbook 4A page 71).

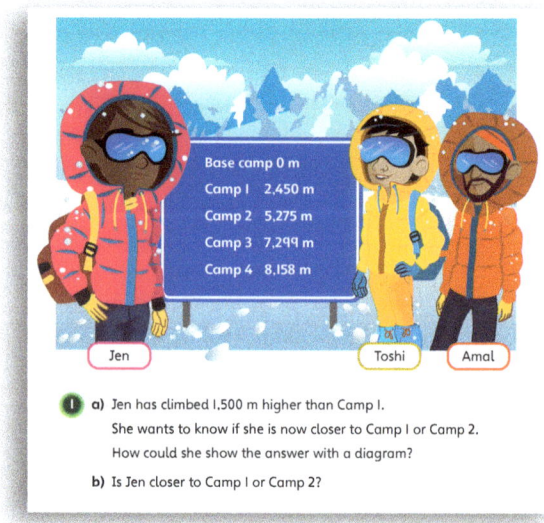

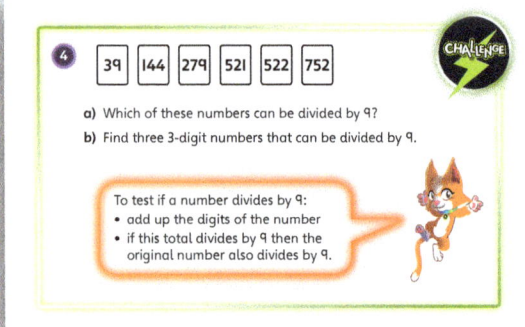

With a question like this (from Unit 5, Lesson 4), you could introduce a game where one child writes a list of numbers where only one is divisible by 9, and their partner has to work out which number it is.

See the bullets above for some general ideas that will help with 'opening out' questions in the books, e.g. 'can you find all the solutions?' type questions.

Other suggestions

Another way of stretching children is through mixed ability pairs, or via other opportunities for children to explain their understanding in their own way. This is a good way of encouraging children to go deeper into the learning, rather than, for instance, tackling questions that are computationally more challenging but conceptually equivalent in level.

Using *Power Maths* with mixed age classes

Overall approaches

There are many variables between schools that would make it inadvisable to recommend a one-size-fits-all approach to mixed age teaching with *Power Maths*. These include how year groups are merged, availability of Teaching Assistants, experience and preference of teaching staff, range in pupil attainment across years, classroom space and layout, level of flexibility around timetables, and overall organisational structure (whether the school is part of a trust).

Some schools will find it best to timetable separate maths lessons for the different year groups. Others will aim to teach the class together as much as possible using the mixed age planning support on *ActiveLearn* (see the lesson exemplars for ways of organising lessons with strong/medium/weak correlation between year groups). There will also be ways of adapting these general approaches. For example, offset lessons where Year A start their lesson with the teacher, while Year B work independently on the practice from the previous lesson, and then start the next lesson with the teacher while Year A work independently; or teachers may choose to base their provision around the lesson from one year group and tweak the content up/down for the other group.

Key strategies for mixed age teaching

The mixed age teaching webinar on *ActiveLearn* provides advice on all aspects of mixed age teaching, including more detail on the ideas below.

Developing independence over time
Investing time in building up children's independence will pay off in the medium term.

Clear rationale
If someone asked, 'Why did you teach both Unit 3 and 4 in the same lesson/separate lessons?', what would your answer be?

Designing a lesson
1. Identify the core learning for each group
2. Identify any number skills necessary to access the core
3. Consider the flow of concepts and how one core leads to the other

Challenging all children
The questions are designed to build understanding step by step, but with careful thought about the purpose of each question you can tweak them to increase the challenge.

Multiple years combined
With more than two years together, teachers will inevitably need to use the resources flexibly if delivering a single lesson.

Enjoy the positives!

Comparison deepens understanding and there will be lots of opportunities for children, as well as misconceptions to explore. There is also in-built pre-teaching and the chance to build up a concept from its foundations. For teachers there is double the material to draw on! Mixed age teachers require a strong understanding of the progression of ideas across year groups, which is highly valuable for all teachers. Also, it is necessary to engage deeply with the lesson to see how to use the materials flexibly – this is recommended for all teachers and will help you bring your lesson to life!

List of practical resources

Year 4C Mandatory resources

Resource	Lesson
Hundredths grids	**Unit 11** Lessons 1, 7
Metre ruler	**Unit 11** Lesson 4
Multilink cubes	**Unit 11** Lesson 7
Number cards	**Unit 11** Lesson 1
Number lines (from 0 to 1)	**Unit 11** Lesson 7
Paper (squared)	**Unit 16** Lesson 3
Place value counters	**Unit 11** Lessons 2, 5
Place value counters (1s and tenths, 0·1)	**Unit 11** Lesson 1
Place value counters (blank)	**Unit 11** Lesson 7
Place value equipment	**Unit 11** Lessons 3, 4
Rulers	**Unit 15** Lessons 1, 2, 3, 4, 5
Ten frames (blank)	**Unit 11** Lesson 1
Weighing scales	**Unit 11** Lesson 5

Year 4C Optional resources

Resource	Lesson
2D polygons (plastic or card)	**Unit 14** Lesson 6
2D shapes	**Unit 14** Lessons 2, 3, 4, 5
2D shapes (range)	**Unit 14** Lessons 1, 7, 8
24-hour clock times (examples from everyday life: computer clock, timetables, etc.)	**Unit 13** Lesson 4
Axis grid (large)	**Unit 15** Lesson 6
Calendars (or year planners)	**Unit 13** Lesson 5
Cards for pair games (set: half with pictures of different shapes, half with names of different shapes)	**Unit 14** Lesson 6
Chalk	**Unit 16** Lesson 4
Chess board	**Unit 16** Lesson 6
Clock faces	**Unit 14** Lesson 1
Clocks (analogue)	**Unit 13** Lessons 3, 4, 5
Clocks (digital)	**Unit 13** Lessons 3, 4, 5
Coins (plastic)	**Unit 11** Lesson 4 **Unit 12** Lessons 1, 2, 3, 4, 5, 6
Computer geometry package	**Unit 16** Lessons 2, 3, 4, 5, 6
Counters	**Unit 15** Lesson 6
Crayons	**Unit 12** Lesson 2
Elastic bands	**Unit 14** Lesson 8
Flashcards	**Unit 13** Lesson 5
Geoboards (with elastic bands)	**Unit 14** Lessons 4, 8
Geostrip kit	**Unit 14** Lesson 4
Help envelopes	**Unit 15** Lesson 3
Internet access	**Unit 16** Lesson 1
Lolly sticks (or straws)	**Unit 14** Lesson 8
Maps (simple)	**Unit 16** Lesson 1
Mirrors	**Unit 14** Lessons 7, 8
Multilink cubes	**Unit 15** Lessons 1, 2
Number cards	**Unit 13** Lessons 3, 4, 5
Number lines	**Unit 15** Lessons 3, 4, 5
Paper (large pieces of)	**Unit 15** Lesson 6
Paper (squared)	**Unit 15** Lessons 3, 4, 5 **Unit 16** Lessons 3, 4
Paper squares	**Unit 14** Lessons 1, 6
Part-whole model (large, laminated)	**Unit 11** Lesson 1
Place value counters	**Unit 11** Lesson 6
Place value grids	**Unit 11** Lesson 7 **Unit 12** Lesson 3
Rulers	**Unit 14** Lessons 2, 5 **Unit 16** Lesson 3
Set squares	**Unit 14** Lesson 2
String (pieces of)	**Unit 13** Lesson 1
Tape	**Unit 16** Lesson 4
Timers or stopwatches (digital)	**Unit 13** Lesson 2
Triangles (range of different)	**Unit 14** Lesson 3

Getting started with *Power Maths*

As you prepare to put *Power Maths* into action, you might find the tips and advice below helpful.

STEP 1: Train up!

A practical, up-front full day professional development course will give you and your team a brilliant head-start as you begin your *Power Maths* journey. You will learn more about the ethos, how it works and why.

STEP 2: Check out the progression

Take a look at the yearly and termly overviews. Next take a look at the unit overview for the unit you are about to teach in your Teacher Guide, remembering that you can match your lessons and pacing to match your class.

STEP 3: Explore the context

Take a little time to look at the context for this unit: what are the implications for the unit ahead? (Think about key language, common misunderstandings and intervention strategies, for example.) If you have the online subscription, don't forget to watch the corresponding unit video.

STEP 4: Prepare for your first lesson

Familiarise yourself with the objectives, essential questions to ask and the resources you will need. The Teacher Guide offers tips, ideas and guidance on individual lessons to help you anticipate children's misconceptions and challenge those who are ready to think more deeply.

STEP 5: Teach and reflect

Deliver your lesson — and enjoy!

Afterwards, reflect on how it went… Did you cover all five stages? Does the lesson need more time? How could you improve it? What percentage of your class do you think mastered the concept? How can you help those that didn't?

Unit 11
Decimals 2

Mastery Expert tip! 'It is essential that children have an understanding of what a decimal looks like visually. I find it best to avoid using base 10 blocks for representing decimals, as this often leads to confusion. A hundredths grid offers a more successful representation.'

Don't forget to watch the Unit 11 video!

WHY THIS UNIT IS IMPORTANT

In the previous unit, children were introduced to decimals. This unit builds on the last by exploring decimals in more depth. Children first find number bonds of tenths and hundredths to 1 and show how this links to their number bonds to 10 and 100. They start to represent decimals on place value grids and use these grids to help them partition and compare decimals. At this stage, children focus on comparing decimals with the same number of digits. Children begin to round decimals to the nearest whole number by considering their position on a number line. Children then progress to using diagrams to understand the decimal equivalents of simple fractions, such as a half and a quarter. Along with the previous unit, these lessons should provide children with a solid introduction to decimals and their link to place value and fractions. This unit is fundamental to further work in Years 5 and 6 on decimals.

WHERE THIS UNIT FITS

→ Unit 10: Decimals (1)
→ **Unit 11: Decimals (2)**
→ Unit 12: Money

This unit builds on children's work in Year 4 on decimals and links closely to all their work on place value and fractions so far.

Before they start this unit, it is expected that children:
- know the decimal equivalent of $\frac{1}{10}$ and $\frac{1}{100}$
- can draw, model and write any number of tenths and hundredths using a hundredths grid, ten frame or bead string
- understand that a tenth arises from dividing 1 by 10 and a hundredth arises from dividing 1 by 100
- understand the use of the decimal point and where it should be placed.

ASSESSING MASTERY

By the end of the unit, children will be able to find the number bond to 1 of a decimal with up to two decimal places. They should be able to round numbers to the nearest whole number and order decimals with the same number of decimal places by comparing digits. Finally, children will know and understand decimal equivalents of simple fractions such as a half and a quarter.

COMMON MISCONCEPTIONS	STRENGTHENING UNDERSTANDING	GOING DEEPER
When finding a number bond to 1, children may add on too much. For example, children may write 0·47 in 0·63 + ☐ = 1.	Remind children of their bonds to 100 and draw the link to number bonds to 1. In addition, children should be able to use a hundredths grid or bead string to help them visually identify these number bonds.	Using 10 blank place value counters and a place value grid from 10s to hundredths, how many different numbers can children make? What is the greatest number? What is the smallest number?
When comparing decimals, children may compare digits that do not have the same place value. For example, when comparing 23·6 and 9·7 they may compare the 2 (tens) and 9 (ones) as opposed to 2 tens and 0 tens.	Use a number line to help children locate decimals.	Encourage children to explore missing digits in numbers that are in order, such as: 2·☐5 < 2·4☐ How many different solutions can children find? Now try: 2·☐5 < 2·4☐ < ☐·45

Unit 11: Decimals 2

UNIT STARTER PAGES

Use these pages to introduce the unit focus to children as part of a whole-class discussion. You can use the characters to explore different ways of thinking and working, too.

STRUCTURES AND REPRESENTATIONS

Hundredths grid: This is an important representation when children are learning to identify hundredths. Children can use a hundredths grid to work out the missing number.

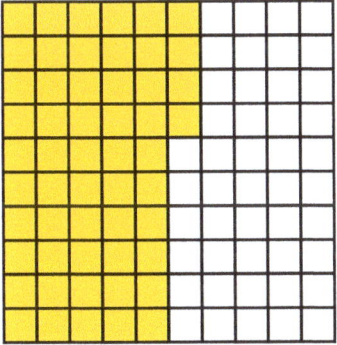

Number line: It is important for children to learn to position a number with one decimal place on a number line. They will learn that, to round a number to the nearest whole number, they need to look at the tenths digit.

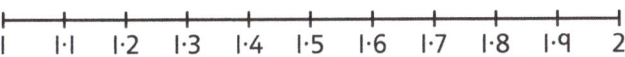

KEY LANGUAGE

There is some key language that children will need to know as part of the learning in this unit.

- tens (10s), ones (1s), tenths, hundredths, fraction
- decimal point, decimal place, 0·1, 0·01
- equivalent, number bond, equivalent fraction
- whole number, digit
- rounding, round up, round down, multiply (×), divide (÷)
- greater than (>), less than (<), equal to (=), smallest, lightest, greatest, heaviest, capacity
- order, compare, statement, ascending, descending, convert
- part-whole, place value, bar model

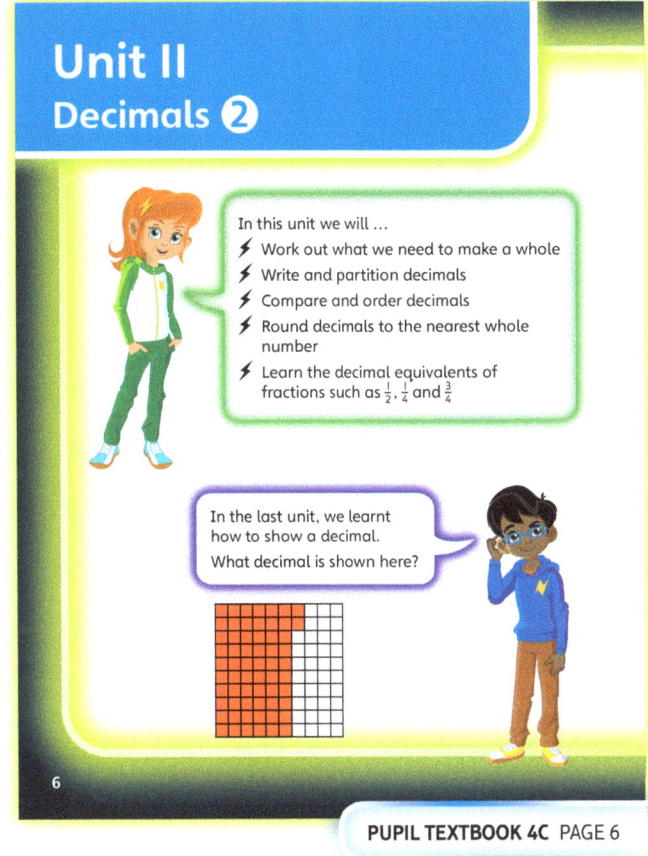

PUPIL TEXTBOOK 4C PAGE 6

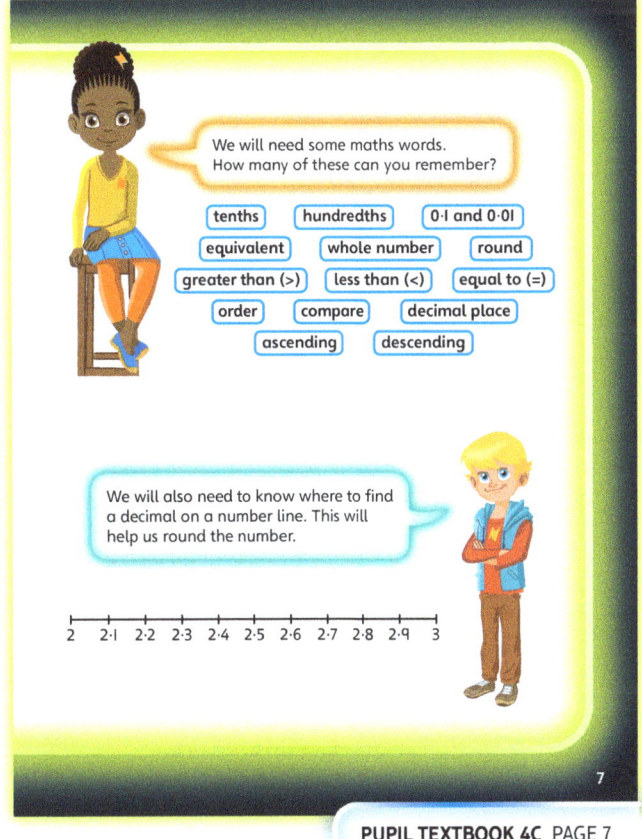

PUPIL TEXTBOOK 4C PAGE 7

Unit 11: Decimals (2), Lesson 1

Make a whole

Learning focus

In this lesson, children will understand that given a number of tenths or hundredths they can make the number bond up to 1.

Before you teach

- Do children know their number bonds to 10 and 100?
- Can children represent tenths on a ten frame and hundredths on a hundredths grid?
- Can children represent tenths and hundredths on a part-whole model?

NATIONAL CURRICULUM LINKS

Year 4 Number – fractions (including decimals)

Recognise and write decimal equivalents of any number of tenths or hundredths.

ASSESSING MASTERY

Children can find the number bond to 1 using a ten frame and hundredths grid and can write them onto a part-whole model.

COMMON MISCONCEPTIONS

Children may not be secure with their number bonds to 10 and 100 and may miscalculate the number that makes the number bond to 1. For example, they may think that, if they had 0·36, they would need 0·74 to make the number bond to 1. Ask:

- What number do you need to add to make 1? Or 10? Or 100? How do you know?

STRENGTHENING UNDERSTANDING

Provide children with a ten frame and hundredths grid. When dealing with tenths and hundredths, encourage children to say them aloud to highlight the value of the digits and to count in tenths or hundredths when making a whole. For example, 0·8 is '8 tenths' or 0·45 is '45 hundredths'.

GOING DEEPER

Ask children to make a whole using three numbers instead of two. Give them one number and ask how many different ways they can make a whole. For example, 0·2 + ☐ + ☐ = 1. This could be represented on a part-whole model. Also encourage children to link making a whole to subtraction, such as 1 – 0·72 = ☐.

KEY LANGUAGE

In lesson: tenths, hundredths, whole, part-whole, statement, number bond

STRUCTURES AND REPRESENTATIONS

Hundredths grid, part-whole model, bar model, ten frame

RESOURCES

Mandatory: hundredths grid, blank ten frames, number cards, 1s and tenths (0·1) place value counters

Optional: large laminated part-whole model

 In the eTextbook of this lesson, you will find interactive links to a selection of teaching tools.

Quick recap

Count on and back together in fraction steps of tenths as a class. Repeat with different starting numbers.

Unit 11: Decimals (2), Lesson 1

Discover

WAYS OF WORKING Pair work

ASK

- Question 1 a): *What is the value of the 7 in 0·7 kg?*
- Question 1 a): *How could you represent 0·7?*
- Question 1 b): *What number is shown here?*
- Question 1 b): *How could you represent 0·46?*

IN FOCUS Encourage children to use resources and model each question in a concrete way. Children may use a hundredths grid or a ten frame to work out the missing number. Some children may need to count up in tenths or hundredths. For example, to get the number bond to 1 for 0·46, some children may individually count 54 squares on a hundredths grid. Encourage children to use a more efficient method, such as identifying that there are 5 columns of ten and then 4 ones.

PRACTICAL TIPS Ensure children have tenths counters and ten frames. Since Jamie has 0·7 kilograms of strawberries, ask children to show the value of the 7 using their counters on the ten frame.

ANSWERS

Question 1 a): Jamie needs another 0·3 kg of strawberries.

Question 1 b): Alex needs another 0·54 kg of strawberries.

PUPIL TEXTBOOK 4C PAGE 8

Share

WAYS OF WORKING Whole class teacher led

ASK

- Question 1 a): *What number are you starting with? How can you use a tenths grid to show this? What do you need to look at to help you make a whole?*
- Question 1 b): *Can you see how this works on a part-whole model?*

IN FOCUS In question 1 a), show children the tenths grid of 0·7 (7 tenths) and count aloud as a class so that they know it is 0·7. Can children explain why the number bond to 1 is 0·3? In question 1 b), show children the hundredths grid of 0·46. Explain a more efficient way of identifying this as 0·46 without counting each individual hundredth. For example, show children that there are 4 columns of ten and 6 ones. Can children explain why the number bond to 1 is 0·54 without having to count each hundredth? Encourage children to see the link to the number bonds to 100.

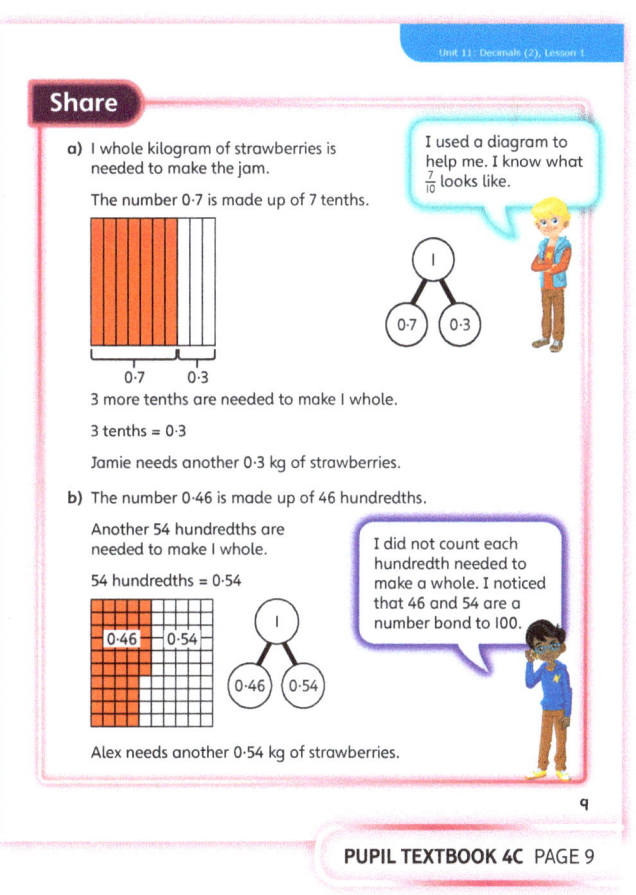

PUPIL TEXTBOOK 4C PAGE 9

Think together

WAYS OF WORKING Whole class teacher led (I do, We do, You do)

ASK
- Question ②: *What numbers are shown here? Can you represent these on a hundredths grid? What number is needed to make a whole?*
- Question ③ a): *What amounts of water does Jamilla have? What do they add up to? What number is needed to make the whole 1 litre?*

IN FOCUS Questions ① and ② look at making a whole from tenths and hundredths, which are represented using ten frames, hundredths grids and part-whole models. Encourage children to make their own representations for each question. Ensure children are aware that they are dealing with tenths and hundredths and not whole numbers when calculating the number bond to 1. Count up in tenths and say the numbers aloud to reinforce this.

STRENGTHEN To support understanding, represent question ③ using an actual jug and cups, counters or a hundredths grid. Children could also use two different colours to represent the two different cups and help them calculate the number bond to 1.

DEEPEN Ask children to give more than one answer for question ③ c). Ask children if it is possible to give an answer that has tenths and hundredths in it. Can they give examples?

ASSESSMENT CHECKPOINT Can children successfully represent their answers on a hundredths grid and on part-whole models?

ANSWERS

Question ① a): 0·4

Question ① b): 0·2

Question ① c): 0·17

Question ② a): 1 — 0·1, 0·9 b): 1 — 0·5, 0·5 c): 1 — 0·27, 0·73 d): 1 — 0·99, 0·01

Question ③ a): Jamilla needs 0·3 l more.

Question ③ b): Luis needs 0·44 l more.

Question ③ c): Various answers are possible, for example:
0·1 + 0·9, 0·2 + 0·8 and so on (tenths add to 10).
0·25 + 0·75, 0·45 + 0·55 and so on (hundredths add to 100).

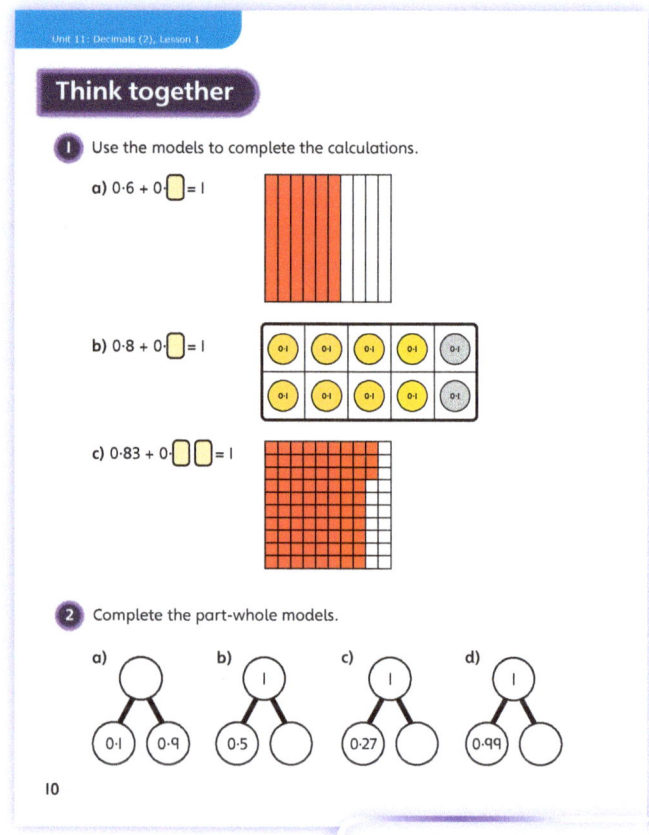

PUPIL TEXTBOOK 4C PAGE 10

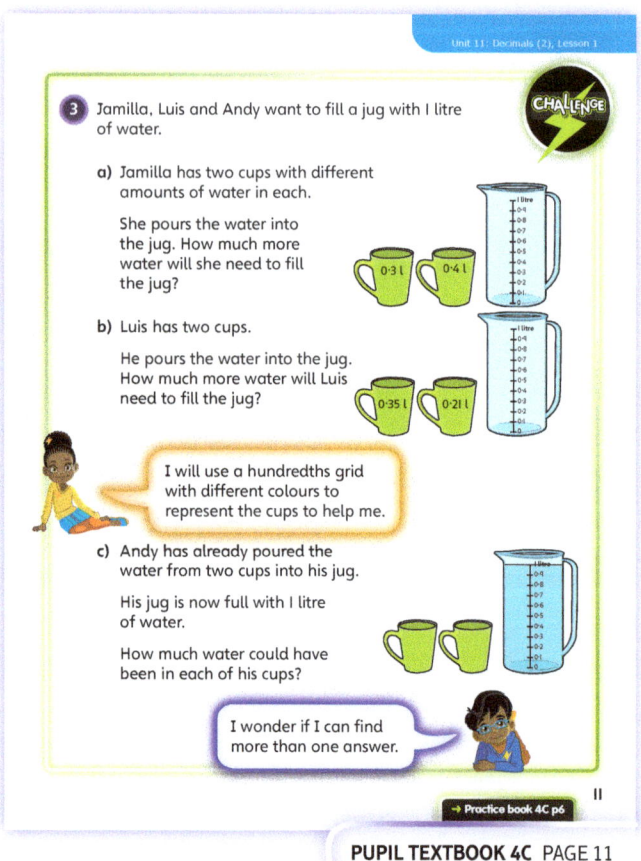

PUPIL TEXTBOOK 4C PAGE 11

Unit 11: Decimals (2), Lesson 1

Practice

WAYS OF WORKING Independent thinking

IN FOCUS Question ③ consolidates the representations on part-whole models. Children can use place value counters to physically replicate the part-whole models in the questions. They can then manipulate the counters to make the number bonds to 1.

STRENGTHEN In question ⑤, children can use a hundredths grid to replace the bar models. This may help them to see more easily how to make a whole. When diagrams are not given, encourage children to use concrete resources to make their own representations.

DEEPEN Explore question ⑥ further by asking children if there are any different digits they could use that would still make the number sentences correct. Can they explain why? Question ⑦ can also be explored further. Ask children to identify different ways to complete the cross diagram. Challenge children to create their own version of this question and share it with a partner.

ASSESSMENT CHECKPOINT Children should now be confident in using a ten frame, hundredths grid or a part-whole model to make a whole if they are given a number of tenths or hundredths. Ask children to model one of the parts of question ③, explaining why they would place certain counters in certain sections of the part-whole model. Do they use sound reasoning and demonstrate a deep understanding when explaining their thinking?

ANSWERS Answers for the **Practice** part of the lesson can be found in the *Power Maths* online subscription.

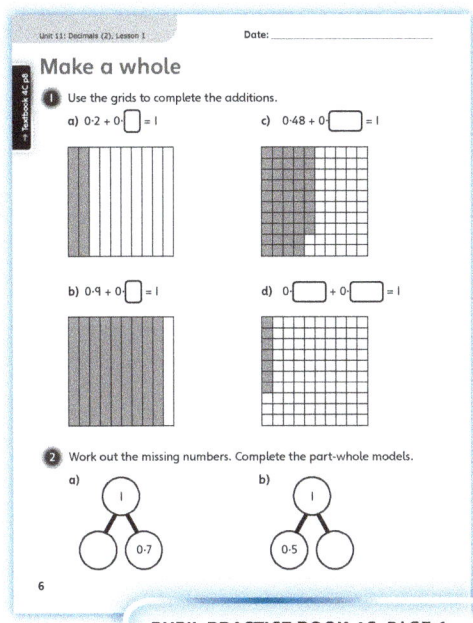

PUPIL PRACTICE BOOK 4C PAGE 6

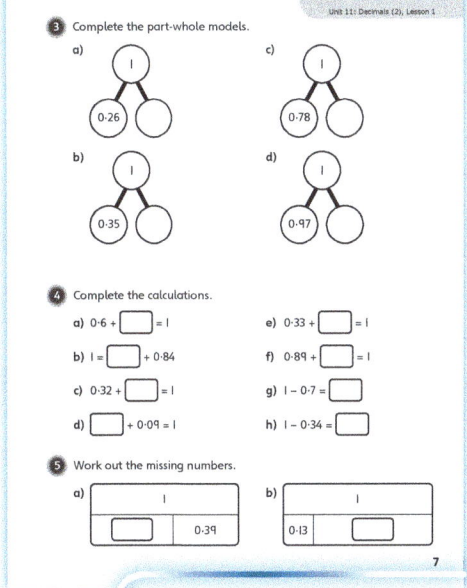

PUPIL PRACTICE BOOK 4C PAGE 7

Reflect

WAYS OF WORKING Independent thinking

IN FOCUS This activity presents a common misconception in order to check children's understanding of how to make a whole when given a number of hundredths for one part. Children should see links with the number bonds to 100 and can use this to explore what mistake has been made.

ASSESSMENT CHECKPOINT Children can identify the correct bond to 1 and can confidently explain their decision using the correct vocabulary and sound reasoning.

ANSWERS Answers for the **Reflect** part of the lesson can be found in the *Power Maths* online subscription.

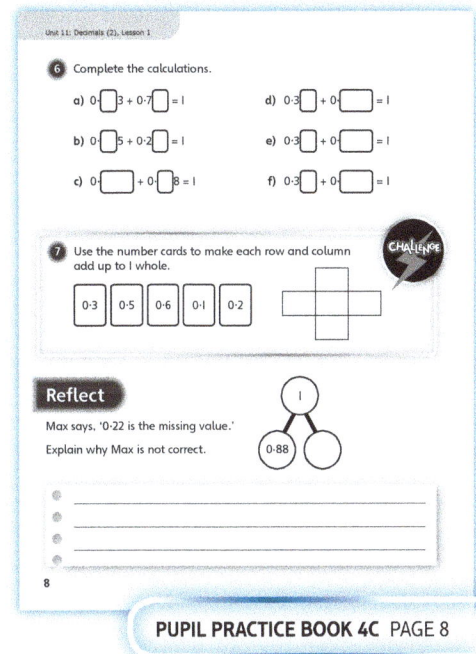

PUPIL PRACTICE BOOK 4C PAGE 8

After the lesson ⏸

- Are children confident with tenths and hundredths?
- Can children make the number bonds to 1 using a ten frame, hundredths grid or part-whole model?

45

Unit 11: Decimals (2), Lesson 2

Partition decimals

Learning focus
In this lesson, children will learn that a number with up to two decimal places can be made up of some 10s, 1s, tenths and hundredths.

Before you teach
- Can children represent 1-, 2- and 3-digit numbers using a place value grid?
- Do children know the place value of each digit in whole numbers?

NATIONAL CURRICULUM LINKS

Year 4 Number – fractions (including decimals)

Recognise and write decimal equivalents of any number of tenths or hundredths.

ASSESSING MASTERY

Children can represent numbers with up to two decimal places using counters and a place value grid and, given a pictorial representation, can write a number with up to two decimal places. Children recognise that a number up to two decimal places can be made up of some 10s, 1s, tenths and hundredths.

COMMON MISCONCEPTIONS

Children may confuse the place value and size of a number. They may, for example, see 2 ones and 7 hundredths as 2·7, missing that the value of the tenth is 0. Ask:
- *How would you write 2 tenths and 7 hundredths? Are there any 0s in this number? What does the 0 represent?*

STRENGTHENING UNDERSTANDING

Children who need support with representing numbers up to two decimal places should recap representing 1-digit numbers. Ask children to show a 1-digit number on a place value grid. Explain that we can now add some tenths and this will give us a number with one decimal place. Next, explain that we can also add some hundredths and this will create a number with two decimal places. Encourage children to write out some numbers in full – for example, 7·23 can be written out in full as 7 ones, 2 tenths and 3 hundredths. Children can then represent each part on a place value grid.

GOING DEEPER

Ask children to represent the number 5·63 in different ways. For example, do they represent this as 5 ones, 6 tenths and 3 hundredths or 5 ones and 63 hundredths? Ask children to explain why these are equal.

KEY LANGUAGE

In lesson: hundreds, tens (10s), ones (1s), tenths (0·1), hundredths (0·01), decimal place

STRUCTURES AND REPRESENTATIONS

Place value grid, bar model, hundredths grid, part-whole model

RESOURCES

Mandatory: place value counters

 In the eTextbook of this lesson, you will find interactive links to a selection of teaching tools.

Quick recap

Challenge children to identify the value of each digit in the number 5·55.

Unit 11: Decimals (2), Lesson 2

Discover

WAYS OF WORKING Pair work

ASK

- Question 1 a): *What is the value of the 2? What is the value of the 3? What is the value of the 7?*
- Question 1 a): *How can you tell how many 1s, tenths and hundredths Lexi has used?*
- Question 1 a): *What number has Lexi made?*
- Question 1 b): *How can you partition your number? How can you tell how many 10s and how many 1s there are? What about how many tenths and how many hundredths?*

IN FOCUS Question 1 b) provides children with a number and asks them to make a representation of it on a part-whole model. Encourage children to partition the number into ones, tenths and hundredths and discuss how many parts their part-whole model will have.

PRACTICAL TIPS Encourage children to use counters and a place value grid or a hundredths grid to represent Lexi's number from question 1. Encourage children to partition the number into 1s, tenths and hundredths until they see that Lexi has made a mistake.

ANSWERS

Question 1 a): The ones and tenths are correct, but Lexi has only 6 hundredths instead of 7.

Question 1 b): 2·37 = 2 + 0·3 + 0·07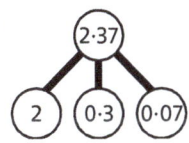

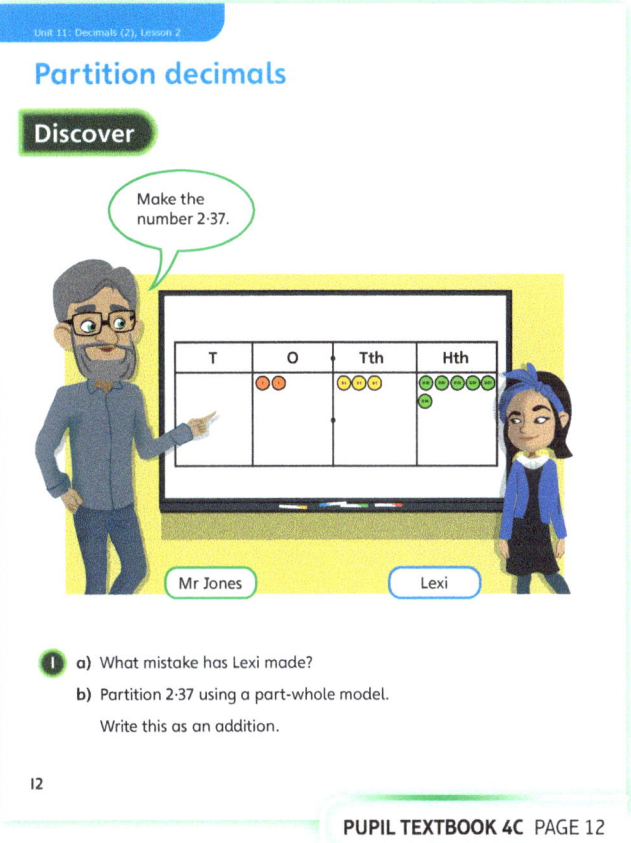

PUPIL TEXTBOOK 4C PAGE 12

Share

WAYS OF WORKING Whole class teacher led

ASK

- Question 1 a): *What is the number 2·37 made up of? Which parts of the number has Lexi got correct? What is Lexi's mistake?*
- Question 1 b): *Why do you not have a part for 10s?*

IN FOCUS Show children the diagram of 2·37 correctly represented on the place value grid. Can children explain why the value of the 3 is 3 tenths and why the value of the 7 is 7 hundredths? Explain that the first number after the decimal point tells us how many tenths there are and the second number after the decimal point tells us how many hundredths there are.

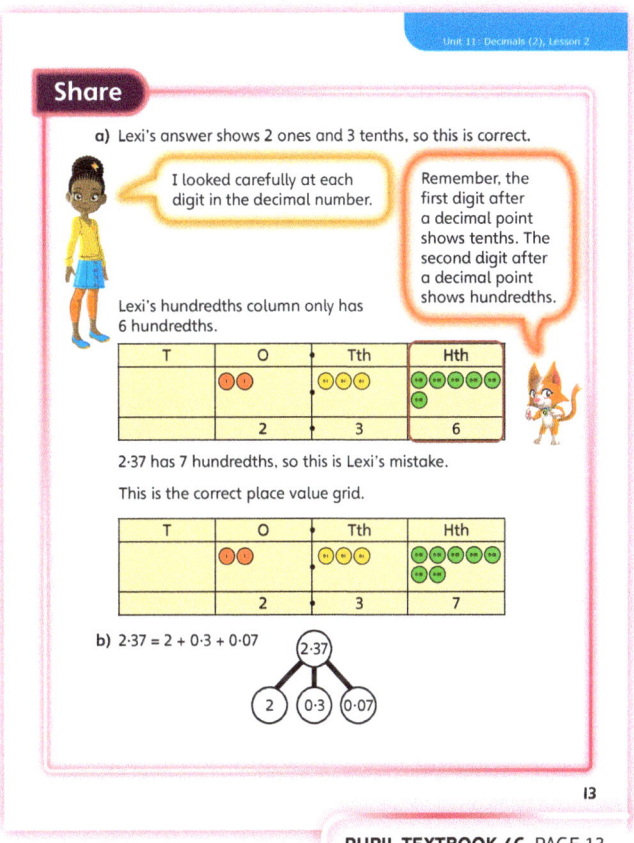

PUPIL TEXTBOOK 4C PAGE 13

Think together

WAYS OF WORKING Whole class teacher led (I do, We do, You do)

ASK

• Question ① a): *What is the value of the 5, the 4 and the 9?*
• Question ① b): *What is the value of the 0, the 2 and the 6?*
• Question ②: *What does each part represent? What is the whole? How do you know?*
• Question ③: *What number has Ebo shown? Which number is the placeholder in 20·12? Why do you need to include 0 as a placeholder in this way?*

IN FOCUS In question ③, children write decimals from numbers they have created themselves, using a place value grid and five counters. It highlights the importance of 0 and when we do and do not need to include it. Can children explain why 12·2 and 12·20 have the same value?

STRENGTHEN To support understanding, represent all the numbers on a place value grid and ask children to write the value at the bottom of each place value heading. Separate the 10s, the 1s, the tenths and the hundredths. Clearly associate each digit with the particular place value and say this aloud. For example, 0·7 is 7 tenths. This will help children understand the numbers.

DEEPEN Give children numbers using place value counters (but not a grid). Provide the numbers out of order (not arranged as 10s, 1s, tenths and hundredths) and ask children to write down the number shown. This will help them understand that the order the parts are presented in does not matter, but the value does.

ASSESSMENT CHECKPOINT Can children represent numbers up to two decimal places on a place value grid? Do children understand that a number up to two decimal places is made up of some 10s, 1s, tenths and hundredths?

ANSWERS

Question ① a): 5·49 is equal to 5 ones, 4 tenths and 9 hundredths. 5·49 = 5 + 0·4 + 0·09

Question ① b):

O	Tth	Hth
	0·1 0·1	0·01 0·01 0·01 0·01 0·01 0·01

0·26 is equal to 0 ones, 2 tenths and 6 hundredths. 0·26 = 0·2 + 0·06

Question ②: a) 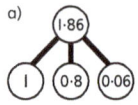 b) 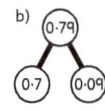 c)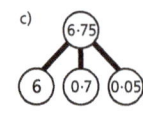

Question ③: There are many possible answers, including whole numbers, for example:
50, 5, 41, 14, 32, 23, 40·1, 40·01, 30·2, 30·02, 20·3, 20·03, 20·12, 20·21, 31·1, 31·01, 30·11, 3·11, 22·1, 22·01, 21·2, 21·02, 12·11, 12·2, 12·02, 0·5, 4·1, 1·4, 3·2, 2·3, 0·05, 0·41, 0·14, 0·32, 0·23, 4·01, 1·04, 3·02, 2·03, 10·22, 10·13, 10·31, 10·4, 10·04, 11·12, 11·21, 13·1, 13·01, 1·31, 1·13, 2·21, 2·12

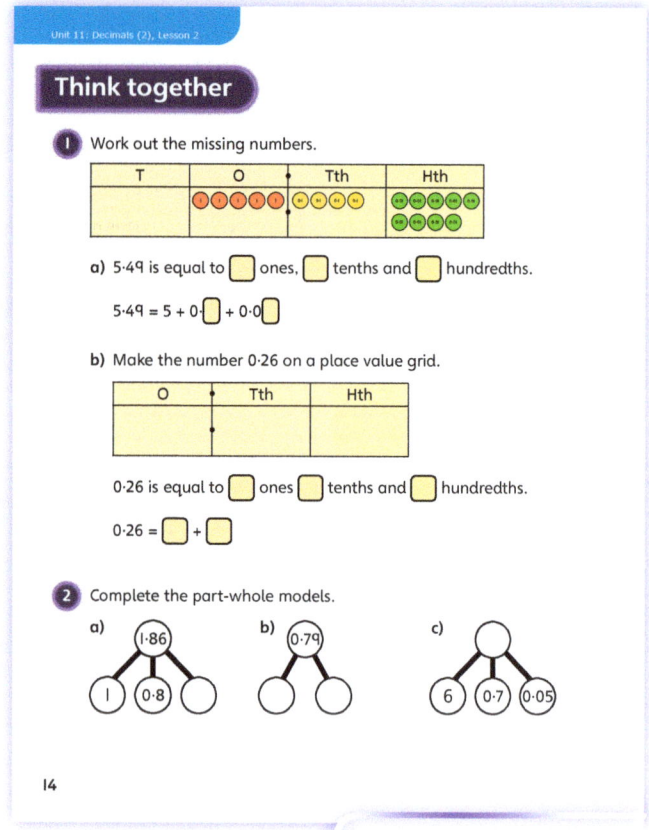

PUPIL TEXTBOOK 4C PAGE 14

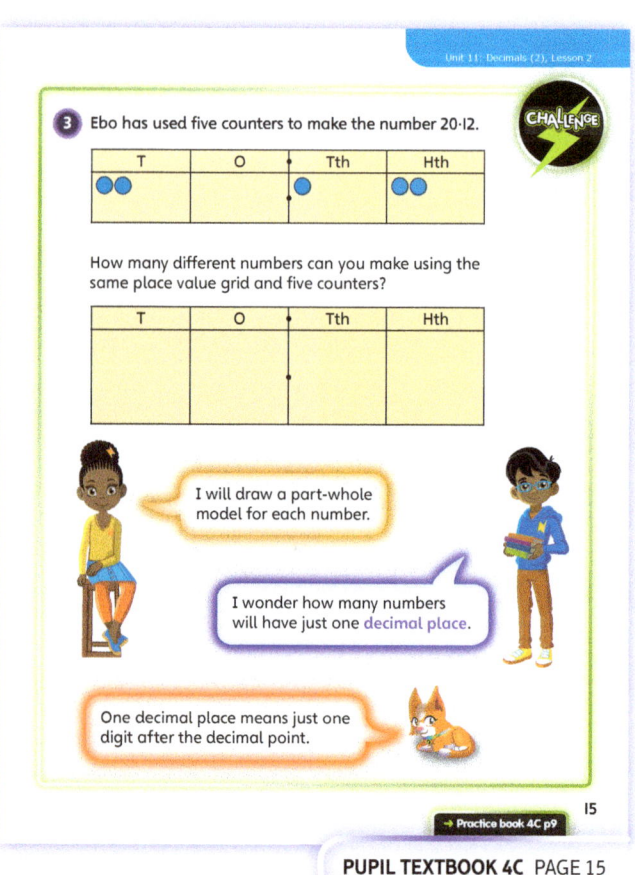

PUPIL TEXTBOOK 4C PAGE 15

Unit 11: Decimals (2), Lesson 2

Practice

WAYS OF WORKING Independent thinking or pair work

IN FOCUS Questions 1 to 6 aim to consolidate children's understanding of representations of numbers up to two decimal places. Children can make their own representations and should understand that a number is made up of 10s, 1s, tenths and hundredths and that these can be shown and written in different ways.

STRENGTHEN Children can use place value grids and counters to represent the numbers. Present them with some numbers that are not given in the order of 10s, 1s, tenths and hundredths, and encourage children to reorder them.

DEEPEN Question 7 can be explored further by asking children what other clues they could write for each of these numbers. They then choose their own number with two decimal places and give clues to a partner who tries to guess it.

ASSESSMENT CHECKPOINT Children should be confident in representing numbers up to two decimal places using a place value grid and a part-whole model. They should also be able to write the number when presented with a representation of it.

ANSWERS Answers for the **Practice** part of the lesson can be found in the *Power Maths* online subscription.

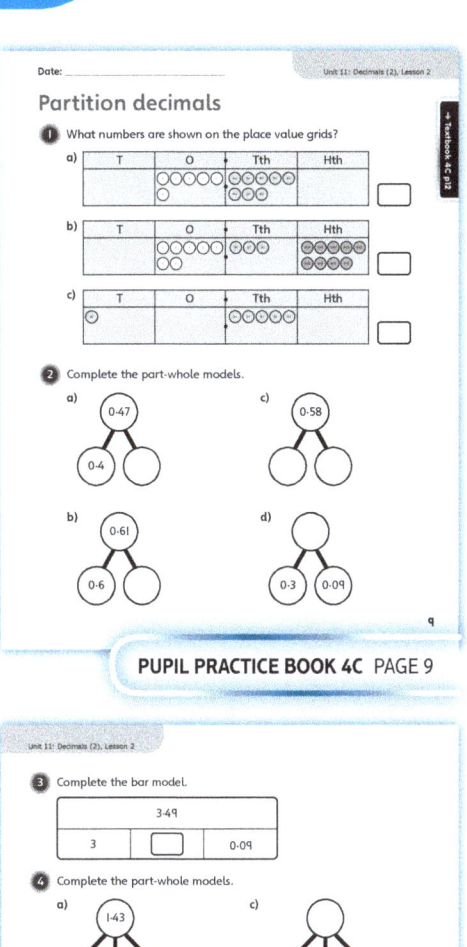

PUPIL PRACTICE BOOK 4C PAGE 9

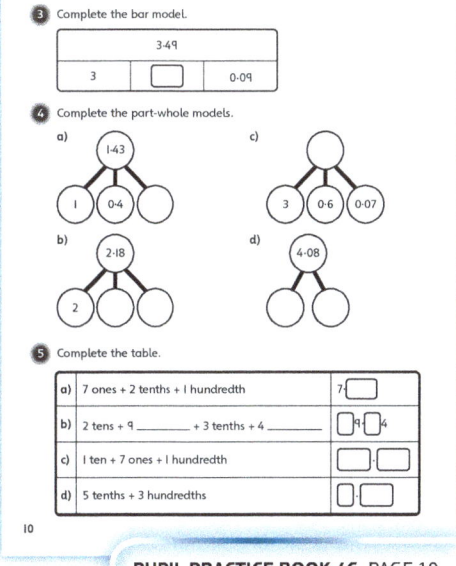

PUPIL PRACTICE BOOK 4C PAGE 10

Reflect

WAYS OF WORKING Independent thinking

IN FOCUS This question checks for understanding of place value. Encourage children to write a number with some 10s, some 1s, some tenths and some hundredths. They could also choose a number that includes a 0 in one of the parts.

ASSESSMENT CHECKPOINT Children explain the value of each digit in the decimal number. They use this to partition the number by showing or drawing a suitable visual representation of their choosing – for example, a part-whole model or counters on a place value grid.

ANSWERS Answers for the **Reflect** part of the lesson can be found in the *Power Maths* online subscription.

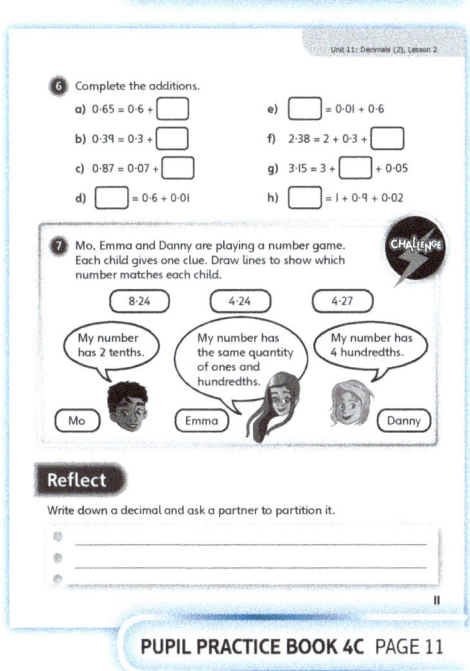

PUPIL PRACTICE BOOK 4C PAGE 11

After the lesson

- Can children represent a number up to two decimal places on a place value grid or part-whole model?
- Can children work out what decimal numbers are represented by given representations?

49

Unit 11: Decimals (2), Lesson 3

Flexibly partition decimals

Learning focus
In this lesson, children will find a range of different ways to partition a given decimal number.

Before you teach
- Can children partition a decimal number based on place value?
- Can children combine 1s, tenths and hundredths into a decimal number?

NATIONAL CURRICULUM LINKS

Year 4 Number – fractions (including decimals)

Recognise and write decimal equivalents of any number of tenths or hundredths.

ASSESSING MASTERY

Children can explain how a given decimal number may be partitioned in a variety of different ways.

COMMON MISCONCEPTIONS

Children may think partitioning can only be done using the place value columns. Ask:

• *How could you represent the number 7 using some ones and some tenths?*

For example, you could write 7 as 6 ones and 1 one. You could then write the 1 one as 10 tenths. So, 7 = 6 ones + 10 tenths.

STRENGTHENING UNDERSTANDING

Provide place value equipment to support children with partitioning and identifying the value of each digit in a decimal number.

GOING DEEPER

Discuss with children why they can choose to partition a number in a range of different ways, depending on what calculations are needed. Help them to understand when a different way of partitioning might be more helpful than simply partitioning by place value columns (for example, to make a subtraction easier so that no exchange is needed).

KEY LANGUAGE

In lesson: tenth, hundredth, partition

Other language to be used by the teacher: place value, wholes, parts, column

STRUCTURES AND REPRESENTATIONS

Part-whole model, place value grid

RESOURCES

Mandatory: place value equipment

 In the eTextbook of this lesson, you will find interactive links to a selection of teaching tools.

Quick recap

Ask children to partition each of these numbers into their place value parts:

115   11·5   1·15

50

Unit 11: Decimals (2), Lesson 3

Discover

WAYS OF WORKING Pair work

ASK

- Question 1 a): *Which place value counters will you need?*
- Question 1 a): *How many of each counter will you need?*
- Question 1 b): *What is the same and what is different about the two part-whole models?*
- Question 1 b): *How could you group your place value equipment to help you complete the part-whole models?*

IN FOCUS Show children the two part-whole models and discuss that they both have the same whole but the parts are different. Use this to explore the fact that there is more than one way to partition a decimal number. Ask: *How can we find each of the missing numbers?*

PRACTICAL TIPS Ask children to use or draw place value equipment that they can group and regroup as they partition numbers.

ANSWERS

Question 1 a):

T	O	Tth	Hth
	●●●●	●●●	●●●●●●
	4	3	6

Question 1 b):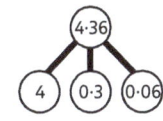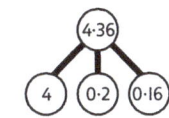

Share

WAYS OF WORKING Whole class teacher led

ASK

- Question 1 a): *What is the value of the digit 3?*
- Question 1 a): *What is the value of the digit 6?*
- Question 1 b): *What is the same and what is different in each part-whole model?*
- Question 1 b): *Can you think of any other ways to partition 4·36?*

IN FOCUS In question 1 a), children use place value counters on a grid to partition the decimal number by place value, giving them the opportunity to identify how many wholes, tenths and hundredths it is made up of. In question 1 b), they then use the part-whole model to explore how to partition the same number in different ways. Refer children to Dexter's comments and discuss how the place value counters can be used to explore many possible ways of partitioning a decimal number such as this one.

51

Unit 11: Decimals (2), Lesson 3

Think together

WAYS OF WORKING Whole class teacher led (I do, We do, You do)

ASK

- Question ❶: *What is the value of the digit 0 in the number 0·45?*
- Question ❷: *There are only two parts in the part-whole model, but there are three digits in the number. How is that possible?*
- Question ❸: *Do you notice any patterns in these sets?*

IN FOCUS Question ❶ requires children to partition a 2-digit decimal into two parts in different ways, whereas question ❷ requires them to partition a 3-digit decimal into two parts in different ways. In question ❸, children complete a series of partitions that are presented as addition sentences. Children should notice that the whole in each set of numbers is the same, and so the list of addition sentences shows that each of these numbers can be partitioned in at least five different ways.

STRENGTHEN Provide place value equipment that children can use to physically manipulate the whole and the parts as they partition.

DEEPEN Challenge children to find six or more different ways to partition the decimal number 3·02.

ASSESSMENT CHECKPOINT Use question ❷ to assess whether children can understand and use four possible variations to flexibly partition a decimal number. Use question ❸ to assess whether children can partition numbers flexibly by drawing part-whole models, and without the need for place value equipment.

ANSWERS

Question ❶ a):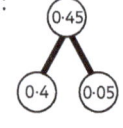

Question ❶ b):

Question ❶ c):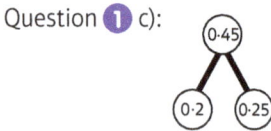

Question ❷: Children should draw part-whole models to show a correct partitioning of 5·26.
For example:
5 + 0·26   5 + 0·2 + 0·06
4 + 1·26   4 + 1·2 + 0·06
5·2 + 0·06   3·2 + 2·06

Question ❸: Set A   Set B
0·89 = 0·8 + 0·09   3·42 = 3 + 0·4 + 0·02
0·89 = 0·7 + 0·19   3·42 = 3 + 0·3 + 0·12
0·89 = 0·6 + 0·29   3·42 = 3 + 0·2 + 0·22
0·89 = 0·4 + 0·49   3·42 = 3 + 0·42
0·89 = 0·1 + 0·79   3·42 = 2 + 1·4 + 0·02

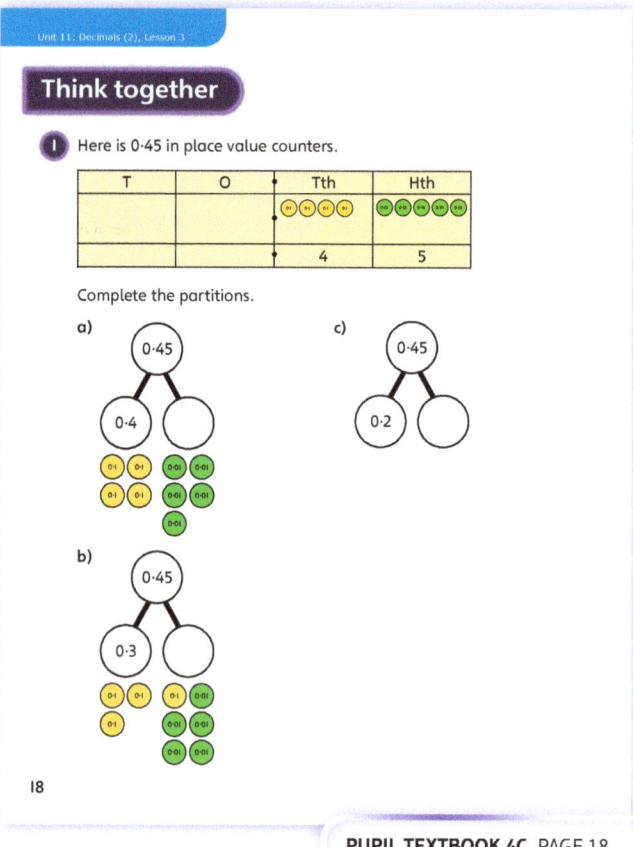

PUPIL TEXTBOOK 4C PAGE 18

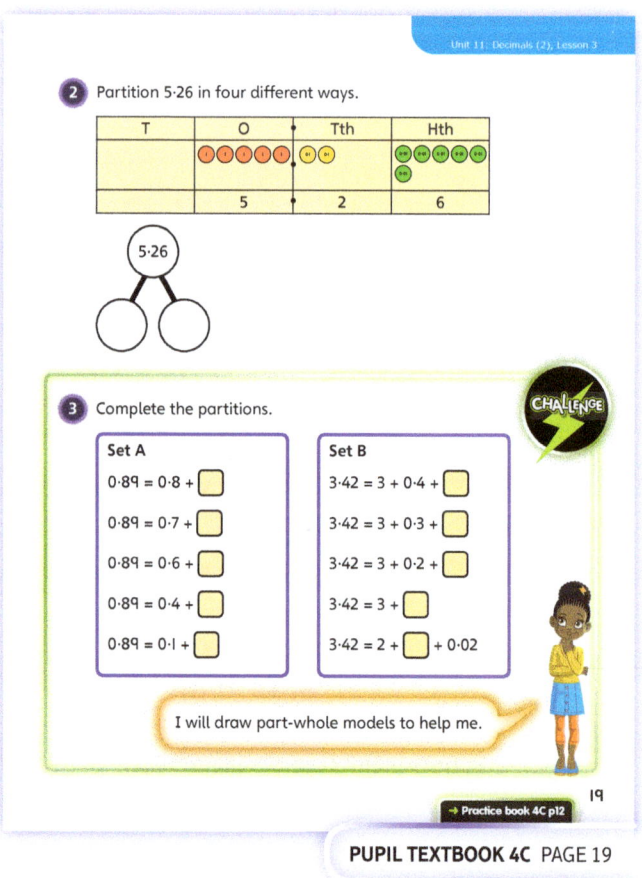

PUPIL TEXTBOOK 4C PAGE 19

52

Practice

WAYS OF WORKING Independent thinking

IN FOCUS In questions ① and ②, children complete part-whole models to partition given decimal numbers into two parts in different ways. In question ①, this is scaffolded with place value counters. In question ③, children partition a 3-digit decimal number in two different ways, again with place value counters as a visual representation.

Question ④ requires children to complete lists of decimal additions that partition a given decimal number in many different ways, thereby showing how flexible partitioning can be.

STRENGTHEN Provide place value equipment for children to use to model and manipulate the decimal numbers throughout. Encourage children to draw a part-whole model to support them in question ④, where necessary.

DEEPEN Ask children to discuss when they think different partitions might be useful. Ask: *What calculation might you be doing if it was helpful to partition the number in this way?* Furthermore, remove some of the place value equipment and ask children to partition numbers simply by drawing part-whole models, and by adding and subtracting.

ASSESSMENT CHECKPOINT Use question ② to assess whether children can understand how to partition a given decimal in several different ways. Use question ④ to assess whether children can flexibly partition decimals when place value equipment is not provided, or where they have to arrange the place value equipment themselves to aid their calculations.

ANSWERS Answers for the **Practice** part of the lesson can be found in the *Power Maths* online subscription.

Reflect

WAYS OF WORKING Independent thinking

IN FOCUS This part of the lesson prompts children to flexibly partition a given decimal number that they have chosen, in as many ways as they can.

ASSESSMENT CHECKPOINT Assess whether children can explain the approaches that they have used to find different ways of partitioning their chosen number.

ANSWERS Answers for the **Reflect** part of the lesson can be found in the *Power Maths* online subscription.

After the lesson

- Did children find more than one way to partition a given decimal number?
- Are there any children who still believe partitioning can only be done by place value?

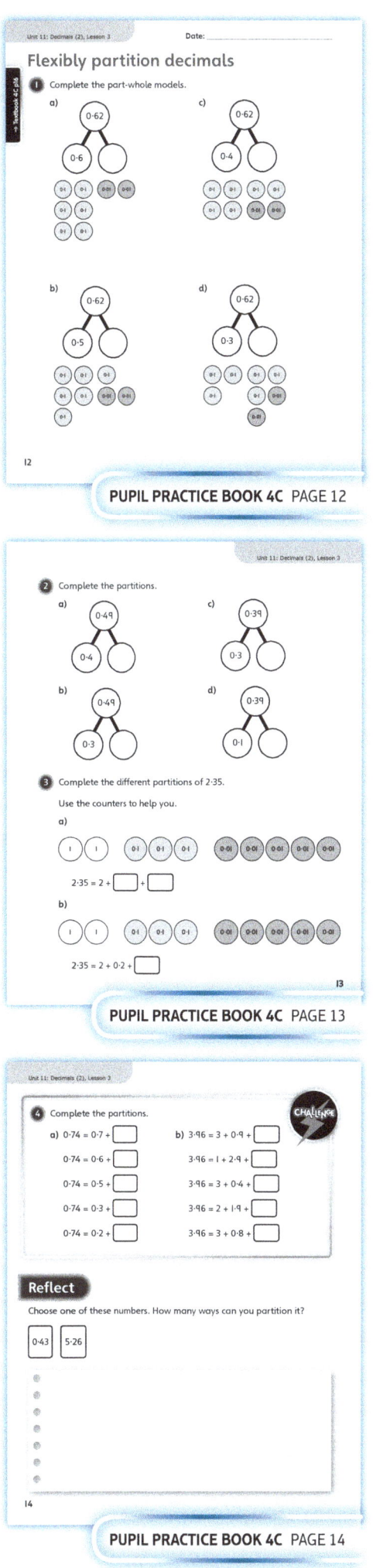

PUPIL PRACTICE BOOK 4C PAGE 12

PUPIL PRACTICE BOOK 4C PAGE 13

PUPIL PRACTICE BOOK 4C PAGE 14

Unit 11: Decimals (2), Lesson 4

Compare decimals

Learning focus

In this lesson, children will compare decimal numbers by looking at the largest place value and then moving to the next largest place value.

Before you teach

- Can children represent decimal numbers in a place value grid?
- Can children compare 2- and 3-digit numbers?
- Are children confident using the inequality signs < and >?

NATIONAL CURRICULUM LINKS

Year 4 Number – fractions (including decimals)

Compare numbers with the same number of decimal places up to two decimal places.

ASSESSING MASTERY

Children can compare decimal numbers using a place value grid and place value counters. They compare decimal numbers by looking at which number has the largest place value.

COMMON MISCONCEPTIONS

Children may not look at the largest place value first when comparing decimal numbers. Ask:
- *Which number has the higher value, 2·17 or 2·71? My number is 5·15. Can you think of a number that is larger than this?*

STRENGTHENING UNDERSTANDING

Recap comparing 2- or 3-digit numbers. Ask children to show a selection of these numbers on a place value grid. Explain that we need to look at the largest place value to help us compare the numbers. If the largest place value does not help us, then we must look at the next largest place value. Encourage children to write the numbers underneath the place value grid.

GOING DEEPER

Ask children to compare decimal numbers that are represented in different ways or that do not have the same number of decimal places. For example, ask: *Which is bigger, 5 ones and 2 tenths or 3 tenths and 5 ones? Which is bigger, 4·5 or 4·25?*

KEY LANGUAGE

In lesson: tens (10s), ones (1s), tenths, hundredths, statement, compare, less than, greater than, decimal, place value

STRUCTURES AND REPRESENTATIONS

Place value grid, hundredths grid

RESOURCES

Mandatory: place value equipment, metre ruler

Optional: plastic coins

 In the eTextbook of this lesson, you will find interactive links to a selection of teaching tools.

Quick recap

Challenge children to make each of these numbers using place value equipment:
2·33   2·03   2·31

Unit 11: Decimals (2), Lesson 4

Discover

WAYS OF WORKING Pair work

ASK

- Question 1 a): *How can you represent Bella and Zac's numbers on a place value grid? How can you tell how many 1s, how many tenths and how many hundredths each number has? How can you decide which number is larger?*
- Question 1 b): *What numbers are you comparing in this question? Why does it not help to compare the 1s and tenths? Which place value do you need to look at?*

IN FOCUS For each question, encourage children to make the numbers with counters on a place value grid. Ask them to partition the numbers into 1s, tenths and hundredths. They should start to see that, to compare the numbers, they first need to look at the largest place value, then the next place value, and so on.

PRACTICAL TIPS Re-create a similar activity in the classroom. Measure two items of similar height and give children the measurements in the same format. For example: *Isabelle's chair is 0·43 metres tall. My chair is 0·49 metres tall.* Ask children to model the heights using a place value grid and counters.

ANSWERS

Question 1 a): 0·67 m < 0·76 m
Zac is correct.

Question 1 b): 0·79 m > 0·76 m.
Zac is correct.

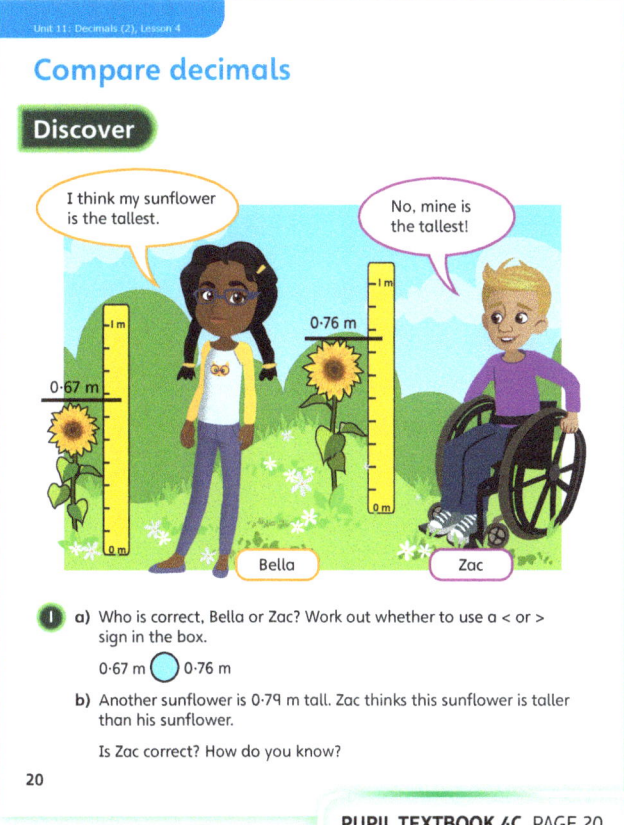

PUPIL TEXTBOOK 4C PAGE 20

Share

WAYS OF WORKING Whole class teacher led

ASK

- Question 1 a): *How can you represent these numbers on place value grids? When comparing the numbers, why do you need to start by looking at the largest place value? How many 1s do the numbers have? Why does this not help you to compare the numbers? Why do you not need to look at the hundredths to compare the numbers?*
- Question 1 a): *What do the < and > signs mean?*
- Question 1 b): *What numbers are you comparing now? Why do you need to look at the hundredths to compare the numbers? Which number is bigger?*

IN FOCUS For question 1 a), model the numbers on a place value grid. Say how many 1s each number has. Can children explain why this does not help them find the answer? Say how many tenths each number has. Can children explain which number is bigger or smaller now? Can children explain why it is not necessary to look at how many hundredths each number has? Discuss the inequality sign and ensure children are able to use it correctly.

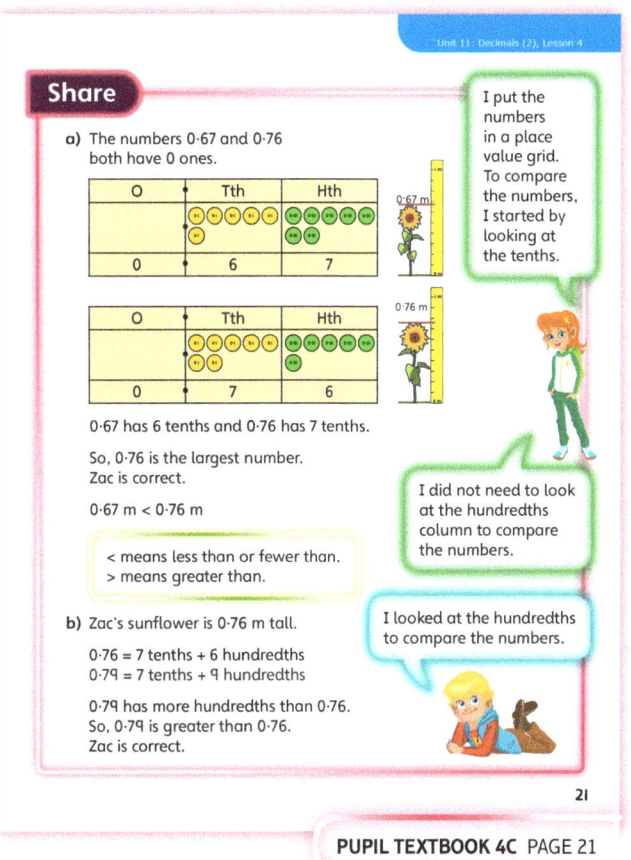

PUPIL TEXTBOOK 4C PAGE 21

Think together

WAYS OF WORKING Whole class teacher led (I do, We do, You do)

ASK

- Question ❶: *What sign means less than? What sign means greater than?*
- Question ❷: *Which digit will you compare first? Do you need to compare any other digits? Why or why not?*
- Question ❸: *How many 1s and tenths are there in 2·4 and 2·7? Who has jumped the farthest on the first attempt?*

IN FOCUS In question ❶, children compare two numbers by looking at the number of counters in each column of the two place value grids. In question ❷, children are given only the numbers and not the representation in a place value grid. Encourage children to make the numbers in a place value grid. Children need to understand that to compare the numbers they need to look at the largest place value first.

STRENGTHEN To support understanding, represent the numbers on a place value grid. Separate the 10s from the 1s from the tenths from the hundredths. Clearly associate each digit with the particular place value. Instead of just displaying the counters in the place value grids, make sure you write the numbers under each place value column; this will help children understand the sizes of the numbers and also help them to compare the numbers.

DEEPEN Provide numbers represented by place value counters that are not given in the order of 10s, 1s, tenths and hundredths. This will help deepen children's understanding that the *order* does not matter but that it is always important to compare the largest place value first.

Ask children to compare numbers that have a different number of decimal places, as in question ❷.

ASSESSMENT CHECKPOINT Children should be able to evaluate decimals by comparing the 1s, tenths and hundredths. Are they able to compare decimal numbers using a place value grid and place value counters? Children need to understand that to compare decimal numbers they need to start by looking at the largest place value.

ANSWERS

Question ❶ a): <

Question ❶ b): <

Question ❶ c): >

Question ❷ a): 0·68 > 0·65

Question ❷ b): 0·38 < 0·45

Question ❷ c): 2·08 < 3·24

Question ❷ d): 16·81 > 6·79

Question ❸ a): Holly jumps further each time.

Question ❸ b): Place value grid with 2 counters in the ones and 4 in the tenths
Place value grid with 2 counters in the ones and 7 in the tenths

Question ❸ c): 2·4 < 2·7

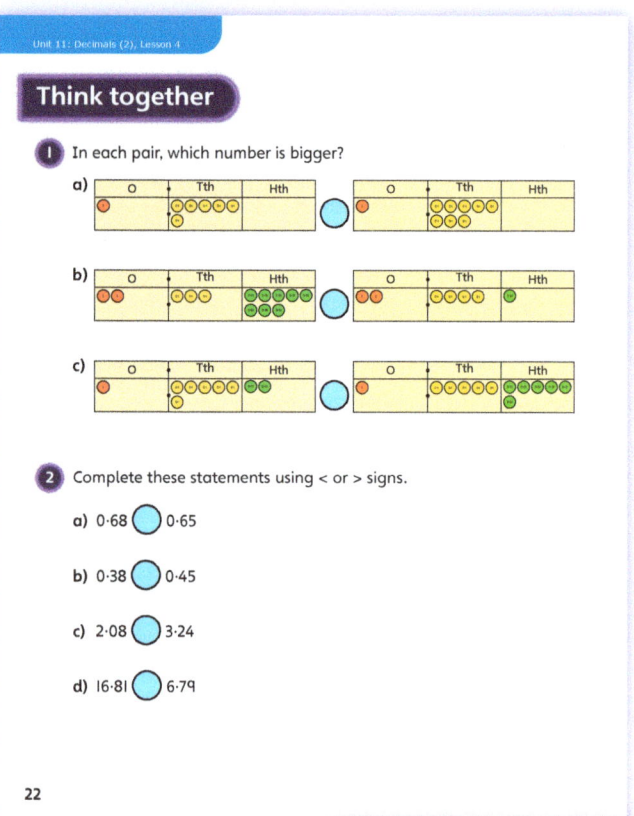

PUPIL TEXTBOOK 4C PAGE 22

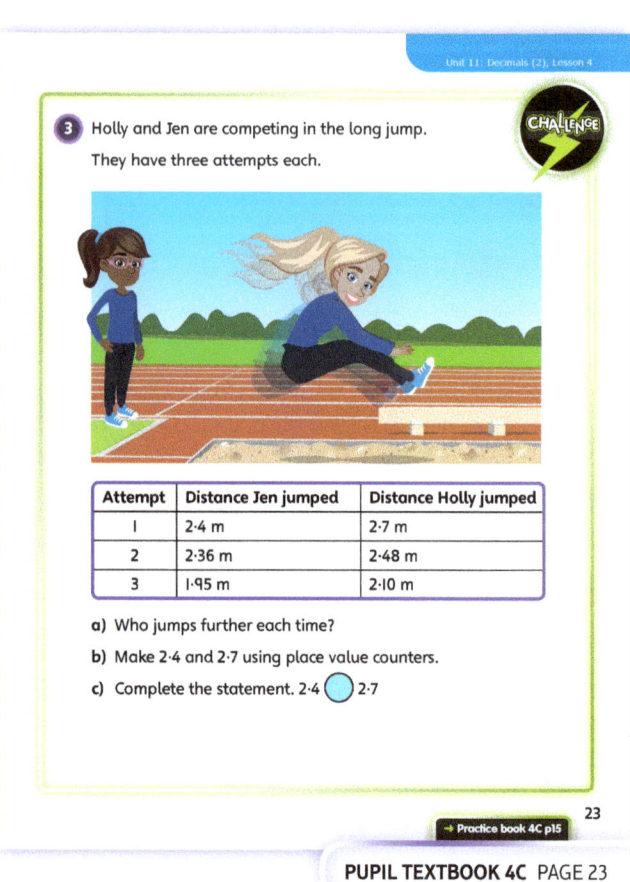

PUPIL TEXTBOOK 4C PAGE 23

Unit 11: Decimals (2), Lesson 4

Practice

WAYS OF WORKING Independent thinking

IN FOCUS Question ❶ asks children to use inequality signs to compare decimal numbers that are represented on the place value grids. Questions ❷ and ❸ are more abstract with no pictorial representations given. Ensure concrete resources are available to children as they may need to make their own representations of the numbers. Question ❽ asks children to consider more deeply the place value of digits within decimal numbers. Finding multiple potential answers will cement this learning.

STRENGTHEN In question ❶, children can use a place value grid with the headings clearly labelled. Assist children in writing out the numbers as decimals when they are not presented in this way.

DEEPEN Comparing decimals can be further explored by giving children numbers that have a different number of decimal places.

Give children two numbers and ask them to give examples of numbers that are in between these values. For instance, which numbers are between 3·1 and 3 ones, 1 tenth and 9 hundredths? Are they able to explain how they know?

THINK DIFFERENTLY Question ❹ highlights the misconception that more counters mean a bigger number. Help children to understand that one tenth counter is worth ten hundredth counters. They need to look at the place value of each counter, rather than the numbers of individual counters, to determine which is bigger.

ASSESSMENT CHECKPOINT Children should now be confident when comparing decimals that have the same number of decimal places using a place value grid.

ANSWERS Answers for the **Practice** part of the lesson can be found in the *Power Maths* online subscription.

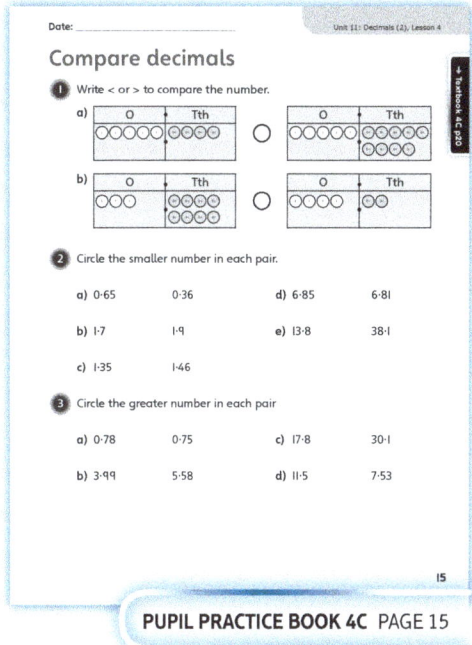

PUPIL PRACTICE BOOK 4C PAGE 15

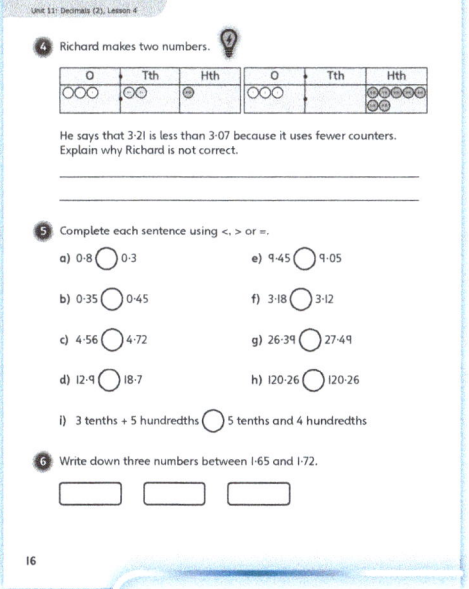

PUPIL PRACTICE BOOK 4C PAGE 16

Reflect

WAYS OF WORKING Pair work

IN FOCUS This **Reflect** question checks children's understanding of comparing decimal numbers. It encourages them to explain the process in their own words. Children may need to use a place value grid to help them construct their explanation.

ASSESSMENT CHECKPOINT Children can explain how to compare decimal numbers. They should realise that they need to start by looking at the largest place value, then the next largest place value, and so on.

ANSWERS Answers for the **Reflect** part of the lesson can be found in the *Power Maths* online subscription.

After the lesson

- Can children compare decimal numbers that have the same number of decimal places?
- Can children work out what numbers are represented by the diagrams in the questions?
- Do children understand that to compare numbers they need to start by looking at the largest place value?

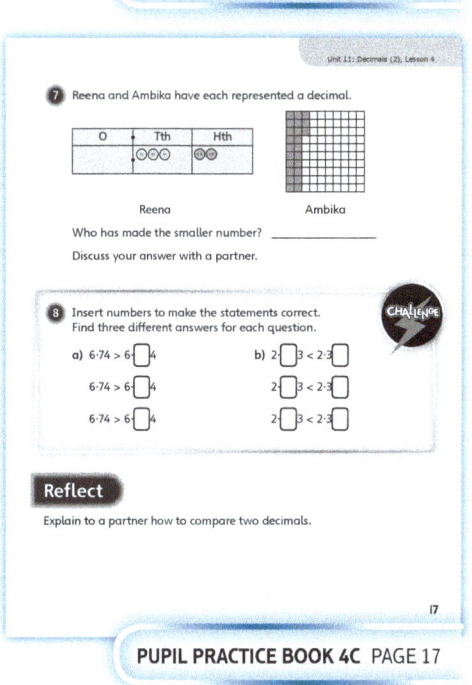

PUPIL PRACTICE BOOK 4C PAGE 17

Unit 11: Decimals (2), Lesson 5

Order decimals

Learning focus
In this lesson, children will order numbers with up to two decimal places.

Before you teach
- Can children represent decimal numbers in a place value grid?
- Can children order whole numbers?
- Could children identify the number if given a number of 10s, 1s, tenths and hundredths?

NATIONAL CURRICULUM LINKS

Year 4 Number – fractions (including decimals)

Compare numbers with the same number of decimal places up to two decimal places.

ASSESSING MASTERY

Children can order decimal numbers using a place value grid and place value counters. They start by looking at the largest place value.

COMMON MISCONCEPTIONS

When comparing decimals, children may not start by looking at the largest place value and then the next largest place value and so on. For example, to order 6·16, 5·09 and 6·12, children must focus on the 1s and then the hundredths. Ask:
- *Will focusing on the tenths help you in comparing these numbers?*
- *Which place value should you look at first when comparing numbers?*

STRENGTHENING UNDERSTANDING

Children who need support ordering decimal numbers should first recap ordering whole numbers. Ask children to show these numbers on a place value grid. Explain that they need to look at the largest place value to help them order the numbers. If this does not help, then they must look at the next largest place value and so on. Encourage children to write out the numbers underneath the place value grid.

GOING DEEPER

Give children some decimal numbers that are in order and ask them to place a number that would fit in the sequence. For example, ask children to think of a decimal number that could fill the gap in this sequence: 5·67, 5·72, ☐, 5·81. Note that this sequence is only about ordering numbers; children are not expected to find common differences. Ask: *Is it possible to give an answer that has only one decimal place?* Ask children to represent their answers on a place value grid. Alternatively, ask children to order numbers that do not have the same number of decimal places.

KEY LANGUAGE

In lesson: tens (10s), ones (1s), tenths, hundredths, smallest, largest, greatest, lightest, heaviest, compare, ascending

STRUCTURES AND REPRESENTATIONS

Place value grid, number line

RESOURCES

Mandatory: place value counters, weighing scales

 In the eTextbook of this lesson, you will find interactive links to a selection of teaching tools.

Quick recap

Discuss and compare these numbers together as a class. Ask: *Which number is greater?*
3·49   3·53

58

Unit 11: Decimals (2), Lesson 5

Discover

WAYS OF WORKING Pair work

ASK

• Question 1 a): *How can you represent the rabbits' masses on a place value grid? How can you tell how many 1s, how many tenths and how many hundredths there are?*
• Question 1 a): *How can you decide which of the three numbers is the smallest? Why does it **not** help to compare the tenths?*
• Question 1 b): *Where would the second heaviest rabbit be in the order from lightest to heaviest? What numbers is this position in between? Which place values need to be the same when working out Flopsy's mass? Is there more than one answer?*

IN FOCUS For each question, encourage children to make the numbers on a place value grid and ask them to partition the numbers into 1s, tenths and hundredths. Children should start to see that to order the numbers they need to look at the largest place value, then the next place value and so on.

PRACTICAL TIPS Re-create the scene in the classroom using classroom objects and scales, or ask children to bring in stuffed animals from home.

ANSWERS

Question 1 a): 1·25 kg   2·11 kg   2·15 kg
                Lily   Bob   Molly

Question 1 b): Flopsy's mass could be 2·12 kg, 2·13 kg or 2·14 kg.

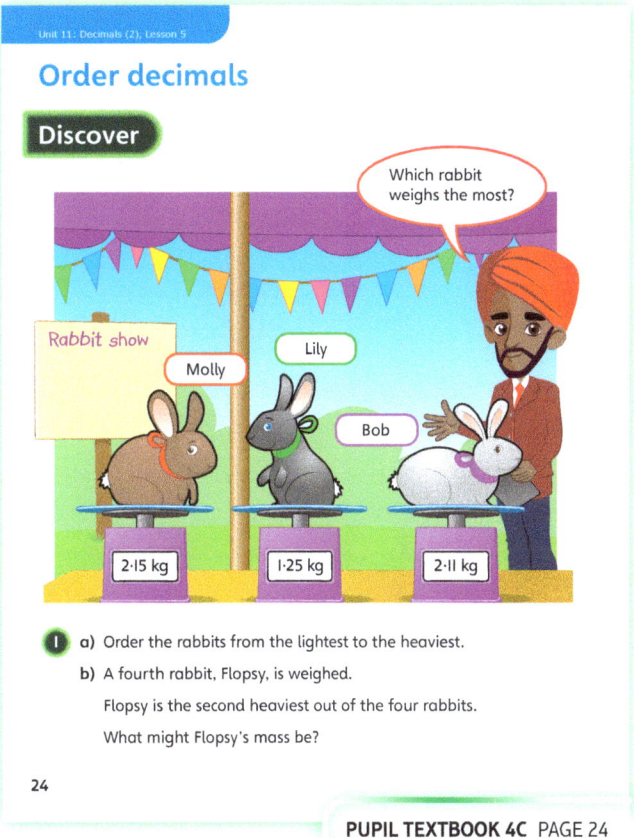

PUPIL TEXTBOOK 4C PAGE 24

Share

WAYS OF WORKING Whole class teacher led

ASK

• Question 1 a): *How have the numbers been represented on the place value grids? What does each counter represent? Why do you need to follow Flo's example and start by looking at the largest place value? How many 1s do the numbers have?*
• Question 1 a): *How do you know that Lily is the lightest rabbit without looking at the tenths or hundredths? Why does it not help to compare the tenths? How many hundredths do the numbers have? How do you know which number is the biggest?*
• Question 1 b): *Which two rabbits is Flopsy's mass between? Why do you need to look at the hundredths to decide on Flopsy's mass? What could Flopsy's mass be? Is there more than one answer?*

IN FOCUS For question 1 a), show children the numbers on a place value grid. Can children explain why this means Lily is the lightest rabbit without having to compare the tenths or hundredths? For 2·15 and 2·11, say aloud how many tenths each number has. Can children explain why comparing the 1s and tenths for these numbers does not help? Say how many hundredths each number has. Can children explain which number is greater or smaller now?

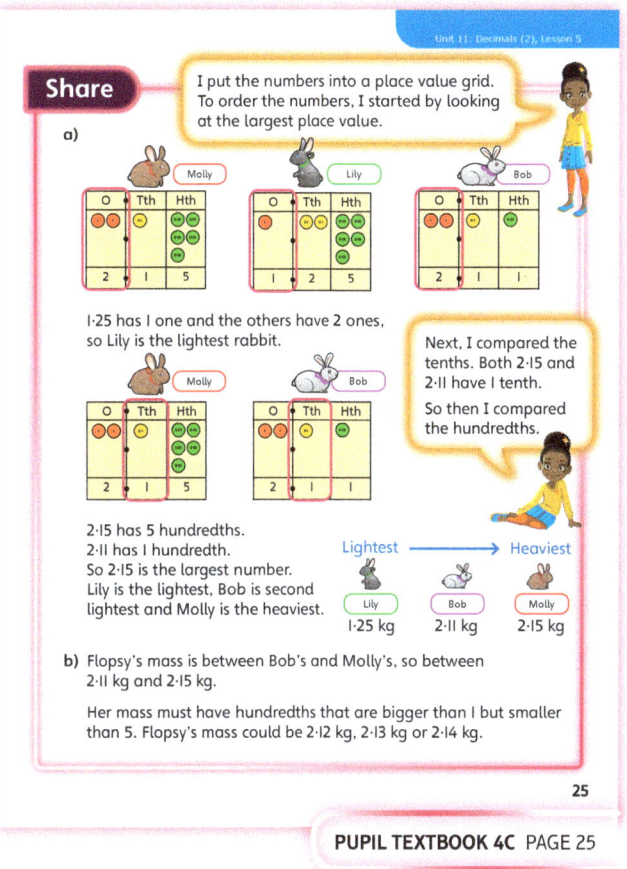

PUPIL TEXTBOOK 4C PAGE 25

Think together

WAYS OF WORKING Whole class teacher led (I do, We do, You do)

ASK
- Question ❶: *How many 1s and tenths does each number have?*
- Question ❷: *How many 10s, 1s, tenths and hundredths does each number have? Which place value is going to help you order the numbers? Do you need to look at all the place values?*
- Question ❸ a): *Can you make each number in a place value grid?*
- Question ❸ b): *Is there more than one possible way to order the numbers? Discuss with a partner.*

IN FOCUS Question ❸ gives children some decimal numbers that are in order and asks them to identify the mistake or fill in the missing digits. Encourage children to make the numbers in a place value grid and write each number as a decimal. For question ❸ b), encourage children to give more than one answer.

STRENGTHEN To support understanding, represent the numbers on place value grids and separate the 10s from the 1s from the tenths from the hundredths. Clearly associate each digit with the particular place value. Instead of just displaying the counters in the place value grids, ensure you also put the numbers under each place value column. This will help children understand the sizes of the numbers and help them order the numbers.

DEEPEN Provide partitioned numbers where one of the place value columns has been left empty. For example, ask children to order: 4 tens and 4 tenths; 4 tens, 4 ones and 4 hundredths; 4 ones, 4 tenths and 4 hundredths. Children may have the misconception that 4 tens and 4 tenths is the smallest as it only contains 2 parts, so this exercise will help them understand the importance of place value. Encourage children to make these numbers in a place value grid.

ASSESSMENT CHECKPOINT Can children order decimal numbers using a place value grid and place value counters? Children should understand that to order decimal numbers they need to start by looking at the largest place value. Children should be able to order decimals by comparing the 1s, tenths and hundredths.

ANSWERS

Question ❶: 1·2, 1·9, 2·1

Question ❷ a): 1·43, 1·53, 2·33

Question ❷ b): 15·62, 19·07, 25·31

Question ❸ a): 9·82 is the largest, so should be first.

Question ❸ b): Various answers are possible, for example:
5·32, 5·33, 5·54, 6·09
5·39, 5·43, 6·54, 6·79

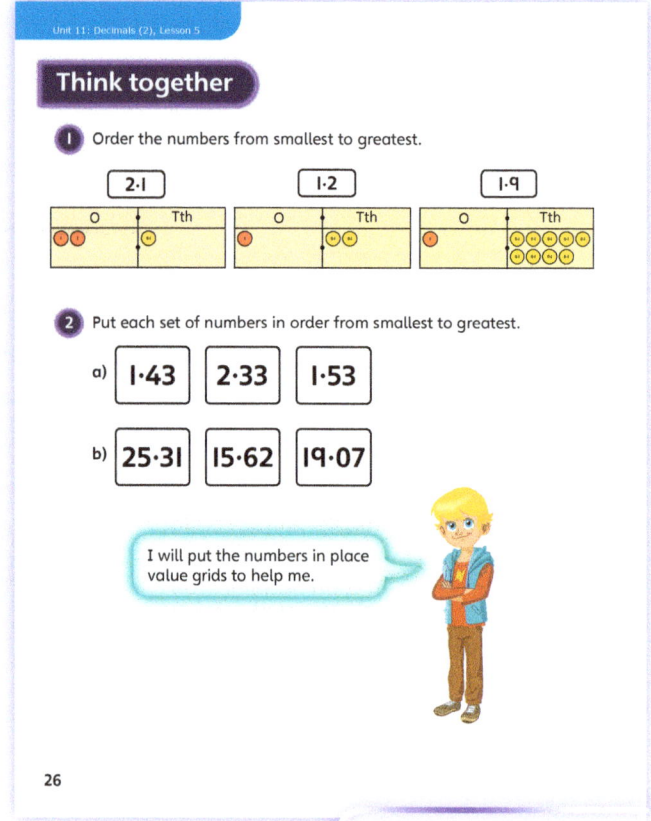

PUPIL TEXTBOOK 4C PAGE 26

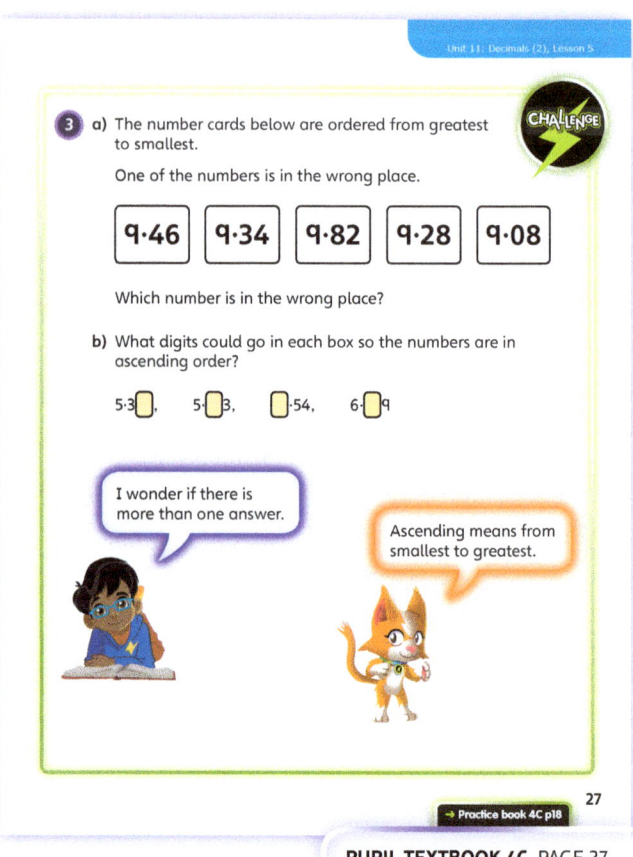

PUPIL TEXTBOOK 4C PAGE 27

Unit 11: Decimals (2), Lesson 5

Practice

WAYS OF WORKING Independent thinking

IN FOCUS Question ❼ encourages children to problem solve and order decimal numbers. Encourage children to make the numbers on a place value grid and manipulate the counters until the numbers are in ascending order.

STRENGTHEN Encourage children to make each number on a place value grid. Spend some time making sure children are secure with question ❶, where they focus on numbers that only involve comparing the tenths. Then progress to subsequent questions where they compare numbers by looking at both tenths and hundredths. Emphasize again the order in which they should compare digits: tens, ones, tenths, then hundredths.

DEEPEN Ask children if they can come up with more than one answer for some of the numbers in question ❼. They should discuss and compare their answers with a partner.

THINK DIFFERENTLY Question ❻ aims to highlight the mistake that the largest number means the fastest time. Encourage children to think about this carefully. It may help them to relate the context to whole numbers in order to unpick this difficult misconception. For example, ask children if it is faster to complete a race in 30 seconds or 40 seconds. Does this mean the larger number is the faster time? Highlight that the context will shape the answer.

ASSESSMENT CHECKPOINT By the end of the **Practice** section, children should be confident in using a place value grid to order decimals that have the same number of decimal places. Successful work in answering question ❹, including modelling the answers in a place value grid with counters and then writing the numbers if need be, should indicate a sound understanding of the concept.

ANSWERS Answers for the **Practice** part of the lesson can be found in the *Power Maths* online subscription.

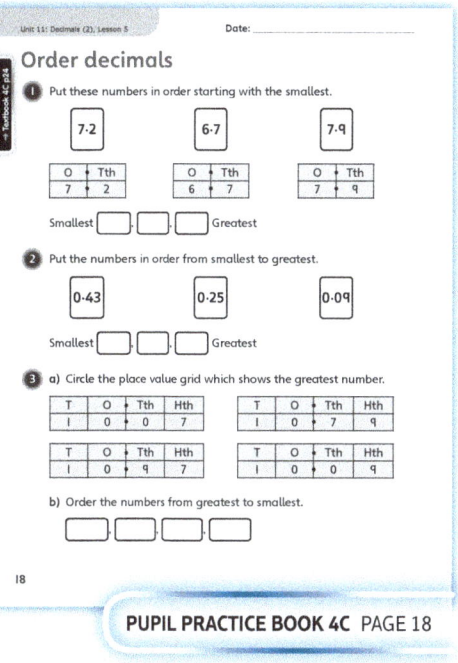

PUPIL PRACTICE BOOK 4C PAGE 18

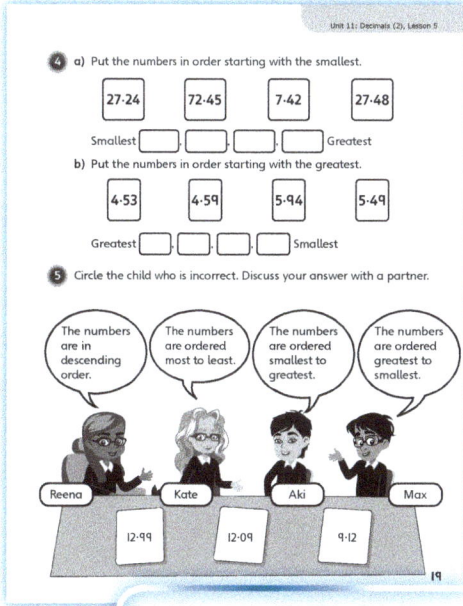

PUPIL PRACTICE BOOK 4C PAGE 19

Reflect

WAYS OF WORKING Pair work

IN FOCUS This question assesses children's understanding of ordering decimal numbers and whether they can describe their reasoning coherently to a partner using mathematical language such as place value, greater than and less than.

ASSESSMENT CHECKPOINT Children can explain how to order decimal numbers. They should realise that they need to start by looking at the largest place value and then the next largest place value and so on.

ANSWERS Answers for the **Reflect** part of the lesson can be found in the *Power Maths* online subscription.

After the lesson

- Can children make numbers in a place value grid to help them order decimal numbers?
- Can children order decimal numbers that have the same number of decimal places?
- Do children understand that to order decimal numbers they need to start by looking at the largest place value?

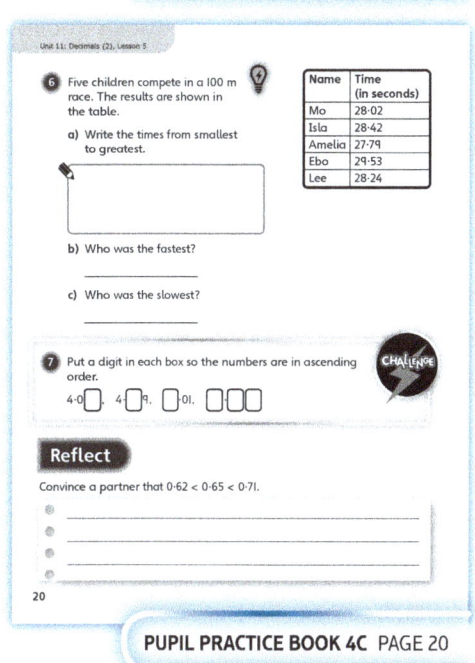

PUPIL PRACTICE BOOK 4C PAGE 20

Unit 11: Decimals (2), Lesson 6

Round to the nearest whole

Learning focus
In this lesson, children will round a decimal to the nearest whole number by looking at the tenths digit. They will place decimal numbers on a number line.

Before you teach
- Do children know that if the place value is 5 or more they round up to the next whole number, 10 or 100?
- Can children identify the tenth digit in a decimal number?
- Can children place decimals with one decimal place on a number line?

NATIONAL CURRICULUM LINKS

Year 4 Number – fractions (including decimals)

Round decimals with one decimal place to the nearest whole number.

ASSESSING MASTERY

Children can round a number with one decimal place to the nearest whole number using a number line. They understand that to round a number to the nearest whole number they need to look at the tenths digit.

COMMON MISCONCEPTIONS

A common misconception occurs when children do not understand that within a number with one decimal place, the tenths digit determines what the number will round to. For example, they may see 8·2 and think it rounds to 9 because 8 is greater than 5. Children need to understand that the number in the tenths column determines the nearest whole number. Ask:
- *What would you round 8·2 to as the nearest whole number? Why? Which is the important place value here?*

Some children may also incorrectly round a number to the nearest 10. For example, some children may round 17·6 to 20. Ask:
- *What do we mean by a whole number? What is the closest whole number to 17·6?*

STRENGTHENING UNDERSTANDING

Children who need support with rounding to the nearest whole number should recap rounding to the nearest 10. For example, ask children to round 27 to the nearest ten and then explain how they did this (by looking at the 1s digit). Explain that we can round to the nearest whole number by looking at the tenths digit. Encourage children to place the number on a number line so they can clearly see the nearest whole number.

GOING DEEPER

Give children a whole number and ask if they can say what the number might have been before it was rounded to the nearest whole. Challenge them to find two or more answers.

KEY LANGUAGE

In lesson: tens (10s), ones (1s), tenths, number line, round up, round down, decimal place, whole number, digit

STRUCTURES AND REPRESENTATIONS

Number line, place value grid, number cards

RESOURCES

Optional: place value counters

 In the eTextbook of this lesson, you will find interactive links to a selection of teaching tools.

Quick recap
Challenge children to identify three numbers that are greater than 1 but less than 2.

Unit 11: Decimals (2), Lesson 6

Discover

WAYS OF WORKING Pair work

ASK
- Question 1 a): *How many grams of sugar are in one serving of cereal?*
- Question 1 a): *Can you place 6·8 on a number line?*
- Question 1 b): *Can you place 1 on a number line? Which numbers would round to 1?*
- Question 1 b): *What does '1 decimal place' mean?*

IN FOCUS In question 1 a), encourage children to find or write the number on a number line. Some children may need support deciding which whole numbers 6·8 lies between. Encourage children to look at the tenths when rounding to the nearest whole number. They should see that Mo is correct.

PRACTICAL TIPS Re-create this activity by looking at the labels on various empty cereal packets or food wrappers and rounding some of the values to the nearest whole number.

ANSWERS

Question 1 a): Mo is correct. The amount of sugar, 6·8 g, is closer to 7 g than 6 g.

Question 1 b): The smallest possible amount of salt is 0·5 g.

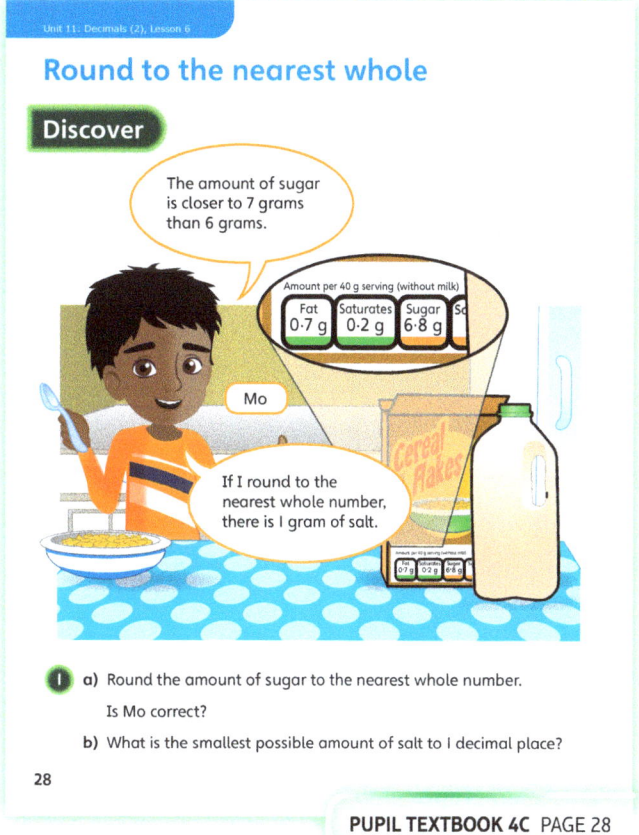

PUPIL TEXTBOOK 4C PAGE 28

Share

WAYS OF WORKING Whole class teacher led

ASK
- Question 1 a): *Which whole number is 6·8 closer to: 6 or 7? Which part of the number helps you decide?*
- Question 1 b): *Do you need to look at the numbers below or above 1? How do you know?*

IN FOCUS For question 1 a), show children the number line from 6 to 7 and explain that we need to look at the tenths. If the number of tenths is 5 or more, then we round up to the next 1. Remind children that a tenth is the first number after the decimal point.

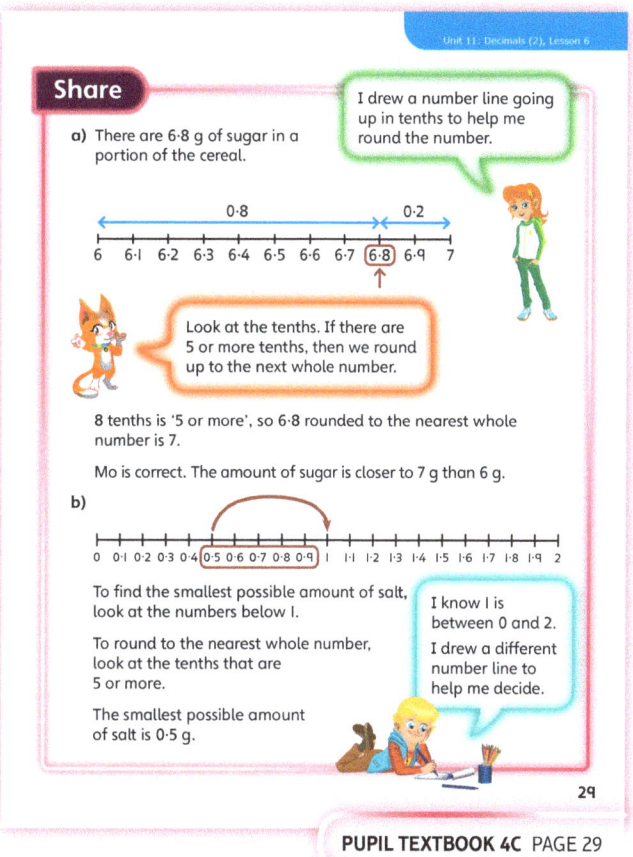

PUPIL TEXTBOOK 4C PAGE 29

Think together

WAYS OF WORKING Whole class teacher led (I do, We do, You do)

ASK

- Question ① a): *What is the value of the tenths digit in the number 4·2? Is 4·2 closer to 4 or 5?*
- Question ① b): *Which whole numbers does 5·6 lie between? What do you do when the tenths digit is 5 or more?*
- Question ②: *Will each number round up or down to the nearest whole number? How do you know?*
- Question ③: *Can you place each of the numbers on a number line? Which numbers round to 8?*

IN FOCUS Question ③ challenges children to explore the misconception that all the given decimal numbers will round to the same whole number. Encourage children to mark each number on the number line and to identify which numbers are closer to 8 and which are closer to 9.

STRENGTHEN To support understanding in question ③, represent each number on a number line and ask children to decide which whole number it is closer to. Encourage children to always identify the tenths digit and decide if it is 5 or more.

DEEPEN Give children a decimal number that rounds to the same number whether it is rounded to the nearest whole number, nearest 10 or nearest 100. For example, 199·7, rounded to the nearest whole number is 200. It is also 200 when rounded to the nearest 10 or the nearest 100. Ask children to explore other numbers that follow this pattern. Extend this to see if children can think of a number that rounds to the same number when rounded to the nearest whole and 10 but a different number when rounded to the nearest 100. For example, 19·6 rounds to 20 when rounded to the nearest whole number or nearest 10, but when rounded to the nearest 100 it is 0. Can they explain why this is? What are the smallest and largest numbers they can think of that this would work for?

ASSESSMENT CHECKPOINT Can children round numbers to the nearest whole number using a number line? Children need to understand that to round a number with one decimal place to the nearest whole number, they need to look at the tenths digit.

ANSWERS

Question ① a): 4

Question ① b): 6

Question ① c): 13

Question ②:
Previous		Next
3	3·2	4
4	4·5	5
0	0·7	1
11	11·8	12

Question ③ a): Jamilla is not correct.
7·5, 7·7 and 7·9 round up to 8, as all the tenths are 5 or above and 7 is less than 8.
8·1 rounds down to 8, as 1 < 5.
8·5 rounds up to 9, since 5 and above rounds up.

Question ③ b): 8·2, 8·3 and 8·4 round down to 8. 7·6 and 7·8 round up to 8. Children may suggest numbers with 2 decimal places.
The smallest is 7·5, the largest is 8·49.

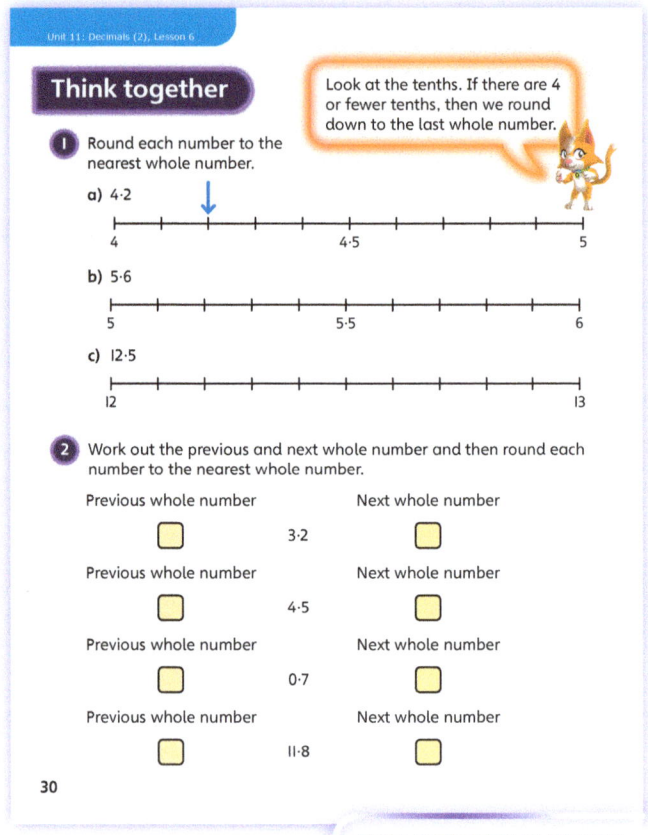

PUPIL TEXTBOOK 4C PAGE 30

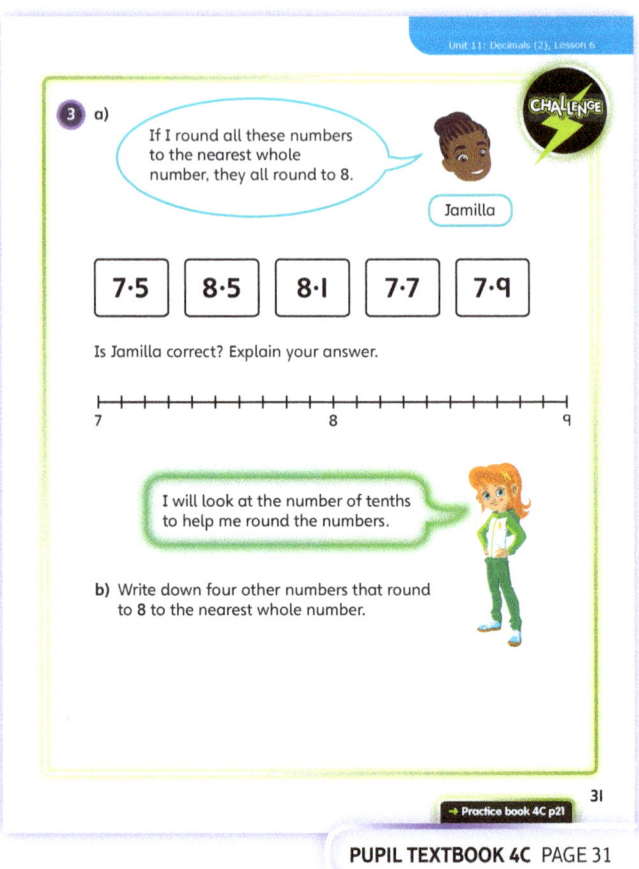

PUPIL TEXTBOOK 4C PAGE 31

Unit 11: Decimals (2), Lesson 6

Practice

WAYS OF WORKING Independent thinking

IN FOCUS Question ❻ reinforces the value of the tenths and that they need to be 5 or more to round up to the next whole number and 4 or less to round down to the previous one. Encourage children to explain why their answers round to 80.

STRENGTHEN Children can place the numbers on a number line before writing their answers when possible. When number lines are not given, persuade them to draw one of their own and label it going up in tenths.

DEEPEN Explore question ❺ further by asking children to come up with more than one answer when possible. Ask children what the smallest and largest value would be to go in each blank box. Can they explain their answers?

ASSESSMENT CHECKPOINT Children should now be confident in rounding a decimal number to the nearest whole number. They should also be able to write the numbers on a number line. Successful responses to questions ❶ a) to c) will demonstrate their confidence in these skills.

ANSWERS Answers for the **Practice** part of the lesson can be found in the *Power Maths* online subscription.

Reflect

WAYS OF WORKING Independent thinking

IN FOCUS This activity checks children's understanding of rounding to the nearest whole number. Children may need to use a number line to help them formulate their response. They should be confident in their explanation that if the tenths digit is 5 or more, they round up to the next whole number.

ASSESSMENT CHECKPOINT Children should answer that the number 43·6 rounds to 44 as the nearest whole number. As part of their explanation, they should describe how the tenths are used to determine this, as 6 tenths is '5 or more'.

ANSWERS Answers for the **Reflect** part of the lesson can be found in the *Power Maths* online subscription.

After the lesson ⏸

- Can children represent a number with 1 decimal place on a number line?
- Can children round a number with 1 decimal place to the nearest whole number?

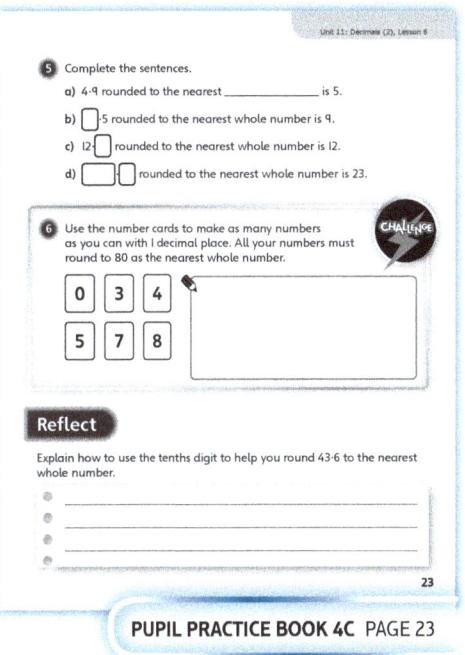

PUPIL PRACTICE BOOK 4C PAGE 23

Unit 11: Decimals (2), Lesson 7

Halves and quarters as decimals

Learning focus
In this lesson, children will represent fractions and decimals using a number line and a hundredths grid. They will learn the decimal equivalents for $\frac{1}{2}$, $\frac{1}{4}$ and $\frac{3}{4}$.

Before you teach
- Can children represent a fraction on a number line and on a hundredths grid?
- Can children represent hundredths on a hundredths grid?
- Do children know what equivalent means?

NATIONAL CURRICULUM LINKS

Year 4 Number – fractions (including decimals)

Recognise and write decimal equivalents to $\frac{1}{4}$, $\frac{1}{2}$ and $\frac{3}{4}$.

ASSESSING MASTERY

Children can write the decimal equivalents for $\frac{1}{2}$, $\frac{1}{4}$ and $\frac{3}{4}$ and can accurately represent them on a number line and hundredths grid.

COMMON MISCONCEPTIONS

Some children will make the mistake of taking the numbers in the fraction and changing them into a decimal. They may, for example, think that $\frac{1}{4}$ = 1·4. Children need to understand what the fraction is telling them (for example, 1 out of 4 equal parts) in order to find its decimal equivalent. Show children representations of fractions and decimals on a hundredths grid and number line in order to secure this understanding and avoid the misconception. Ask:
- *Look at the denominator of this fraction. How many equal parts do we need to divide 10 tenths or 100 hundredths into to find the decimal equaivalent? How do you know?*

STRENGTHENING UNDERSTANDING

Strengthen understanding of the decimal equivalents of $\frac{1}{4}$ and $\frac{3}{4}$ by showing them on a hundredths grid. First, have children practise shading in $\frac{1}{4}$ and $\frac{3}{4}$, then talk about the decimal equivalents. It may be necessary to use a place value grid to show, for example, 25 hundredths as a decimal.

GOING DEEPER

Ask children to make decimal equivalents for fractions that are equivalent to $\frac{1}{2}$, $\frac{1}{4}$ and $\frac{3}{4}$. For example, ask children to find the decimal equivalent of $\frac{2}{4}$. Ask questions such as: *What fraction is equivalent to 5 tenths?*

KEY LANGUAGE

In lesson: fraction, decimal, tenths, hundredths, part, equivalent, equivalent fraction

Other language to be used by the teacher: whole, whole number

STRUCTURES AND REPRESENTATIONS

Hundredths grid, number line, bar model

RESOURCES

Mandatory: hundredths grid, number line from 0 to 1, multilink cubes, blank place value counters

Optional: place value grid

 In the eTextbook of this lesson, you will find interactive links to a selection of teaching tools.

Quick recap

Draw a number line from 0 to 1 and ask children to indicate the position of $\frac{1}{2}$, $\frac{1}{4}$ and $\frac{3}{4}$ on the line. Then discuss the position of decimals such as 0·1, 0·9 and 0·5.

Unit 11: Decimals (2), Lesson 7

Discover

WAYS OF WORKING Pair work

ASK

- Question 1 a): *Ebo says that 0·5 is the same as $\frac{1}{2}$. What does $\frac{1}{2}$ mean?*
- Question 1 a): *How can you represent $\frac{1}{2}$?*
- Question 1 b): *What fraction full is Amelia's jug?*
- Question 1 b): *How can you represent $\frac{3}{4}$?*

IN FOCUS This part of the lesson focuses on the decimal equivalents of $\frac{1}{2}$ and $\frac{3}{4}$. Begin by recapping with children what a fraction means. $\frac{1}{2}$ is 1 out of 2 equal parts and $\frac{3}{4}$ is 3 out of 4 equal parts.

PRACTICAL TIPS For each question, encourage children to make their own representation of the fraction. Children may use a number line or a hundredths grid to represent the fraction.

ANSWERS

Question 1 a): Ebo is correct, $\frac{1}{2}$ is equivalent to 0·5.

Question 1 b): $\frac{3}{4}$ is equivalent to 0·75.

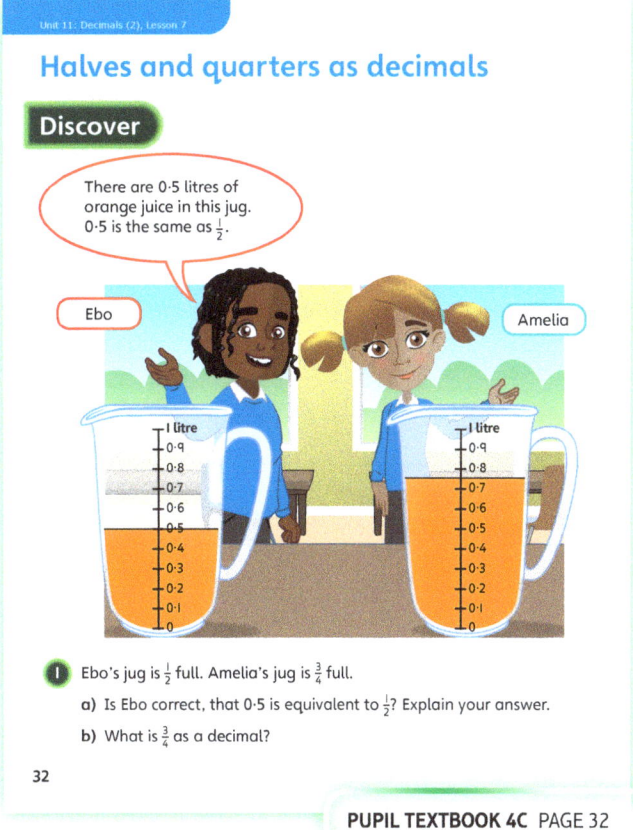

PUPIL TEXTBOOK 4C PAGE 32

Share

WAYS OF WORKING Whole class teacher led

ASK

- Question 1 a): *How full is Ebo's jug? How can you use a number line to show this?*
- Question 1 b): *What does $\frac{3}{4}$ mean? How can you use a hundredths grid to show this? What do you need to look at to help you change the fraction to a decimal?*

IN FOCUS Discuss where $\frac{3}{4}$ is on the number line. Explain that $\frac{3}{4}$ is exactly half-way between 0·7 and 0·8. Can children explain why this is 0·75? This is where some children may give an answer of 7·1. Avoid this misconception by showing children the hundredths grid. Can children see that $\frac{3}{4}$ is shaded? Discuss how many small squares are shaded. Encourage children to say this as 75 hundredths. Can children explain why $\frac{3}{4}$ is equivalent to 0·75? A place value grid may be needed to remind children what 75 hundredths looks like as a decimal.

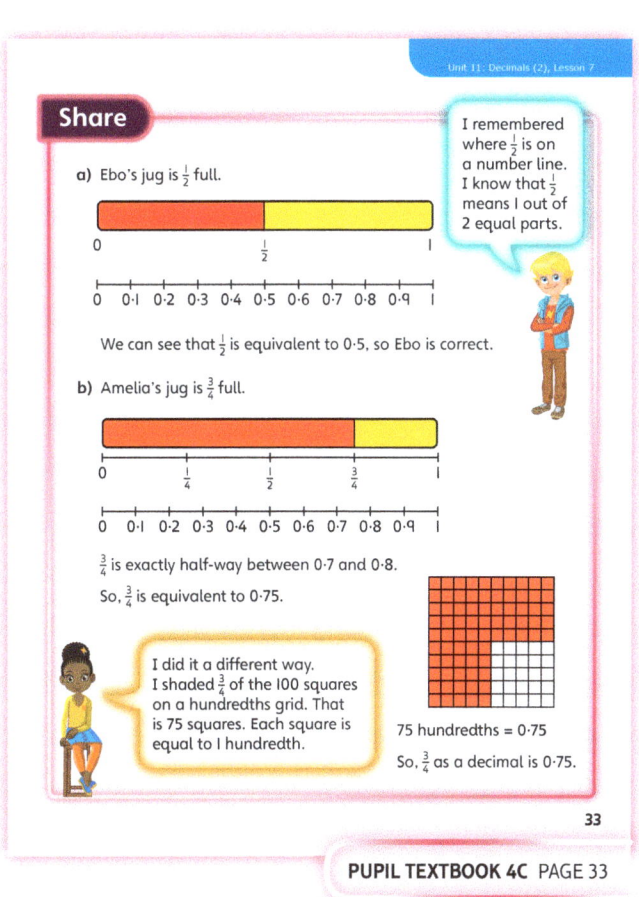

PUPIL TEXTBOOK 4C PAGE 33

67

Unit 11: Decimals (2), Lesson 7

Think together

WAYS OF WORKING Whole class teacher led (I do, We do, You do)

ASK
- Question ❶: *Can you see $\frac{1}{4}$ on the hundredths grid? How many hundredths are shaded in? What is 25 hundredths as a decimal?*
- Question ❷: *How many hundredths are shaded? How many tenths are shaded? What is 5 tenths as a decimal?*
- Question ❸ a): *Can you write each diagram as a fraction or a decimal?*
- Question ❸ b): *What diagram could you draw to show each of these fractions?*

IN FOCUS Questions ❶ and ❷ look at using the hundredths grid to write the decimal equivalents for $\frac{1}{4}$ and $\frac{1}{2}$. Encourage children to make their own representations for each question. Ensure children are aware that they are dealing with hundredths and not whole numbers when looking at the hundredths grid. Say the numbers aloud to reinforce this.

STRENGTHEN To support understanding, ensure children have access to and use hundredths grids. For question ❸ b), encourage children to look at question ❸ a) to help them think of different ways of representing each of the decimal numbers.

DEEPEN For question ❸ b), encourage children to represent $\frac{1}{4}$, $\frac{1}{2}$ and $\frac{3}{4}$ in as many different ways as they can, including equivalent fractions. Ask: *How can you show that $1\frac{1}{2}$ is the same as $1\frac{2}{4}$?*

ASSESSMENT CHECKPOINT Questions ❶ and ❷ will provide an indication of whether children can accurately represent their answers on a hundredths grid and then translate their work with the physical resources into a more abstract written format.

ANSWERS

Question ❶: $\frac{1}{4} = 0.25$

Question ❷: $\frac{1}{2}$ is equivalent to 50 hundredths.
$\frac{1}{2}$ is equivalent to 5 tenths.
$\frac{1}{2} = 0.5$

Question ❸ a): 3·4 does not show $\frac{3}{4}$.

Question ❸ b): 1·25, 1·5, 1·75

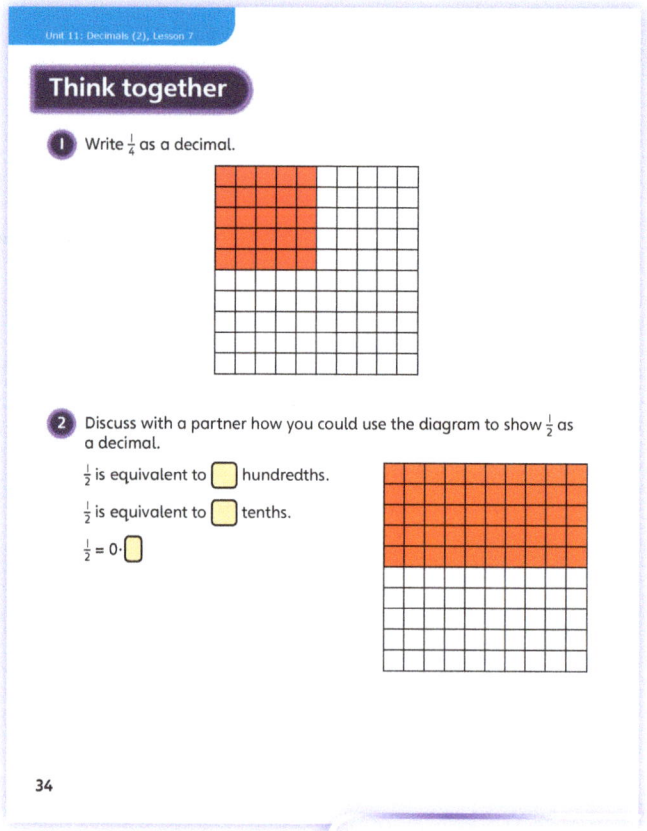

PUPIL TEXTBOOK 4C PAGE 34

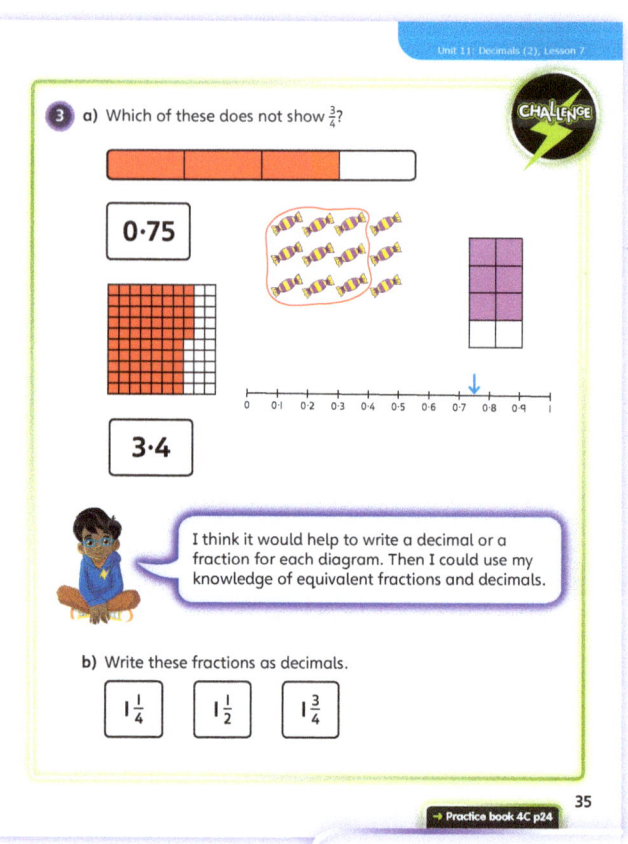

PUPIL TEXTBOOK 4C PAGE 35

Unit 11: Decimals (2), Lesson 7

Practice

WAYS OF WORKING Independent thinking

IN FOCUS Question ⑤ consolidates the equivalence of 0·5 and $\frac{1}{2}$. Children could work out $\frac{1}{2}$ of 12, but discuss with them whether this is necessary. Ask children what they know about $\frac{1}{2}$ and 0·5. What can they say about the number of apples each child has? This should reinforce the equivalence of $\frac{1}{2}$ and 0·5.

STRENGTHEN For all questions where diagrams are not provided, encourage children to make their own representations. For question ②, encourage children to sketch as many different diagrams as they can to represent $\frac{3}{4}$. Ask: *How do your diagrams help you to see that $\frac{3}{4}$ is not the same as 3·4?*

DEEPEN Question ⑥ can be explored further by asking children to draw a different visual representation for each of the decimals in the table.

THINK DIFFERENTLY Question ④ provides an alternative representation. Encourage children to convert the decimals to fractions and think about how they would shade the decimals in.

ASSESSMENT CHECKPOINT By the end of **Practice**, children should be confident in writing the decimal equivalents for $\frac{1}{2}$, $\frac{1}{4}$ and $\frac{3}{4}$ using a hundredths grid and a number line. Their responses to question ③ should indicate their level of understanding and highlight any areas where further practice may be necessary.

ANSWERS Answers for the **Practice** part of the lesson can be found in the *Power Maths* online subscription.

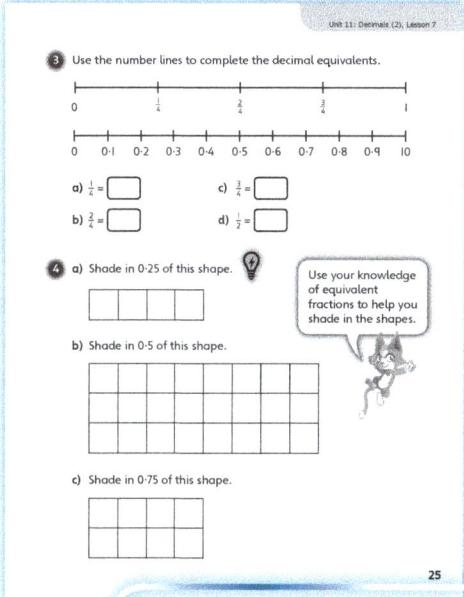

PUPIL PRACTICE BOOK 4C PAGE 24

PUPIL PRACTICE BOOK 4C PAGE 25

Reflect

WAYS OF WORKING Independent thinking

IN FOCUS In this part of the lesson, children must demonstrate the equivalence of 0·75 and $\frac{3}{4}$. Suggest that they shade the hundredths grid. Do children understand what they need to do and how many squares need to be shaded?

ASSESSMENT CHECKPOINT Children should use the hundredths grid provided to show that 0·75 is equivalent to $\frac{3}{4}$. Children should recognise that $\frac{3}{4}$ is 75 hundredths and shade the squares accordingly. They should then be able to write this as 0·75.

ANSWERS Answers for the **Reflect** part of the lesson can be found in the *Power Maths* online subscription.

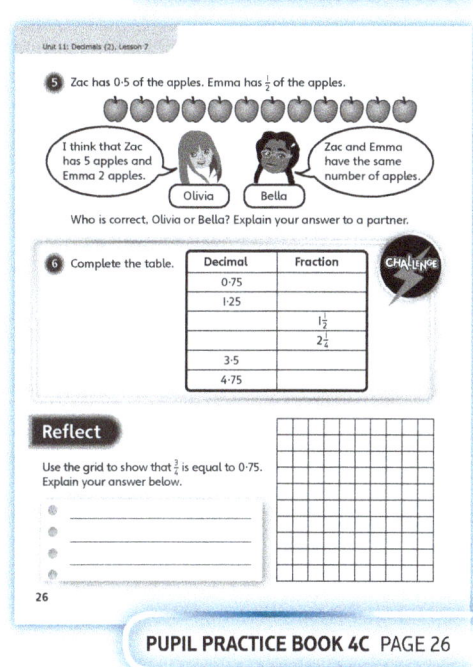

After the lesson

- Can children show the decimal equivalents for $\frac{1}{2}$, $\frac{1}{4}$ and $\frac{3}{4}$ on a hundredths grid?
- Can children locate and write the decimal equivalents for $\frac{1}{2}$, $\frac{1}{4}$ and $\frac{3}{4}$ on a number line?

PUPIL PRACTICE BOOK 4C PAGE 26

Unit 11: Decimals (2)

End of unit check

Don't forget the unit assessment grid in your *Power Maths* online subscription.

WAYS OF WORKING Group work adult led

IN FOCUS These questions are designed to draw out particular misconceptions or misunderstandings. Question ② assesses whether children know what 2 ones, 5 tenths and 3 hundredths look like when written as a number.

In question ③, the hundredths are in the middle of the three parts. Children need to see that they must write the tenths in the empty part on the right.

In question ④, children should first look at the ones, then the tenths, then the hundredths digits. Can they see that 4·2 is bigger 3·79, even though 3·79 has more digits?

In question ⑤, can children see that 6·5 does not round to 6, even though the first digit is 6?

ANSWERS AND COMMENTARY By the end of the unit, children will be able to find the number bond to 1 of a decimal with two decimal places. They will be able to round numbers to the nearest whole number and order decimals with the same number of decimal places by comparing digits. Finally, children will know and understand decimal equivalents of simple fractions such as a half and a quarter.

The completed table for question ⑥ is below:

Fraction	Decimal
$\frac{1}{4}$	0·25
$\frac{1}{2}$	0·5
$\frac{3}{4}$	0·75
$1\frac{1}{2}$	1·5
$1\frac{3}{4}$	1·75
$2\frac{1}{2}$	2·5
$3\frac{1}{4}$	3·25

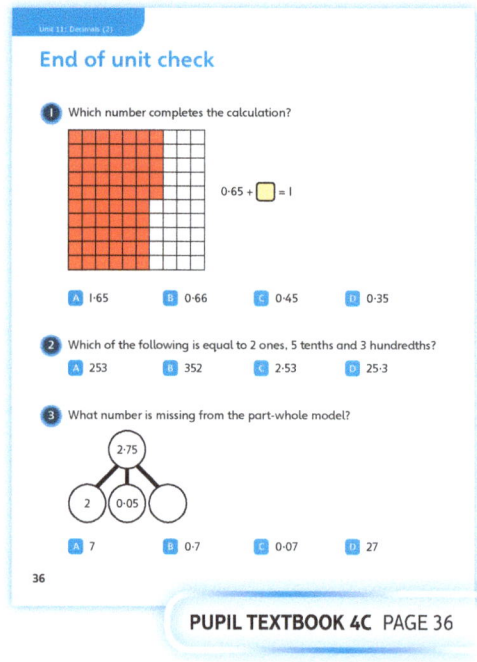

PUPIL TEXTBOOK 4C PAGE 36

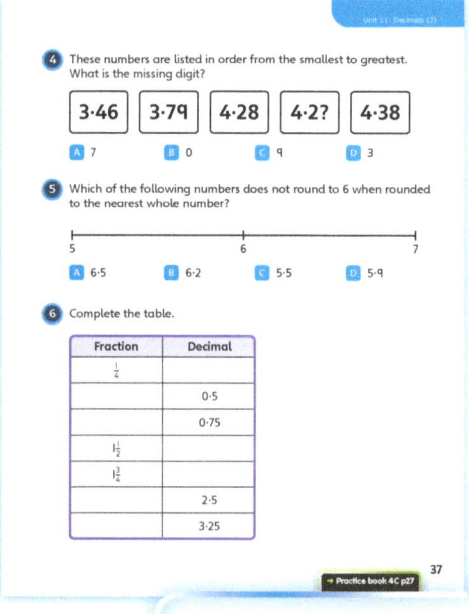

PUPIL TEXTBOOK 4C PAGE 37

Q	A	WRONG ANSWERS AND MISCONCEPTIONS	STRENGTHENING UNDERSTANDING
1	D	A suggests children added together the 1 and 0·65. B suggests they just added 1 to 65.	For question ①, children should count the squares. Encourage children to count in 10s, not 1s, where possible. For question ②, children might find a place value grid and counters help them better understand the value of the number. For question ⑤, children should place the numbers on a number line to help them.
2	C	B suggests children have confused tenths with 10s and hundredths with 100s. D suggests children are confused about where to put the decimal point.	
3	B	A and C suggest children have made a place value error.	
4	C	A, B and D suggest children are unsure about hundredths.	
5	A	C and D suggest children do not understand the '5 or above' rule of rounding up.	
6	see above	Incorrect conversions suggest that children need more work with number lines and fractions strips to understand the equivalence of decimals and fractions. These topics will be covered again as they progress in their studies.	

Unit 11: Decimals (2)

My journal

WAYS OF WORKING Independent thinking

ANSWERS AND COMMENTARY Children may make the numbers on a place value grid to help them understand the size of the numbers and what each digit in each number represents. Encourage children to read the numbers aloud. They should take care not to read the two digits after the decimal as a double digit, so they should avoid saying 'zero point twenty-seven' for '0·27' and instead say 'zero point two seven'. Children may also compare just two of the numbers, as opposed to finding similarities and differences about all three.

What is the same? Children may offer answers such as:
- They are all greater than 0.
- They all contain the digits 2 and 7.
- All the numbers have a decimal point in them.
- Two of the numbers have two numbers after the decimal (the other just has one).
- 7·2 and 7·20 are equivalent.

What is different?
- One number does not show any hundredths.
- Two numbers start with a 7, the other one does not.

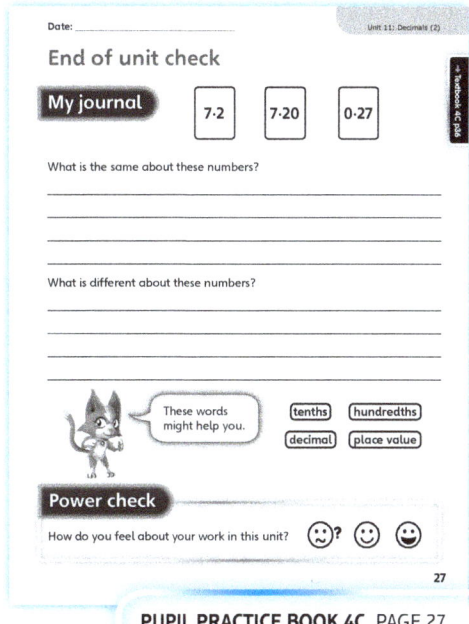

PUPIL PRACTICE BOOK 4C PAGE 27

Power check

WAYS OF WORKING Independent thinking

ASK
- *Can you partition a decimal into ones, tenths and hundredths?*
- *Can you partition a decimal in a different way?*
- *Can you explain how to round a number with one decimal place to the nearest whole number?*
- *Are you able to put some decimals in order?*

Power puzzle

WAYS OF WORKING Pair work or small groups

IN FOCUS This puzzle focuses on children understanding and applying the number bonds of tenths to make 1. Children may draw on their knowledge of bonds to 10 when identifying pairs. They should notice that there is a symmetry to the patterns on their number lines due to commutativity. They can then explore similar patterns with number bonds of hundredths to make 1.

ANSWERS AND COMMENTARY

0 + 1, 0·1 + 0·9, 0·2 + 0·8, 0·3 + 0·7, 0·4 + 0·6, 0·5 + 0·5

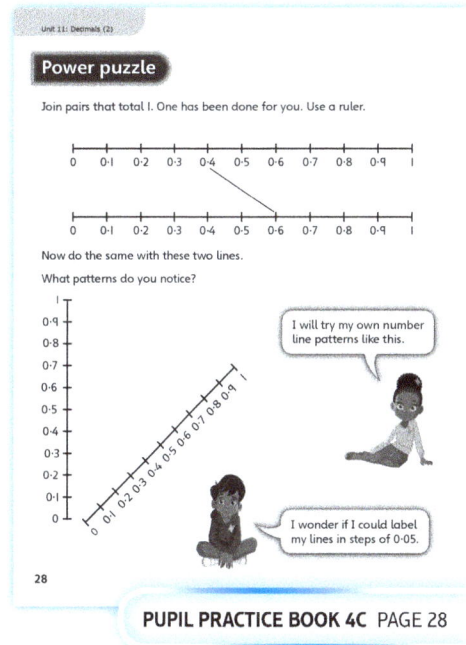

PUPIL PRACTICE BOOK 4C PAGE 28

After the unit

- Can children find the number bond of a decimal to 1? Can they accurately represent a decimal on a place value grid or other representation?
- Can children round a number to the nearest whole number and compare and order numbers that have the same number of decimal places?
- Can children use a hundredths grid to explain why $\frac{1}{2}$ is equivalent to 0·5? Can they explain why $\frac{1}{4}$ is the same as 0·25 and why $\frac{3}{4}$ is the same as 0·75?

Strengthen and **Deepen** activities for this unit can be found in the *Power Maths* online subscription.

71

Unit 12
Money

Mastery Expert tip! 'Children have only just been formally introduced to the decimal point in the previous unit so spend time introducing these key concepts. I re-created a lot of shopping scenes in class, with plenty of £·p price tags, and encouraged children to add mentally and find the change!'

Don't forget to watch the Unit 12 video!

WHY THIS UNIT IS IMPORTANT

This unit is the first time children are introduced to the £·p notation. Children will learn that the decimal point separates the pounds from the pence. They will estimate total costs and will start to add and subtract simple amounts of money, but without needing to add decimals formally. Children will know already that 100p is equal to £1 and will use this knowledge to help them with their addition. They will go on to multiply and divide amounts of money and solve word problems about money.

WHERE THIS UNIT FITS

→ Unit 11: Decimals (2)
→ **Unit 12: Money**
→ Unit 13: Time

Children have already worked with money and been formally introduced to decimals. Now they will learn how to write about money using £·p. Children should already be confident in knowing that 100p is equal to £1 and should be able to work out how much money is shown in notes and coins.

Before they start this unit, it is expected that children:
- know how to convert between pounds and pence
- can write and interpret decimal numbers with tenths and hundredths
- can use a variety of methods to count amounts of money.

ASSESSING MASTERY

By the end of the unit, children will be able to record money using the £·p notation. They will understand that the decimal point separates pounds and pence. They will know how to convert between pounds and pence and vice versa. They will be able to write money such as 3p in £s and will estimate totals when the price of an item is close to a whole number of pounds. They will compare and order amounts of money to work out the cheapest and most expensive items. Finally, children will be able to use the four operations to solve money-based problems, such as calculating which offer gives the better deal.

COMMON MISCONCEPTIONS	STRENGTHENING UNDERSTANDING	GOING DEEPER
Children may incorrectly write amounts of money when they have money less than £1. For example, children may write 3p as £0·30.	Encourage children to think of the difference between amounts such as £3, 30p and 3p. Link their knowledge of numbers with tenths and hundredths as decimals. Use a place value table to help children find the correct place for each digit.	Explore the minimum number of coins children need to make particular amounts or ask how many ways they can make this amount. For example, children could use their knowledge of times-tables to find all the ways of making 50p using coins of smaller value.
Children think that more coins equals a greater amount of money.	Children should make amounts using pennies. For example, to show that 1 × 50p coin is worth more than 8 × 5p coins, ask children to select the correct number of pennies (or 5p coins) that make up each amount and compare.	Explore what it means to find an under estimate and an over estimate. Ask children why, when adding amounts of money, it might be useful to over estimate if they have just £20 to spend.

Unit 12: Money

UNIT STARTER PAGES

Introduce the unit using whole class discussion. Use simple amounts of money to give children examples of comparing, ordering and what it means to have change. Ask children which of Flo's words they are familiar with and use terminology in sentences about money.

STRUCTURES AND REPRESENTATIONS

Number lines: These are used to add amounts. Children will benefit from seeing the addition and jumps of money using this model.

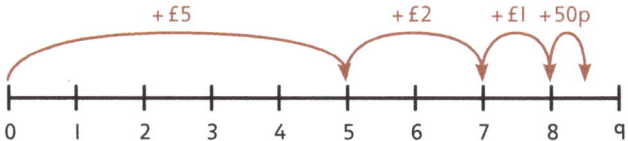

Column addition and subtraction: Adding and subtracting amounts of money using the column method allows children to use familiar methods to work with money.

46p + 85p = ☐   500 – 179 = ☐

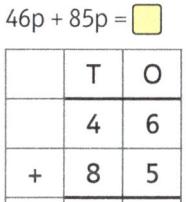

KEY LANGUAGE

There is some key language that children will need to know as part of the learning in this unit:

→ notes, coins
→ pounds (£), pence (p)
→ add (+), subtract (–)
→ change
→ order
→ greater than (>), less than (<)
→ cheaper, more expensive, same price
→ estimate, over estimate, under estimate
→ total

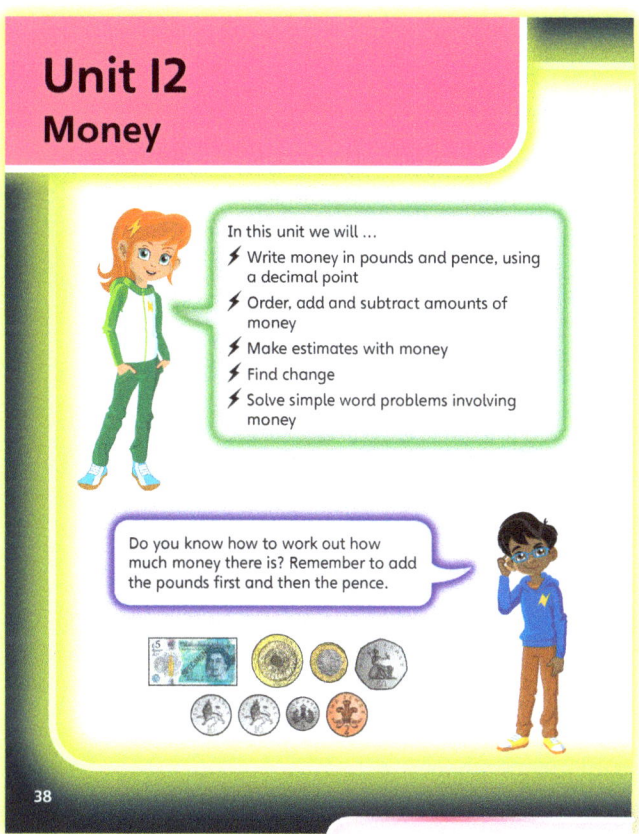

PUPIL TEXTBOOK 4C PAGE 38

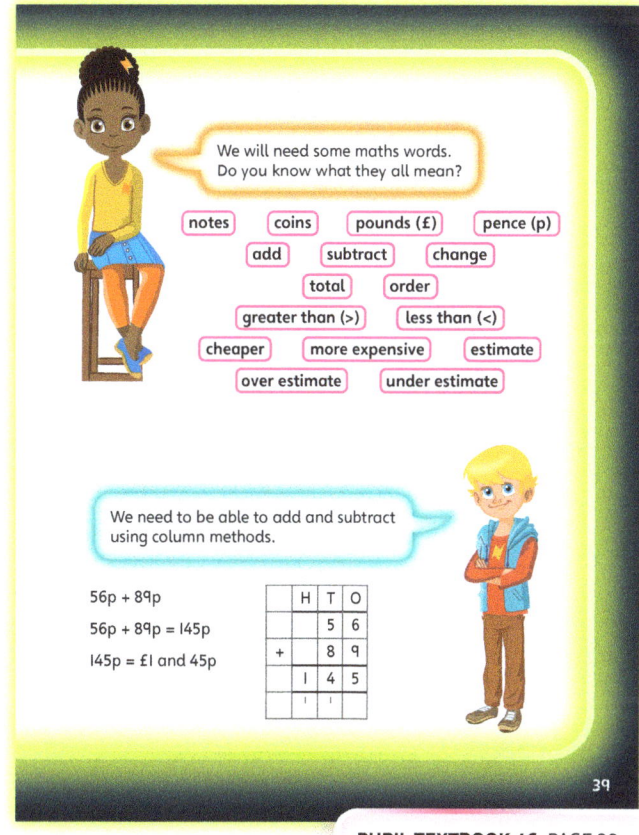

PUPIL TEXTBOOK 4C PAGE 39

Unit 12: Money, Lesson 1

Write money using decimals

Learning focus

In this lesson, children will focus on the place value of coins and amounts when recording in pounds. Children will make links between fractions of a pound and converting to decimals with two decimal places.

Before you teach

- Do children have an effective strategy for counting coins and finding totals?
- Can children record totals in pence, pounds and pence, and pounds?
- Do children know there is 100p in £1?

NATIONAL CURRICULUM LINKS

Year 4 Measurement – money

Estimate, compare and calculate different measures, including money in pounds and pence.

ASSESSING MASTERY

Children can count and write totals in pounds to two decimal places. Children understand that pence are made up of tenths and hundredths and can identify and record tenths and hundredths in totals they work out. They can explain the difference between each place value column in an amount and what each column is worth.

COMMON MISCONCEPTIONS

Children may not see the importance of 0 as a placeholder and may incorrectly write amounts. Ask:
- *Have you remembered to use 0 as a placeholder? Why is this important?*

STRENGTHENING UNDERSTANDING

Provide children with tens strips, hundredths grids and plastic coins to help them identify tenths and hundredths. To help children to identify which digit is the tenth or the hundredth, they may benefit from writing the amounts on a place value grid.

GOING DEEPER

To deepen understanding, ask children to explore and explain the relationships between pounds, tenths and hundredths. Ask children to look for different ways to make amounts, looking at how tenths and hundredths could be made using different coins.

KEY LANGUAGE

In lesson: pence (p), pounds (£), equal

Other language to be used by the teacher: amount, total, price, decimal point, tenth, hundredth, fraction

STRUCTURES AND REPRESENTATIONS

Hundredths grids, tens strips (that is, one row of the hundredth grid)

RESOURCES

Optional: plastic coins

 In the eTextbook of this lesson, you will find interactive links to a selection of teaching tools.

Quick recap

Challenge children to choose and draw coins that have a total value of 83p. Then, challenge children to find 83p in another way.

74

Unit 12: Money, Lesson 1

Discover

WAYS OF WORKING Pair work

ASK

- Question 1 a): *What coins does Emma have? How many coins does Emma have? How many 1p coins make £1?*
- Question 1 b): *How many 1p coins does Danny have? Did you need to count each coin individually? How could you write that as a fraction? How could you write that as a decimal?*

IN FOCUS In question 1 a), remind children that 100p is equal to £1 so they do not need to count each individual penny. Question 1 b) highlights children's understanding of place value and whether they are aware of tenths and hundredths when recording amounts less than £1 as a decimal.

PRACTICAL TIPS Provide children with a hundredths grid filled with 1p coins. Images of Emma and Danny's filled hundredths grid may also be useful.

ANSWERS

Question 1 a): Emma has 100 pence = £1·00.

Question 1 b): Danny has 43 pence = £0·43.

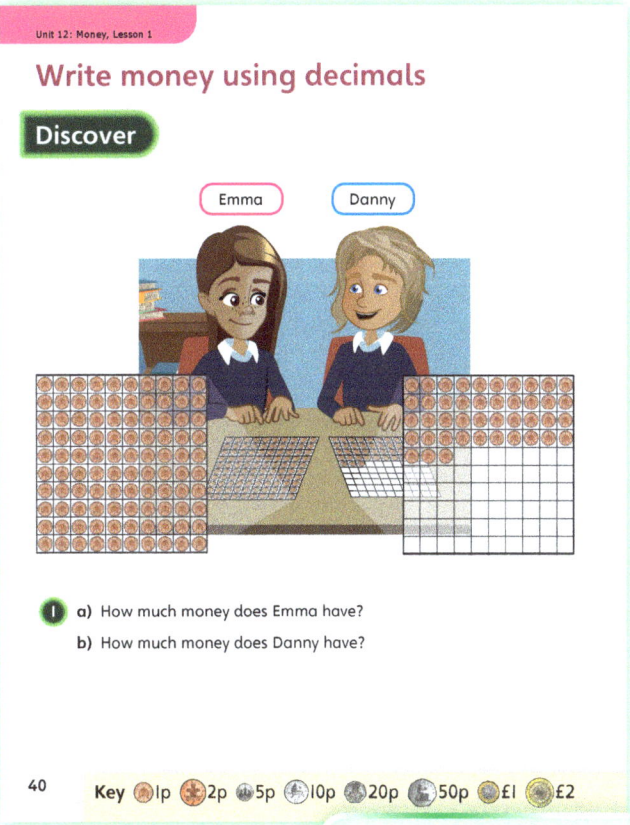

PUPIL TEXTBOOK 4C PAGE 40

Share

WAYS OF WORKING Whole class teacher led

ASK

- Question 1 a): *What do you know about 100 pennies? How are you going to record Emma's amount?*
- Question 1 b): *What will be the quickest way to find the total of Danny's coins? How are you going to record Danny's amount?*
- Question 1 b): *How do you record this in pounds? What goes before the decimal point? What goes after the decimal point?*

IN FOCUS For question 1 a), discuss the layout of the grid and how this can help children work out the total. To work out the total of coins in question 1 b), children may need to count the coins individually. Some children could be encouraged to use the layout of the hundredths grid – there are four full rows plus three, therefore 43 coins. Can children use the hundredths grid to write this as $\frac{43}{100}$ of £1 (that is, 43 hundredths of a pound)? See if children can work out that the decimal equivalent of $\frac{43}{100}$ is 0·43 since there are 4 tenths and 3 hundredths. Help them see that this is £0·43.

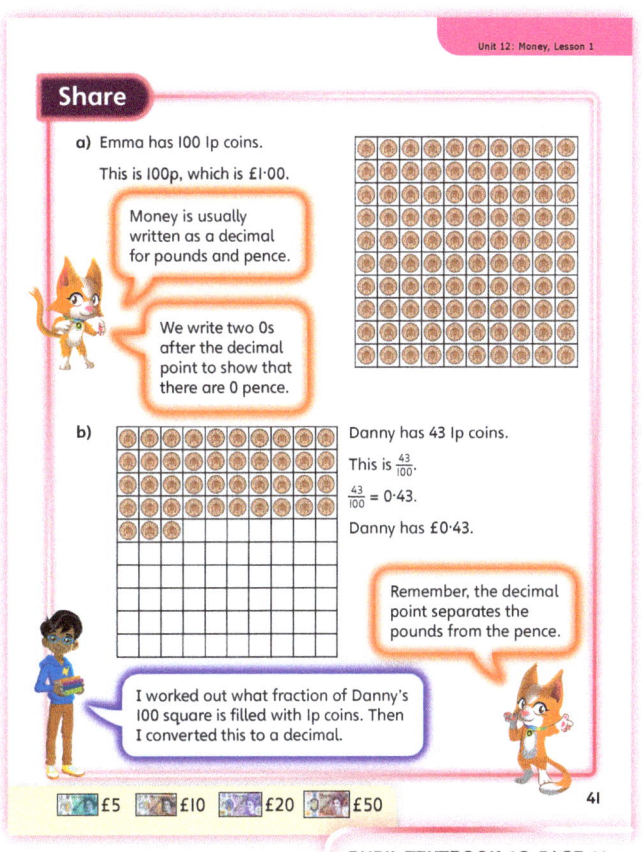

PUPIL TEXTBOOK 4C PAGE 41

75

Unit 12: Money, Lesson 1

Think together

WAYS OF WORKING Whole class teacher led (I do, We do, You do)

ASK

- Question ❶: *How many 1p coins are there? How can you count the number of coins on the grids? What is the worth of the 1p coins on the grid? How can you write the amount of coins as a fraction? What would these fractions look like as decimals? Where will the decimal points go?*
- Question ❷: *What coins are in each box? Are there any pounds? How many pounds? How much is there in pence? How many tenths? How many hundredths? What will they look like as decimals?*
- Question ❸: *How many pounds are there in each price? How many pence are there? What does the decimal point mean? Is there more than one way you could make that amount?*

IN FOCUS Question ❷ requires children to find totals and write them correctly to two decimal places. Encourage children to think carefully about the tenths and hundredths in terms of how many 10p coins and 1p coins they could have. This will help them write the amounts using decimal points correctly.

STRENGTHEN For question ❶, have coins available for children so they can make the relevant amount and count the number of pence. In question ❷, it may help children to write the pence after the decimal point if they first write the pence as a fraction. When completing question ❸, children may need to use real coins to move, rearrange and make the given amounts.

DEEPEN For question ❶, encourage children to find multiple strategies for working out how much money is on the grid. For question ❷, ask children to show each amount as tenths or hundredths on a hundredths grid. For question ❸, deepen understanding further by encouraging children to work out what other amounts they could make with the given coins using their knowledge of tenths and hundredths.

ASSESSMENT CHECKPOINT Children should now be able to write correctly tenths and hundredths as a decimal. They should understand that $\frac{1}{100}$ of £1 is 1p and use this to express amounts of money, including those less than £1, using the £·p notation.

ANSWERS

Question ❶ a): £0·55

Question ❶ b): £0·20

Question ❷ a): £3·30

Question ❷ b): £3·03

Question ❷ c): £0·03

Question ❷ d): £0·35

Question ❸: £0·50: 50p or 20p + 20p + 5p + 5p
£1·50: £1 + 50p or £1 + 20p + 20p + 5p + 5p
£2·30: £1 + 50p + 50p + 20p + 5p + 5p
£1·05: 50p + 50p + 5p or £1 + 5p

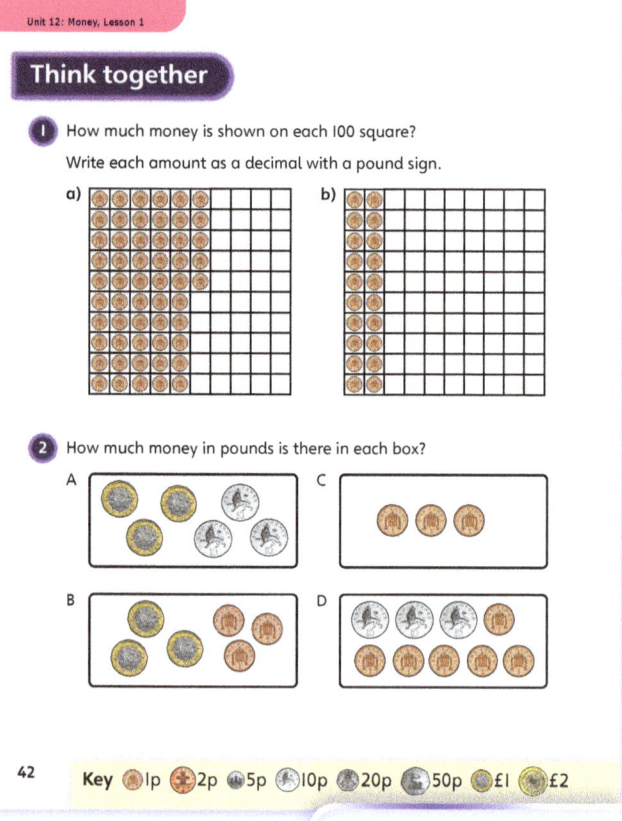

PUPIL TEXTBOOK 4C PAGE 42

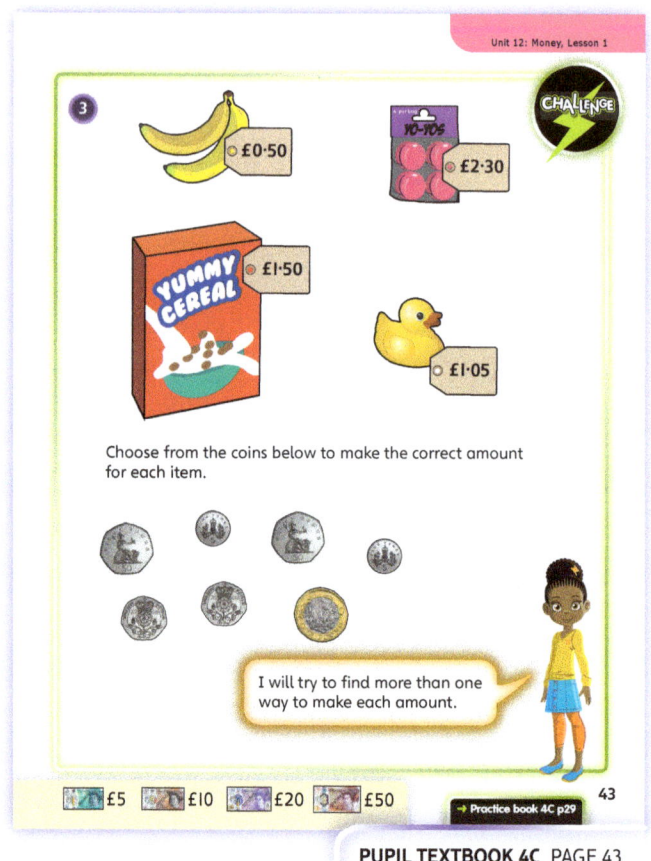

PUPIL TEXTBOOK 4C PAGE 43

76

Unit 12: Money, Lesson 1

Practice

WAYS OF WORKING Independent thinking

IN FOCUS Question ① requires children to write amounts of money as a decimal. Children may feel they need to count every 1p coin on the hundredths grid, but encourage them to look for more efficient ways to find the total. Question ② introduces 10p coins on tens strips to reinforce the concept of 10p as $\frac{1}{10}$ of £1. In question ⑥, children re-visit fractions of an amount, which they studied in Unit 9. Give children hundredths grids to work from and make sure they understand that the denominator tells them how many parts the grid must be divided into. For $\frac{3}{10}$, children must consider the hundredths grid as 10 rows, since it is only being split into 10. They could shade 3 of these rows to show them the fraction they need to find. For $\frac{3}{100}$, children should see the hundredths grid as 100 squares. Reinforce that one square of the hundredths grid represents 1 pence, and each row represents 10 pence.

STRENGTHEN Before starting to work out question ③, encourage children to look for any coins that could be used together to make tenths. Provide hundredths grids, tens strips and plastic coins so children can record the pence after the decimal point accurately. Initially, children may need to work out the tenths first, followed by the hundredths.

DEEPEN Encourage children to find different ways to make the same amounts in question ④ and identify how many tenths and hundredths there are for each version.

THINK DIFFERENTLY Question ⑤ explores the misconception of not including the placeholder zero in the hundredths place when an amount of money only has tenths.

ASSESSMENT CHECKPOINT Children should now be able to add coins together and identify whole pounds, tenths and hundredths in an amount to record the total correctly in pounds. Assess whether children can choose appropriate coins to make given pounds, tenths and hundredths. Do children understand the link between tenths and hundredths?

ANSWERS Answers for the **Practice** part of the lesson can be found in the *Power Maths* online subscription.

Reflect

WAYS OF WORKING Independent thinking

IN FOCUS This question will highlight children's understanding of tenths and hundredths and how they relate to pence. Children should identify that both amounts have the same number of pounds but different tenths and hundredths.

ASSESSMENT CHECKPOINT Assess children's explanations of the difference in tenths and hundredths. Can children identify that the amounts have the same number of whole pounds but a different number of tenths and hundredths?

ANSWERS Answers for the **Reflect** part of the lesson can be found in the *Power Maths* online subscription.

After the lesson

- Do children recognise pence as tenths and hundredths?
- Can children record amounts correctly, thinking about the tenths and hundredths?
- Can children discuss the value of each digit in a given amount?

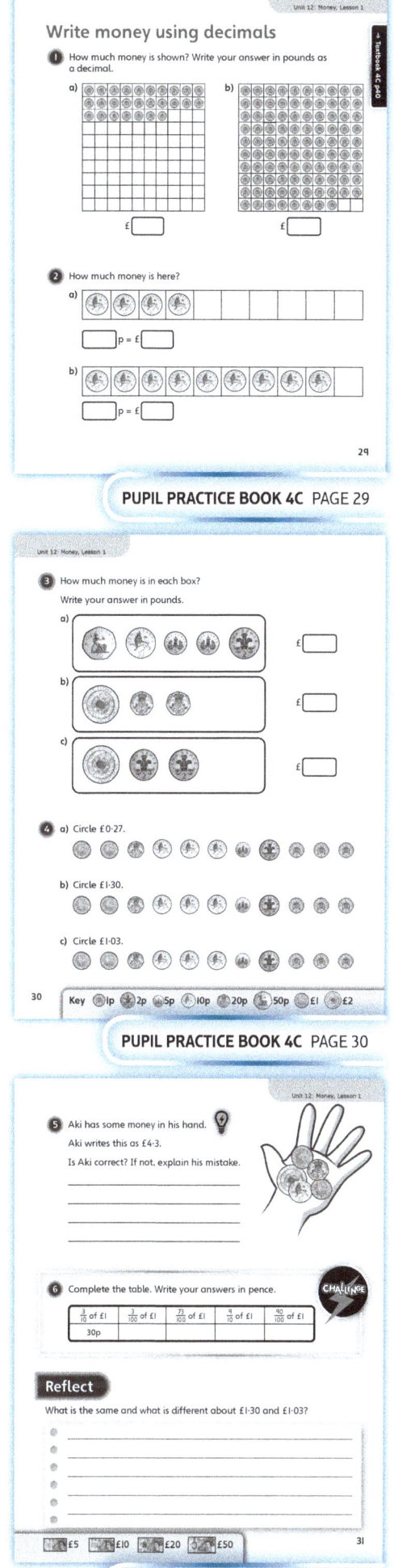

PUPIL PRACTICE BOOK 4C PAGE 29

PUPIL PRACTICE BOOK 4C PAGE 30

PUPIL PRACTICE BOOK 4C PAGE 31

77

Unit 12: Money, Lesson 2

Convert between pounds and pence

Learning focus

In this lesson, children will add pence, crossing the pound boundary, and pounds and pence. Children will write totals as pence, pounds and pence, and with a decimal point.

Before you teach

- Do children recognise British coins and notes?
- Do children know how much each coin and note is worth?
- Do children know basic equivalence (ten 10p coins make £1, two 5p coins make 10p)?

NATIONAL CURRICULUM LINKS

Year 4 Measurement – money

Estimate, compare and calculate different measures, including money in pounds and pence.

ASSESSING MASTERY

Children will understand that there are 100p in £1 and will explore various ways of making a pound and other totals by adding a range of coins together. Children will be confident writing totals in pence, pounds and pence, and with a decimal point.

COMMON MISCONCEPTIONS

When recording amounts, children may not be clear where and when to use the signs '£', 'p' and '·'. Ask:
- *What does the £ sign represent? What does the p sign represent? Where should £ be used? Where should p be used?*
- *Do we use the decimal point when we write a price in pence only, or in pounds and pence? What does the decimal point separate?*

STRENGTHENING UNDERSTANDING

Strengthen understanding by providing children with physical coins to move around, pair up and count. A number line or hundredths grid will help children with addition. Hundredths grids are particularly useful to show reaching £1 and crossing the boundary.

GOING DEEPER

Challenge children to find a range of methods or come up with a variety of ways to make a given total.

KEY LANGUAGE

In lesson: pence (p), pounds (£), decimal point

Other language to be used by the teacher: coins, total, altogether, one hundred, multiples

STRUCTURES AND REPRESENTATIONS

Part-whole models

RESOURCES

Optional: plastic coins, crayons

 In the eTextbook of this lesson, you will find interactive links to a selection of teaching tools.

Quick recap

Challenge children to choose and draw coins that have a total value of £1·35.

Unit 12: Money, Lesson 2

Discover

WAYS OF WORKING Pair work

ASK

- Question 1 a): *What coins does Bella have? How are you going to find the total? Could you make the coins easier to count?*
- Question 1 b): *What does 'pounds' mean? How will the total look different in pounds and pence?*

IN FOCUS In questions 1 a) and b), children must recognise the value of each coin and add them together correctly. Question 1 b) will highlight whether children know there are 100p in £1 and whether children understand and can use the pound sign and decimal point.

PRACTICAL TIPS Recreate the **Discover** scene of Bella counting her pounds and pence. Give children plastic coins matching the coins Bella has.

ANSWERS

Question 1 a): Bella has 236p in total.

Question 1 b): Bella has £2·36 in total.

PUPIL TEXTBOOK 4C PAGE 44

Share

WAYS OF WORKING Whole class teacher led

ASK

- Question 1 a): *Are there different ways to make 100p? How many groups of 100p can you make using the coins that Bella has? What coins are left over? How can you count these left over coins?*
- Question 1 b): *How many pence are there in £1? If 100p make £1, how many pounds will 200p be? How do you write £2? Where does the pound sign go?*
- Question 1 b): *What units do you use for the 36? Why is the 36 in pence and not pounds? What does the decimal point tell you? Do you need the £ sign when using a decimal point? Do you need the p sign when using a decimal point?*

IN FOCUS Ensure children understand that there are 100p in £1, and therefore 200p are equivalent to £2. Explain that the 36p remains in pence because it is less than 100p and you can only exchange for £1 at 100p. Using a decimal point ensures children understand that it comes after the whole pounds.

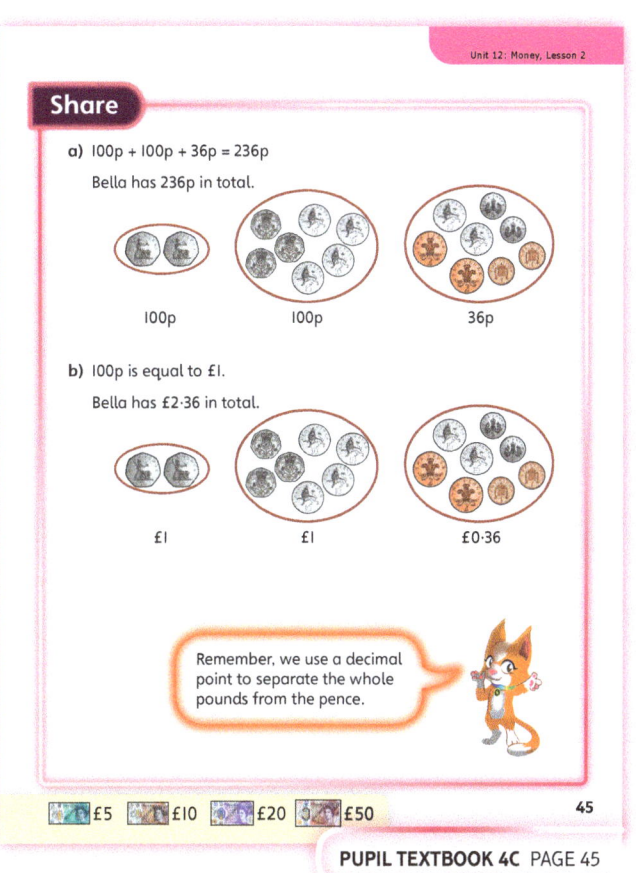

PUPIL TEXTBOOK 4C PAGE 45

79

Think together

WAYS OF WORKING Whole class teacher led (I do, We do, You do)

ASK

- Question ❶: *Can you make the coins easier to count by making pounds? How many pounds are there? How many coins are left that do not make one pound? What is the total of these coins in pence?*
- Question ❷: *How many whole pounds are there on each price tag? How can you tell? How many pence are left over? Where will you put the decimal point?*
- Question ❸: *What is the same and what is different about £10, £1, £0·10 and £0·01?*

IN FOCUS In question ❷, help children to see that, because all prices are written in pence, they have to look at the digit in the hundreds column to determine how many whole pounds (that is, how many lots of 100p) there are in each price. Children might also realise that they divide by 100 to convert pence to pounds. You might want to use a place value grid to recap dividing by 100, emphasising that each digit moves 2 places to the right. Question ❸ gives children the opportunity to explore the value of all coins and some notes when expressed in pounds as a decimal. Discuss which coins worth are less than £1 and which coins or notes are worth more than £1 and how this will be reflected in the decimal notation. Look for children who do not use 0 as placeholder or put it in the wrong place.

STRENGTHEN Children may find it beneficial having plastic coins available to move around and group into 100s or other amounts. In order to group coins to make 100p, children may find it helpful to use a hundredths grid. Encourage children to use number bonds to 10 or use the larger coins first to help them make 100p.

DEEPEN Challenge children to find alternative ways of making 100p and to explain which way they found the most efficient and why.

ASSESSMENT CHECKPOINT Check to see if children can find totals of a range of coins and whether they can write amounts in pence, pounds and pence, and pounds. Do children know when it is appropriate to use the '£', 'p' and '·' signs and why? Do they know that 100p and £1 are equivalent and can they find an efficient way to make 100p given a range of coins?

ANSWERS

Question ❶ a): 114p

Question ❶ b): £1·14

Question ❷: £1·50   £3·03
              £2·99   £0·90

Question ❸ a): 1p = £0·01   2p = £0·02   5p = £0·05
              10p = £0·10   20p = £0·20   50p = £0·50
              £1 = £1·00   £2 = £2·00   £5 = £5·00
              £10 = £10·00 £20 = £20·00

Question ❸ b): Neither child is correct, as money is written with 2 decimal places.
              1p = £0·01 and 10p = £0·10

Unit 12: Money, Lesson 2

Practice

WAYS OF WORKING Independent thinking

IN FOCUS Question ❺ focuses on equivalence. Children must convert amounts from pence to pounds and vice versa. Children are expected to convert both ways so will need to think carefully whether they are dividing or multiplying by 100.

STRENGTHEN Children need to keep a running total when completing question ❸. To help children keep track of the amount, encourage the use of a hundredths grid or number line. Encourage children to make the whole pounds first and regularly add up their notes and coins so far. To complete questions ❹ to ❻, children might need to use plastic coins or draw coins, circle amounts to 100p or £1, or used coloured crayons to pair up bonds to 100.

DEEPEN For question ❷, ask children to find different ways of making 100p using the given coins and then to explain which is the most efficient method and why. Use question ❷ to deepen understanding and ask children to investigate different ways to make the given amounts.

ASSESSMENT CHECKPOINT Assess whether children can add pounds and amounts under 100p together. Children should be secure in their knowledge that 100p makes £1 and should be able to choose suitable coins to make a given amount.

ANSWERS Answers for the **Practice** part of the lesson can be found in the *Power Maths* online subscription.

Reflect

WAYS OF WORKING Independent thinking

IN FOCUS This section gives children a final chance to reflect on the three different ways to record amounts. Children will be able to use the images to work out one way of writing the total, then use their knowledge of multiplying or dividing by 100 to convert. The question also requires children to use their knowledge of the '£', 'p' and '·' signs.

ASSESSMENT CHECKPOINT Children should now be aware of the three different ways of recording amounts and be able to convert from pence to pounds and from pounds to pence. Do children have an efficient method for grouping coins? Can they use appropriate signs correctly?

ANSWERS Answers for the **Reflect** part of the lesson can be found in the *Power Maths* online subscription.

After the lesson

- Can children add coins and record the total in pence, pounds and pence, and pounds?
- Do children know how and when to use '£', 'p' and '·'?
- Can children divide and multiply by 100 to convert from pence to pounds and vice versa?

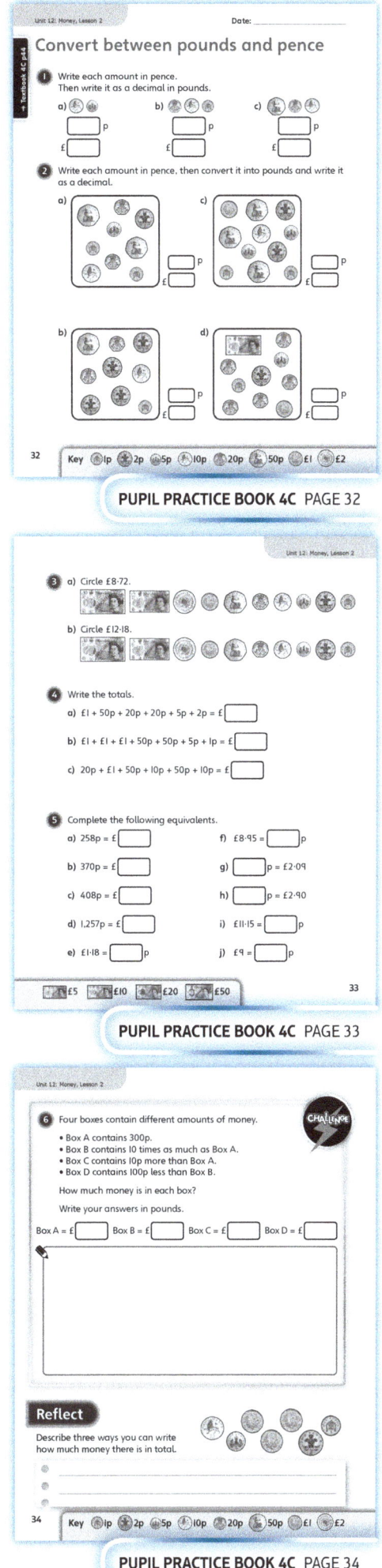

PUPIL PRACTICE BOOK 4C PAGE 32

PUPIL PRACTICE BOOK 4C PAGE 33

PUPIL PRACTICE BOOK 4C PAGE 34

Unit 12: Money, Lesson 3

Compare amounts of money

Learning focus
In this lesson, children will identify, compare and put in order the most and least expensive items and amounts of money. Children will convert prices and amounts in a variety of notations into a common unit.

Before you teach
- Can children read prices and amounts in various notations?
- Can children convert between units?
- Do children understand vocabulary linked to ordering?

NATIONAL CURRICULUM LINKS

Year 4 Measurement – money

Estimate, compare and calculate different measures, including money in pounds and pence.

ASSESSING MASTERY

Children can convert a mixture of notations into a common unit, identify the most and least expensive item and identify the greatest and least amount of money. Children can order prices and amounts from greatest to least and from least to greatest.

COMMON MISCONCEPTIONS

When converting notations, children may mix up whether they are multiplying by 100 or dividing by 100 and so wrongly identify which is the most or the least. Ask:
- *What calculation do you need to use to change an amount to pounds or pence? How do you know which is the most? How do you know which is the least?*

STRENGTHENING UNDERSTANDING

Give children access to plastic coins so that they can make given amounts. Looking at physical representations of what is the same and what is different about the amounts may make it easier for children to compare (for example, both amounts have two 50p coins, but this one has an extra 10p coin as well so it must be bigger). When ordering totals, encourage children to set amounts out on a number line to make the order very visual.

GOING DEEPER

Encourage children to work between units rather than converting every amount into a common notation. Ask children about their decisions. Discuss their understanding of worth and order and ensure their explanations correctly use mathematical vocabulary linked to ordering money.

KEY LANGUAGE

In lesson: convert, most, greatest, least, more than (>), less than (<), order

Other language to be used by the teacher: price, total, amount, units, common, ascending, descending

STRUCTURES AND REPRESENTATIONS

Number lines

RESOURCES

Optional: plastic coins, place value grid

 In the eTextbook of this lesson, you will find interactive links to a selection of teaching tools.

Quick recap
Ask children to write each of these amounts in decimal form as pounds and pence:
57p   250p   205p

82

Discover

WAYS OF WORKING Pair work

ASK
- Question 1 a): *What does more expensive mean? Are the prices all recorded in the same way?*
- Question 1 b): *How much does each item cost? How much does Isla have to spend? Which items cost less than £5? What are you looking for in each price?*

IN FOCUS In question 1 a), children may look at the amount of pounds in each item and mentally use their knowledge of 100p = £1 to compare the items. Some children may convert the prices into pounds or pence so that they can compare the items more easily.

PRACTICAL TIPS Set up the shop scenario using toys and price tags and provide children with a variety of plastic coins and notes.

ANSWERS

Question 1 a): The football is more expensive than the colouring pencils.

Question 1 b): Isla could buy any items that cost £5·00 or 500p or less.
Isla could buy the football or both the colouring pencils and the notepad.

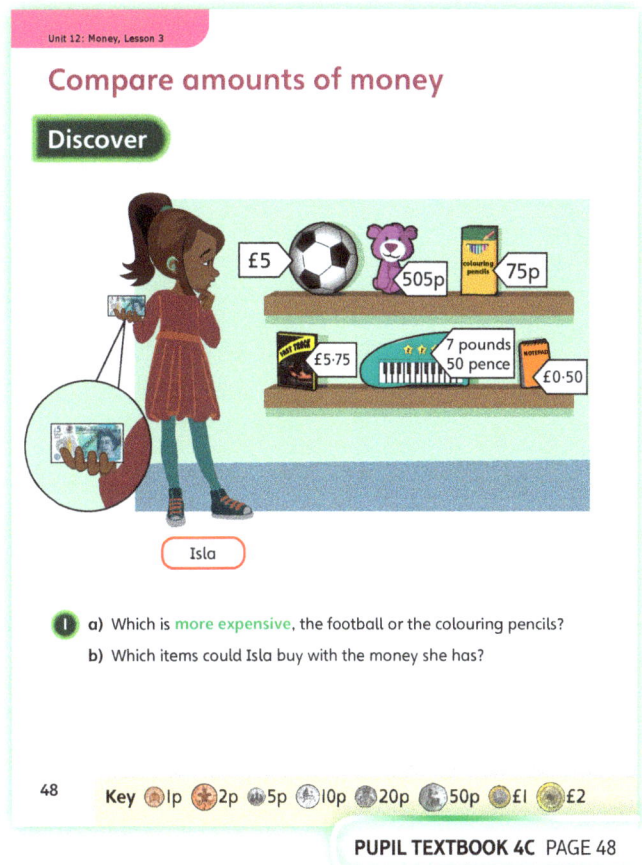

PUPIL TEXTBOOK 4C PAGE 48

Share

WAYS OF WORKING Whole class teacher led

ASK
- Question 1 a): *Are these items priced in the same units? Can you convert them into the same units? How do you convert from pence to pounds? How do you write prices in pounds? How do you convert from pounds to pence? How do you write prices in pence?*
- Question 1 b): *What is this note worth in pounds? What is this note worth in pence? Which items are less than £5 or 500p? Which items are the same as £5 or 500p? Which items are more than £5 or 500p?*

IN FOCUS In question 1 b), some children may want to convert the £5 into pence and others may want to convert the items in pence into pounds. Discuss why both of these options would be possible and whether one is more efficient than the other. Encourage children to then explain why certain items can be eliminated.

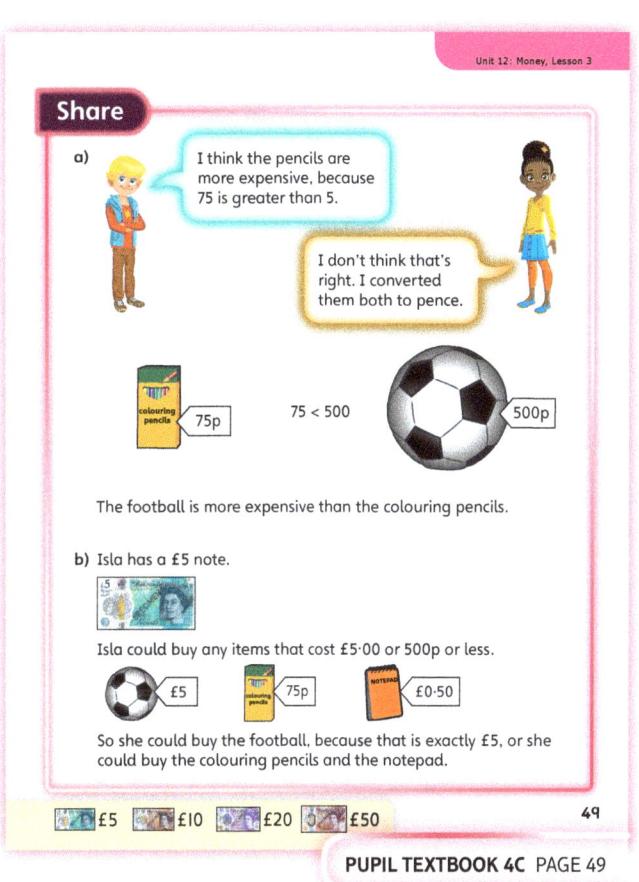

PUPIL TEXTBOOK 4C PAGE 49

Unit 12: Money, Lesson 3

Think together

WAYS OF WORKING Whole class teacher led (I do, We do, You do)

ASK

- Question ①: *What are the prices of each of the items? What does cheapest mean? What does most expensive mean?*
- Question ②: *How much are Alex's coins worth altogether? How do you write Alex's amount in pounds? How do you write Alex's amount in pence? Which items could Alex **not** buy?*
- Question ③: *How much money does each child have? Why would having a note make Max think he has the most? Why would having the most coins make Richard think he has the most?*

IN FOCUS Question ③ can be used to highlight children's understanding of the worth of a coin or note. It will also highlight possible misconceptions – for example, the bigger the coin, the more you have; or the more coins you have, the larger the amount.

STRENGTHEN For question ①, encourage children to make prices with coins and notes in order to identify and compare how many pounds and pence each item costs. To strengthen understanding of question ②, encourage children to write down the coins Alex has in pounds and then in pence. Children could also use individual coins to buy certain items (for example, using the £1 for the comic or car).

DEEPEN Deepen understanding of question ② by asking children what combinations of items Alex could buy with £5. Children could also calculate how much extra she would need if she wanted to buy all the items. Additionally, when looking at the misconceptions for question ③, ask children to use examples of coins and notes to prove the misconceptions are incorrect.

ASSESSMENT CHECKPOINT Children should now be able to identify the most and least expensive by converting into the same notation and correctly compare and order prices following set criteria. Ensure children can identify which items are more than, less than or the same as the total given. Children should also recognise common misconceptions related to money and be able to explain why the misconceptions are incorrect.

ANSWERS

Question ① a): The dinosaur comic is the cheapest.

Question ① b): The engine is the most expensive.

Question ① c): Order from least expensive to most expensive:
comic, 59p; car, £0·99; movie, 595p; doll, £5·99; engine, 9 pounds 95 pence

Question ②: Alec has £6·50, so could buy everything except the engine.

Question ③: Max has not taken into account the value of the rest of his coins.
Richard does have the most money, but not because he has more coins. Someone with fewer coins could have more than Richard has, for example, four £2 coins = £8·00 is more than Richard's nine coins which total £6·70.

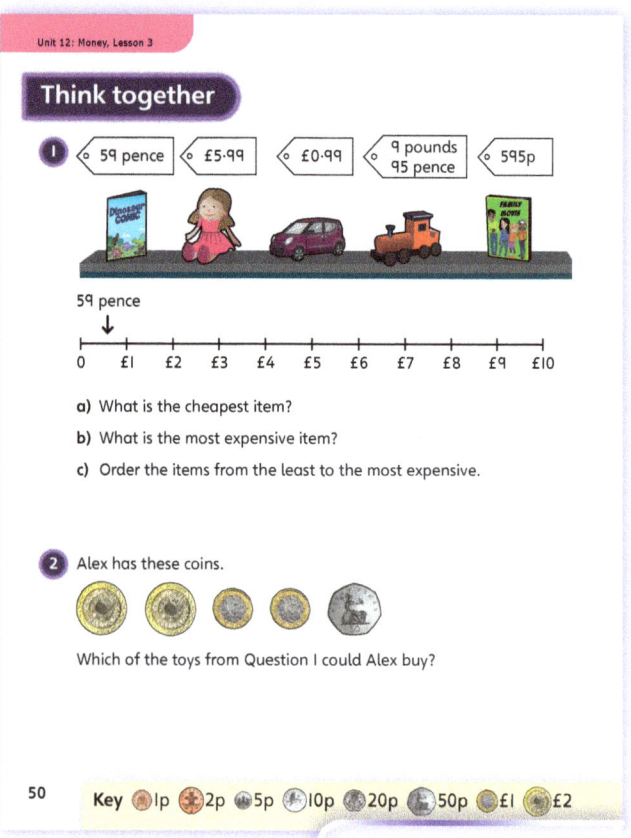

PUPIL TEXTBOOK 4C PAGE 50

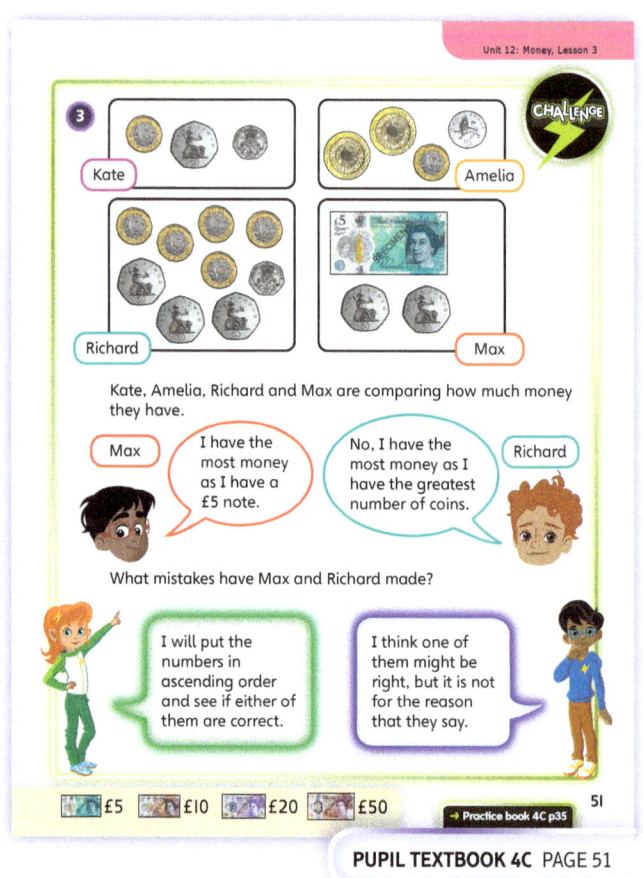

PUPIL TEXTBOOK 4C PAGE 51

Unit 12: Money, Lesson 3

Practice

WAYS OF WORKING Independent thinking

IN FOCUS Question ❶ allows children to convert or compare mentally using their secure knowledge of 100p = £1. Children can show their understanding of the language and what a total is worth by explaining how they know which is the most or least expensive.

STRENGTHEN Encourage children to convert different amounts into the same units or to make them using plastic coins. Children may also find it beneficial to set amounts out on a number line in order to compare.

DEEPEN Deepen understanding of question ❼ by asking children to explain how they knew which money bag belonged to which child after reading the clues. Children could also explain why specific money bags could not belong to other children based on the clues given. Ask children to write different clues that would reveal whose money bag was whose.

ASSESSMENT CHECKPOINT Children should have an understanding of the vocabulary 'most expensive' and 'least expensive', be able to identify the most or least expensive from a list of totals and be able to justify their choices. They should also be able to identify amounts greater than, less than, or equal to a given amount and to order prices to specific criteria.

ANSWERS Answers for the **Practice** part of the lesson can be found in the *Power Maths* online subscription.

Reflect

WAYS OF WORKING Independent thinking

IN FOCUS In this **Reflect** activity, children use their knowledge of place value, conversions and the inequality signs in order to compare amounts of pounds and pence.

ASSESSMENT CHECKPOINT Children should identify that Isla is incorrectly showing £3 as 3p in the statement and be able to explain that £3 is 300p, which is larger than 257p, or that 257p is £2·57, which is less than £3.

ANSWERS Answers for the **Reflect** part of the lesson can be found in the *Power Maths* online subscription.

After the lesson

- Can children identify, compare and order amounts according to given criteria?
- Can children use the inequality signs to compare amounts?
- Can children identify and discuss common misconceptions related to comparing and ordering money?

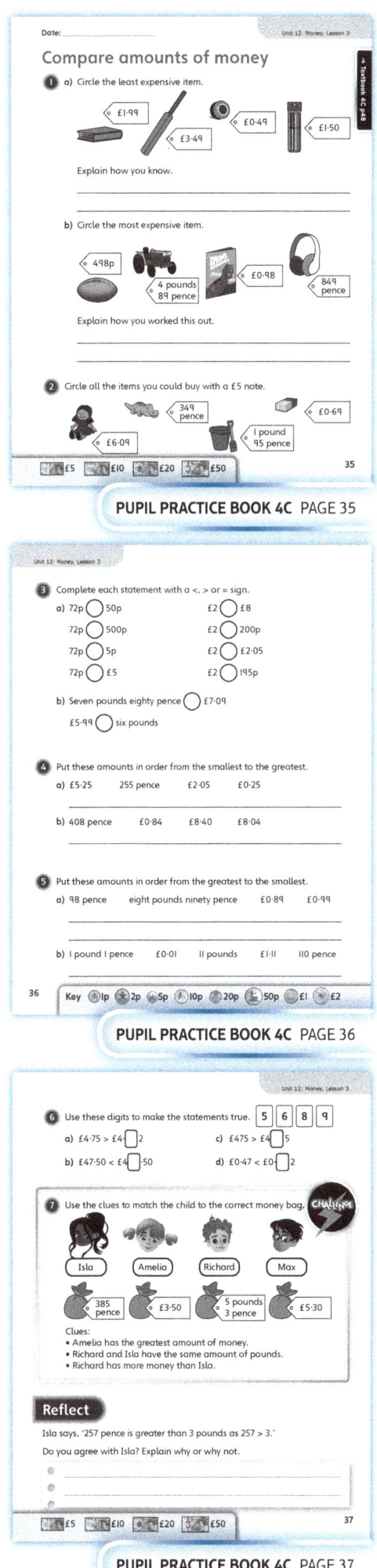

PUPIL PRACTICE BOOK 4C PAGE 35

PUPIL PRACTICE BOOK 4C PAGE 36

PUPIL PRACTICE BOOK 4C PAGE 37

Unit 12: Money, Lesson 4

Estimate with money

Learning focus
In this lesson, children will make estimates, look at differences between prices and work out how much money remains. Children will explore over and under estimates depending on how prices were adjusted.

Before you teach
- Are children confident rounding whole numbers to the nearest 10 and 100?
- Do children know what 'estimate' means?
- Can children confidently add multiples of 10 and 100?

NATIONAL CURRICULUM LINKS

Year 4 Measurement – money

Estimate, compare and calculate different measures, including money in pounds and pence.

ASSESSING MASTERY

Children can confidently use estimated amounts to estimate totals. Children can find the difference between prices and determine if there is enough money to purchase given items. Children can also determine if an estimate is an over or under estimation.

COMMON MISCONCEPTIONS

Children may not understand that after making an estimate, the answer is not exact. Ask:
- *Have you calculated using an estimate? How could you find the exact answer instead?*

STRENGTHENING UNDERSTANDING

Providing children with a range of number lines with various scaffolds and place value grids will support any children who are still not confident with making sensible estimates. When calculating with estimates, children may benefit from using a blank number line, a number track of multiples of 10p or 100p, or having the money to manipulate. Also getting children to make the exact price and the estimated price with play money will give them a good visual that, when estimating, they are working with a 'little more' or a 'little less' than the exact answer.

GOING DEEPER

With each question answered, some children may be able to calculate the exact amount as well as work out the difference between the exact answer and their estimated answer. Some children may also be able to work out where the difference came from.

KEY LANGUAGE

In lesson: nearest, estimate, **over estimate**, **under estimate**, 10p, £1, total, most, least

Other language to be used by the teacher: closest, approximately, different, more, less, left

STRUCTURES AND REPRESENTATIONS

Number lines

RESOURCES

Optional: plastic coins

 In the eTextbook of this lesson, you will find interactive links to a selection of teaching tools.

Quick recap

Challenge children to use a mental strategy to complete this addition:

9 + 19 + 29

Unit 12: Money, Lesson 4

Discover

WAYS OF WORKING Pair work

ASK

- Question 1 a): *How many pounds are in each price? How many tenths? How many hundredths?*
- Question 1 b): *Why is it a good idea to use an estimate rather than calculating the actual total for these prices?*

IN FOCUS Question 1 b) requires children to estimate the total of the three given prices. Children will need to look at the number of pounds and pence in each price in order to identify the nearest whole number. They can then use this to make a sensible estimate of the total.

PRACTICAL TIPS Set up the supermarket scene with corresponding items and prices. Provide children with plastic coins to help them make estimates and find totals.

ANSWERS

Question 1 a): Each item has 99p in the pence part of the price.
But they all have different numbers of pounds in the pounds part of the price.

Question 1 b): £1 + £2 + £3 = £6
A good estimate is £6.

Share

WAYS OF WORKING Whole class teacher led

ASK

- Question 1 a): *Which whole number is each price closest to?*
- Question 1 b): *How can you use the estimated prices to find an approximate total? Why is the total going to be an estimate and not exact?*

IN FOCUS For question 1 a), encourage children to explain how they knew where to position each price on the number line. Ask: *What do you notice about the number of pounds? The number of pence? Is each price much nearer to one number than another on the number line?* In question 1 b), discuss what operation is needed to find the total. Encourage children to compare adding the exact prices and adding multiples of 100p, then discuss which is quicker.

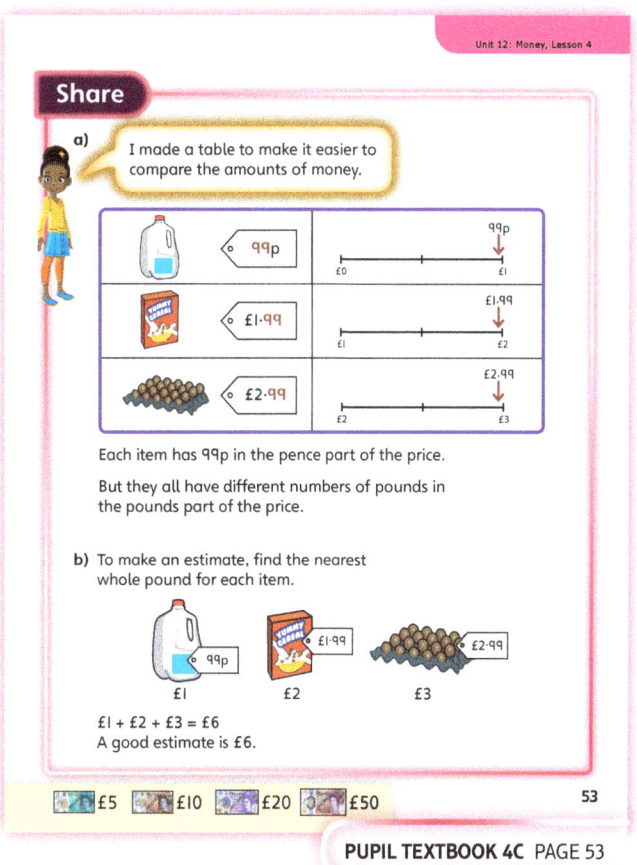

Think together

WAYS OF WORKING Whole class teacher led (I do, We do, You do)

ASK
- Question ❶: *How many pounds are in each price? How many pence? Which item costs approximately £4?*
- Question ❷: *Which whole number of pounds is each price closest to? When might it be useful to estimate the cost of any one particular item?*
- Question ❸: *What do you need to do with the rounded prices to find the totals? How are you going to add these rounded prices?*

IN FOCUS In question ❸, children investigate the accuracy of estimating. Discuss when children may make an over estimate and when they may make an under estimate. Ask: *Why would you need to know if your estimate is more or less than the actual total?*

STRENGTHEN For question ❸, encourage children to note which prices they estimated up and which they estimated down in order to work out whether their approximate total is an over or under estimate. This will give children a clear idea of whether they added or subtracted from the exact prices.

DEEPEN For question ❸, ask children to calculate the exact cost and comment on how good their estimate was. Look together at Ash's comment and discuss how children could also estimate to the nearest 10p to find a better estimate of the total.

ASSESSMENT CHECKPOINT Children should now be able to identify why an estimated answer is an over or under estimate. They should also be able to explain why estimating to the nearest £1 could be less accurate than estimating to the nearest 10p.

ANSWERS

Question ❶: The cap costs approximately £5. Accept answers that the sunglasses are approximately £5. Ensure children can explain their reasoning for choosing this item.

Question ❷: Various responses are possible for both individual items and combined totals, for example:
50p + £19 + £50 + £50 = £119·50
50p + £20 + £50 + £50 = £120·50

Question ❸ a): £1·50 + £4 + £2·50 = £8

Question ❸ b): Over estimate as all the prices have been rounded up.
If children have rounded to the nearest pound, their estimate will be £1 + £4 + £2 = £7, which is an under estimate, as two prices have been rounded down quite significantly.

PUPIL TEXTBOOK 4C PAGE 54

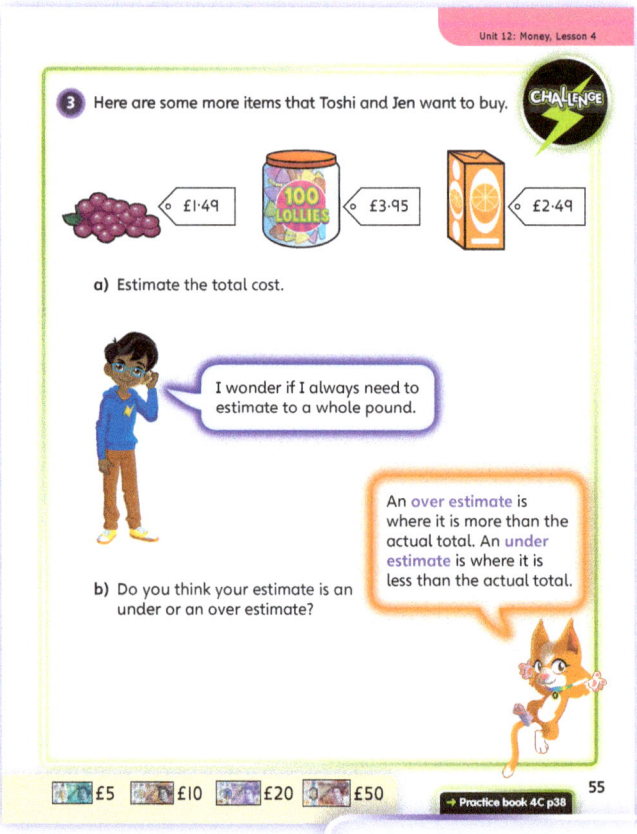

PUPIL TEXTBOOK 4C PAGE 55

Unit 12: Money, Lesson 4

Practice

WAYS OF WORKING Independent thinking

IN FOCUS In question ❶, children identify the nearest whole number of pounds for some given prices in order to demonstrate an understanding of sensible estimates. Children can then use this in question ❷ where they write their own estimates.

STRENGTHEN Encourage the use of a number line to help children add pounds and pence accurately. In question ❷, encourage children to think about whether rounding each price to the nearest pound would give a good estimate for the price of that item. If rounded to the nearest pound, the price of the donut is £2·00, but if rounded to the nearest 10p, the price is £1·50, which is a far better estimate. Ask: *How might a more accurate estimate help you decide what you can afford to buy whilst shopping?* In question ❸, support children by encouraging them to record whether they estimated each item up or down. This will enable them to assess the accuracy of their estimated total. Similarly, for question ❻, encourage children to work through the stages of estimating to the nearest whole pound. This will make it clearer why Lexi does not have enough money for all the items.

DEEPEN Deepen understanding of question ❻ by asking children to create all possibilities of the items Lexi could buy with £20 and explain why certain groups of items can and cannot be purchased when estimating the total. Also challenge children to work out the exact cost of all the items and then find out how much extra Lexi would need to buy them all.

THINK DIFFERENTLY Question ❺ allows children to use what they have learnt over previous lessons to help them find an approximate answer. Children need to make decisions about what their estimate will be and how accurate this will make their answer.

ASSESSMENT CHECKPOINT Responses to question ❻ will identify whether children are confident identifying whether an approximate total will be an over or under estimate. Do children recognise that how prices are estimated will affect the total?

ANSWERS Answers for the **Practice** part of the lesson can be found in the *Power Maths* online subscription.

Reflect

WAYS OF WORKING Independent thinking

IN FOCUS This question allows children to explore what they need to know about prices in order to make appropriate estimates to the nearest whole number of pounds and to the nearest 10p.

ASSESSMENT CHECKPOINT Children's answers to this section will highlight whether they truly understand how to estimate money. Can children explain why estimating to the nearest pound is useful? Can children explain why estimating to the nearest pound is not always useful?

ANSWERS Answers for the **Reflect** part of the lesson can be found in the *Power Maths* online subscription.

After the lesson

- Do children know that estimated prices will not be exact?
- Can children recognise an over or under estimation and explain why it has occurred?
- Do children understand when it is appropriate to estimate money?

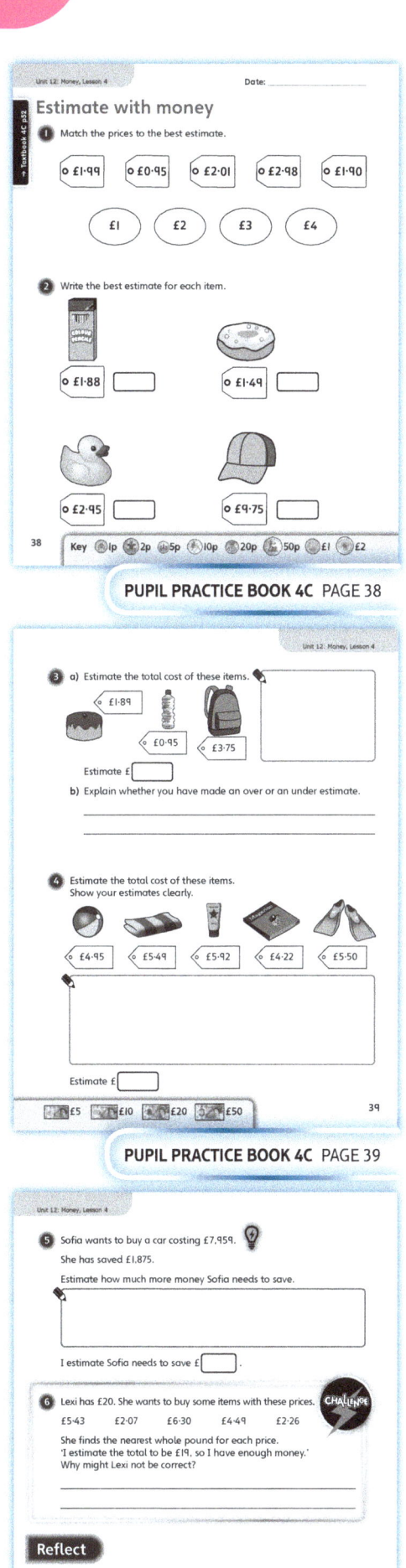

Unit 12: Money, Lesson 5

Calculate with money

Learning focus
In this lesson, children will solve problems involving pounds and pence. They will solve addition and subtraction problems and work out change.

Before you teach
- Do children recognise and understand vocabulary linked to addition and subtraction?
- Do children have strategies for addition and subtraction (such as counting on using number lines, or using the column method)?
- Do children know what change is?

NATIONAL CURRICULUM LINKS

Year 4 Measurement – money

Estimate, compare and calculate different measures, including money in pounds and pence.

ASSESSING MASTERY

Children can find totals of coins and amounts by partitioning into pounds and pence. They can use a number line to find the difference and can work out change. Children can look at the structure of problems and identify multiple steps, relevant information and what given information fits into a pictorial representation and a calculation.

COMMON MISCONCEPTIONS

Children may not understand why they are recombining pounds and pence when adding amounts (for example, they may want to write £5 and 36p rather than £5·36). Ask:
- *Look at the pounds and pence answer individually. Why can they not be the final answers? How can you come to the final answer?*

STRENGTHENING UNDERSTANDING

Using plastic coins to find totals helps children to identify the pounds and pence within amounts and add like amounts together more easily. Having coins available to place in the jumps on the number lines will also benefit understanding of totalling up the jumps. Showing children calculations and problems as pictorial representations such as bar models or part-whole models allows children to examine and become familiar with the structure of questions, to see what information is needed and to understand the best method for finding the answer.

GOING DEEPER

Expose children to a variety of methods for adding and subtracting with money and investigate the suitability of certain methods for certain questions. Encourage children to create rules or guidance for when to use specific methods and ask them to explain and discuss their choices for and against methods depending on the numbers given or the structure of the question.

KEY LANGUAGE

In lesson: change, total, add, pounds, pence

Other language to be used by the teacher: count, altogether, partition, recombine, subtract, find the difference, nearest 10p, nearest £1

STRUCTURES AND REPRESENTATIONS

Number lines, bar models

RESOURCES

Optional: plastic coins

 In the eTextbook of this lesson, you will find interactive links to a selection of teaching tools.

Quick recap

Ask: *What do you have to add to each of these amounts to make £1?*
20p   50p   85p   17p   51p

Unit 12: Money, Lesson 5

Discover

WAYS OF WORKING Pair work

ASK

- Question 1 a): *How much does each item cost? What are you going to do to find the total cost? What sort of calculation will you use to find the total cost? What method are you going to use to add?*
- Question 1 b): *How much did Alex spend? What is change? Why does Alex need some? What sort of calculation is finding change? What method are you going to use to subtract?*

IN FOCUS In question 1 b), ensure children understand the concept of change and that they are required to subtract. Some children may convert £4·25 to 400p and £5·00 to 500p and then use a column method to calculate 500 – 425. Other children may prefer to find the difference by counting on from £4·25 to £5·00 using a number line. This is the method shown in **Share**. Watching children find the answers for questions 1 a) and b) will give a good indication of their current understanding, confidence and strategies for adding and subtracting money.

PRACTICAL TIPS Place the items and corresponding price tags to match **Discover** at the front of the classroom and place a bowl of coins on each table in the classroom for children to use throughout the lesson.

ANSWERS

Question 1 a): The total cost is £4·25.

Question 1 b): Alex will get 75p change.

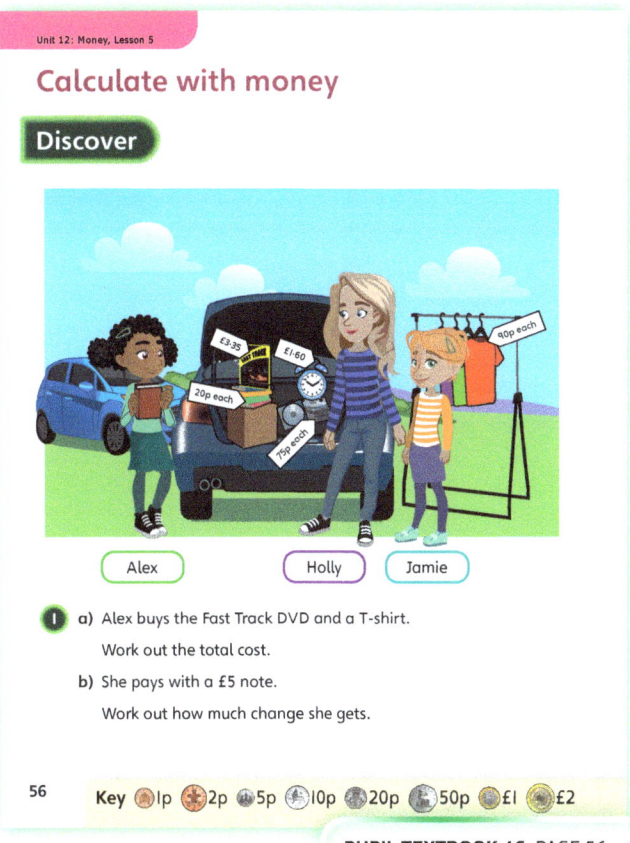

PUPIL TEXTBOOK 4C PAGE 56

Share

WAYS OF WORKING Whole class teacher led

ASK

- Question 1 a): *Why has Flo converted both prices to pence? How are you going to add the two prices together? Is Flo's method the most efficient?*
- Question 1 b): *What did Alex pay with? Where does that amount go in your calculation? What method are you going to use to work out Alex's change? Are there any other methods for working out change?*

IN FOCUS Discuss children's various methods for adding and subtracting money, as well as the vocabulary used in each question and how it gives an idea of what calculation is needed. In question 1 a), children are required to add amounts together to find the total cost. Some children may choose to add the coins together to find the total cost, whereas others may add the prices of the items – for example, by using the column method.

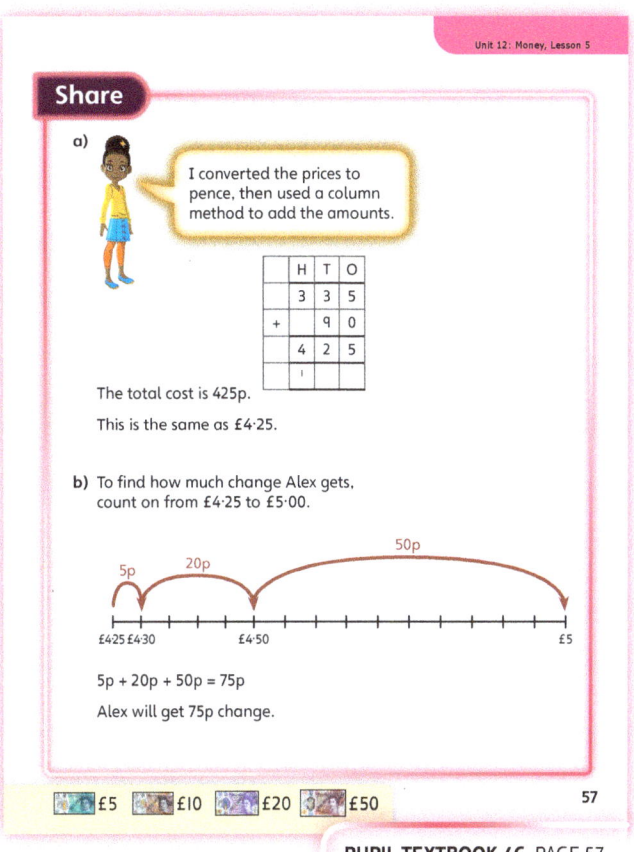

PUPIL TEXTBOOK 4C PAGE 57

Think together

WAYS OF WORKING Whole class teacher led (I do, We do, You do)

ASK

- Question ❶: *What sort of calculation is needed to find a total cost? Would it be easier to partition the prices into pounds and pence? How do you recombine the pounds and pence for your final answer?*
- Question ❷: *What operation do you need to use to find change? If you calculate the change by counting on using the number line, which point on the number line do you start at? How do you get from £2·35 to £3 on the number line? How do you get from £3 to £10 on the number line? How do you combine these two amounts?*
- Question ❸: *Are the questions asking you to do the same thing? Which words in each question tell you what sort of a calculation it is? Where would the information you have been given go in a calculation?*

IN FOCUS In question ❷, discuss with children why they are counting on to find an answer, even though finding change is a subtraction calculation. Question ❸ explores the structure of subtraction questions and how the context can affect which method is most efficient.

STRENGTHEN To help partition the prices into pounds and pence for question ❶, encourage children to make the amounts out of plastic coins. This will make it easier for children to see how many pounds or pence are in each price. In question ❷, children could place or draw coins onto the number line. This will also help them add the amounts together from the jumps.

DEEPEN Deepen understanding of question ❷ by encouraging children to find as many different ways to make the change using notes and coins as possible. Then, ask children to explain what makes the problems different in question ❸.

ASSESSMENT CHECKPOINT Assess children's strategies for problem solving. Can children link totals or change to the correct mathematical calculations? Do children understand why partitioning into pounds and pence makes it easier to add? Can children recombine the pounds and pence?

ANSWERS

Question ❶ a): £4·95

Question ❶ b): £4·15

Question ❷: £7·65

Question ❸: Both questions involve subtraction from £5. Ambika's question is about how much change she gets, given the amount she spends (£2·32). Bella's question is about the amount spent, given the change she gets (£1·54).

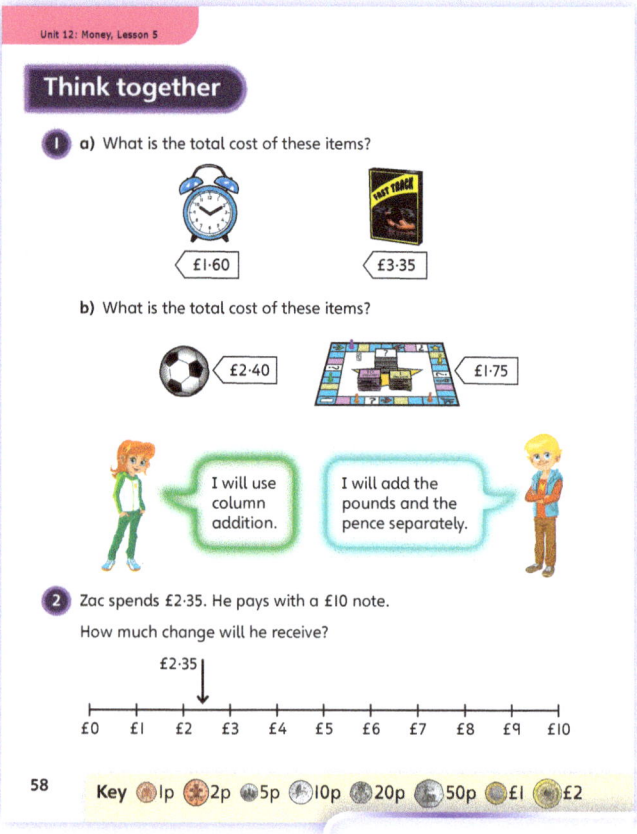

PUPIL TEXTBOOK 4C PAGE 58

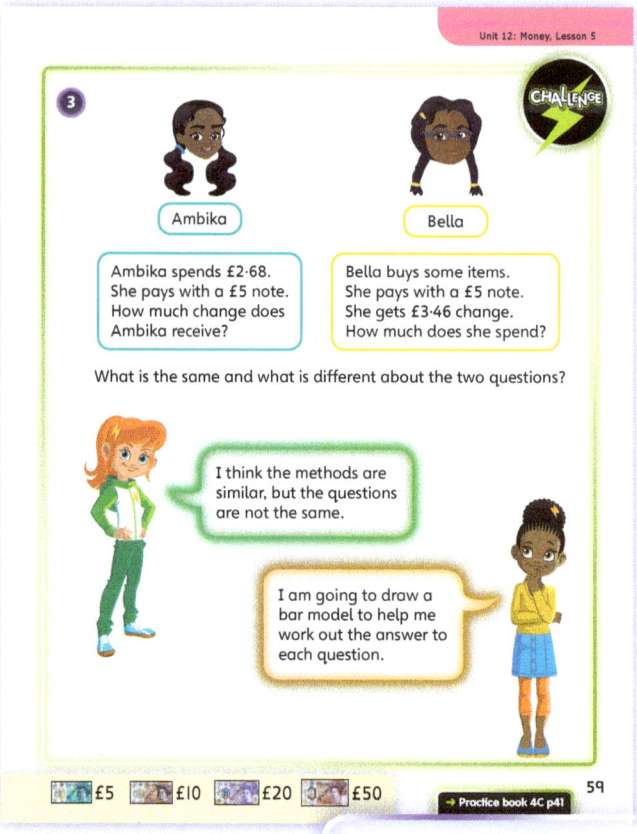

PUPIL TEXTBOOK 4C PAGE 59

Unit 12: Money, Lesson 5

Practice

WAYS OF WORKING Independent thinking

IN FOCUS In question ①, children partition pounds and pence to find totals. Ensure children understand that question ① c) requires them to partition the amounts found in questions ① a) and b) again and work out the total.

STRENGTHEN Provide plastic coins to pile up in pounds and pence to help children to partition and add together. Having the coins may allow children to spot any bonds to 100 and exchange coins for £1 coins. As well, blank number lines will help with addition and subtraction.

DEEPEN Deepen understanding by changing the information in question ⑥ slightly. For example, Lexi could have a different amount of money, she may wish to buy more than one of each item, the change cannot contain any £1 coins, and so on. Challenge children to explore how this affects their current answer.

ASSESSMENT CHECKPOINT Ensure children can use appropriate methods to find totals and change. Children should now be confident partitioning and recombining amounts into pounds and pence in multi-step problems.

ANSWERS Answers for the **Practice** part of the lesson can be found in the *Power Maths* online subscription.

Reflect

WAYS OF WORKING Independent thinking

IN FOCUS In this question, the information is not given in the order that children will need to use it. Children should demonstrate their understanding of adding amounts to find totals and work out change.

ASSESSMENT CHECKPOINT This question requires children to use different methods within one problem and will therefore show how secure they are with each individual method. Do children know which numbers need to be used in which calculation? Do children know the order the calculations need to be done in?

ANSWERS Answers for the **Reflect** part of the lesson can be found in the *Power Maths* online subscription.

After the lesson

- Can children find the total of coins and prices by partitioning into pounds and pence?
- Can the children decide on suitable jumps on a number line to count on or work out change?
- Can children move between methods within one problem or question?

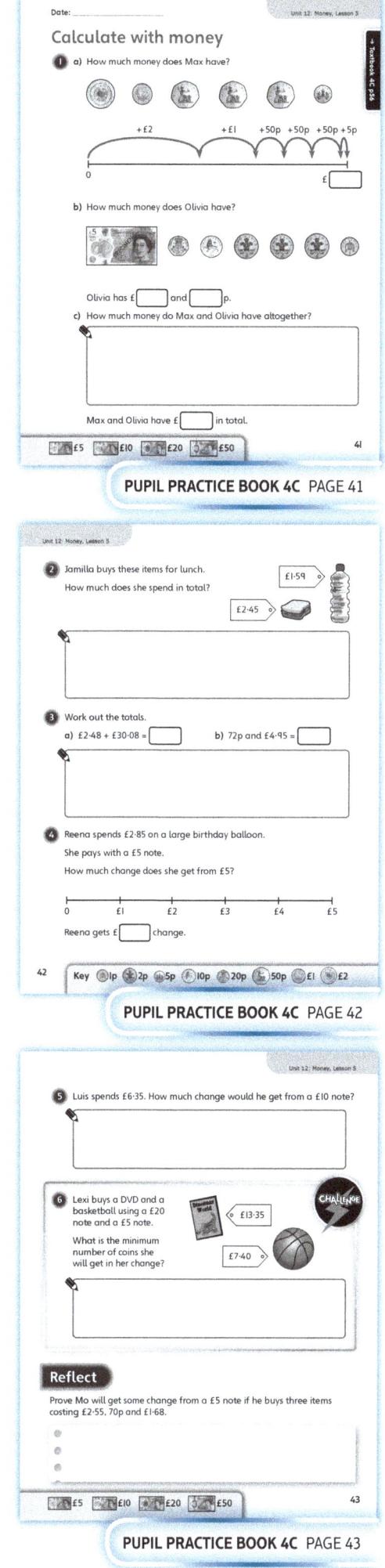

93

Unit 12: Money, Lesson 6

Solve problems with money

Learning focus
In this lesson, children will use previously learnt strategies and methods to solve multi-step problems with money.

Before you teach
- Can children solve addition, subtraction, multiplication and division calculations related to money?
- Can children use different methods to do the above calculations?
- Can children break problems down into manageable steps?

NATIONAL CURRICULUM LINKS

Year 4 Measurement – money

Estimate, compare and calculate different measures, including money in pounds and pence.

ASSESSING MASTERY

Children can identify small steps within a larger problem, picking out key information or using the structure of the problem to work out what mathematical calculation is needed. Children can use previously learnt methods and strategies to find answers and use their working out to agree or disagree with statements.

COMMON MISCONCEPTIONS

Multi-step problems can cause confusion. Encourage children to mark up or highlight key information in the problem. Ask:
- *What information do you have? What information do you need to find the answer? How can you find this information?*

STRENGTHENING UNDERSTANDING

Using a range of bar models, part-whole models and number lines helps children visualise the amounts, make links and recognise the operations required. Using plastic coins to represent money and objects or pictures to represent items will help strengthen understanding. Used against abstract calculations, coins and items help children to understand what is happening in each step.

GOING DEEPER

Children can explore a range of methods and structures in this lesson, allowing them to develop more flexibility with their working and apply the methods they feel are most suitable for each problem they are presented with. Building on the amount of flexibility enables children to independently develop their own 'rules' about when to use certain methods.

KEY LANGUAGE

In lesson: multiply, divide, explain, add, greater than (>)

Other language to be used by the teacher: problem, small steps, parts, key information, structure, calculate, subtract, find the difference, prove, less than (<)

STRUCTURES AND REPRESENTATIONS

Bar models, part-whole models, number lines

RESOURCES

Optional: plastic coins

 In the eTextbook of this lesson, you will find interactive links to a selection of teaching tools.

Quick recap

Challenge children to solve this money word problem:
You pay with a £10 note for an item that costs £4. How much change do you need?

94

Unit 12: Money, Lesson 6

Discover

WAYS OF WORKING Pair work

ASK

- Question 1 a): *What does 'cheapest' mean? What prices do you know? How can you work out the cost of 3 single buns?*
- Question 1 b): *What does 'best deal' mean? How else could Max buy 6 buns? How can you work out the cost of 2 packs of 3? How can you work out the cost of 6 individual buns?*

IN FOCUS Question 1 a) requires children to multiply prices then compare amounts. Which option children choose for Kate to buy will highlight their understanding of the word 'cheapest' and what an amount is worth. In question 1 b), children need to find the three possibilities for purchasing 6 buns, multiply the relevant prices and then compare the three results to decide whether Max could have paid less for the same items.

PRACTICAL TIPS Display the food items to re-enact the stall in the **Discover** image. Have plastic coins available for children to use.

ANSWERS

Question 1 a): £1·95 > £1·50 so it is cheaper for Kate to buy the pack of 3 buns.

Question 1 b): 6 single buns = £3·90
2 packs of 3 buns = £3
£3 < £3·50, Max could have had a better deal.

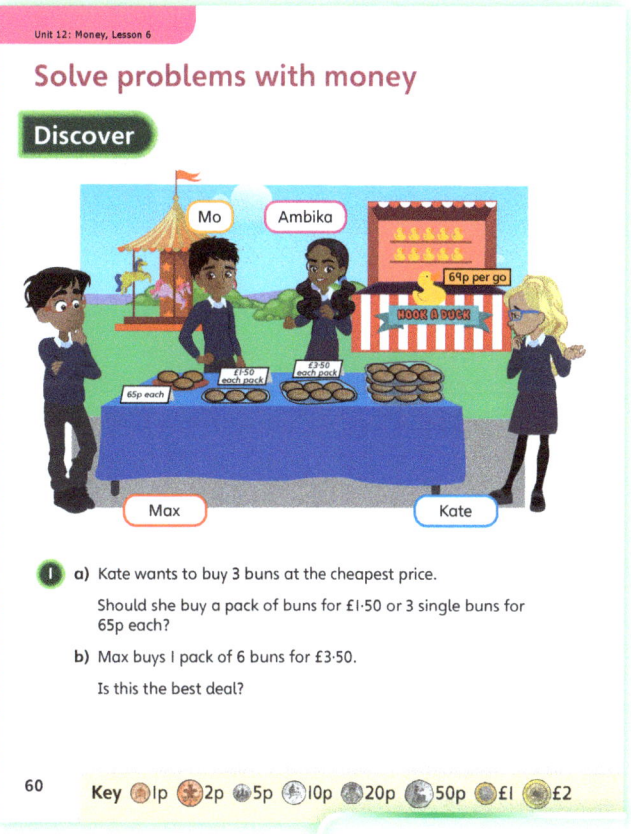

PUPIL TEXTBOOK 4C PAGE 60

Share

WAYS OF WORKING Whole class teacher led

ASK

- Question 1 a): *How can you make 65 easier to multiply? How could you partition 65? What do you need to do with your partitioned answers? What do you need to do with the prices for a 3-pack and 3 single buns?*
- Question 1 b): *How will you know if Max got the best deal? Was the pack of 6 the most expensive? Was there a cheaper option?*

IN FOCUS For question 1 b), discuss what 'best deal' means and ask children to give ideas of other ways Max could buy 6 buns. Children should identify what sort of a calculation this would be and offer their methods. For Max's other option, show children 2 packs of buns and discuss the easiest way to find the cost. Once the class has the cost of all three options, discuss whether buying the 6-pack was the best deal.

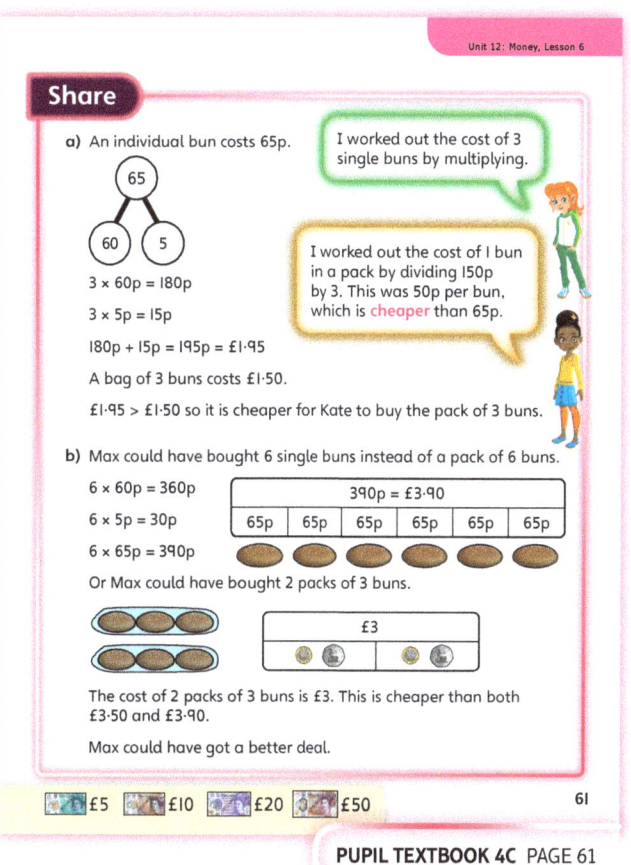

PUPIL TEXTBOOK 4C PAGE 61

Think together

WAYS OF WORKING Whole class teacher led (I do, We do, You do)

ASK

- Question ①: *What method will you use to work out the price of 3 goes? What multiplication facts can you use to help you work out 3 × 60? What else do you need to work out to answer the question?*
- Question ②: *What is the first thing you need to work out? What calculation will help you work out how much Bella spent? What is the second part of the problem asking you to solve?*
- Question ③: *How can you compare 4 cookies and 6 cookies? How could you work out the cost of 1 cookie from each bag? What can you see about the prices of the single cookies? Does this mean that Lee is correct or incorrect?*

IN FOCUS For question ①, encourage children to identify the two parts to the problem – finding the total Kate spent and then the change she would receive. To answer question ② a), children must use a 'find the difference' method. To solve question ② b), children need to use the answer to ② a) and divide it by 10.

STRENGTHEN When using the number line in question ①, some children may find it easier to record the coins in the jumps as well as the number. For question ② a), encourage children to use plastic coins to make £6·60 and then investigate what other coins they need to reach £10. For question ② b), encourage children to set the information out in a bar model, as it will make the need to divide more obvious. To aid children in recognising the division element of question ③, encourage children to show the information in a bar model.

DEEPEN Once children have worked out Kate's change in question ①, encourage them to calculate how many more goes on Hook-a-Duck Kate could afford. In question ②, challenge children to use the information they have worked out to reason about other amounts. For example: 'If 10 tickets cost £3·40, I know that 5 tickets would cost £1·70'; or 'If I know 1 ticket costs 34p and 10 tickets cost £3·40, I know that 11 tickets would cost £3·74'.

ASSESSMENT CHECKPOINT Assess whether children recognise each step in a multi-step problem. Can children link information to the correct operation? Can children use appropriate methods and strategies to find answers?

ANSWERS

Question ①: 3 × 60p = 180p
3 × 9p = 27p
3 × 69p = 207p
Kate receives £2·93 change from £5.

Question ② a): £3·50

Question ② b): 35p

Question ③: 4 for £2·40 = 60p each
6 × 60p = £3·60
£3·60 > £3·36
Lee is not correct, 6 for £3·36 is the better deal. Some children may instead work out that 6 for £3·36 = 56p each, which is better than 60p each.

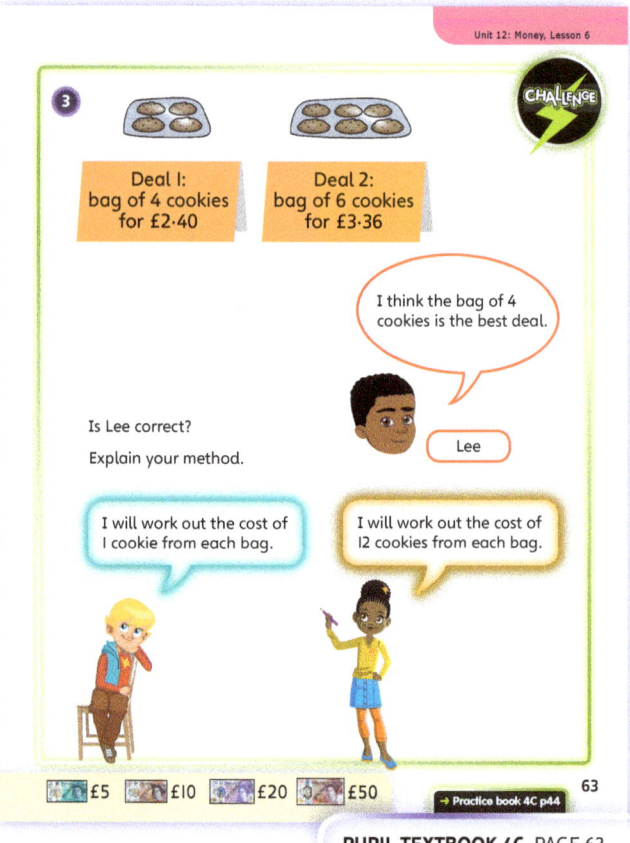

PUPIL TEXTBOOK 4C PAGE 62

PUPIL TEXTBOOK 4C PAGE 63

Unit 12: Money, Lesson 6

Practice

WAYS OF WORKING Independent thinking

IN FOCUS Question ❶ requires children to multiply an amount, then find the change using a 'find the difference' method. For question ❷ a), children need find the difference to work out how much Aki spent. Questions ❸ and ❹ require children to solve calculations with multiplication and division, then compare their answers to find the cheapest options.

STRENGTHEN For questions ❶ and ❷, using plastic coins and creating bar models will show children the amounts and required calculations more clearly. For questions ❸ and ❹, prompt children to work out both calculations before making any claims. A bar model will highlight the division element of question ❻.

DEEPEN Before finding the exact answer to question ❺, challenge children to create a list of solutions that would not be possible and give reasons why.

THINK DIFFERENTLY Question ❺ assesses children's understanding of place value and ability to add.

ASSESSMENT CHECKPOINT Assess whether children can identify what operations are necessary and whether they are able to break down a problem into more manageable steps. Can children use answers from previous questions or earlier parts of the problem to find answers? Can children prove or disprove theories using information they have worked out?

ANSWERS Answers for the **Practice** part of the lesson can be found in the *Power Maths* online subscription.

Reflect

WAYS OF WORKING Independent thinking

IN FOCUS This question is open-ended and children can give a wide range of answers as long as they can explain their reasons and back up their thinking. Children need to realise that for a pack to be cheaper, they need to charge less than 55p × 4.

ASSESSMENT CHECKPOINT The question will highlight children's understanding of comparative language. Do children understand that cheaper means a lower price? Can children work out the cost of 4 single bread rolls by multiplying? Can children clearly explain why they have chosen a lower price than the answer they calculated?

ANSWERS Answers for the **Reflect** part of the lesson can be found in the *Power Maths* online subscription.

After the lesson

- Can children break a problem up into small steps?
- Can children use their information to reason?
- Can children explain and use working out to agree or disagree with theories?

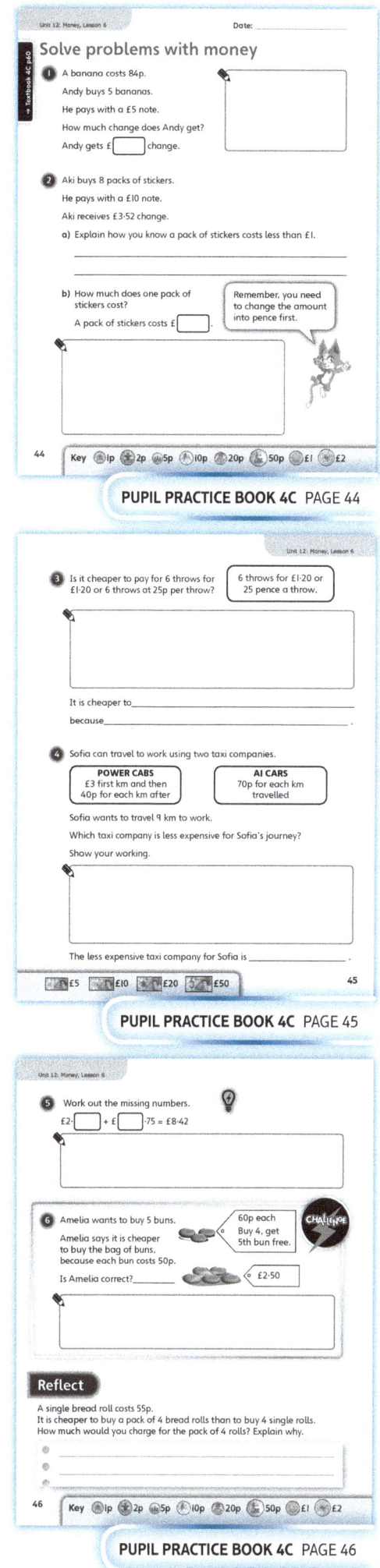

PUPIL PRACTICE BOOK 4C PAGE 44

PUPIL PRACTICE BOOK 4C PAGE 45

PUPIL PRACTICE BOOK 4C PAGE 46

End of unit check

> **Don't forget the unit assessment grid in your *Power Maths* online subscription.**

WAYS OF WORKING Group work adult led

IN FOCUS

- Question ❶ assesses whether children can find how much money is shown. Encourage children to count in pounds and pence separately. Children should give their answer in terms of £s.
- In question ❷, children are asked to write an amount that is less than £1 in £s to check their understanding of what is one of the most difficult concepts in this unit. Ensure they use the zero placeholder correctly in £0·03.
- In question ❹, children are given the amount of change and asked to work out a cost. Show children that working out the change if they are given the amount something costs is the same as working out the amount something costs if they are given the amount of change. This can be shown by counting on using a number line or bar model.
- In the SATs-style questions, children use their knowledge of multiplication and division to solve problems. In question ❽, children first need to find the cost of the pear by noticing that on the top line there is an extra pear. They can then use the cost of the pear to work out the cost of the apple.

ANSWERS AND COMMENTARY

Children who have mastered the concepts in this unit will be able to record money using the £·p notation, understand that a decimal point separates pounds and pence and will know how to convert between pounds and pence. They will be able to estimate totals, compare amounts of money and order amounts of money to work out the cheapest and most expensive items; and they will be able to solve multi-step money problems.

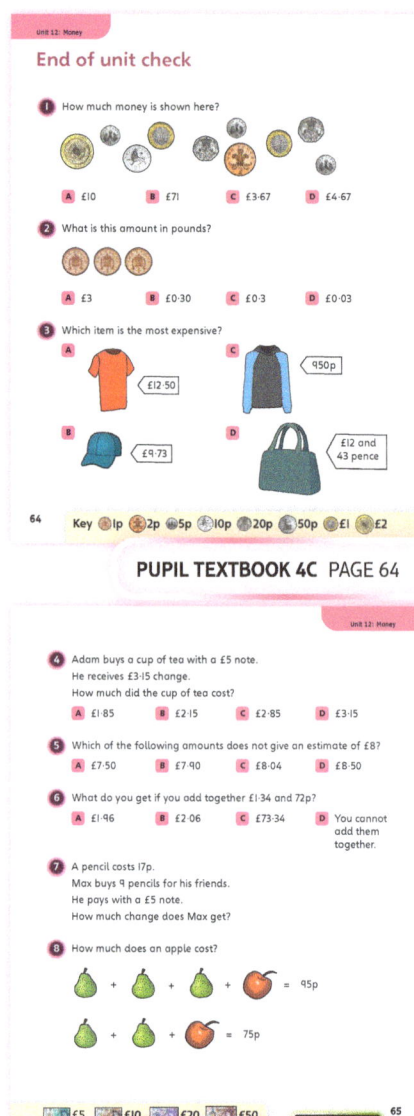

PUPIL TEXTBOOK 4C PAGE 64

PUPIL TEXTBOOK 4C PAGE 65

Q	A	WRONG ANSWERS AND MISCONCEPTIONS	STRENGTHENING UNDERSTANDING
1	D	A suggests children have just counted the number of coins. C suggests children think that the £2 is worth only £1.	Encourage children to use coins and notes to help them count out the amounts. A number line can be used to help children find the total of some coins and notes given. Children should be told to start with the greatest notes or coins first. For adding and subtracting amounts of money, children may use coins and place value equipment alongside the abstract calculation. Encourage children to convert amounts to pence before adding and then convert back to pounds at the end.
2	D	A suggests children have just put £s in front. B or C suggest children have not understood how to use the zero placeholder correctly to show that 3p is 3 hundredths of a pound.	
3	A	D suggests children think that £12·50 is less than £12·43, because 43 is greater than 5.	
4	A	C suggests children have subtracted £3 from £5 to give £2, then subtracted 15p from 100p to give 85p, and then added the two results together. This would mean that Adam started with £6.	
5	D	A suggests children think they must round 50p down to the previous pound.	
6	B	C suggests children forgot to use the decimal point.	
7	£3·47	Children may forget that they then need to subtract 17p × 9 from £5 to find the change.	
8	35p	Children may divide the price by the number of fruit without considering that the pears and apples cost different amounts.	

Unit 12: Money

My journal

WAYS OF WORKING Independent thinking

ANSWERS AND COMMENTARY The answer is £2·06. This activity asks children to add two amounts of money. The question raises the issue that children cannot add together decimals at this moment. Children should be confident with changing these amounts to pence and then using column addition or other methods to add two 3-digit numbers. Once children have added the amounts, remind them about the final step: it is important that children convert their final answer to pounds. Some children may want to explore the method of adding the pounds first and then adding the pence.

Power check

WAYS OF WORKING Independent thinking

ASK

- Do you feel confident finding how much money is shown in notes and coins?
- Can you write amounts of money in pounds using £·p?
- Can you confidently estimate with amounts of money and understand when it might be useful to do this?
- Do you feel confident when adding and subtracting amounts of money?
- Can you find change by counting on or subtracting?

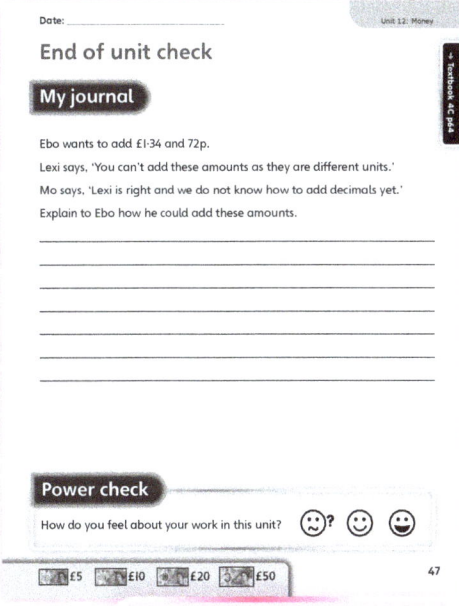

PUPIL PRACTICE BOOK 4C PAGE 47

Power puzzle

WAYS OF WORKING Independent thinking

IN FOCUS This **Power puzzle** brings together children's work on problem solving with their knowledge of money. Encourage children to extract the relevant information. For question ❶, children have been given a bar model. Ask children to explain why the bar model represents the situation. Ask: *What do you know the total is? How many parts do you have altogether? What do you know about each part? How can you find the value of each part?*

For questions ❷ and ❸, encourage children to draw similar bar models to help them determine the steps they need to take to solve the problem. The problems get increasingly more complicated.

ANSWERS AND COMMENTARY

Question ❶: A toaster costs £24. A kettle costs £48.

Question ❷: The radio costs £85.

Question ❸: A pair of speakers costs £51.
A pair of headphones costs £17.
A camera costs £87.

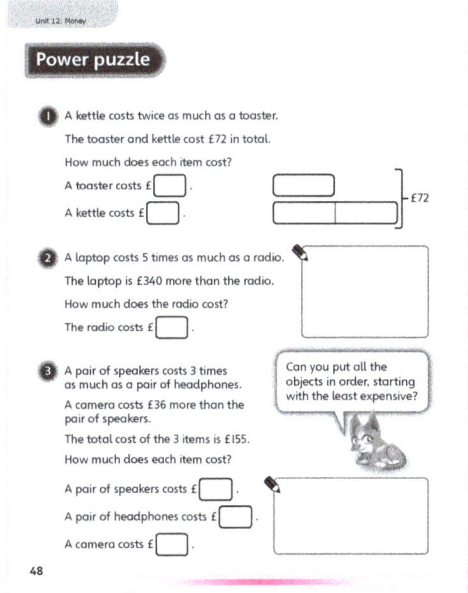

PUPIL PRACTICE BOOK 4C PAGE 48

After the unit

- Can children write amounts of pounds and pence using the £·p notation?
- Can children convert between pounds and pence?
- Can children compare and order amounts of money?

Strengthen and **Deepen** activities for this unit can be found in the *Power Maths* online subscription.

Unit 13
Time

Mastery Expert tip! 'I found that this unit was a great opportunity to introduce several clocks into the classroom – a 12-hour and a 24-hour digital clock as well as the existing analogue clock on the wall. Seeing the time represented in these different ways throughout the school day helped children to build natural connections between them.'

Don't forget to watch the Unit 13 video!

WHY THIS UNIT IS IMPORTANT

This unit will develop children's ability to convert between units of time. Children will apply their knowledge of existing facts (for example, the number of minutes in an hour) when expressing a period of time using a different unit of measurement. Children will also be introduced to the concept of the 24-hour clock, learning to state the time as both a 12- and 24-hour clock time. Children will solve problems using these new concepts and prior learning, including word problems.

WHERE THIS UNIT FITS

→ Unit 12: Money
→ **Unit 13: Time**
→ Unit 14: Geometry – angles and 2D shapes

This unit builds on the concepts of time learned in Year 3 Unit 13, particularly when telling time to the minute. Children will link their prior knowledge of facts to bar models that will help them convert between units.

Before they start this unit, it is expected that children:
- can read and write times to the nearest minute
- know the number of seconds in a minute, minutes in an hour and hours in a day
- understand how to express 12-hour times digitally, including using the terms am and pm.

ASSESSING MASTERY

Children who have mastered this unit will be able to convert between seconds and minutes, and between minutes and hours. They will also be able to convert between longer periods of time expressed in days, weeks, months and years. They will use these different units of measurement in their description of times with confidence. They will be able to express times in both analogue and digital forms, including 24-hour clock times. Children will apply these elements confidently to solve mathematical problems.

COMMON MISCONCEPTIONS	STRENGTHENING UNDERSTANDING	GOING DEEPER
Children may consider only the numerical value of periods of time without understanding the significance of their units (for example: 1 week and 4 days equals 1 + 4 = 5 days).	Display calendars and year planners in the classroom. Ask questions that relate a week on the calendar to the number of days, or the year on the year planner to the number of months.	Challenge children to make up problems using the calendar and/or the year planner. Encourage them to use as many different units of time as they can.
Children may confuse the numbers on a digital clock with those on an analogue clock face, thinking that 04:11 will have the hands pointing to the numbers 4 and 11.	Label 5-minute intervals around a clock face to show the number of minutes in digital form (:00, :05, :10 and so on). Display three different types of clocks (analogue, 12-hour digital and 24-hour digital). Refer to the three clocks over the course of daily routines in order to build connections between these different ways of representing the time.	Challenge children to express times in different ways throughout the day. For example, show only one of three clocks (analogue, 12-hour digital, 24-hour digital) and ask children to give the time as it would be shown on the other clocks.

Unit 13: Time

UNIT STARTER PAGES

Use these pages to introduce the unit focus to children. Use the characters to discuss concepts and phrases that children have not heard before.

STRUCTURES AND REPRESENTATIONS

Analogue clock and digital clock: Pictures of clock faces (both analogue and digital) are used regularly to represent times. They are used to demonstrate times as well as to form the basis of problems to solve. Children will be encouraged to use these representations themselves, completing them to represent different times.

Bar model: This model will help children to represent the equivalence between different units of time. The upper bar can be split into one unit and the lower bar used to show the equivalent parts expressed in another unit. Children can then see the calculation that they need to do to convert one unit into another.

1 minute	1 minute	1 minute
60 seconds	60 seconds	60 seconds

KEY LANGUAGE

There is some key language that children will need to know as part of the learning in this unit:

➔ seconds, minutes, hours
➔ days, weeks, months, years
➔ units of time
➔ convert, equal to (=), compare
➔ 12-hour, 24-hour, am, pm
➔ analogue, digital
➔ bar model

PUPIL TEXTBOOK 4C PAGE 66

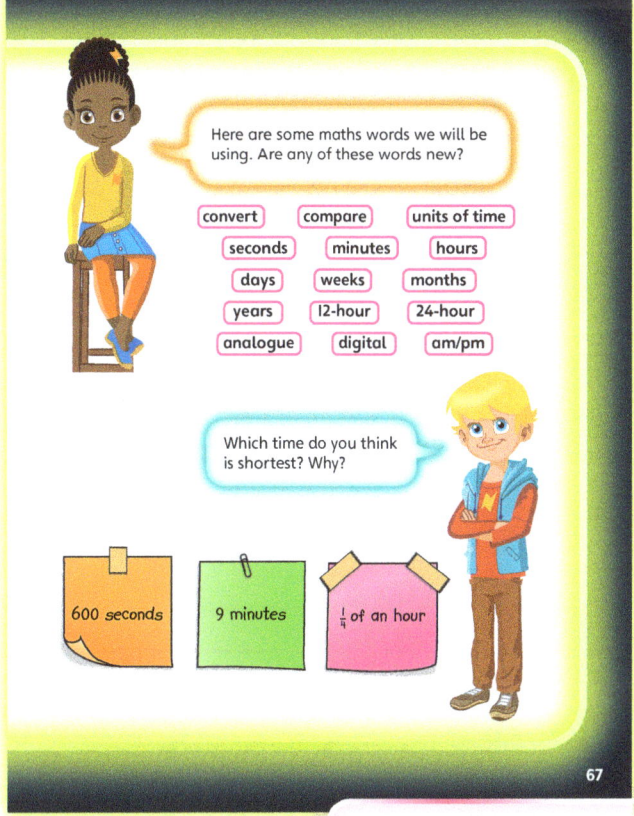

PUPIL TEXTBOOK 4C PAGE 67

Unit 13: Time, Lesson 1

Years, months, weeks and days

Learning focus
In this lesson, children will revise their understanding of the equivalences between years, months, weeks and days, applying their knowledge to convert between units of time.

Before you teach
- How could you use concrete representations (clocks, calendars) to support children?
- Can children recall equivalences of different units of time confidently?

NATIONAL CURRICULUM LINKS

Year 4 Measurement – time

Convert between different units of measure [for example, kilometre to metre; hour to minute].

ASSESSING MASTERY

Children can express 1 week in days and 1 year in months. Children can confidently convert measurements given in these units and apply this skill in problem-solving contexts.

COMMON MISCONCEPTIONS

Children may add the numbers in measurements without considering the units or converting them. For example, 1 week 4 days might be written as 1 + 4 = 5 days. Ask:
- *What is 2 weeks in days? What is 2 weeks and 3 days in days? What did you do to find the answer?*

Children may think of the larger unit of measurement as being worth 10, so they may consider 4 years and 3 months as being equivalent to 43 months. Ask:
- *How many months are in 1 year? How many months are in 2 years? How many months are in 2 years and 1 month?*

STRENGTHENING UNDERSTANDING

Reinforce children's knowledge of multiples of 7 and 12 (useful when converting between days and weeks, and between months and years respectively). Display an unmarked number line split into 50. Choose one group of children to count along the line from 1 to 50. A second group should call out '1', '2' and so on for each group of 7 that is counted. Use the same method to practise identifying multiples of 12.

GOING DEEPER

Give children problems where they need to use their knowledge of the months of the year to convert to days. For example, ask: *Kate has had a book out of the library for the whole of January and February. How many days is this? How many weeks and days is this?*

KEY LANGUAGE

In lesson: unit of time, convert, day, week, month, year

Other language to be used by the teacher: measure

STRUCTURES AND REPRESENTATIONS

Bar model

RESOURCES

Optional: pieces of string

 In the eTextbook of this lesson, you will find interactive links to a selection of teaching tools.

Quick recap
Chant the months of the year together as a class. Then rehearse different ways to remember the number of days in each month.

Discover

WAYS OF WORKING Pair work

ASK

- Questions 1 a) and b): *What sorts of things do we measure in weeks/months/years?*
- Questions 1 a) and b): *We use clocks and timers to measure hours, minutes and seconds. What do we use to measure days, weeks, months and years?*
- Questions 1 a) and b): *What facts do you know about days, weeks, months and years that you can use to convert between these units?*

IN FOCUS Discuss the different units of time that are shown in the picture. Children sometimes do not see weeks, months and years as units of time (like hours, minutes and seconds) because they are not used for telling the time from a clock. Ensure that they understand that these are still units of time, but that they measure longer periods of time. Ask them how they might measure these units (for example, using dates on a computer screen, calendars, wall planners and so on).

PRACTICAL TIPS One way to model the addition of times is to use a timeline. Give children a piece of string and ask them to use sticky labels to create a timeline that labels the information they know about the two dogs' ages. At the left-hand end should be 3 years and 8 months (Lexi's dog's age), then a jump of 1 year and 7 months, followed by 'Max's dog's age' at the other end of the timeline.

ANSWERS

Question 1 a): The new play area will open in 28 days.

Question 1 b): Max's dog is 5 years and 3 months old.

Share

WAYS OF WORKING Whole class teacher led

ASK

- Question 1 a): *What fact do you need to use to convert a period of weeks into days?*
- Question 1 a): *Would you rather work out 4 × 7 or 7 + 7 + 7 + 7 to find the answer?*
- Question 1 b): *Is this an addition or subtraction question?*
- Question 1 b): *The bar model is used for part of the working out. How does it help you?*

IN FOCUS Ensure that children can explain how the bar models have been used to solve each problem. In question 1 a), they should note how 1 week is visually equivalent to 7 days. Children should understand that bar models provide a useful way of modelling equivalences. In question 1 b), check that children understand that the bar model is being used for *part* of the question (to split up 15 months into years and months), not the whole question. They should also realise that an addition is required to solve this question. They need to add on 1 year and 7 months to the age of Lexi's dog.

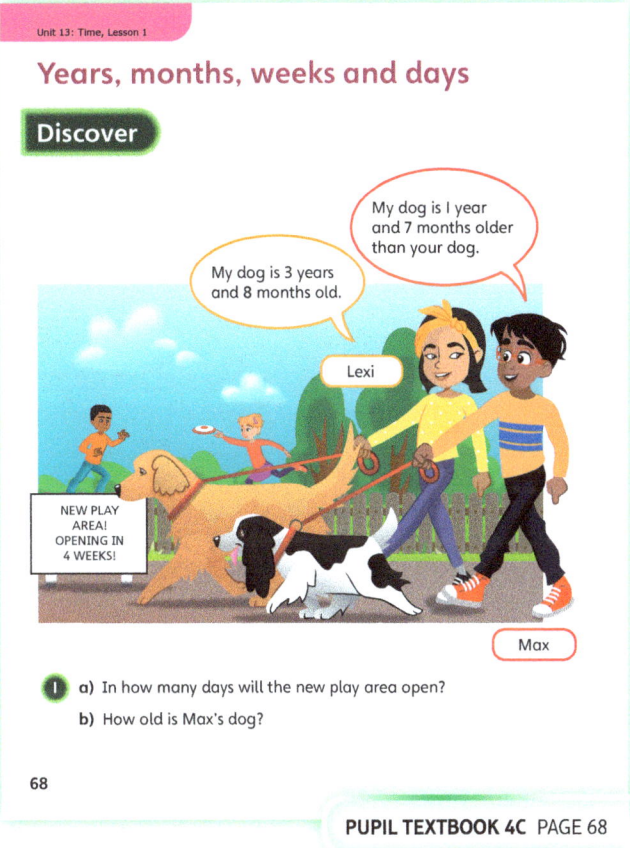

PUPIL TEXTBOOK 4C PAGE 68

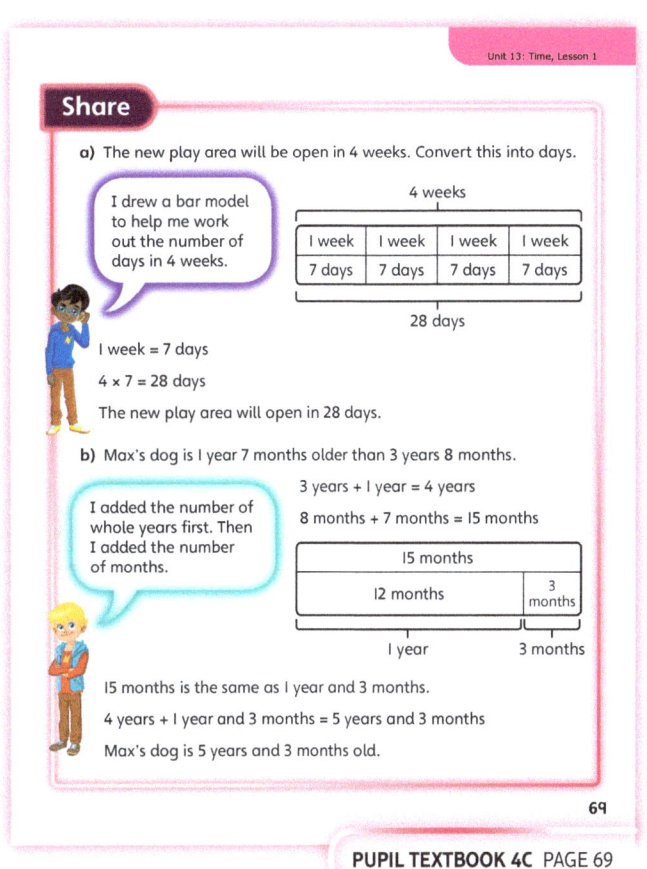

PUPIL TEXTBOOK 4C PAGE 69

Think together

WAYS OF WORKING Whole class teacher led (I do, We do, You do)

ASK

- Question ① a): *How is this question similar to question ① b) in Discover?*
- Question ① a): *How does the bar model help you to answer the problem?*
- Question ① a): *Why could the answer not just be '8 years 14 months'?*
- Question ②: *How do you know how many 7-day bars are equal to 35 days? Is there a quick way to find this out?*
- Question ②: *Why do you divide by 7 to find the answer, and not by any other number?*

IN FOCUS In question ① a), make sure that children understand why the bar model is used to convert 14 months into years and months. Ask them to explain why the bar model shows 14 months split into 12 months and 2 months, not 7 and 7 or 13 and 1, for example.

STRENGTHEN In question ②, encourage children to use strips of paper to build up various bar models, exploring the different numbers of days that are formed by blocks of 7 days (1 week). Ask how many weeks are the same as 7 days, 14 days, 21 days … Link this to multiplication facts and guide children towards a quicker way to find the answer – dividing 35 by 7.

DEEPEN Explore question ③ further. Challenge children to teach the correct way of converting years and months into months to someone who has never converted units of time before. Ask: *How can you help them avoid making the kind of mistake Amelia made? What resources or pictures could you use?*

ASSESSMENT CHECKPOINT Use questions ① to ③ to assess whether children can convert between months and years and between weeks and days, supporting their reasoning with pictorial representations (bar models). Look for children who use bar models to recognise the different operations they can use when converting between units of time: division for smaller units (such as months) into larger ones (such as years) and multiplication for larger units (such as years) into smaller ones (such as months).

ANSWERS

Question ① a): Andy is 9 years and 2 months old.

Question ① b): Mo is 10 years and 9 months old.

Question ②: 35 ÷ 7 = 5
5 weeks are the same as 35 days.

Question ③: Amelia is wrong because she thinks that the number of years and months are the same as tens and ones. 4 years are worth 4 × 12, not 4 × 10. 4 years and 3 months = 51 months

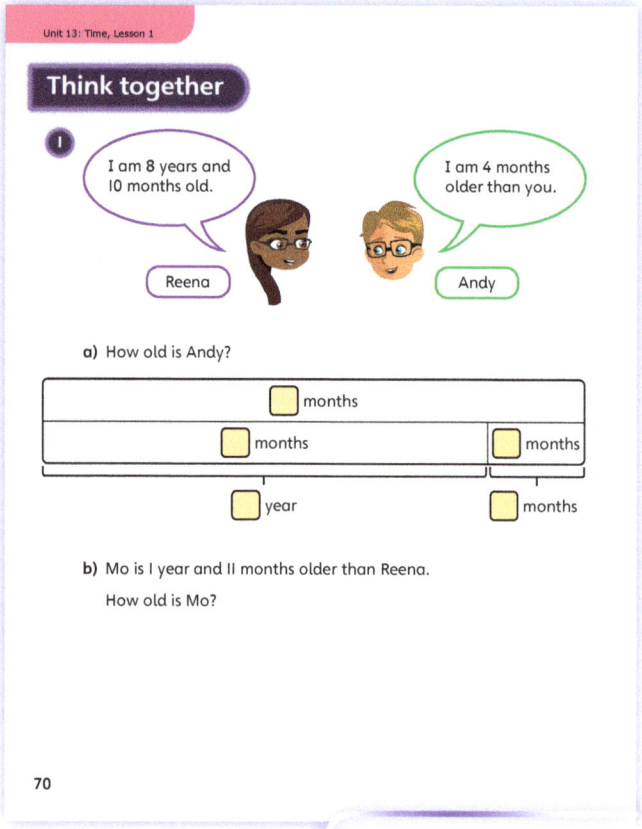

PUPIL TEXTBOOK 4C PAGE 70

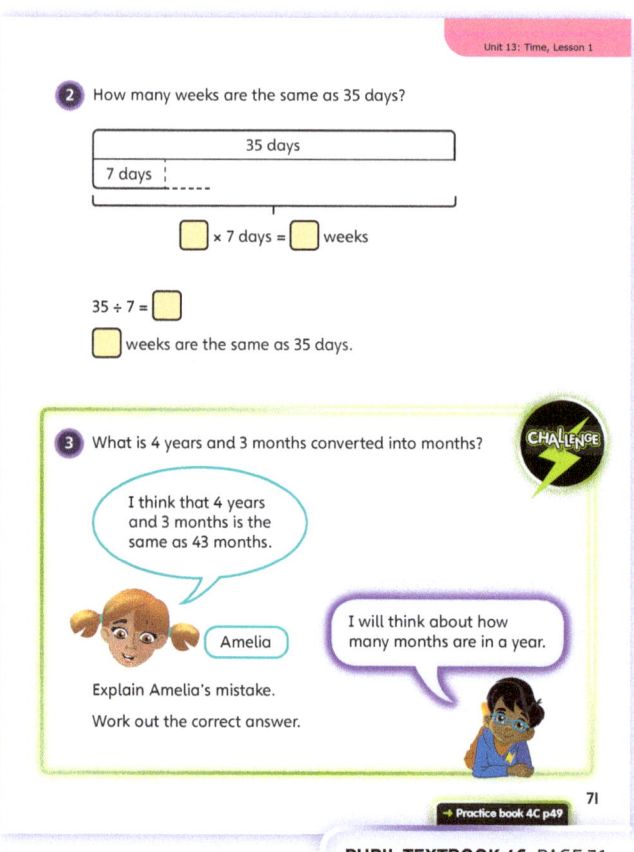

PUPIL TEXTBOOK 4C PAGE 71

Unit 13: Time, Lesson 1

Practice

WAYS OF WORKING Independent thinking

IN FOCUS Question ❶ scaffolds children's understanding of the equivalence of days, weeks, months and years through the use of bar modelling. Children are required to draw the final bar model themselves.

STRENGTHEN In question ❷, children may need reminding that there are 365 days in a year.

If children are finding it difficult to calculate abstractly in question ❹, point out the part of the question that may need converting (in both cases, the second period of time). Then encourage children to use pictorial representations (bar models) to convert the units of time. Ask children to explain how they used their bar models to help work out the calculations.

DEEPEN In question ❻, ask children whether all years have 365 days. Discuss how their calculation needs to change to take account of leap years. Challenge children to devise their own investigations similar to question ❻ – for example, working out the number of weeks they have been attending school. This requires converting from the number of years and months, which can prompt a discussion about how many weeks are in a year and in a month, and whether this is a precise number.

THINK DIFFERENTLY Question ❸ requires children to explore the misconception of using multiplication when trying to convert from days to weeks. Discuss the method that children would use instead and ask them to sketch a bar model to justify their reasoning.

ASSESSMENT CHECKPOINT Use questions ❶ and ❷ to assess whether children are confident in converting between days and weeks, and between months and years. Look for children using pictorial representations (bar models) to support their reasoning. Use question ❺ to check whether children are able to explain which operation to use when converting between different units.

ANSWERS Answers for the **Practice** part of the lesson can be found in the *Power Maths* online subscription.

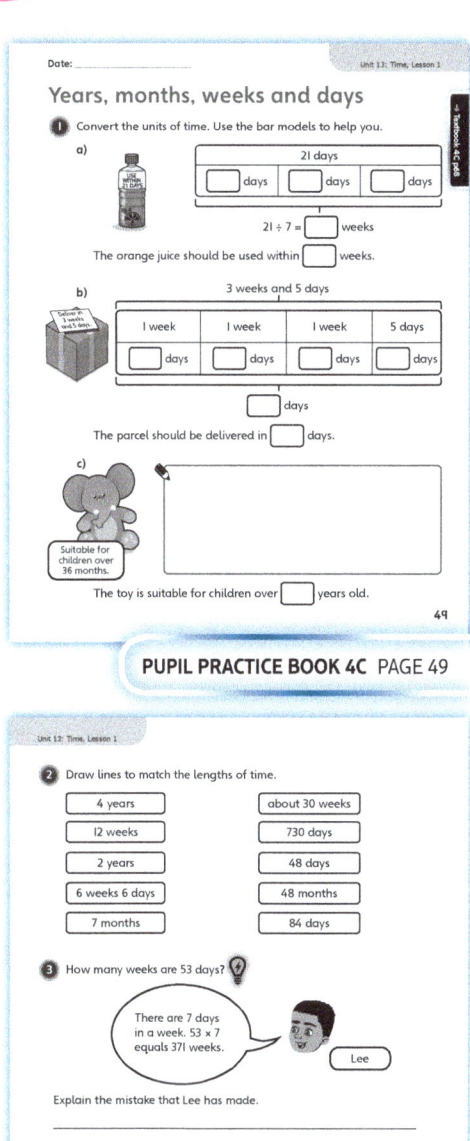

PUPIL PRACTICE BOOK 4C PAGE 49

PUPIL PRACTICE BOOK 4C PAGE 50

Reflect

WAYS OF WORKING Independent thinking

IN FOCUS Explain to children that this sort of conversion is one that people need to do regularly in real life, as babies' ages are often given in months only, even after a year. Ask them to explain how they will use unit conversion to find the answer.

ASSESSMENT CHECKPOINT Children should explain clearly how to convert 20 months into 1 year and 8 months by finding the number of groups of 12 (1 year) in 20 months. This may involve using a pictorial representation, and choosing to use subtraction or division.

ANSWERS Answers for the **Reflect** part of the lesson can be found in the *Power Maths* online subscription.

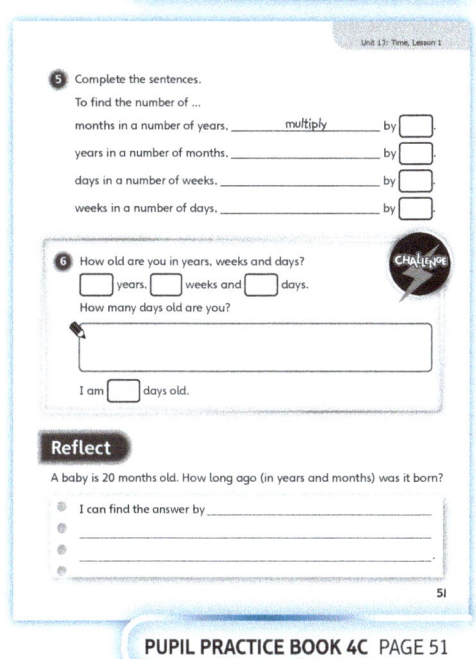

PUPIL PRACTICE BOOK 4C PAGE 51

After the lesson ⏸

- Are children confident converting between days, weeks, months and years?
- What opportunities can you give for children to continue to practise these skills in meaningful, real-life contexts?

Unit 13: Time, Lesson 2

Hours, minutes and seconds

Learning focus
In this lesson, children will revise their understanding of the equivalences between different units of time. They will apply their knowledge to convert between hours, minutes and seconds.

Before you teach
- Can children recall equivalences of different units of time confidently?
- How could you help them to remember these?

NATIONAL CURRICULUM LINKS

Year 4 Measurement – time

Convert between different units of measure [for example, kilometre to metre; hour to minute].

ASSESSING MASTERY

Children can express 1 hour in minutes and 1 minute in seconds. Children can confidently convert measurements given in these units and apply this skill in problem-solving contexts.

COMMON MISCONCEPTIONS

Children may add the numbers in measurements without considering the units or converting them. For example, they might write 1 minute 20 seconds as 1 + 20 = 21 seconds. Ask:
- *What is 2 minutes in seconds? What is 2 minutes and 10 seconds in seconds? What did you do to find the answer?*

STRENGTHENING UNDERSTANDING

To strengthen understanding, use stopwatches to time short activities (slightly more than 1 minute). Ask children to observe what happens when the timer goes beyond 59 seconds. With each time, ask children how they could write the time in seconds. Use bar models to support the equivalence of 1 minute = 60 seconds.

GOING DEEPER

Provide children with results tables that show Olympic race times in minutes and seconds (for example, the 800 metre running race) or in hours and minutes (the marathon). Challenge children to convert these into the smaller unit (for example, converting hours and minutes into simply minutes). They can use these new times to devise their own quiz questions to ask each other.

KEY LANGUAGE

In lesson: unit of time, convert, minute, second, hour

Other language to be used by the teacher: measure

STRUCTURES AND REPRESENTATIONS

Bar model

RESOURCES

Optional: digital timers or stopwatches

 In the eTextbook of this lesson, you will find interactive links to a selection of teaching tools.

Quick recap
Rehearse key time facts. Ask: *How many seconds are in one minute? How many minutes are in one hour? How many hours are in one day?*

Unit 13: Time, Lesson 2

Discover

WAYS OF WORKING Pair work

ASK

• Question 1 b): *What is the difference between the two timers?*
• Question 1 b): *In 1 second's time, what will each timer show?*
• Question 1 b): *What fact do you know about minutes and seconds that you can use to help compare the times?*

IN FOCUS Ensure that children are given the opportunity to explain their answer to question 1 b). Encourage children to use reasoning to justify their explanations. Children should also be encouraged to explore different methods to find the answer. For example, they may suggest drawing a bar model to help them count up in intervals of 60 seconds. You might also want to explore how the 6 times table can help them here, and follow this up with Dexter's comment in **Share**.

PRACTICAL TIPS Provide children with stopwatches to revise the concept of minutes and seconds, particularly observing how their stopwatches behave when 60 seconds is reached. Use timers to illustrate the concept of counting down.

ANSWERS

Question 1 a): 1 minute is equal to 60 seconds.

Question 1 b): 3 minutes 20 seconds = 200 seconds, so both timers show the same time until launch.

PUPIL TEXTBOOK 4C PAGE 72

Share

WAYS OF WORKING Whole class teacher led

ASK

• Question 1 a): *Why do you think you need to convert times into the same unit to compare them?*
• Question 1 b): *How does the bar model represent the controller's and the astronaut's timers? What would you expect to see if the times are the same?*
• Question 1 b): *Dexter mentions using the 6 times-table to help multiply by 60. How can this help?*

IN FOCUS Ensure that children are able to explain how the bar models have been used to solve the problem, noting how 1 minute is visually shown to be equivalent to 60 seconds. In question 1 b), ask: *How does the bar model show that 3 minutes 20 seconds is the same as 200 seconds? Can you explain how the 6 times-table can help you with this question?* Children might suggest that counting in 6s to 20 (6, 12, 18) helps them to count in 60s to 200 (60, 120, 180).

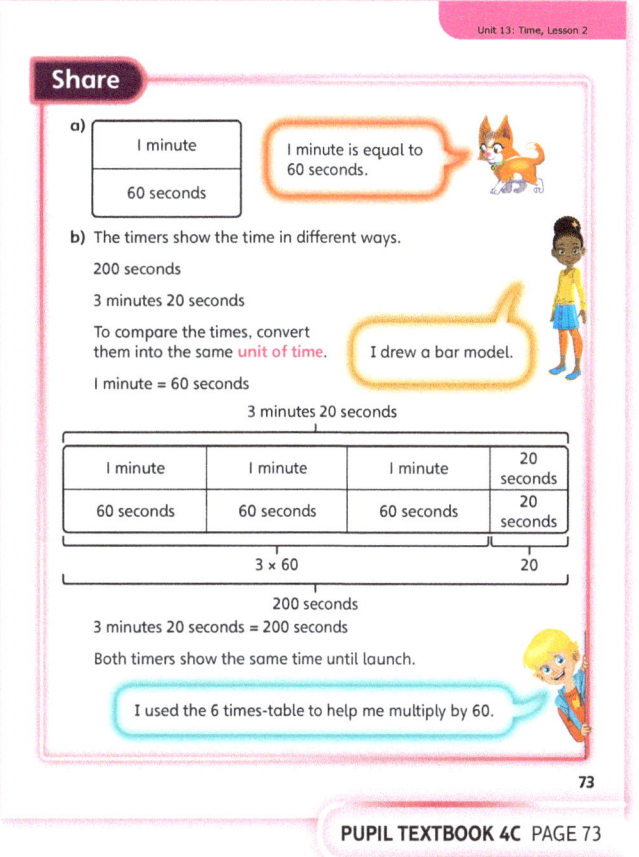

PUPIL TEXTBOOK 4C PAGE 73

107

Think together

WAYS OF WORKING Whole class teacher led (I do, We do, You do)

ASK

- Question ①: *Explain the question using your own words. How does the bar model help you to answer the problem?*
- Question ①: *What is the same and what is different about the bars in the bar model?*
- Question ②: *How would you complete a bar model to show this?*
- Question ②: *How do you know how many whole 60-second bars fit within 280 seconds? Is there a quick way to find this out? How many seconds are there left over?*

IN FOCUS In question ①, children should use the given bar model to convert 2 minutes 50 seconds into seconds. This involves multiplying 60 × 2 and adding 50, and is the same process which they used in **Share** question ① b). In question ②, children use the reverse process because they need to convert a time in seconds into minutes and seconds. They first need to count up in intervals of 60 until they reach 240 seconds (4 minutes). They can then calculate 280 – 240 using column division, or find the difference by counting on, to determine that the timer on the left should show 4 minutes 40 seconds.

In question ③, children are no longer using minutes and seconds, but are instead using hours and minutes. Ensure that children are able to explain *why* converting hours into minutes is similar to converting minutes into seconds, as well as *how*, since there are 60 seconds in 1 minute and also 60 minutes in an hour.

STRENGTHEN To emphasise the equivalence between 1 minute and 60 seconds, provide children with base 10 equipment and ask them to group the equipment in 6s (with each group of 6 tens representing 1 minute). These can be used in questions ① and ② to support children's understanding of the two units of time.

DEEPEN In question ②, ask children how they would draw the bar model if the correct timer was the one on the left. Challenge children to solve this type of problem without drawing a bar model.

ASSESSMENT CHECKPOINT Use questions ① to ③ to assess whether children can convert between minutes and seconds and between hours and minutes. Look for clear explanations of how they are using the bar models to represent their conversions.

ANSWERS

Question ①: 2 minutes = 2 × 60 seconds = 120 seconds
120 seconds + 50 seconds = 170 seconds
The two timers do not show the same time.

Question ②: The timer on the left should show 4 minutes 40 seconds.

Question ③: 5 hours and 10 minutes = 310 minutes
This is similar to converting minutes into seconds because there are the same number of minutes in 1 hour as there are seconds in 1 minute (60).

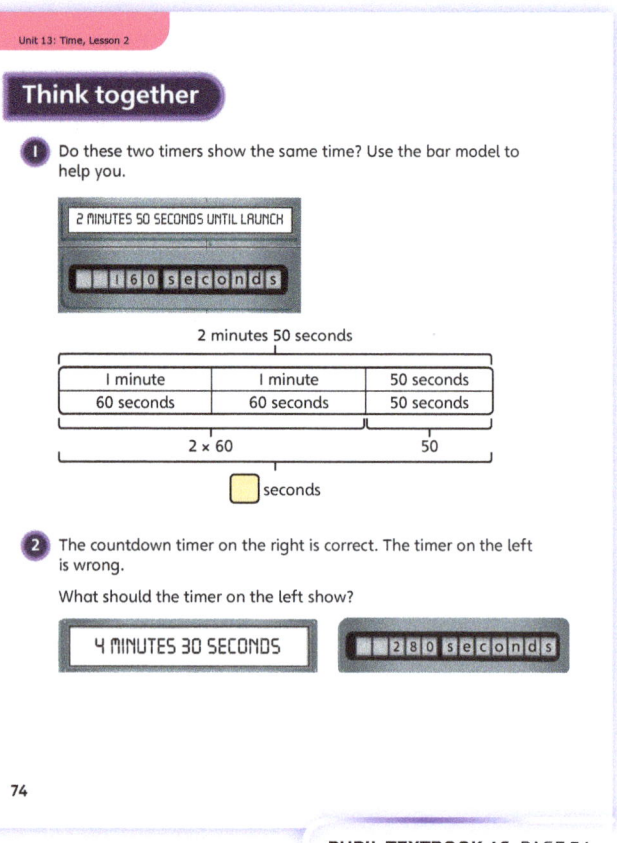

PUPIL TEXTBOOK 4C PAGE 74

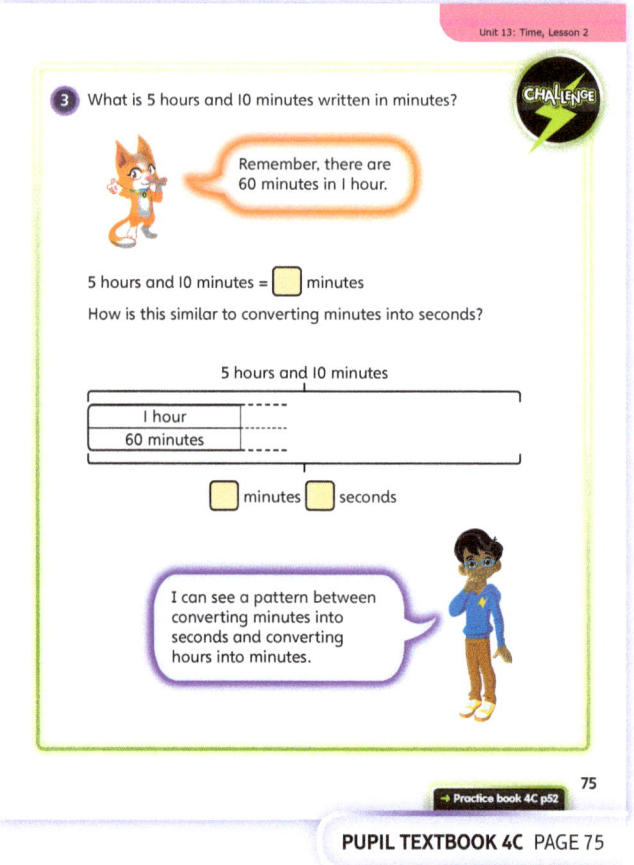

PUPIL TEXTBOOK 4C PAGE 75

Unit 13: Time, Lesson 2

Practice

WAYS OF WORKING Independent thinking

IN FOCUS Question ❶ develops children's understanding of the process to convert minutes to seconds and hours to minutes. In questions ❶ a) and b), children convert from a larger unit of time to a smaller one, so will need to multiply by 60 at some stage in their working. In question ❶ c), children convert from a smaller unit of time to a larger one. They may consider which multiple of 60 is close to 157 (that is, 120) and then subtract 120 from 157. Alternatively, they may repeatedly subtract 60 from 157 until the answer is less than 60. They can draw their own bar models to find each of the missing times.

STRENGTHEN For children finding it difficult to convert one unit into the other, it may be beneficial to get them to make their own bar models out of pieces of coloured card. They could write 1 minute on the front of each piece and 60 seconds on the reverse (or 1 hour on the front and 60 minutes on the reverse). Having formed a bar model that matches the information they know, they could turn all the cards over to find the answer.

DEEPEN In question ❺, children are required to calculate the number of seconds in 1 hour. Give children similar problems – for example, to find the number of hours in a week. Ask them to explain whether they could find the number of hours in a month from the number of weeks in a month.

THINK DIFFERENTLY Question ❸ asks children to use a different method to apply their knowledge of converting between minutes and hours. Encourage children to use repeated subtraction of 60 to work out each film's length in terms of hours and minutes. Challenge them to investigate the duration of their own favourite films.

ASSESSMENT CHECKPOINT Use questions ❶ and ❸ to assess whether children can convert between units of time. Check whether they are confident using different methods; they should be able to apply both times-tables facts (6 times-tables to help identify multiples of 60) and subtraction methods (repeatedly subtracting 60).

ANSWERS Answers for the **Practice** part of the lesson can be found in the *Power Maths* online subscription.

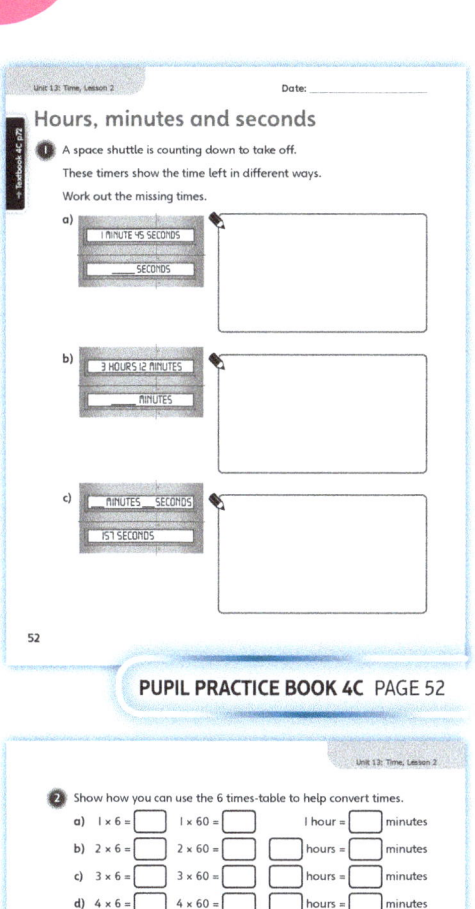

PUPIL PRACTICE BOOK 4C PAGE 52

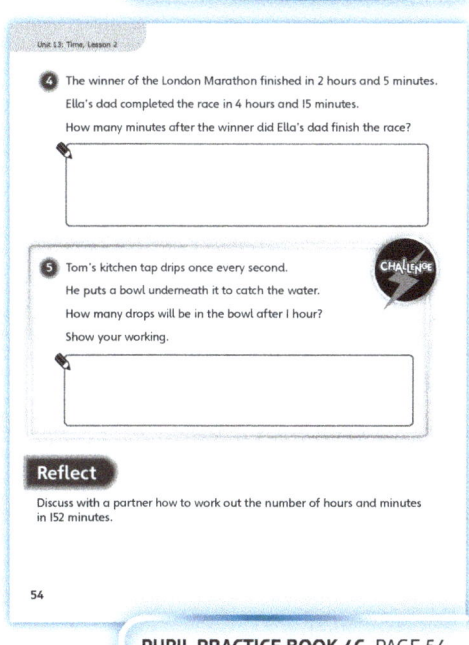

PUPIL PRACTICE BOOK 4C PAGE 53

Reflect

WAYS OF WORKING Pair work

IN FOCUS Use this question to check children's methodology. Pay attention to the way that children approach the conversion. Some may look for the nearest multiple of 60 to find the number of hours, others may repeatedly subtract 60. Ask children to share their working and ask whether it matters which method they used. Ask how they would have converted if they had been given the number of hours and minutes and then asked to give the time in minutes.

ASSESSMENT CHECKPOINT Check that children are able to convert the given time accurately and to explain their method.

ANSWERS Answers for the **Reflect** part of the lesson can be found in the *Power Maths* online subscription.

After the lesson

- Were children confident explaining their reasoning in this lesson?
- Do children have the confidence to apply what they have learnt in this lesson to convert between different units of time?

PUPIL PRACTICE BOOK 4C PAGE 54

Unit 13: Time, Lesson 3

Convert between analogue and digital times

Learning focus
In this lesson, children will convert between analogue and digital times.

Before you teach
- How confident are children when reading analogue times to the nearest minute?
- What opportunities are there for you to refer to both analogue and digital times throughout the school day to embed the concepts learnt in this lesson?

NATIONAL CURRICULUM LINKS

Year 4 Measurement – time

Convert between different units of measure [for example, kilometre to metre; hour to minute].

ASSESSING MASTERY

Children can confidently convert between analogue and digital 12-hour times to the nearest minute. They can apply this skill when problem solving.

COMMON MISCONCEPTIONS

Children may misunderstand the relationship between the numbers on a digital clock face and the numbers on an analogue clock face. For example, they may represent the digital time 6:10 as one hand pointing to the number 6 and the other hand pointing to the number 10. Similarly, children may represent the analogue time ten past 7 as 7:02 because these are the two numbers the hands are pointing to. Ask:
- *What do the numbers on each side of the colon in a digital time represent? How would you show this time on an analogue clock face?*

STRENGTHENING UNDERSTANDING

To help children build connections between analogue and digital times, consider times to the nearest five minutes. Provide children with large analogue clock faces and ask them to place number cards next to each number to show the digital equivalent in minutes. For example, the number 1 on the clock face represents 5 minutes past and so is represented by :05 in a digital time. Turn this into a quick-fire question and answer game where children point to the correct part of the analogue clock for minutes given in a digital time (such as :45).

GOING DEEPER

Show children different 'minutes to' analogue times. Challenge them to write the times in three different ways. For example, three minutes to four might be written as '3:57', 'fifty-seven minutes past 3' or 'three minutes to 4'. This will further consolidate children's understanding of the links between digital and analogue times.

KEY LANGUAGE

In lesson: unit of time, convert, analogue, digital, am, pm, hour, minute, 12-hour

STRUCTURES AND REPRESENTATIONS

Analogue clock, digital clock

RESOURCES

Optional: analogue clocks, digital clocks, number cards

 In the eTextbook of this lesson, you will find interactive links to a selection of teaching tools.

Quick recap
Use an analogue clock face to make different times to the nearest 5 minutes. Ask children to read the times or to make them on their own clock faces.

Discover

WAYS OF WORKING Pair work

ASK

- Question 1 a): *Look at the two types of clock face shown. What is the same? What is different?*
- Question 1 a): *How does the spy with the watch know her watch is wrong?*
- Question 1 a): *What time does the park clock say it is?*
- Question 1 b): *How far will the minute hand move in an hour and a half? How far will the hour hand move?*
- Question 1 b): *How will the hours digit change on the digital clock? How will the minutes digit change?*

IN FOCUS When considering question 1 b), encourage children to discuss how both methods of showing the time will change over the course of an hour (for example, the minute hand on the analogue clock moving once around the clock face, or the hours digit on the digital watch increasing by 1). Extend the question to consider how the clocks will change over the course of one and a half hours.

PRACTICAL TIPS Provide children with practice clock faces with movable hands, and with number cards for modelling digital watches. Call out different times and challenge them to set their clocks to the correct time as quickly as possible. Move from times to the nearest five minutes to times to the nearest minute.

ANSWERS

Question 1 a): The time on the watch should say 3:07 pm.

Question 1 b): Analogue:  Digital: 4:37 pm

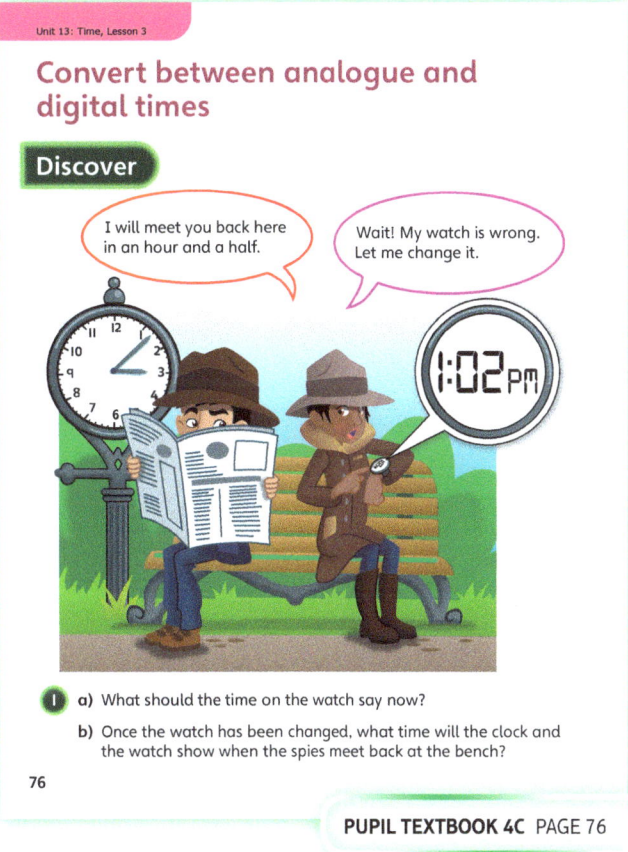

Share

WAYS OF WORKING Whole class teacher led

ASK

- Question 1 a): *What do the letters 'am' and 'pm' mean? The digital watch shows that it is a pm time – how else can you tell this fact?*
- Question 1 b): *What happens to both types of clock when the time crosses into a new hour?*
- Question 1 b): *What would the analogue clock show in (10 minutes/half an hour/one hour/an hour and a half)?*
- Question 1 b): *What would the digital watch show in (10 minutes/half an hour/one hour/an hour and a half)?*

IN FOCUS When answering question 1 b), ensure that children recognise that the number of minutes past the hour increases by 30, as half an hour equals 30 minutes. Give examples that cross the hour boundary. For example, ask: *What time will the spies need to meet if the time now is 3:50 pm?* In these cases, children will need to partition 30 and complete two additions – one to get to 4 o'clock (+ 10) and one to add the remainder of the 30 minutes (+ 20) after 5 o'clock.

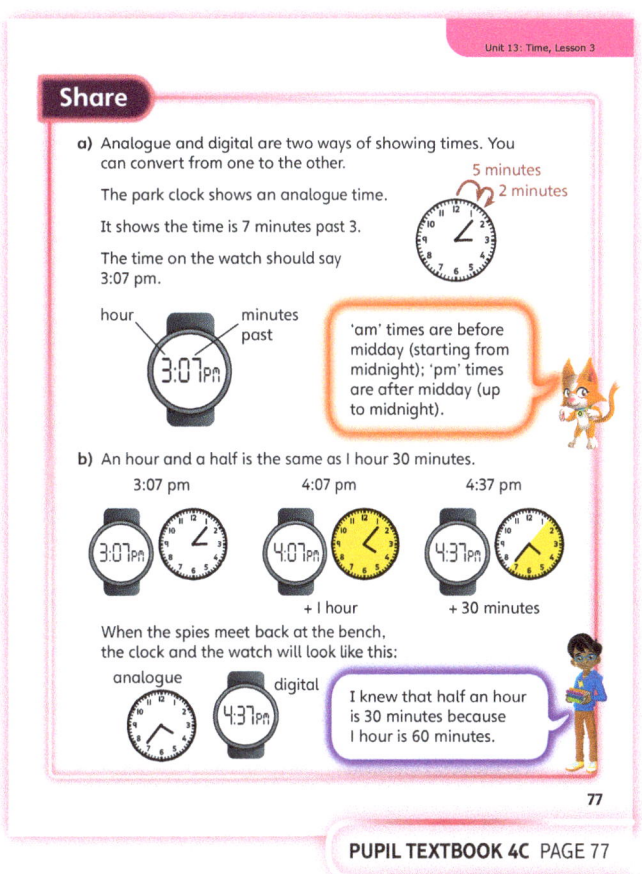

111

Think together

WAYS OF WORKING Whole class teacher led (I do, We do, You do)

ASK

- Question ❶: *How could you say twenty to 9 in a different way? Why is this important?*
- Question ❶: *Why doesn't the digital version of twenty to 9 have the number 20 or 9 in it?*
- Question ❷: *There are two ways to say the time on the first clock. What are they? Which one is the most helpful when finding the correct digital clock that goes with it?*
- Question ❷: *Do the am or pm letters make a difference to how you answer the question?*

IN FOCUS The times in question ❷ test children's understanding of the two numbers in a digital time. For example, the analogue clock showing twenty-one minutes past 5 might be matched incorrectly to the digital time 4:05 am because children believe that the numbers on the clock face towards which the hands are pointing should be the same as the ones in the digital time.

STRENGTHEN In questions ❶ and ❷, provide children with digit cards and analogue clock faces with movable hands. These will enable children to physically model the times in both analogue and digital formats.

DEEPEN Question ❸ requires children to convert a digital time to analogue and use reasoning to explain incorrect answers that are based on common misconceptions. The key error here is that children may not be able to recognise the meaning of each number either side of the colon in a digital time. Challenge children to think of other common misconceptions. They could make up similar problems to question ❸, with one correct match and two incorrect matches, and swap with a partner to explain the mistakes.

ASSESSMENT CHECKPOINT Use question ❷ to assess whether children can convert digital times to analogue and vice versa. They should be able to express digital times in different ways, particularly being able to describe times that are both minutes past and minutes to the hour (for example, 4:50 as 'fifty minutes past 4' and 'ten to 5').

ANSWERS

Question ❶: Twenty to 9 is the same as forty minutes past 8.

 Analogue: Digital: 8:40 am

Question ❷: a) 7:51 pm b) 5:21 pm c) 8:10 am d) 4:05 am

Question ❸ a): Alex's clock face matches the digital time.

Question ❸ b): Jamilla thinks 6:10 am means six minutes past 10 and has drawn this time instead. Bella has mixed up the minute and the hour hands.

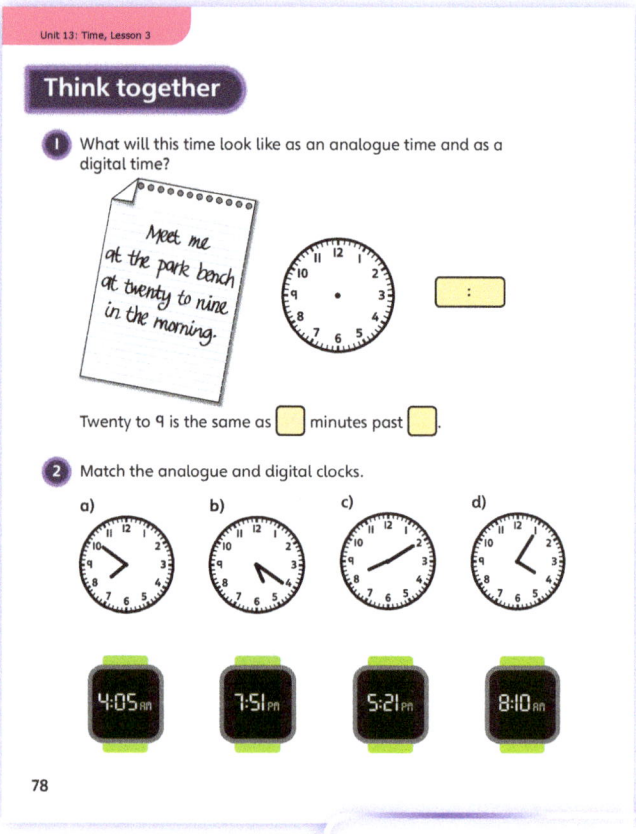

PUPIL TEXTBOOK 4C PAGE 78

PUPIL TEXTBOOK 4C PAGE 79

Unit 13: Time, Lesson 3

Practice

WAYS OF WORKING Independent thinking

IN FOCUS In question 2, children are given times written in words and are required to represent these on both analogue and digital clocks. In order to avoid making any of the usual errors, children should consider carefully all the information available to them in the written times. For example, what is the hour and what are the minutes? Is it a time to the hour or past the hour? Is it an am time or a pm time?

STRENGTHEN To support children as they attempt to convert each written time in question 2 into analogue and digital, suggest that they underline the important words in the message. Provide analogue clock faces for them to model each time before copying onto the blank clock face provided. If necessary, ask questions to guide them to the relevant information on the clock face that is needed to make each part of the digital time.

DEEPEN Use question 4 to deepen children's understanding and reasoning skills. Ask children whether there are any incorrect digital times that they can make using the given digits. For example, digital times that are formatted incorrectly (63:5) or that refer to impossible times (3:65). Give children different sets of number cards to make *possible* times, including sets of four cards where two are 0, 1 or 2.

THINK DIFFERENTLY In question 3, children revise what the digits in a digital time represent by considering a time where the same number has different meanings in the analogue and digital representations. Ask children whether they can think of any other examples where one of the hands on a clock face points to a digit in the digital time, but where they both represent different things.

ASSESSMENT CHECKPOINT Use questions 1 and 2 to assess whether children can convert between analogue and 12-hour digital times. They should recognise what both sets of digits either side of the colon in a digital time represent and be able to express 'minutes to' digital times in different ways (for example, 6:42 as 'eighteen minutes to 7').

ANSWERS Answers for the **Practice** part of the lesson can be found in the *Power Maths* online subscription.

Reflect

WAYS OF WORKING Independent thinking

IN FOCUS Children need to explain what the numbers in a digital time represent. Children should be able to describe how to use the hour hand on the analogue clock to determine the first number shown on the digital display, and then use the minute hand to determine the number of minutes *past* the hour, which will give them the number of minutes that should be shown on the digital display. Children should be able to give an example, particularly in the case where they would normally read 'minutes to' on the analogue clock. For example, '10 minutes to 4' would be shown as 3:50 on the digital clock.

ASSESSMENT CHECKPOINT Look for children who are able to describe accurately how to convert an analogue time into a digital time.

ANSWERS Answers for the **Reflect** part of the lesson can be found in the *Power Maths* online subscription.

After the lesson

- In the next lesson children will convert between 24-hour digital times and analogue times. Do children have the confidence to apply what they have learnt in this lesson in a new context?

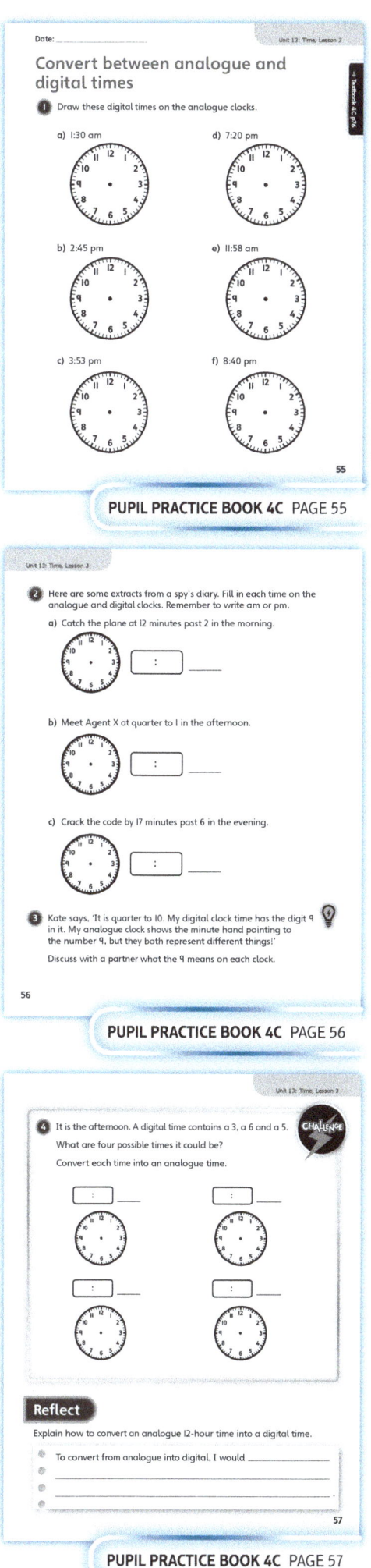

PUPIL PRACTICE BOOK 4C PAGE 55

PUPIL PRACTICE BOOK 4C PAGE 56

PUPIL PRACTICE BOOK 4C PAGE 57

Unit 13: Time, Lesson 4

Convert to the 24 hour clock

Learning focus
In this lesson, children will convert between 12-hour and 24-hour times expressed on both analogue and digital clocks.

Before you teach
- Are children confident when relating 12-hour digital times to analogue times?
- Can children recall what is meant by a 24-hour time and why they are used?

NATIONAL CURRICULUM LINKS

Year 4 Measurement – time

Convert between different units of measure [for example, kilometre to metre; hour to minute].

ASSESSING MASTERY

Children can confidently convert between analogue and digital 24-hour times to the nearest minute. They apply this skill when problem solving.

COMMON MISCONCEPTIONS

Children may think, because 17:00 can be said as '17 hundred hours', there are 100 minutes in an hour. Ask:
- *How many hours go by between 13:00 and 14:00? How many minutes is this?*

Children may interchange minutes and hours from digital times. For example, they may read 16:05 as sixteen minutes past 5 – this error often occurs because analogue times are said in this order (minutes past hour). Ask:
- *If a clock shows 13:07, what time is it? Can you make this time on an analogue clock?*

STRENGTHENING UNDERSTANDING

To support children's understanding of 24-hour clock times in different contexts, present times in different ways (clock on computer, times in different parts of the world, flight departure times). Discuss the way that these 24-hour times are formatted. Choose individual times and ask children to say these times and to represent them on an analogue clock.

GOING DEEPER

Explore possible misconceptions and encourage children to consider the advice they would give to someone making that particular error. For example, show children an analogue clock displaying twenty-five past 3. Explain that this is an afternoon time. Ask children to think of wrong answers someone might give if asked to write this time as a 24-hour digital time and how they would correct their mistakes.

KEY LANGUAGE

In lesson: convert, analogue, digital, **12-hour** time, **24-hour** time, hour, minute, am, pm

STRUCTURES AND REPRESENTATIONS

Analogue clock, digital clock

RESOURCES

Optional: analogue clocks, digital clocks, number cards, examples of 24-hour clock times from everyday life (computer clock, timetables, etc.)

 In the eTextbook of this lesson, you will find interactive links to a selection of teaching tools.

Quick recap
Rehearse the language of telling the time on an analogue clock. Ask: *What is the difference between 'quarter to 4' and 'quarter past 4' on a clock face? Why don't we say '45 minutes to 7?'*

Unit 13: Time, Lesson 4

Discover

WAYS OF WORKING Pair work

ASK

- Question 1 a): *Compare these digital times with the ones in the last lesson. What is the same? What is different?*
- Question 1 a): *How can a digital time show more than 12 hours when there are only 12 hours on a clock face?*
- Question 1 b): *How could you say each time in a different way?*

IN FOCUS Ensure that the picture provides an opportunity for children to revise the characteristics of 24-hour times and to explore the differences between 24-hour digital times and the 12-hour digital times they used in the previous lesson. Check that children understand what is meant by a '24-hour time'.

PRACTICAL TIPS Provide digital clocks (or use online digital clocks) for children to practise exploring 24-hour clock times. Ask children to make the different times in the picture. As they move from one time to the other, children should notice how the 24-hour clock behaves (for example, the hours go to 00 when moving on from 23).

ANSWERS

Question 1 a): The first two digits show the hour (from 00 up to 23). The last two digits show the number of minutes past (from 00 up to 59).

Question 1 b): The correct watch shows 15:52.

PUPIL TEXTBOOK 4C PAGE 80

Share

WAYS OF WORKING Whole class teacher led

ASK

- Question 1 a): *Look at the list of digital times. What do you notice about the way that the digital times are written?*
- Question 1 a): *How would you write each time as a 12-hour time?*
- Question 1 b): *What advice would you give to someone looking at an analogue clock who wanted to convert it into a 24-hour digital time?*
- Question 1 b): *What would each digital time look like on an analogue clock face? Which one is the same as the clock in the picture?*

IN FOCUS Use both analogue and digital clocks (or number cards) for children to model both sets of times. The physical acts of moving the hands of the clock and altering the digits in a digital time will ensure that children build connections between the two formats. It is particularly important to spend time considering 24-hour times after 12 pm (where the hour digits will be greater than 12), and where the number of minutes are after half past (where the digital time uses the number of minutes *past* even though the time would normally be read as a number of minutes *to*).

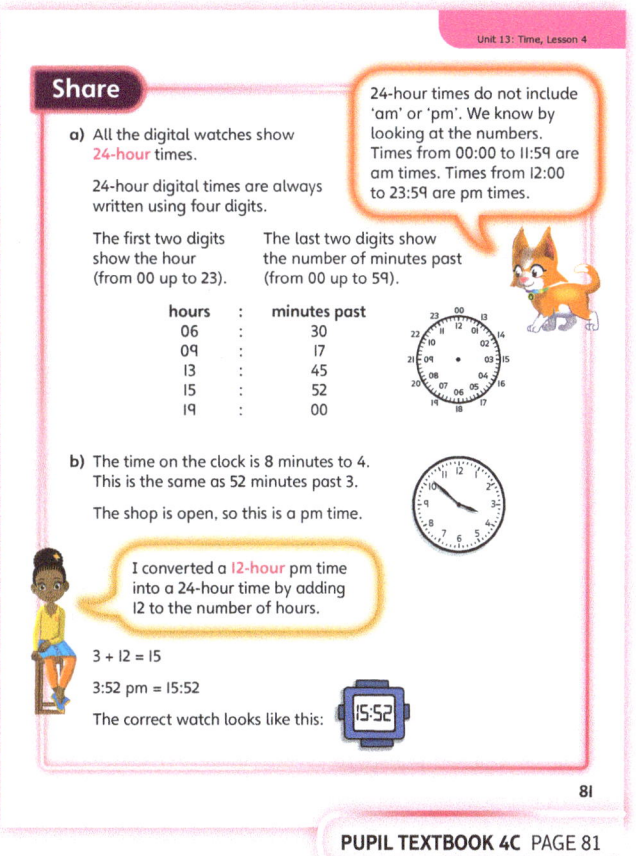

PUPIL TEXTBOOK 4C PAGE 81

115

Think together

WAYS OF WORKING Whole class teacher led (I do, We do, You do)

ASK
- Question ❶: *What do you need to find out from an analogue time to convert it into a digital time?*
- Question ❶: *Explain how to convert a 12-hour am or pm time into a 24-hour digital time.*
- Question ❷: *Why do you think this question gets you to focus on the number of minutes past the hour, rather than the number of minutes to?*

IN FOCUS In question ❷, ask children what they notice about the answer boxes given for the 24-hour time. Children should identify that there is no space for am or pm and also that there are spaces for four digits (both of which are features of 24-hour times). Ask how their answer would differ if this time was in the afternoon.

STRENGTHEN Provide analogue clocks with movable hands and number cards for children to model their answers. Emphasise the 'minutes to' elements of a clock face and also how 'to' times can also be said as 'minutes past' times. If helpful, use flashcards to reinforce children's understanding of these two ways of expressing times (for example, show 'twenty to 5' and expect children to respond with 'forty minutes past 4').

DEEPEN After children have identified the mistake in question ❹, ask them to give further mistakes that could be made when converting between different formats of times in real life. Ask: *Look at the time on your 24-hour digital watch. Now adjust the time on your analogue clock to match it. What mistakes might you make if you did this? What if you wanted to set your digital watch by looking at the analogue clock in your classroom?*

ASSESSMENT CHECKPOINT Use questions ❶ and ❷ to assess whether children can convert between analogue and 24-hour digital times.

ANSWERS

Question ❶ a): The clock shows twelve minutes past 8.
As a 12-hour time, this is written as 8:12 am.
As a 24-hour time, this is written as 08:12.

Question ❶ b): The clock shows thirteen minutes to 12.
As a 12-hour time, this is written as 11:47 pm.
As a 24-hour time, this is written as 23:47.

Question ❷: Quarter to 5 is the same as forty-five minutes past 4.
Analogue: 24-hour digital: 04:45

Question ❸ a): Mo's watch would show 06:35.

Question ❸ b): Mo's watch would show 18:35.

Question ❹: Isla has treated it as a pm time. It is the morning, so she does not need to add 12 to the number of hours. To convert 7:28 am into a 24-hour time, Isla needs to write a 0 at the start of the time so it has four digits and to remove the letters 'am' as these are not needed. The 24-hour time is 07:28.

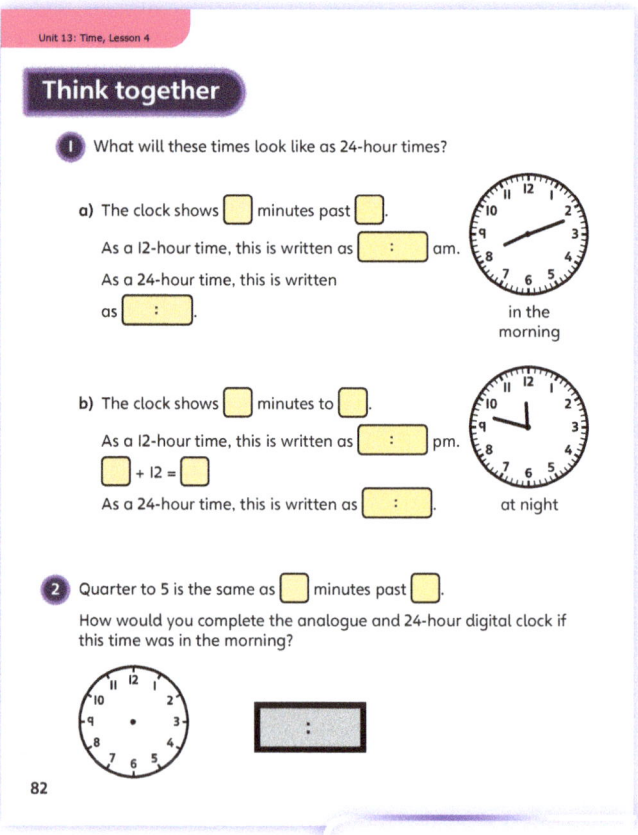

PUPIL TEXTBOOK 4C PAGE 82

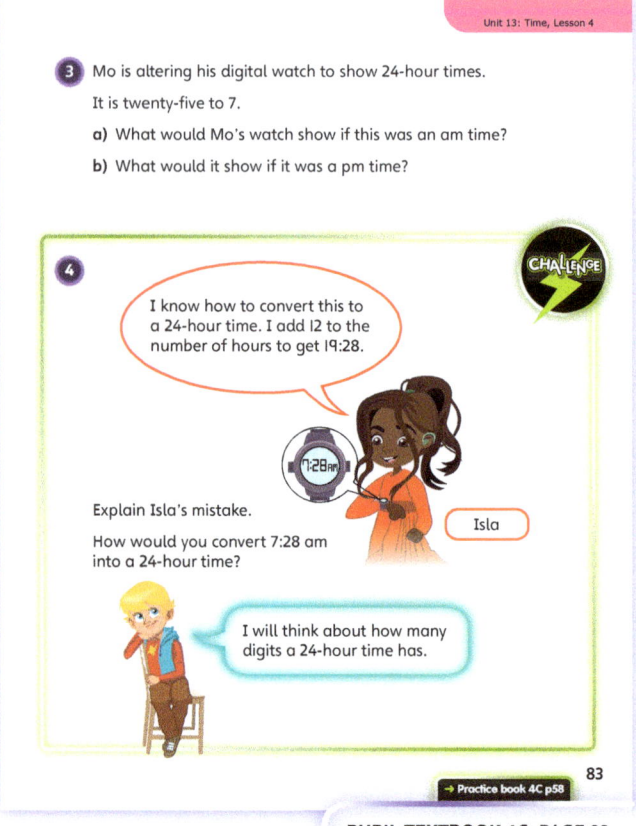

PUPIL TEXTBOOK 4C PAGE 83

Unit 13: Time, Lesson 4

Practice

WAYS OF WORKING Independent thinking

IN FOCUS Question ❶ challenges children to convert various different times (expressed in words and as 12-hour digital times) into both analogue and 24-hour digital formats. Ask children how each time shows what part of the day it is describing. Ask them to explain why this is important when writing the time on an analogue or 24-hour digital clock.

STRENGTHEN As question ❹ is more abstract in nature, ask children what they might do to help visualise the current time and then the time $1\frac{1}{2}$ hours later. Ask them what they could use to count on one and a half hours from 2:17. Provide access to analogue and digital clocks for children to model the question.

DEEPEN Use the open-ended task in question ❺ to deepen children's understanding of converting between 24-hour and 12-hour times. Ask questions about the times they make: for example, whether they are before or after midday or how this affects how they will work out the 12-hour times. Challenge children to come up with examples of times that are not correct and to then explain why not (for example: 24:11 because 24-hour clock times go to 00 after 23; or 4:40 because all 24-hour times need four digits).

ASSESSMENT CHECKPOINT Use questions ❶ and ❷ to assess whether children can convert between analogue and 24-hour digital times as well as between 12-hour and 24-hour digital times. They should be able to use their understanding of the digital format to identify what each set of numbers means, applying this knowledge when moving between analogue and digital times. Children should be confident when representing am and pm times using 24-hour notation.

ANSWERS Answers for the **Practice** part of the lesson can be found in the *Power Maths* online subscription.

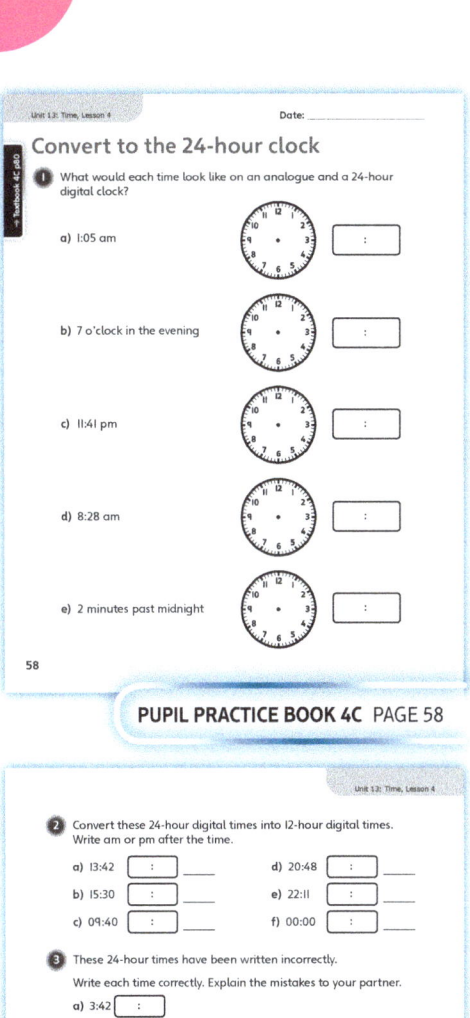

PUPIL PRACTICE BOOK 4C PAGE 58

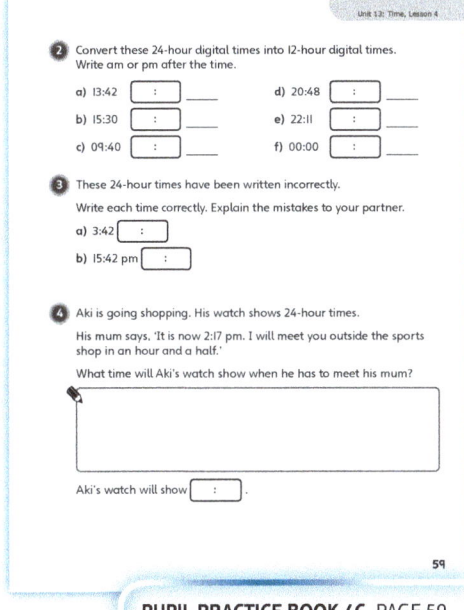

PUPIL PRACTICE BOOK 4C PAGE 59

Reflect

WAYS OF WORKING Independent thinking

IN FOCUS Give children the opportunity to consider the different representations of time they have worked with. Ask them to describe the features of 12-hour times and 24-hour times, and how they would convert between them. Children may find it useful to refer back to previous pages in the Textbook to help explain their ideas.

ASSESSMENT CHECKPOINT Look for children who are able to explain that they need to identify whether the 12-hour time is an am or pm time and how to convert each of these into 24-hour times. Children's reasoning should make mention of the concepts they have covered so far – for example, that 24-hour clock times always contain four digits.

ANSWERS Answers for the **Reflect** part of the lesson can be found in the *Power Maths* online subscription.

After the lesson
- Have children made connections between the past two lessons when converting using digital times?
- How will you reinforce these connections during the next lesson when problem solving?

PUPIL PRACTICE BOOK 4C PAGE 60

Unit 13: Time, Lesson 5

Problem solving – convert units of time

Learning focus
In this lesson, children will apply their knowledge of units of time to problem-solving contexts. They will use mathematical reasoning, choosing when and how to convert between units of time or between analogue and digital times in order to solve problems.

Before you teach
- Are children confident converting between units of time?
- Are children confident problem solving and reasoning?

NATIONAL CURRICULUM LINKS

Year 4 Measurement – time

Convert between different units of measure [for example, kilometre to metre; hour to minute].

ASSESSING MASTERY

Children can solve time-based problems confidently, including where they are required to convert between units of time and/or between times shown on analogue and digital clocks.

COMMON MISCONCEPTIONS

Children may think that 24-hour times in a problem are not correct because there are only 12 numbers on a clock face. Ask:
- *Why might the time 16:10 look unusual to some people? Is it written correctly? What does it mean?*

Children may think that, because two pieces of information in a problem are given using different units of time, they are unconnected. Ask:
- *Can you highlight the units of time mentioned in this problem? How can you make them easier to compare?*

STRENGTHENING UNDERSTANDING

To strengthen understanding, ensure that children use the structures and representations that they have been using throughout the unit. Suggest that they underline the parts of the problem that are most important. Ask them whether they can say the problem in a different way. Provide blank bar models and analogue and digital clocks to help children model each problem and to help them deepen their understanding.

GOING DEEPER

Provide children with data that shows the number of hours/days/weeks/months that it has taken various explorers to complete their journeys. Challenge children to devise their own problems based on this information. The simplest form of question may be a straightforward conversion from one unit into another. Encourage children, however, to come up with more complicated multi-step questions including information of their own.

KEY LANGUAGE

In lesson: convert, seconds, minutes, hours, days, weeks, months, years, analogue, digital, 12-hour, 24-hour, compare

Other language to be used by the teacher: unit of time, measure, slower, quicker

STRUCTURES AND REPRESENTATIONS

Bar model, analogue clock, digital clock

RESOURCES

Optional: calendars or year planners, flashcards, analogue clocks, digital clocks, number cards

 In the eTextbook of this lesson, you will find interactive links to a selection of teaching tools.

Quick recap
Rehearse a selection of key time facts. For example, ask: *How many hours are in one day? How many days are in one week? How many weeks are in one year? How many days are in one year?*

Unit 13: Time, Lesson 5

Discover

WAYS OF WORKING Pair work

ASK

- Question 1: *Why is it important for the explorers to be able to convert times accurately? Can you think of another example when it might be important?*
- Question 1: *What different units of time can you see in the picture?*
- Question 1: *What facts do you know about these units of time? How many days are in 1 week? How many days/weeks are in 1 month? (How does this depend on the month?) How many days/weeks/months are in 1 year?*

IN FOCUS Explore the different units of time mentioned in the picture. Ask children to list them and then revise the equivalence of each unit. Use the opportunity to discuss the different lengths of months. Encourage children to suggest when different units of time might be important during an expedition. Can they think of one example for each unit of time?

PRACTICAL TIPS Provide pairs of children with calendars or year planners and encourage them to role-play the parts of the explorers. For example, they can use the calendars to mark the current date and when they might expect to run out of woolly socks. It does not matter which month they use as the questions do not specify this information. Using calendars in this way should help children to visualise the equivalence between 7 days and 1 week (or 1 row down on the calendar) and between 12 months and 1 year (or 1 whole calendar).

ANSWERS

Question 1 a): The explorers have been training for $2\frac{1}{2}$ years.

Question 1 b): Toshi does have enough socks to make it to the North Pole, because three weeks (or 21 days) of socks is greater than the 20 days left of travelling.

Share

WAYS OF WORKING Whole class teacher led

ASK

- Question 1: *Describe what each part of the question is asking you to do in as few words as possible.*
- Question 1: *It is easier to compare two periods of time if they have been converted to use the same unit. Does it matter which unit you choose?*
- Question 1 b): *Dexter and Flo suggest two different methods. Explain how they reach the same answer.*

IN FOCUS Both questions employ bar models in order to represent the problem visually. Ask children to explain how the bar models have been used to help solve the problems. Ask them whether they could work out the answers without using a bar model.

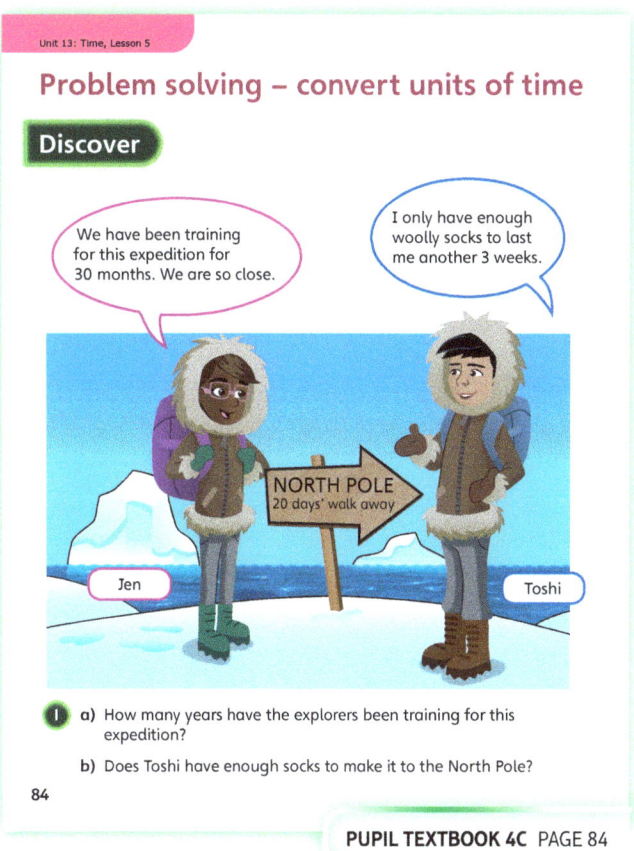

PUPIL TEXTBOOK 4C PAGE 84

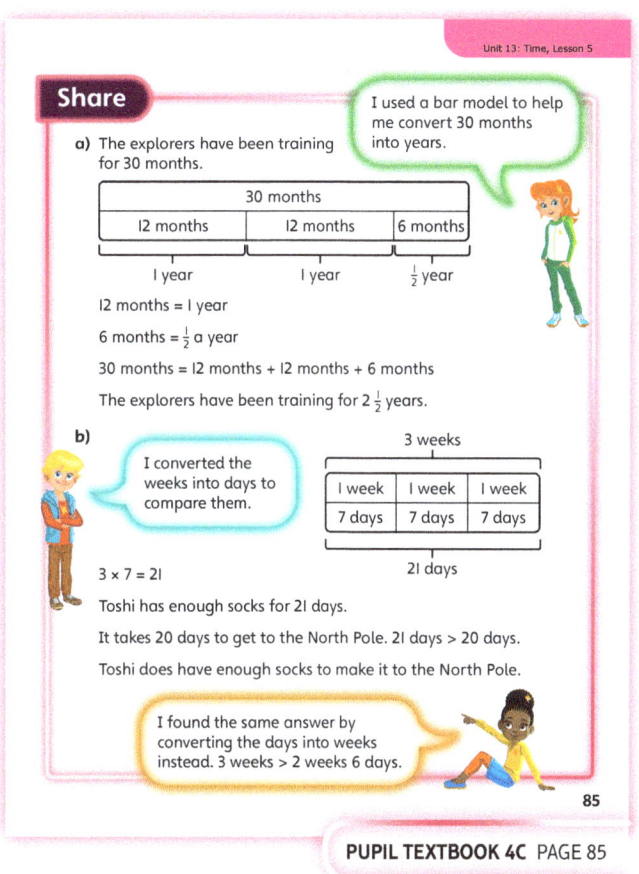

PUPIL TEXTBOOK 4C PAGE 85

119

Unit 13: Time, Lesson 5

Think together

WAYS OF WORKING Whole class teacher led (I do, We do, You do)

ASK

- Question ❶: *Why is the bar model useful?*
- Question ❶: *Is the quicker time the one with the larger or smaller number of seconds?*
- Question ❶: *Flo mentions a different way to convert the times. What do you think it is?*
- Question ❷: *What is the difference between the two methods of finding the answer?*
- Question ❷: *Is the tin that needs to be used first the one with the longer or shorter 'Use by' date?*

IN FOCUS Question ❷ takes children through two methods of finding the answer (by converting either 30 days into weeks, or 4 weeks into days, so that both labels are expressed in the same units of measurement). Initially, show children the problem without showing them the bar model in question ❷ a). Ask: *How could you convert 30 days to weeks? How could you convert 4 weeks to days?* Their differing methods can lead to a class discussion.

STRENGTHEN To strengthen children's understanding of the connections between units of time, use flashcards with equivalent times on each side (for example, 1 minute on the front and 60 seconds on the back). Children can then use these flashcards to form their own bar models.

DEEPEN The problems in this section all allude to two ways of finding the answer (converting either of the two times so that it is the same as the other and can therefore be compared more easily). Ask children whether it matters which unit they decide to convert. Some children may find it easier to go from large units to small units as the operation used is multiplication rather than division. Give children several pairs of times to investigate.

ASSESSMENT CHECKPOINT Use questions ❶ to ❸ to assess whether children are confident in solving problems that involve conversion and comparison. Ensure children are able to explain clearly why and how they are using bar models to help them solve each problem.

ANSWERS

Question ❶: (3 × 60) + 14 = 180 + 14 = 194 seconds
194 seconds < 203 seconds
3 minutes 14 seconds is a quicker time than 203 seconds.
Jen is quicker than Toshi.

Question ❷ a): Tin A = Use by 4 weeks 2 days
Tin B = Use by 4 weeks
Tin B needs to be used first.

Question ❷ b): Tin A = Use by 30 days
Tin B = Use by 28 days
Tin B needs to be used first.

Question ❸: Children's answers will vary but should involve converting one of the given measurements so that the unit of time is the same.

Question ❸ a): 3 hours and 45 minutes is 225 minutes, so it is longer than 200 minutes.

Question ❸ b): $4\frac{1}{2}$ years is 54 months, so it is longer than 50 months.

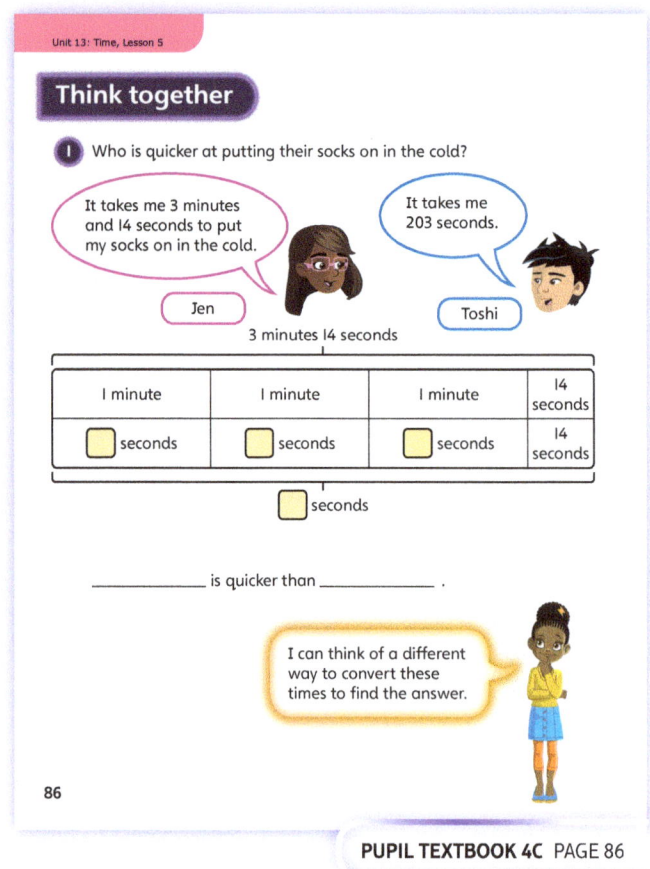

PUPIL TEXTBOOK 4C PAGE 86

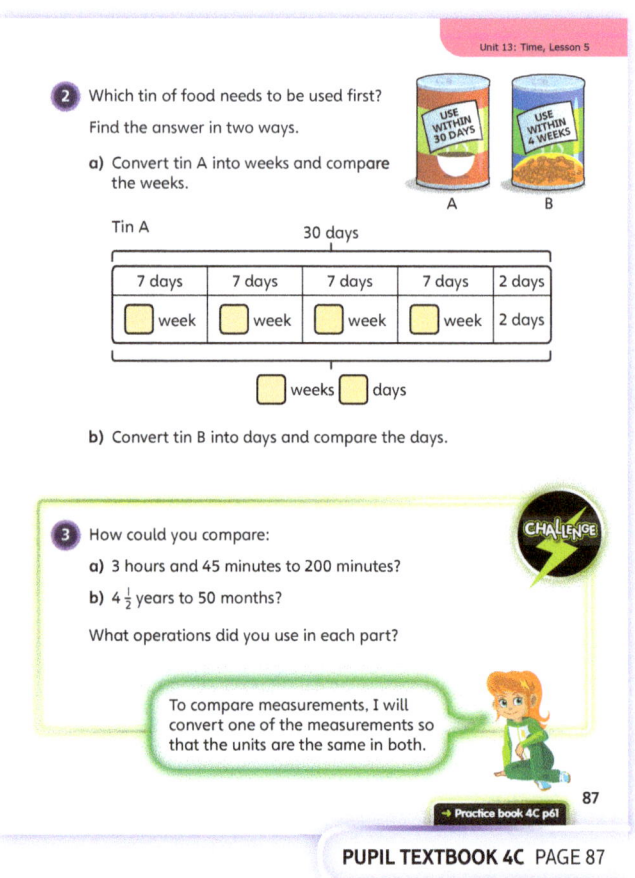

PUPIL TEXTBOOK 4C PAGE 87

Unit 13: Time, Lesson 5

Practice

WAYS OF WORKING Independent thinking

IN FOCUS In question ❶, children explore the relationship between weeks and days in the context of a mountain climb. The climb consists of four stages, the times for which are given in tabular form. Spend time asking children questions about the data in the table – the time taken to complete a stage, the time taken to complete two or three consecutive stages, and so on – so that they become familiar with what is being represented.

STRENGTHEN With children who need further support for question ❷, begin by asking them to look at the third column of the table – what unit of time is the answer to be given in? Children should then work backwards and look at the second column. If children are unsure how to convert between seconds, minutes and hours, encourage them to look back at the bar models they used in the Textbook.

DEEPEN Ask children to make up similar questions to question ❺. Children could, for example, base their questions on local bus times. They could write questions for a partner to answer, such as: *Megan lives at 'place A' and wants to meet her friends at the mall at 13:30. What time should she catch the bus from her house?* Encourage children to solve problems using both 12-hour and 24-hour times.

THINK DIFFERENTLY In question ❹, children are presented with the ages of babies. The ages are given for the first two babies (using different units of time) and related clues are given for the remaining two. Children are expected to convert one of the first two babies' ages and then solve the clues so that each age is now given in the same unit of time.

ASSESSMENT CHECKPOINT Use questions ❶ to ❸ to assess whether children are confident when approaching and solving time-based problems where they are required to convert between units of time and/or between times shown on analogue and digital clocks. They should display reasoning skills and be able to explain appropriate methods and thinking with confidence.

ANSWERS Answers for the **Practice** part of the lesson can be found in the *Power Maths* online subscription.

Reflect

WAYS OF WORKING Pair work

IN FOCUS This activity provides an opportunity to check children's methodology. They should begin by thinking individually and deciding on a method to use. Then they should explain this method to a partner. In their explanations, children should include the equivalence of 1 year and 12 months and describe how they would use this information to help. Ask children whether they used the same method as their partner, and whether their answers were the same.

ASSESSMENT CHECKPOINT Look for children who describe clearly and accurately how to convert 108 months into years.

ANSWERS Answers for the **Reflect** part of the lesson can be found in the *Power Maths* online subscription.

After the lesson

- How did children respond mathematically to the problems and how did the mathematical processes they used flow and develop during the lesson?
- Do you feel that children are ready to move on?

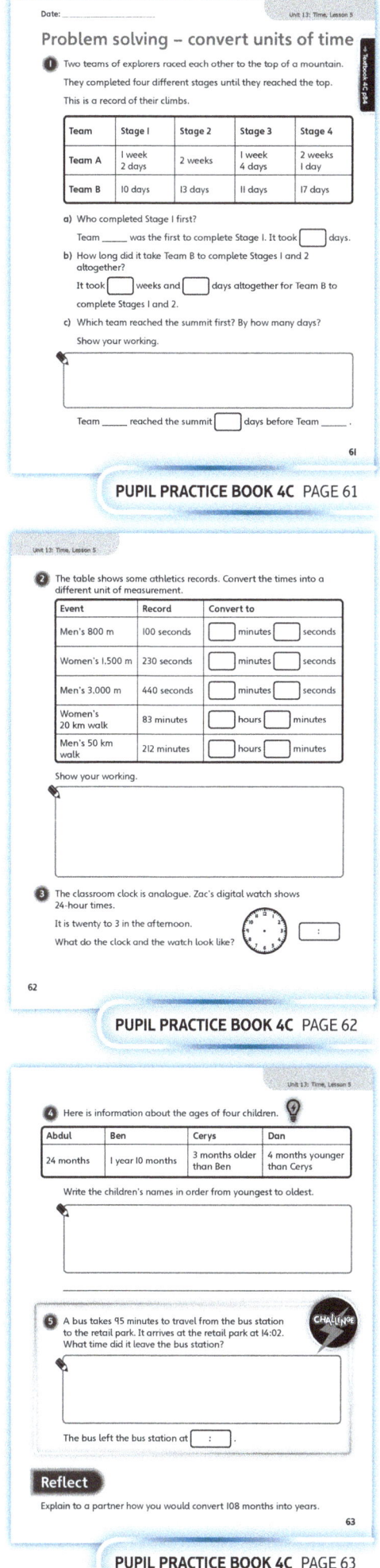

Unit 13: Time

End of unit check

Don't forget the unit assessment grid in your Power Maths online subscription.

WAYS OF WORKING Group work adult led

IN FOCUS

- Questions 1 and 2 assess children's ability to convert measurements of time: seconds into minutes and weeks into days.
- Questions 3 and 4 assess children's ability to convert and compare times represented in different ways (including analogue clocks and 12-hour and 24-hour digital clocks).
- Question 5 assesses children's ability to convert between units of time in a problem-solving context.
- Question 6 is a SATs-style question where conversion between units of time (minutes and seconds) is necessary to solve the problem.

ANSWERS AND COMMENTARY

Children who have mastered the concepts in this unit will be able to convert between seconds, minutes and hours, and between days, weeks, months and years. They will confidently use these units of measurement in their descriptions of times. They will be able to express times in both analogue and digital forms, including 24-hour clock times. Children will apply these elements to confidently solve mathematical problems.

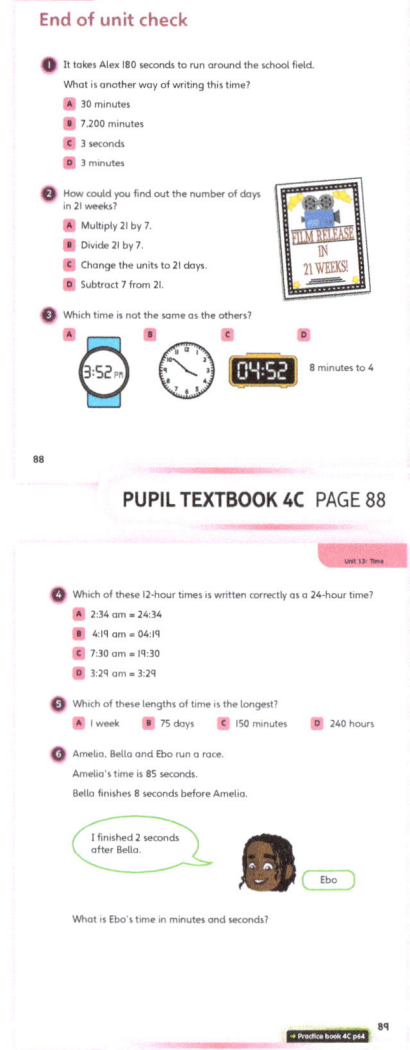

PUPIL TEXTBOOK 4C PAGE 88

PUPIL TEXTBOOK 4C PAGE 89

Q	A	WRONG ANSWERS AND MISCONCEPTIONS	STRENGTHENING UNDERSTANDING
1	D	A suggests the child has divided by 6 instead of 60. B suggests the child has multiplied instead of divided. C suggests the child has correctly calculated the answer, but confused the units of time.	Play matching pairs games using flashcards, where children are required to match times expressed in different units. Provide three different types of clocks in the classroom (analogue, 12-hour digital and 24-hour digital). Use the following activities to build connections between the three ways of showing the time: • At various times during the school day, ask children to express the time in these three different ways. • Cover up one or two of the clocks and encourage children to predict what they show. • Alter one of the clocks so that it shows the wrong time. Ask children to identify which clock is wrong and what it should show.
2	A	B or D suggest the child has used the incorrect operation. C suggests the child does not understand that a calculation is needed to convert between units of time.	
3	C	A, B or D suggest the child has incorrectly identified the common time.	
4	B	A suggests the child does not realise that 24-hour clock times revert to 00:00 after passing 23:59. C suggests the child has added 12. D suggests the child is not aware that 24-hour times must have four digits.	
5	B	A or C suggest the child has incorrectly converted the units of time before comparing them. D suggests the child has chosen the largest number.	
6	1 minute 19 seconds	Some children may get the right answer in seconds, but then not manage to convert it to minutes and seconds correctly.	

Unit 13: Time

My journal

WAYS OF WORKING Independent thinking

ANSWERS AND COMMENTARY

Children's answers will vary depending on their age (which may be more, equal to or less than 100 months). Their responses should show one of the following methods:
- Children could convert 100 months into years and months and then compare this with their own age. For example: *I know I have been alive less than 100 months because 100 months is the same as 8 years and 4 months (100 divided by 12 is 8 remainder 4). I am 8 years and 2 months old, so I have been alive less than 100 months.*
- Children could convert their own age into months and then compare this with 100 months. For example: *I know that I have been alive less than 100 months because I am 8 years and 2 months old. This is the same as 98 months (8 multiplied by 12 is 96 plus another 2 months equals 98).*

To help children work out how to answer the question, ask:
- *Write your age down. Is it written in the same units as the number you want to compare it to? How can you convert either your age or the number in the question so that they are written in the same units?*

Power check

WAYS OF WORKING Independent thinking

ASK
- *What did you know about converting between different units of time before you began this unit?*
- *Do you think you would be able to convert between an analogue time and a 12-hour or 24-hour digital time on your own?*

Power puzzle

WAYS OF WORKING Independent thinking or pair work

IN FOCUS The purpose of this **Power puzzle** is for children to move seamlessly between different units of time, finding equivalent pairs until there is one square left. Children should shade each pair differently. When they reach the final square, a final challenge might be to invent a match that could go with it.

ANSWERS AND COMMENTARY

The pairs are as follows:
- 06:56 matched with 6:56 am
- 3 hours 46 minutes matched with 226 minutes
- 60 months matched with 5 years
- Analogue clock showing four minutes to 6 matched with 17:56
- 8 weeks 4 days matched with 60 days
- 4 years 11 months matched with 59 months
- Analogue clock showing 10 past 1 matched with 13:10

The remaining, unmatched square is: 01:02.

After the unit

- How did children respond to the materials and approaches used during the unit?
- How do you feel that the unit assessment went?

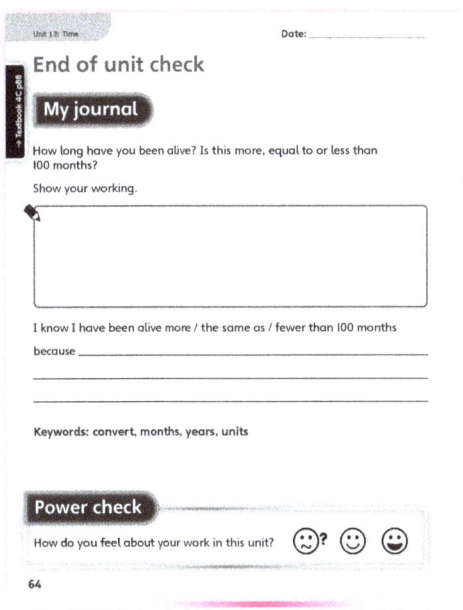

PUPIL PRACTICE BOOK 4C PAGE 64

PUPIL PRACTICE BOOK 4C PAGE 65

Strengthen and **Deepen** activities for this unit can be found in the *Power Maths* online subscription.

Unit 14
Geometry – angles and 2D shapes

Mastery Expert tip! 'When I taught this unit, I made sure children were able to have as much experience with hands on manipulatives (such as 2D shapes, or straws/ sticks that can be used to make shapes or angles) as possible. It made their ability to visualise shapes far stronger.'

Don't forget to watch the Unit 14 video!

WHY THIS UNIT IS IMPORTANT

This unit develops children's understanding of certain types of 2D shapes and their properties. Children begin by learning about three types of angles: acute, obtuse and right angles. They will use right angles as a way of recognising when angles are acute or obtuse. Children will then compare and order angles in ascending and descending order. Children then learn about different types of triangles and different types of quadrilaterals. Children will be encouraged to apply all they have learnt to deduce facts about shapes and solve shape-based problems and puzzles.

Children will then learn about how shapes can be regular or irregular and will discover what this means and how it relates to the angles they have been learning about.

Finally, children will develop their understanding of symmetry, both inside and outside of shapes, and will complete symmetrical shapes and patterns.

WHERE THIS UNIT FITS

→ Unit 13: Time
→ **Unit 14: Geometry – angles and 2D shapes**
→ Unit 15: Statistics

This unit builds upon the previous work children have done on recognising and identifying the basic properties of 2D shapes from Year 3. Children learnt to recognise angles as a turn and learnt about right angles. This unit also builds upon previous work children did on types of lines in Year 3, where they learnt about horizontal and vertical lines, including symmetry and parallel and perpendicular lines.

Before they start this unit, it is expected that children:
- recognise and identify the basic properties of 2D shapes
- use basic vocabulary of shapes to describe 2D shapes
- recognise angles as a turn
- recognise horizontal and vertical lines of symmetry.

ASSESSING MASTERY

Children will demonstrate mastery by being able to recognise and order acute, obtuse and right angles with confidence, explaining how right angles can help them to do so. They will be able to name and describe the different types of triangles and quadrilaterals, clearly explaining the similarities and differences. In the case of quadrilaterals, they will be able to point out where a shape may fit under more than one heading. Children will be able to complete shapes and patterns across lines of symmetry in different orientations and will be able to apply their knowledge and understanding to solve problems.

COMMON MISCONCEPTIONS	STRENGTHENING UNDERSTANDING	GOING DEEPER
Children may incorrectly identify irregular polygons as regular, most commonly an oblong rectangle. They may fail to correctly identify the names of irregular polygons. For example, a 5-sided shape is called a pentagon even if it is not regular. It may look very different to a regular pentagon.	Provide children with opportunities to explore and sort a variety of triangles and polygons, discussing their similarities and differences. Help children to classify the shapes by the number of sides they have, rather than whether or not they look similar to one another.	Children could explore ways of creating different triangles and quadrilaterals by cutting them up or combining them.
Identifying all lines of symmetry can be challenging and some children may only identify those that bisect angles or bisect sides.	Allow children to draw and cut out different types of triangles and quadrilaterals and fold them in order to find the lines of symmetry. Also, provide mirrors so children can see the reflections of complex designs.	

Unit 14: Geometry – angles and 2D shapes

UNIT STARTER PAGES

Talk through the key learning points, mentioned by the characters, and the key vocabulary. Do children have any misconceptions? Do they understand what the vocabulary means? A classroom display showing all of the key information will support children throughout this unit.

STRUCTURES AND REPRESENTATIONS

2D shapes: In this unit, children will learn more about the properties of 2D shapes, including whether they are regular or irregular and about the internal angles of shapes.

Angles: In this unit, children will be introduced to acute, obtuse and right angles.

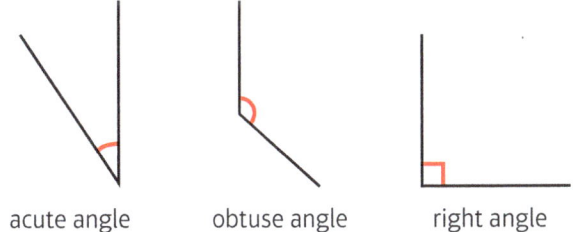

acute angle   obtuse angle   right angle

KEY LANGUAGE

There is some key language that children will need to know as part of the learning in this unit:

- angle, acute, obtuse, right angle, quarter turn, half turn, interior angles, exterior angles
- quadrilateral, square, rectangle, rhombus, parallelogram, trapezium, pentagon, hexagon, octagon, hexadecagon, kite arrowhead, polygon, circle
- triangle, isosceles, equilateral, scalene
- regular, irregular, side length, length, perimeter
- symmetric, symmetrical, symmetry, line of symmetry, horizontal, vertical, diagonal, reflective symmetry, sequence, pattern
- sort, group, compare, order, properties
- shape, vertices, parallel

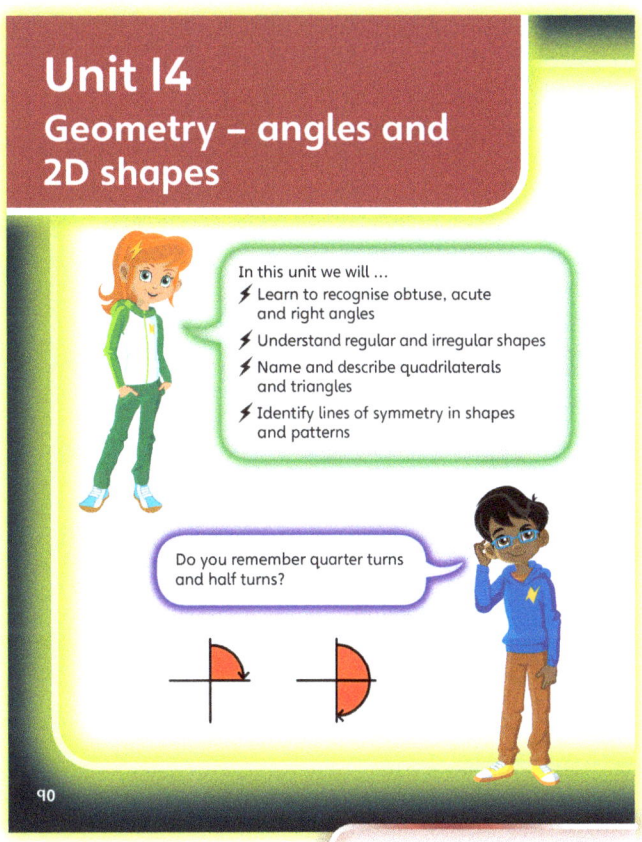

PUPIL TEXTBOOK 4C PAGE 90

PUPIL TEXTBOOK 4C PAGE 91

Unit 14: Geometry – angles and 2D shapes, Lesson 1

Identify angles

Learning focus
In this lesson, children will compare angles and identify acute, obtuse and right angles.

Before you teach
- Are children aware that angles are a measure of a turn around a point?
- How secure are children in describing turns?
- What practical opportunities can you provide for children to explore turns in relation to acute, obtuse and right angles?

NATIONAL CURRICULUM LINKS

Year 4 Geometry – properties of shapes

Identify acute and obtuse angles and compare and order angles up to two right angles by size.

ASSESSING MASTERY

Children can identify right angles as a quarter turn and understand that angles less than a quarter turn are acute and that angles greater than a quarter turn but smaller than a half turn are obtuse. They can begin to apply this knowledge to describing the angles within 2D shapes.

COMMON MISCONCEPTIONS

Children may need support to identify the type of angle when the orientation means that neither line is vertical or horizontal. Ask:
- *What if you rotated the angle so that one line was horizontal (straight across) or vertical (straight up)? Would that make it easier to see what type of angle it is?*

STRENGTHENING UNDERSTANDING

Strengthen children's understanding by providing them with a square or a quarter circle so that they have a right angle that they can physically compare to other angles.

GOING DEEPER

Challenge children by giving them a paper square and asking them to draw two lines that join the opposite corners of the square. Ask: *Can you identify each angle? Are they acute, obtuse or right angles?*

KEY LANGUAGE

In lesson: angle, corner, size, larger, smaller, quarter turn, right angle, half turn, obtuse, acute, clock hand, point, shape, vertices, facing

Other language to be used by the teacher: 2D

STRUCTURES AND REPRESENTATIONS

Angles, clock faces

RESOURCES

Optional: a range of 2D shapes, paper squares, clock faces

 In the eTextbook of this lesson, you will find interactive links to a selection of teaching tools.

Quick recap
Ask children to identify right angles in shapes that they can find around the classroom.

Discover

WAYS OF WORKING Pair work

ASK

- Question 1 a): *Can you see any angles that are the same?*
- Question 1 a): *Do the angles of the bench match any angles in the garden?*
- Question 1 b): *How would you describe the different angles?*

IN FOCUS Question 1 b) encourages children to compare the different angles. Children may not remember the terms acute and obtuse, so encourage children to describe them in relation to the right angles.

PRACTICAL TIPS Get children to stand and make quarter turns in both directions so that they get a 'feel' of what a right angle is. Ask them to make a turn less than a right angle and a turn between a quarter turn and a half turn.

ANSWERS

Question 1 a): The bench can fit in corners a and b.

Question 1 b): Same:
All of the angles measure the turn between two hedges of the garden.

Different:
Angle a is a quarter turn or a right angle.
Angle b is larger than a right angle.
Angle c is smaller than a right angle.

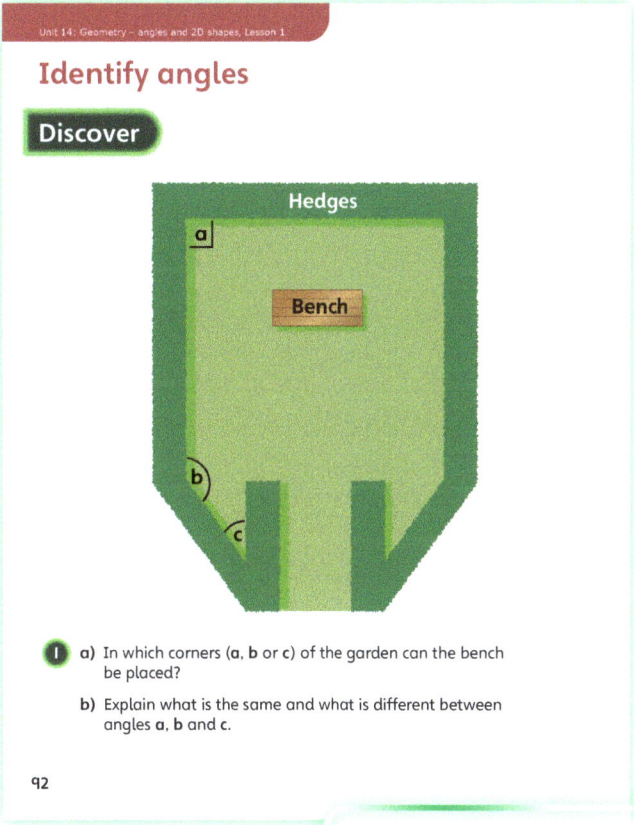

PUPIL TEXTBOOK 4C PAGE 92

Share

WAYS OF WORKING Whole class teacher led

ASK

- Question 1 a): *Why can the bench fit in corner b but not corner c?*
- Questions 1 a) and b): *What can you say about the angles of the bench?*
- Questions 1 a) and b): *Are there any other shapes that have the same angles as the bench?*

IN FOCUS Sparks' comment gives children the vocabulary of obtuse and acute and defines these terms in comparison to a quarter turn. It is important that children understand this definition. Therefore, provide children with the opportunity to compare angles practically with a right angle, for example using the corner of a square as a right angle. Ask: *Can you find any acute or obtuse angles around the classroom?*

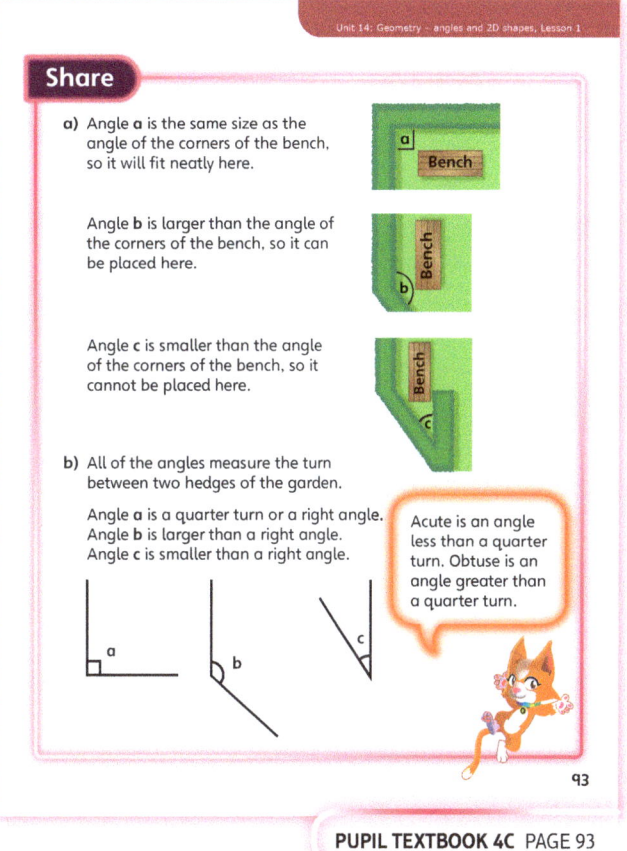

PUPIL TEXTBOOK 4C PAGE 93

Think together

WAYS OF WORKING Whole class teacher led (I do, We do, You do)

ASK

- Question ①: *Can you describe the angles on the bench?*
- Question ② a): *Is an acute angle greater than or less than a right angle?*
- Question ③ a): *If the hour hand stays pointing to 12, which numbers could the minute hand point to so that the clockwise angle between the two hands is acute?*

IN FOCUS For question ③ a), children should assume that the hour hand stays pointing to 12 and the minute hand turns. The angle they should consider is the smaller of the two angles formed between the two hands, since the larger angle will always be a reflex angle (that is, an angle greater than 180°), and children have not learnt about these yet. Children could use clocks to explore this question in order to reinforce their understanding. They will discover that there are two ways that the hands can make a right angle, and various ways that they can make acute or obtuse angles. Some children may give possibilities for obtuse angles that go beyond half a turn. It is important that children understand that obtuse means between a quarter and a half turn.

STRENGTHEN For question ①, provide children with 2D shapes to represent the bench. This enables children to physically compare the angles between the hedges with the angles of the bench.

DEEPEN Explore with children how there are two angles formed between the hands of a clock: the angle moving clockwise and the angle moving anticlockwise. Make sure children can visualise both angles and mark them on a sketch. Ask: *Can both these angles be acute at the same time? Can they both be obtuse? Why not? As one gets bigger, what happens to the the other one?*

ASSESSMENT CHECKPOINT Questions ① and ② will demonstrate whether children can compare angles with a right angle. Question ③ will demonstrate whether children are able to identify acute, obtuse and right angles.

ANSWERS

Question ①: The bench will fit in corners b, c and d.

Question ② a):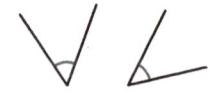

Question ② b):

Question ② c): The right angle is in a).

Question ③ a): i) Numbers 1, 2, 10 and 11 will show an acute turn. ii) Numbers 3 and 9 will show a right angle turn. iii) Numbers 4, 5, 6, 7 and 8 will show an obtuse turn.

Question ③ b): Top: right angle, sides: obtuse angles; bottom: acute angle.

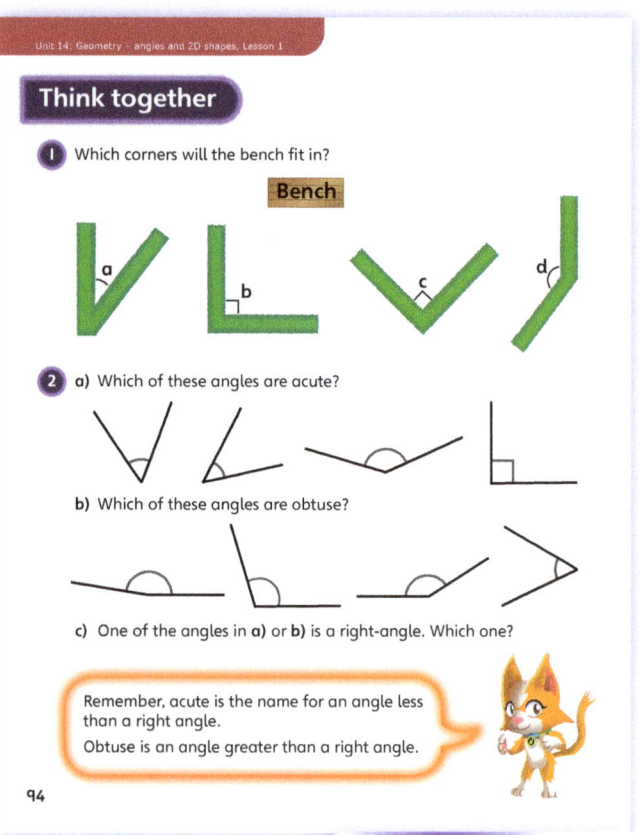

PUPIL TEXTBOOK 4C PAGE 94

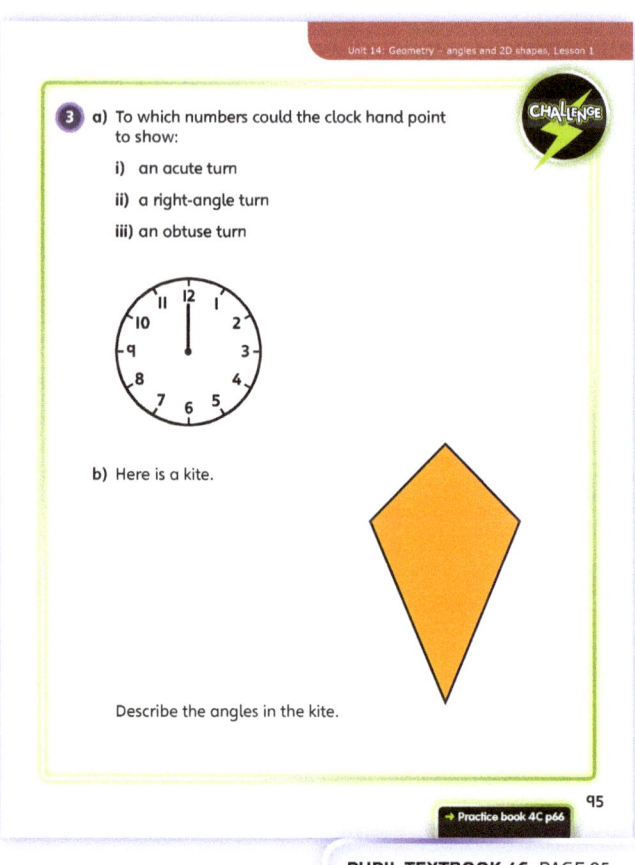

PUPIL TEXTBOOK 4C PAGE 95

Unit 14: Geometry – angles and 2D shapes, Lesson 1

Practice

WAYS OF WORKING Independent thinking

IN FOCUS Question ③ looks at sorting shapes by their types of angles. Children not only need to identify the types of angles in the shapes but also to sort the shapes based on two criteria.

STRENGTHEN Using squared paper, ask children to draw a shape with only right angles, only obtuse angles or only acute angles. They can use a 2D square to check their angles.

DEEPEN Challenge children by providing them with a range of 2D shapes and asking them to sort them based on their angles. Ask: *Can you sort the shapes in different ways?*

ASSESSMENT CHECKPOINT Children should now be confident identifying and drawing acute, obtuse and right angles. Question ③ will demonstrate whether children can identify angles within different 2D shapes.

ANSWERS Answers for the **Practice** part of the lesson can be found in the *Power Maths* online subscription.

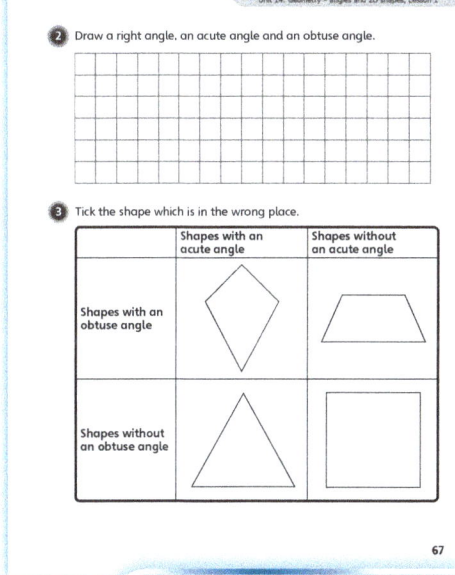

PUPIL PRACTICE BOOK 4C PAGE 66

PUPIL PRACTICE BOOK 4C PAGE 67

Reflect

WAYS OF WORKING Independent thinking

IN FOCUS This section asks children to give a definition for each of the three types of angles, in their own words. This will help to secure their understanding of acute, obtuse and right angles.

ASSESSMENT CHECKPOINT This section will demonstrate if children understand the definitions of acute, obtuse and right angles.

ANSWERS Answers for the **Reflect** part of the lesson can be found in the *Power Maths* online subscription.

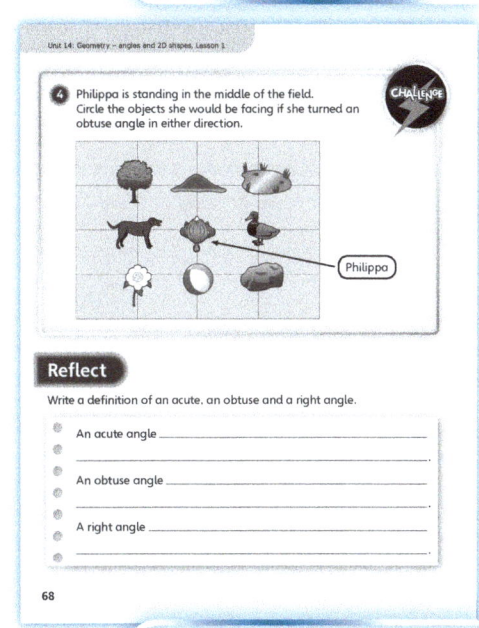

PUPIL PRACTICE BOOK 4C PAGE 68

After the lesson

- Were children able to relate angles to turns around a point?
- Are children secure in identifying the three types of angle?

Unit 14: Geometry – angles and 2D shapes, Lesson 2

Compare and order angles

Learning focus
In this lesson, children will identify acute and obtuse angles, using what they already know about angles. They will compare the sizes of angles and use their comparisons to order them.

Before you teach
- Are children confident at recognising angles inside and outside of a shape?
- Can children reliably identify right angles?

NATIONAL CURRICULUM LINKS

Year 4 Geometry – properties of shapes

Identify acute and obtuse angles and compare and order angles up to two right angles by size.

ASSESSING MASTERY

Children can use what they know about angles to identify acute, obtuse and right angles accurately. They will be able to recognise which angles are larger or smaller than others and use their understanding to put them in ascending or descending order of size.

COMMON MISCONCEPTIONS

Children may think that a right angle is obtuse as it is not smaller than 90°. Ask:
- *What did you call this angle in the previous lesson? Is the angle you are looking at larger or smaller than a right angle?*

STRENGTHENING UNDERSTANDING

Take photos of children holding their arms wide, above their head, at different angles. Ask: *Can you order the pictures from the person who has their arms the widest to the person who has their arms held the least wide?*

GOING DEEPER

Challenge children by giving them a sequence of angles, ordered in ascending or descending order. Take one of the angles out, leaving a missing angle space in the sequence. Ask: *Was the angle I took away acute, obtuse or a right angle?* Ask children to draw the missing angle. To follow on, explain to children that this is not the only angle that could fit into the angle sequence at this point. Challenge children to draw another angle that could fit into the sequence here. The angle they draw could be any size between the two angles on either side of it in the sequence.

KEY LANGUAGE

In lesson: acute, greater, smaller, right angle, larger, obtuse, sort, groups, compare, order, smallest, largest, fewest, most, four-sided, shape, size, interior, pattern, ascending

Other language to be used by the teacher: descending, triangle, equilateral triangle, pentagon, hexagon, octagon, rectangle, polygon

STRUCTURES AND REPRESENTATIONS

Angles, 2D shapes

RESOURCES

Optional: 2D shapes, rulers, set squares

 In the eTextbook of this lesson, you will find interactive links to a selection of teaching tools.

Quick recap
Ask children to identify acute and obtuse angles in items that they can find around the classroom.

Unit 14: Geometry – angles and 2D shapes, Lesson 2

Discover

WAYS OF WORKING Pair work

ASK

- Question 1 a): *How can you tell which ramp will allow for the higher jump?*
- Question 1 a): *What is the same and what is different about the two ramps?*
- Question 1 a): *Can you see any other angles in the pictures?*
- Question 1 b): *Would Emma's plank still work as a ramp if the box it leans on is taller than Emma? What about if the plank is pointing directly upwards?*

IN FOCUS Use this opportunity to remind children of right angles and discuss how the ramps they can see in the picture are similar and different to the angles they have met before. Encourage children to recognise how the ramps are set to smaller angles than a right angle.

PRACTICAL TIPS Give children the opportunity to create ramps as shown in the picture. This could also be linked to a science or PE lesson.

ANSWERS

Question 1 a): Emma's ramp will allow for the higher jump.

Question 1 b): A ramp set at a right angle would not work.

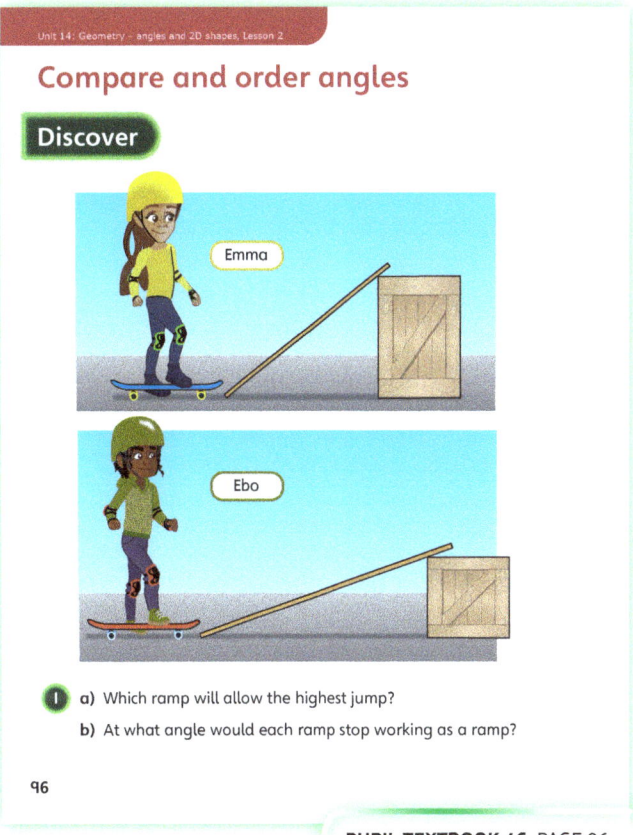

PUPIL TEXTBOOK 4C PAGE 96

Share

WAYS OF WORKING Whole class teacher led

ASK

- Question 1 a): *What part of the ramp did you look at to find the angle?*
- Question 1 a): *How did you know which angle was bigger?*
- Question 1 a): *Why will a bigger angle give the child a higher jump?*
- Question 1 b): *Why would a right angle not function as a ramp?*
- Question 1 b): *Can you explain why an obtuse angle will work as a ramp in the opposite direction?*

IN FOCUS It will be important in this part of the lesson to make sure children are able to explain the properties of each of the three types of angles they are studying: acute, obtuse and right angles. Ensure that children understand that an obtuse angle is greater than a right angle but less than a straight line.

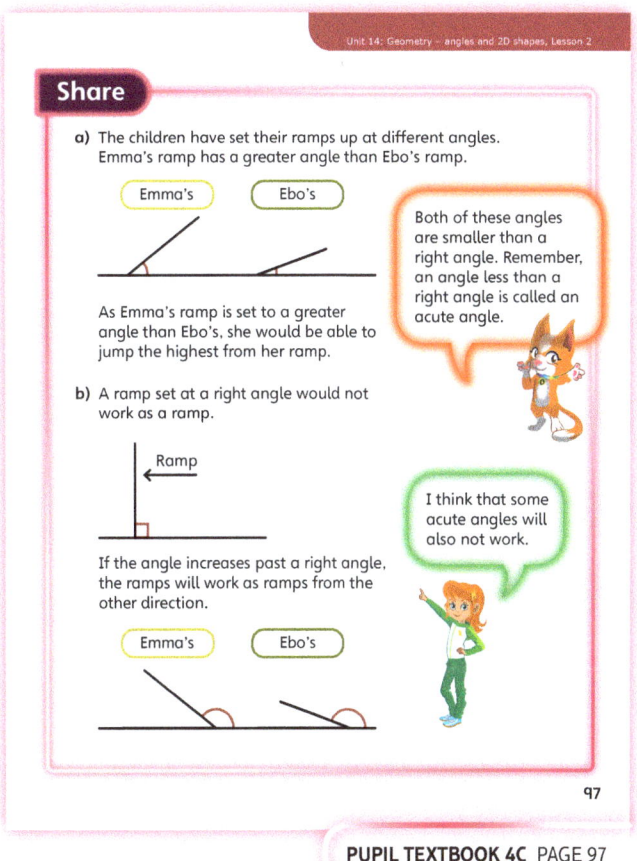

PUPIL TEXTBOOK 4C PAGE 97

131

Unit 14: Geometry – angles and 2D shapes, Lesson 2

Think together

WAYS OF WORKING Whole class teacher led (I do, We do, You do)

ASK
- Question ❶: *What types of angles can you see?*
- Question ❶: *How will you know which are acute angles, which are obtuse angles and which are right angles?*
- Question ❷: *Which angles will be easiest to sort first?*
- Question ❸: *Which angles will you look at in each shape?*

IN FOCUS At this point in the lesson, children begin to order angles based on size. Use questions ❶ and ❷ to discuss how the task of ordering angles can be broken down into two smaller steps, first sorting into type, then ordering them accurately.

STRENGTHEN To help children find which angles are larger or smaller than a right angle, offer them set squares to use. Ask: *How can you use the right angle on the set square to help you find acute and obtuse angles?*

DEEPEN Question ❸ deepens children's understanding of angles within shapes. Children should recognise how angles found in shapes can be acute, obtuse or right angles. Challenge children by asking questions such as: *Are all the obtuse angles in each of the shapes the same? What would happen to the shape you drew if you used larger acute angles? What about smaller?*

ASSESSMENT CHECKPOINT Children should be able to use their understanding of right angles to identify whether they are looking at an acute or an obtuse angle. Through observation, they should be able to order angles in ascending and descending order with more confidence.

ANSWERS

Question ❶ a): The first angle is the smaller angle.

Question ❶ b): The second angle is the larger angle.

Question ❶ c): The first angle is the smaller angle.

Question ❷: d, a, c, b

Question ❸ a): Fewest to most acute angles: C, A, B
Fewest to most right angles: C, B, A
Fewest to most obtuse angles: B, A, C

Question ❸ b): Bottom left angle, top angle, right angle

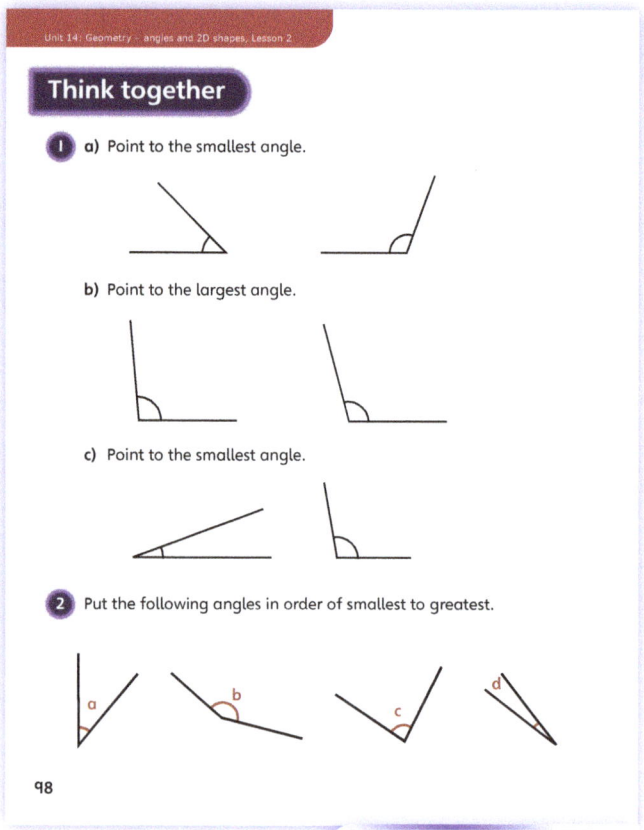

PUPIL TEXTBOOK 4C PAGE 98

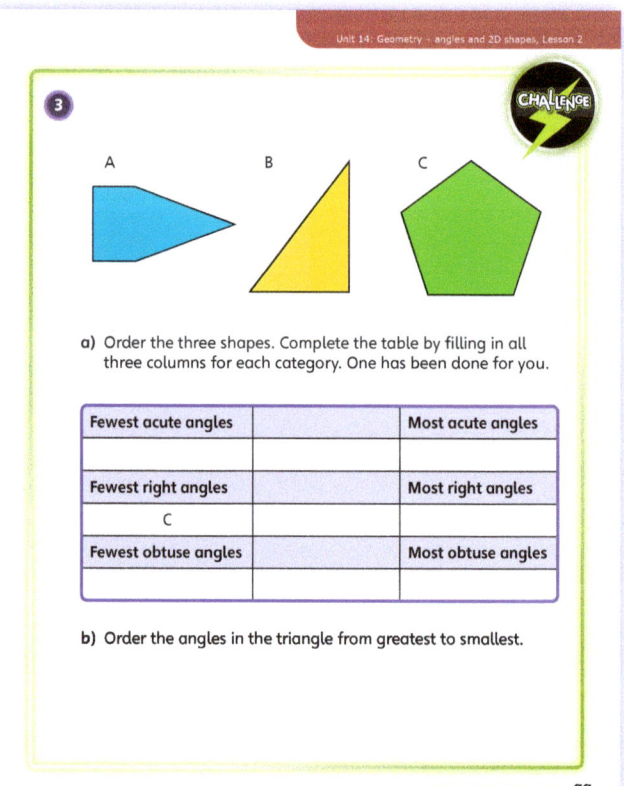

PUPIL TEXTBOOK 4C PAGE 99

Unit 14: Geometry – angles and 2D shapes, Lesson 2

Practice

WAYS OF WORKING Independent thinking

IN FOCUS In question ❶, children have to determine which angle is either the smaller or the larger angle by sight. In each part, this is made slightly more tricky by the fact that the angles are the same type (that is, they are either both acute or both obtuse angles). Encourage children to look closely at the angle and read each question part carefully to make sure they know whether to look for the smallest or the largest angle. In questions ❷ and ❸, children extend this concept to ordering three or four angles by size. You might encourage children to begin by identifying acute angles, right angles and obtuse angles to help them order by size. In question ❹, children's answers will vary, but the angles should be in ascending order and ideally include an acute angle, a right angle and an obtuse angle.

STRENGTHEN If children are finding it difficult to compare the angles by sight in questions ❷ and ❸, ask: *Are there any angles you can recognise easily? How can you use those angles to help you begin to order the rest?*

DEEPEN In question ❺, children are given the opportunity to make a link between the number of sides of a regular polygon and the size of its interior angles. Ensure children understand that an interior angle is one formed inside a shape at a vertex. Help children to see that the greater the number of sides, the greater the interior angle. Draw the following shapes on the board: a hexagon, an octagon (8 sides), a decagon (10 sides), and a 20-sided shape. Ask: *As the number of sides increases, what do these shapes start to look like?* Establish that they look more like circles as the number of sides increases. Informally, children can think of a circle as a shape with infinitely many sides. The sizes of the interior angles never increase to become greater than an obtuse angle.

ASSESSMENT CHECKPOINT Children should be able to identify and order acute, obtuse and right angles with confidence. They should be able to arrange angles fluently in both ascending and descending order and be able to explain clearly how their understanding of right angles can help them.

ANSWERS Answers for the **Practice** part of the lesson can be found in the *Power Maths* online subscription.

Reflect

WAYS OF WORKING Independent thinking or pair work

IN FOCUS Give children time to consider how a right angle helps separate obtuse angles from acute angles. If they have a right-angle template on a piece of card, they can always line it up against an angle to determine whether the angle is smaller or larger than a right angle. They should discuss this with a partner. Once they have done so, children should write their thoughts and share their ideas with the class.

ASSESSMENT CHECKPOINT Children should be demonstrating their understanding that the right angle can be used as a reference point to spot acute and obtuse angles easily.

ANSWERS Answers for the **Reflect** part of the lesson can be found in the *Power Maths* online subscription.

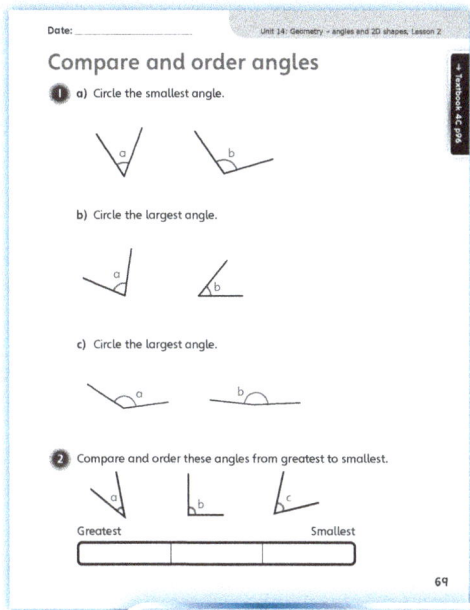

PUPIL PRACTICE BOOK 4C PAGE 69

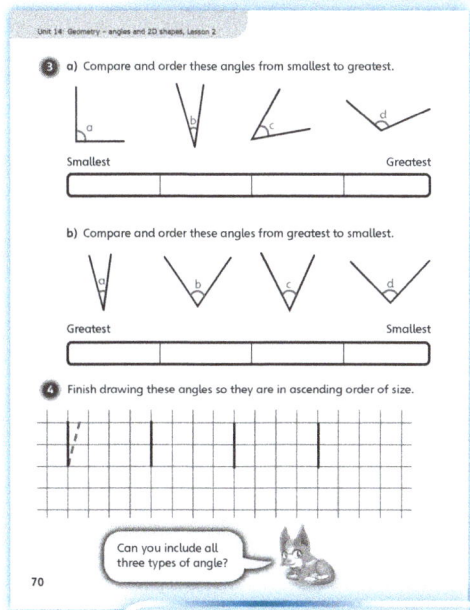

PUPIL PRACTICE BOOK 4C PAGE 70

PUPIL PRACTICE BOOK 4C PAGE 71

After the lesson

- Are children confident with identifying all three types of angles?
- Have children recognised the importance of working systematically when ordering angles?

Unit 14: Geometry – angles and 2D shapes, Lesson 3

Triangles

Learning focus
In this lesson, children will identify the three different types of triangles. They will understand the properties of scalene, isosceles and equilateral triangles in relation to their angles and the length of their sides.

Before you teach
- What knowledge do children have of triangles?
- How secure are children in comparing angles?

NATIONAL CURRICULUM LINKS

Year 4 Geometry – properties of shapes

Compare and classify geometric shapes, including quadrilaterals and triangles, based on their properties and sizes.

ASSESSING MASTERY

Children can identify and classify scalene, isosceles and equilateral triangles. They can identify that equilateral triangles have three sides that are the same length and three angles that are the same size; that isosceles triangles have two sides that are the same length and two angles that are the same size; and that scalene triangles have three sides of different lengths and three angles of different sizes.

COMMON MISCONCEPTIONS

Children may need support to identify the different types of triangles when their orientation is unfamiliar. Ask:
- *Is it easier if you draw the shape and turn it around? Are the sides of the triangle all the same length? Are the interior angles of this triangle all the same?*

STRENGTHENING UNDERSTANDING

Provide children with a range of different triangles that they can sort, either drawn on paper as 2D shapes or photos of shapes. Discuss with children how they might sort them (for example: equilateral, isosceles or scalene; right-angled or non-right-angled). For example, hold up a scalene triangle and ask: *How many other triangles can you find that have three sides all of different lengths?*

GOING DEEPER

Challenge children by giving them a large equilateral triangle (made out of paper) and then asking: *How many different triangles can you find by folding or cutting the paper?*

KEY LANGUAGE

In lesson: classify, triangle, similar, different, isosceles, scalene, equilateral, sides, angles, acute, quarter turn, geoboard, rotated, 90°, equal

Other language to be used by the teacher: longer, shorter, obtuse, half turn, right angle

STRUCTURES AND REPRESENTATIONS

2D shapes

RESOURCES

Optional: a range of different triangles, 2D shapes

 In the eTextbook of this lesson, you will find interactive links to a selection of teaching tools.

Quick recap

Ask children to draw five different examples of triangles. They should then compare their triangles with a partner's, discussing what is the same and what is different. Challenge children to draw an example of a shape that some people might think looks like a triangle but actually is not a triangle. (This is called a non-example, such as an arrowhead shape.)

Unit 14: Geometry – angles and 2D shapes, Lesson 3

Discover

WAYS OF WORKING Pair work

ASK

- Question ❶ a): *Does the shape Ambika makes have the same number of sides as the shape Lee makes? What do you call a 3-sided shape?*
- Question ❶ b): *What can you tell me about the side lengths of Ambika's triangle? How many sides are the same length? What about in Lee's triangle?*
- Question ❶ b): *What can you tell me about the angles in Ambika's triangle/Lee's triangle?*

IN FOCUS Question ❶ b) encourages children to compare the triangles and think about their properties. Prompt children, if necessary, to look at the lengths of the sides and the sizes of the interior angles. This will lay the groundwork for identifying different types of triangles.

PRACTICAL TIPS Provide children with square and rectangular pieces of paper so that they can carry out the folding themselves. They will then be able to directly compare the two triangles.

ANSWERS

Question ❶ a): Ambika and Lee have made triangles.

Question ❶ b): Same: Both triangles have a right angle. Different: When folded, the square makes a triangle that has two equal sides and two equal angles (an isosceles triangle) and the rectangle makes a triangle that has three unequal sides and three unequal angles (a scalene triangle).

PUPIL TEXTBOOK 4C PAGE 100

Share

WAYS OF WORKING Whole class teacher led

ASK

- Question ❶ a): *What type of triangle would you make if you folded the square piece of paper in half a second time?*
- Question ❶ a): *Is it possible to make an equilateral triangle from either piece of paper?*
- Question ❶ b): *Could you draw a third triangle that is different to the two in the question?*

IN FOCUS Question ❶ b) provides definitions of scalene and isosceles triangles. Ensure children understand these definitions. If necessary, get children to measure the sides of the triangles as proof. Give them two identical isosceles triangles and ask them to place one on top of the other. Then, ask them to flip the top triangle over and place it on top of the bottom triangle again. In this way, they should be able to verify that the two base angles of an isosceles triangle are equal.

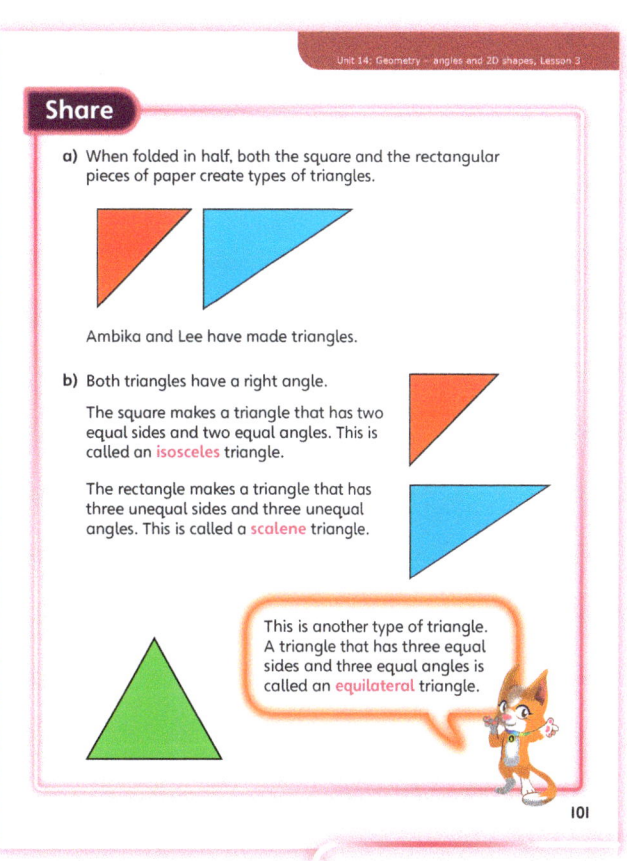

PUPIL TEXTBOOK 4C PAGE 101

135

Unit 14: Geometry – angles and 2D shapes, Lesson 3

Think together

WAYS OF WORKING Whole class teacher led (I do, We do, You do)

ASK

- Question ❶: *Do all isosceles/scalene triangles look the same?*
- Question ❸ a): *How do you know which type of triangle you have created?*
- Questions ❸ a) and b): *How can you be sure that all of your triangles are different?*

IN FOCUS Question ❷ presents children with isosceles triangles that look different both in orientation and in the size of their angles. It is important to highlight that an isosceles triangle is only defined by two equal sides and two equal angles and that therefore isosceles triangles can look quite different from each other. In question ❸, encourage children to make sure that they are not simply creating two of the same triangle in different orientations. Encourage children to turn their boards around and see if they have made a triangle before. Ask: *What can you tell me about the side lengths of this triangle that makes it different to other triangles you made?* Encourage children to work systematically and record their results.

STRENGTHEN Provide children with a range of triangles that they can explore and sort. In order to compare angles within a triangle, children can draw around one triangle and then see if any of the angles match by comparing directly. For question ❶, children could measure the lengths of the sides using a ruler to help determine what type of triangle they are looking at.

DEEPEN After completing question ❸, encourage children to classify the different triangles that they found; for example, equilateral isosceles or scalene, right-angled or non-right-angled. Ask: *Can you join triangles together to make a new triangle? How many equilateral triangles are needed to make a larger equilateral triangle?*

ASSESSMENT CHECKPOINT Children should be able to use a ruler to determine whether the three sides of a triangle are of different lengths, tell the difference between an acute angle and an obtuse angle, and understand the properties of scalene, isosceles and equilateral triangles.

ANSWERS

Question ❶: C is a scalene triangle

Question ❷: A, C and E have three acute angles.

Question ❸ a): There are 8 different triangles that can be made. Each triangle should be different in size or angles and/or length of sides, not just in orientation.

Question ❸ b): Discuss suggestions for how children know as a class. The easiest way would be to draw a number of 3 × 3 geoboards on squared paper and draw one triangle on each, until it is not possible to find any more.

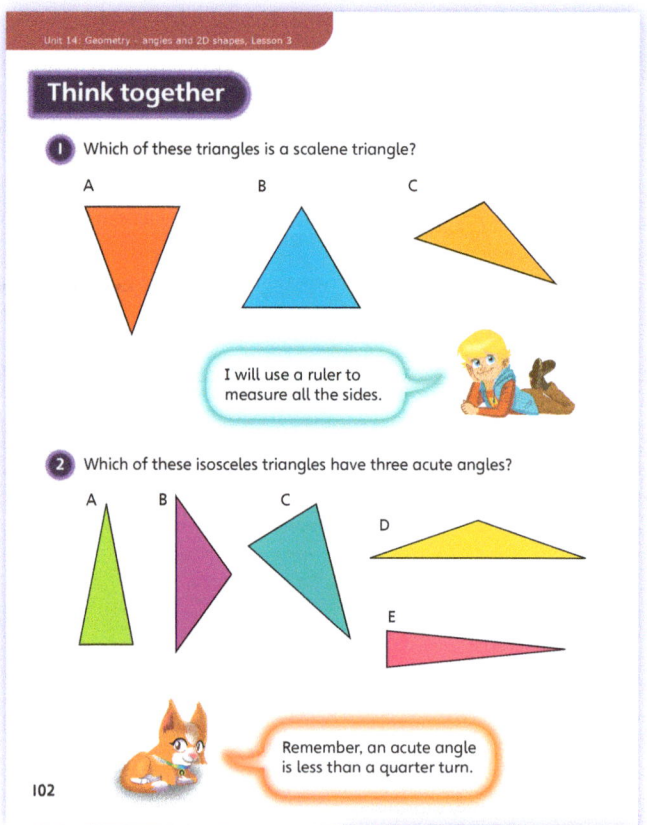

PUPIL TEXTBOOK 4C PAGE 102

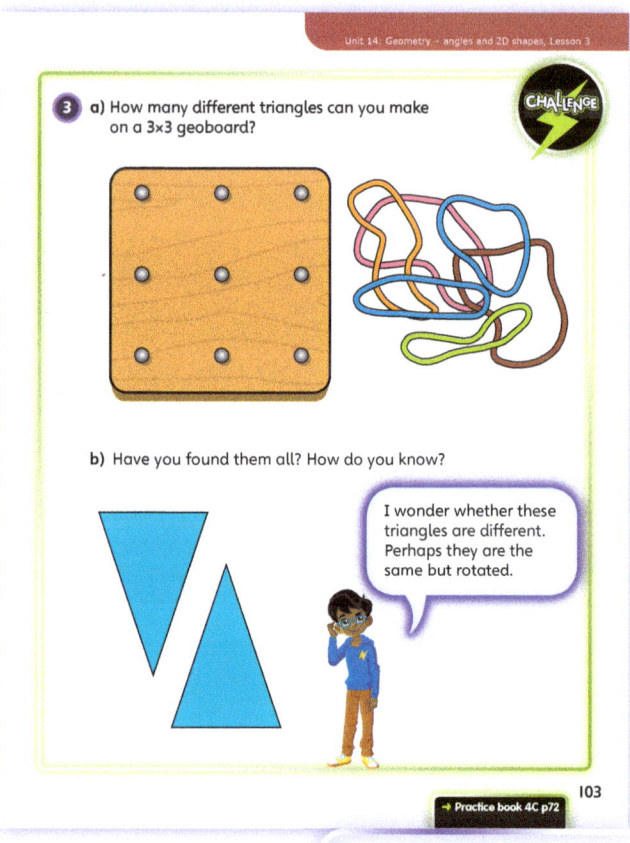

PUPIL TEXTBOOK 4C PAGE 103

Unit 14: Geometry – angles and 2D shapes, Lesson 3

Practice

WAYS OF WORKING Independent thinking

IN FOCUS Question 2 asks children to create a decorative pattern by identifying and shading different types of triangle. They could start by identifying which triangles are identical. Encourage them to define the features of each triangle as they shade them, in order to ensure that they are not just guessing.

In question 4, ensure children do not only look at the smallest types of triangle in the pentagon, but look also at the larger triangles that overlap the smaller triangles. Because of the symmetry of the shape (which will be covered later in the unit), they might also be able to identify which triangles are identical within the pattern, and informally explain why they are identical.

STRENGTHEN Provide children with examples of each type of triangle along with labels and definitions to refer to. They could look around their environment to try to find examples of each type of triangle.

DEEPEN To extend question 4, give children a range of 2D shapes to draw around. Ask: *Which shapes can be divided like the pentagon in the question to create scalene/isosceles/equilateral triangles?*

THINK DIFFERENTLY Question 3 requires children to visualise the types of triangles required. They need to reason that, in order to create an isosceles triangle, they will need to draw lines from the midpoint of one side of the square to the two opposite corners of the square. Children need to have a secure understanding of what makes a triangle an isosceles triangle in order to solve this problem.

ASSESSMENT CHECKPOINT Question 1 will demonstrate whether children can identify equilateral, isosceles and scalene triangles. Question 2 will demonstrate whether children are able to define the types of triangles, to give them the correct properties, and to identify triangles with different dimensions and in different orientations.

ANSWERS Answers for the **Practice** part of the lesson can be found in the *Power Maths* online subscription.

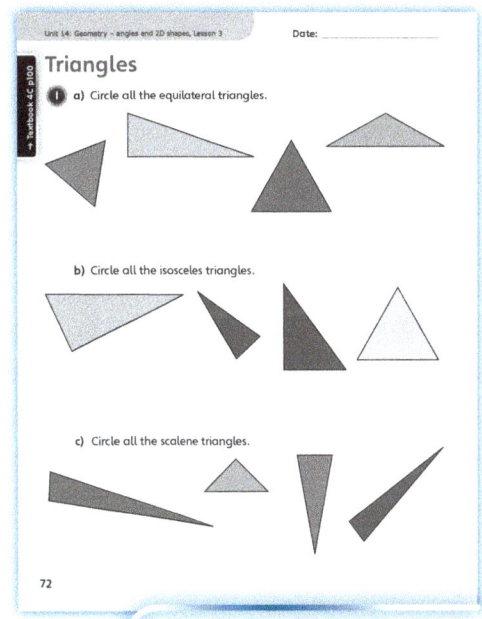

PUPIL PRACTICE BOOK 4C PAGE 72

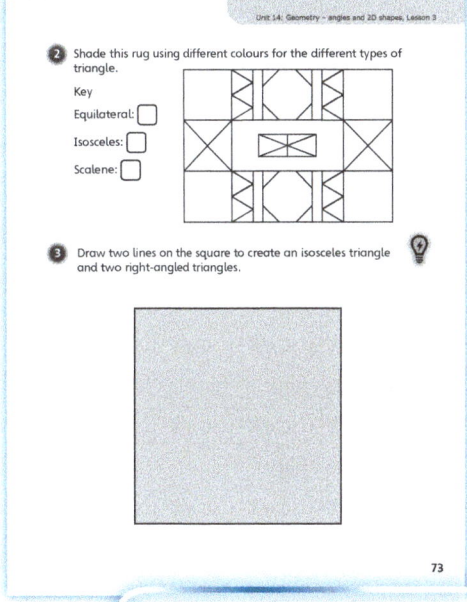

PUPIL PRACTICE BOOK 4C PAGE 73

Reflect

WAYS OF WORKING Pair work

IN FOCUS This section prompts children to discuss the properties of the different types of triangles. This will consolidate their learning from this lesson, or help to identify any misconceptions about the properties of scalene, isosceles and equilateral triangles.

ASSESSMENT CHECKPOINT This section will determine whether children are secure in their understanding of the definitions of each type of triangle.

ANSWERS Answers for the **Reflect** part of the lesson can be found in the *Power Maths* online subscription.

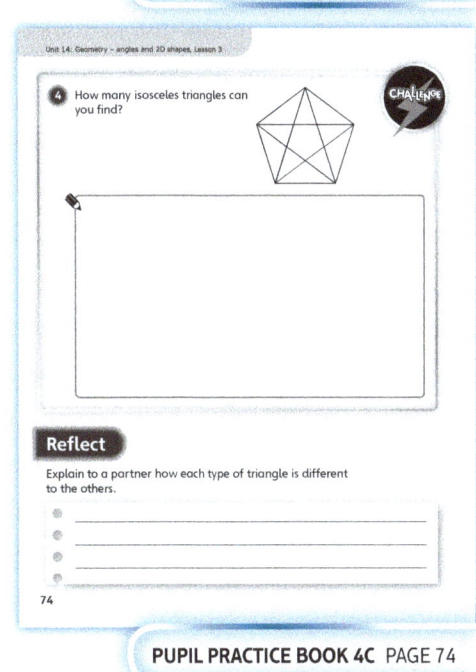

PUPIL PRACTICE BOOK 4C PAGE 74

After the lesson

- Do children have a secure understanding of the differences between the three types of triangles?
- How can you link the learning from this lesson to the next lesson on quadrilaterals?

Unit 14: Geometry – angles and 2D shapes, Lesson 4

Quadrilaterals

Learning focus
In this lesson, children will name, describe and identify quadrilaterals, recognising their similarities and differences. They will use their knowledge to classify and compare quadrilaterals.

Before you teach
- What manipulatives could you provide beyond plastic 2D shapes to help children visualise quadrilaterals?
- How will you link this lesson to children's learning about angles?

NATIONAL CURRICULUM LINKS

Year 4 Geometry – properties of shapes

Compare and classify geometric shapes, including quadrilaterals and triangles, based on their properties and sizes.

ASSESSING MASTERY

Children can confidently identify quadrilaterals, giving each their specific name and describing their properties. They can explain how different quadrilaterals are similar and how they are different, and can use this understanding to solve mathematical problems.

COMMON MISCONCEPTIONS

Children may assume that the word 'quadrilateral' is the name of only one shape. Create a visual reminder, such as a wall display, showing the quadrilaterals children will be studying. Ask:
- *What is similar about all these shapes? What is different?*

STRENGTHENING UNDERSTANDING

Give children a large loop of string. In groups of 4 to 6, ask children to create different four-sided shapes with the loop of string, holding it taut between them. Ask: *Can you draw each shape you make? What do you notice is similar and what is different about your shapes?*

GOING DEEPER

Encourage children to investigate different kinds of quadrilaterals. For example, ask: *Can you find a quadrilateral that only has acute interior angles? Can you find a quadrilateral that only has obtuse interior angles? If you draw two lines through a quadrilateral, what types of triangles can you find?*

KEY LANGUAGE

In lesson: classify, compare, quadrilateral, regular, properties, different, sides, angles, 2D, rhombus, **interior angles**, square, irregular, equal, unequal, parallelogram, parallel, distance, trapezium, sorting circle, rectangle

Other language to be used by the teacher: same, kite, polygon

STRUCTURES AND REPRESENTATIONS

2D shapes

RESOURCES

Optional: 2D shapes, geoboards with elastic bands, geostrip kit

 In the eTextbook of this lesson, you will find interactive links to a selection of teaching tools.

Quick recap
Challenge children to draw three different examples of four-sided shapes. Ask: *Can you name all of your shapes?*

Unit 14: Geometry – angles and 2D shapes, Lesson 4

Discover

WAYS OF WORKING Pair work

ASK
- Question 1 a): *What is the same about the shapes Olivia has made? What is different about them?*
- Question 1 b): *Could she have made any different four-sided shapes?*
- Question 1 b): *Are there any four-sided shapes you already know? Are there any in the picture that you don't recognise?*

IN FOCUS During this part of the lesson it will be important, through discussion, to give children the opportunity to generalise about quadrilaterals. Using the practical tips below will help scaffold these generalisations.

PRACTICAL TIPS Provide children with geostrips or geoboards to create different four-sided shapes. Once they have made two or three shapes, ask: *Can you describe what is similar and what is different about these shapes? Can you compare them with a partner's shapes and describe the similarities and differences?*

ANSWERS

Question 1 a): Olivia's shapes all have four sides but each has different angles.

Question 1 b): A regular quadrilateral with four sides and four angles is a square. The only regular quadrilateral Olivia has is this rectangle:

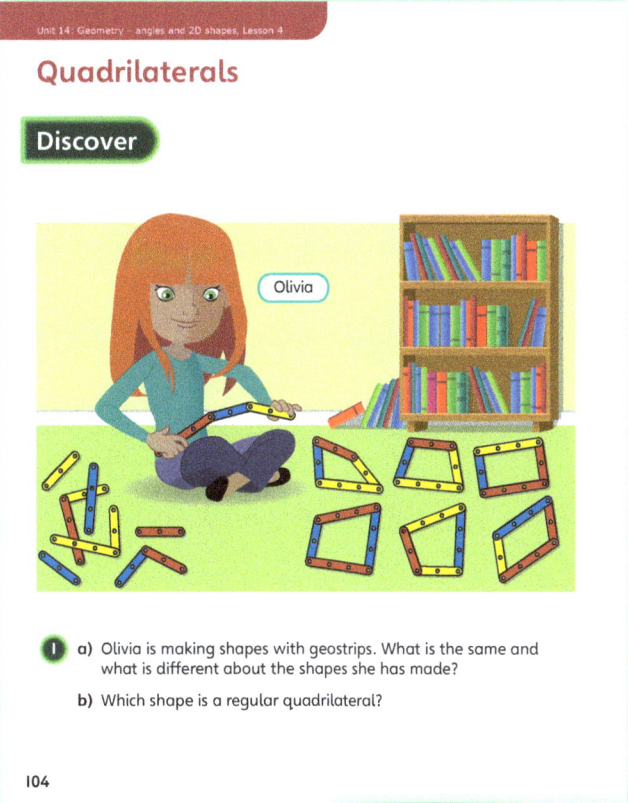

PUPIL TEXTBOOK 4C PAGE 104

Share

WAYS OF WORKING Whole class teacher led

ASK
- Question 1 a): *What is the same about all the sides in every quadrilateral? What is different?*
- Question 1 a): *What is the same about all the angles in a quadrilateral? What is different?*
- Question 1 b): *How is a rhombus different to a square? How is it similar?*
- Question 1 b): *Which quadrilaterals are regular and which are irregular? How do you know?*

IN FOCUS Use this part of the lesson to discuss further the features of the quadrilaterals children have seen or made. Discuss how they each fit with the generalisations children made in the **Discover** section of the lesson. It will be interesting for children to discuss which quadrilaterals are regular and irregular, and discover that a square is the only regular quadrilateral.

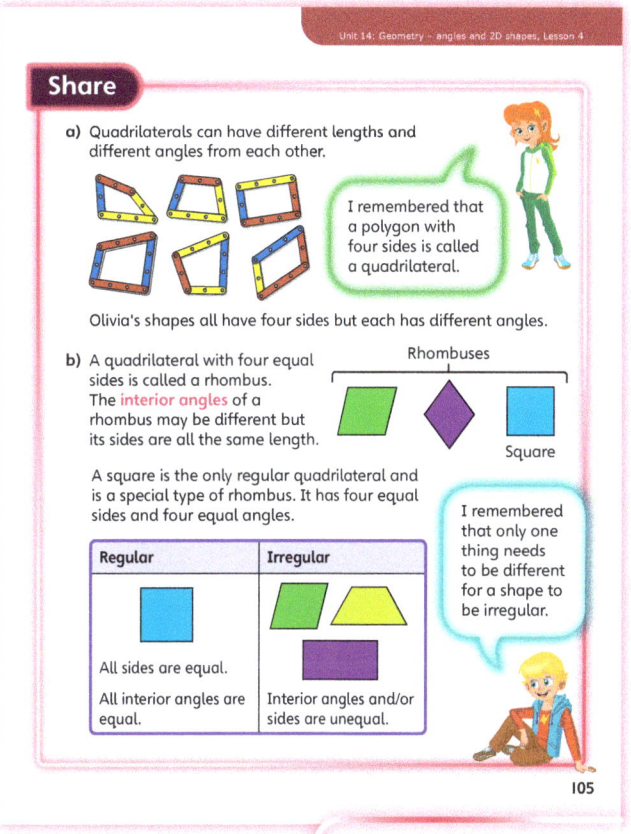

PUPIL TEXTBOOK 4C PAGE 105

139

Unit 14: Geometry – angles and 2D shapes, Lesson 4

Think together

WAYS OF WORKING Whole class teacher led (I do, We do, You do)

ASK
- Question ❶: *What is important about parallel lines?*
- Question ❶: *How can you identify parallel sides?*
- Question ❷: *How many different trapeziums can you draw?*
- Questions ❸ a) and b): *What quadrilaterals have a right angle? Can you find them all?*

IN FOCUS Throughout the activities in this section of the lesson, it will be beneficial to give children the opportunity to explore and create the shapes they are studying using geoboards and/or geostrips.

STRENGTHEN For question ❷, it may help to offer children pictures of different quadrilaterals. Ask: *Which of these quadrilaterals are trapeziums? Can you use the pictures to help you draw your own trapezium?*

DEEPEN When working on question ❸ b), children who have successfully completed the sorting circle could be encouraged to come up with another criterion for a third circle or alternatively, three new criteria. Having done so, they could give their new sorting circle to a partner to sort their quadrilaterals into.

ASSESSMENT CHECKPOINT At this point in the unit, children should recognise quadrilaterals as shapes with four sides and four angles. They should recognise that there are many different types of quadrilaterals and should be able to name some of them with more confidence.

ANSWERS

Question ❶: A, C and D are parallelograms.

Question ❷: Children should accurately draw a different trapezium.

Question ❸ a): Children should be able to create all the quadrilaterals they have studied so far.

Question ❸ b): The quadrilaterals the children have created in part a) should be sorted correctly into the sorting circles.

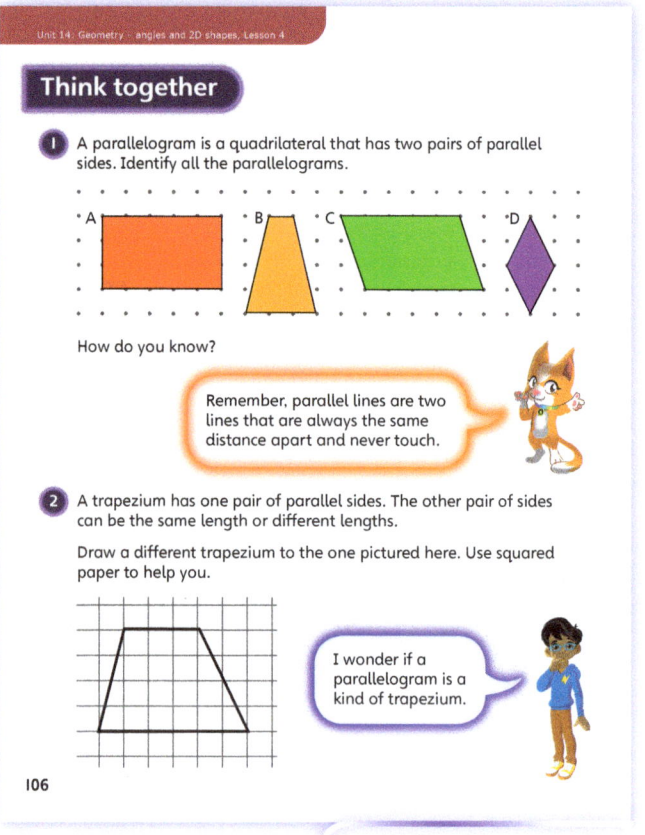

PUPIL TEXTBOOK 4C PAGE 106

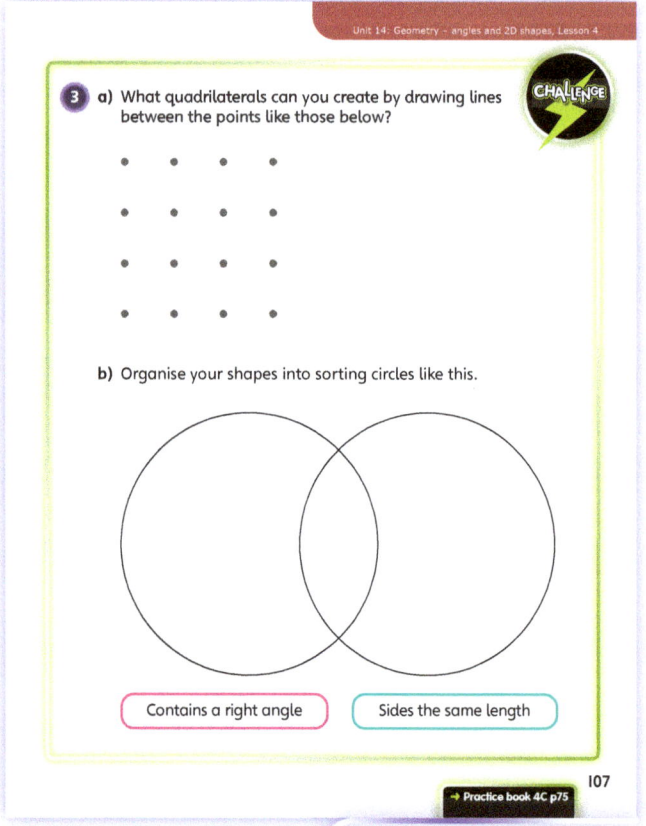

PUPIL TEXTBOOK 4C PAGE 107

Unit 14: Geometry – angles and 2D shapes, Lesson 4

Practice

WAYS OF WORKING Independent thinking

IN FOCUS While solving all the problems in this section of the lesson, ask children to name the shapes they see in each question or those they are drawing themselves. Discuss the properties of each shape and encourage children to link them to the appropriate mathematical shape name.

STRENGTHEN If children have difficulty drawing the quadrilaterals in questions ② and ④ using isometric paper, offer them square dotted paper to help them draw the shapes more easily. Reinforce children's understanding by continuing to encourage them to describe and name each quadrilateral they draw.

DEEPEN If children solve question ④, their learning could be deepened by asking them to create similar challenges for a partner. Ask: *What is the fewest number of clues you can give to someone for them to be able to successfully guess and draw a rhombus?*

ASSESSMENT CHECKPOINT Children should be able to name and describe the different types of quadrilaterals more confidently. They should be able to point out and explain why some quadrilaterals can be categorised under more than one name, for example a square could also be classed as a rhombus, a rectangle or a parallelogram.

ANSWERS Answers for the **Practice** part of the lesson can be found in the *Power Maths* online subscription.

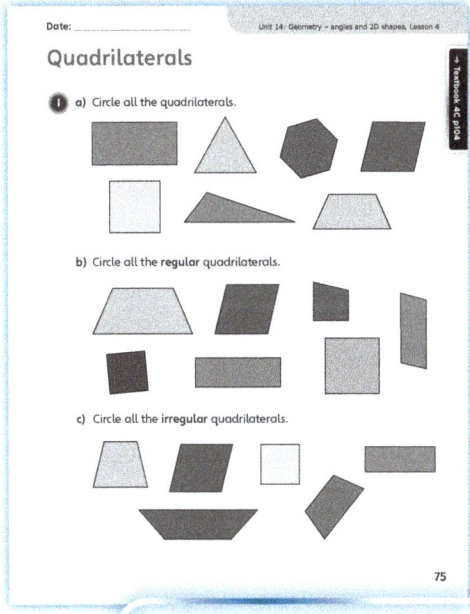

PUPIL PRACTICE BOOK 4C PAGE 75

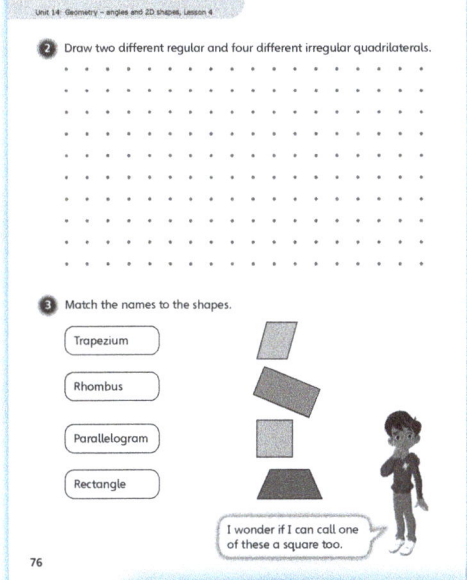

PUPIL PRACTICE BOOK 4C PAGE 76

Reflect

WAYS OF WORKING Pair work

IN FOCUS Give children time to discuss this question. Ask: *Are there any other instances of this kind of scenario that can happen with different quadrilaterals?* If children come up with other examples, encourage them to offer proof to support their ideas.

ASSESSMENT CHECKPOINT Children should be able to explain how the properties of one type of quadrilateral may encompass that of another type of quadrilateral.

ANSWERS Answers for the **Reflect** part of the lesson can be found in the *Power Maths* online subscription.

After the lesson

- How confident are children at naming all the types of quadrilaterals?
- What support will you offer for those children who are still developing their understanding of quadrilateral names and properties?

PUPIL PRACTICE BOOK 4C PAGE 77

Unit 14: Geometry – angles and 2D shapes, Lesson 5

Polygons

Learning focus

In this lesson, children will recognise the similarities and differences between regular and irregular polygons. They will use this vocabulary to help inform their reasoning about 2D shapes.

Before you teach

- How will you ensure that children recognise that they are studying the interior angles of shapes?
- What practical opportunities to find and compare regular and irregular shapes will you provide?

NATIONAL CURRICULUM LINKS

Year 4 Geometry – properties of shapes

Compare and classify geometric shapes, including quadrilaterals and triangles, based on their properties and sizes.

ASSESSING MASTERY

Children can reliably identify regular and irregular shapes. They can explain fluently how the angles and side lengths can make a shape regular or irregular and can explain how only one property needs to be different for a shape to be classed as irregular.

COMMON MISCONCEPTIONS

Children may muddle interior and exterior angles when deciding if a shape is regular or not. Ask:
- *Which angles in a 2D shape have you been looking at? The ones on the inside or outside?*

When studying a shape with an interior angle that is larger than 180° but less than 360°, children may use the exterior angle instead as it will be smaller and more recognisable to them. Ask:
- *Where in the shape do the angles you have been comparing appear? On the inside or outside?*

STRENGTHENING UNDERSTANDING

Before learning the mathematical vocabulary introduced in this lesson, support children by asking them to organise shapes into different categories. For example, ask: *Can you find all the six-sided shapes? What other name do you know for six-sided shapes? What is the same and what is different about these shapes?*

GOING DEEPER

Children should use their learning from Lesson 2 to deepen their understanding in this lesson. Challenge them to draw an irregular hexagon with four acute angles, one obtuse angle and one right angle.

KEY LANGUAGE

In lesson: regular, irregular, hexagonal, hexagon, side length, interior angles, equal, different, 2D

Other language to be used by the teacher: isometric dots, exterior angles, polygon

STRUCTURES AND REPRESENTATIONS

2D shapes

RESOURCES

Optional: 2D shapes, rulers

 In the eTextbook of this lesson, you will find interactive links to a selection of teaching tools.

Quick recap

Explore 2D shapes together as a class. Ask: *How many different 2D shapes can you draw and name?*

Unit 14: Geometry – angles and 2D shapes, Lesson 5

Discover

WAYS OF WORKING Pair work

ASK

- Question 1 a): *What shape tents are on the campsite?*
- Question 1 a): *How do you know that there is more than one hexagon?*

IN FOCUS Encourage children to notice that there are two hexagonal tents. Ask children to convince each other that there are definitely two hexagons. Discuss with children how they can be sure.

PRACTICAL TIPS Encourage children to find as many different versions of one shape around the room as they can. Ask: *Can you find all the pentagons? What do you notice is the same and what is different about these shapes?* Children could be encouraged to take photos of the shapes to sort later.

ANSWERS

Question 1 a): The tent Richard remembers could have been either tent C or D.

Question 1 b): The two hexagons are similar as they both have six sides and six angles. They are different because their side lengths and interior angles are different sizes. One is an irregular hexagon and one is a regular hexagon.

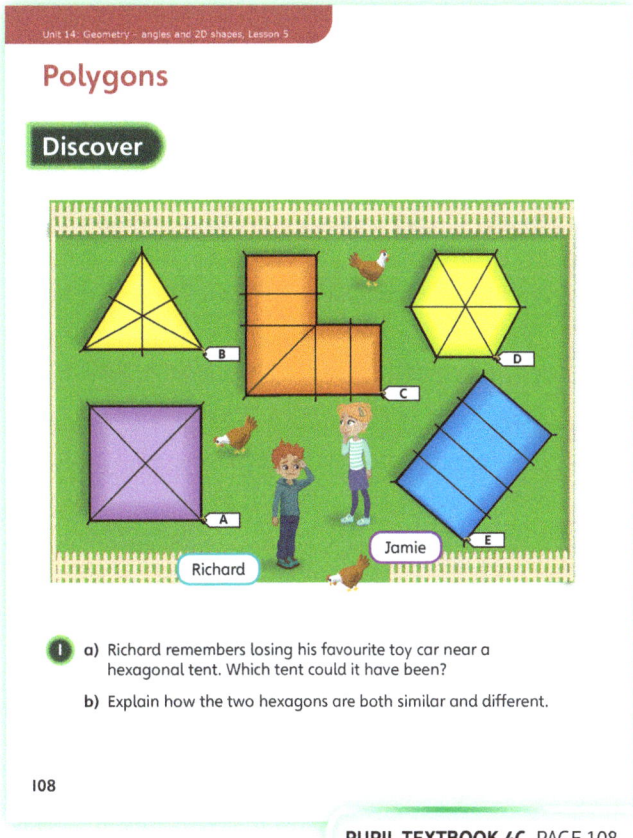

PUPIL TEXTBOOK 4C PAGE 108

Share

WAYS OF WORKING Whole class teacher led

ASK

- Question 1 a): *How did you know which shapes were hexagonal?*
- Question 1 b): *Which hexagonal shape was strange and why?*
- Question 1 b): *Where would you look to find a shape's interior angles?*

IN FOCUS It will be important, during this part of the lesson, to make sure children are comfortable with what an 'interior angle' is and where it can be found. Remind children that 2D shapes are called polygons and that interior angles are found inside a shape. For example, the irregular hexagon (a compound L shape) has a three-quarter turn interior angle, as well as smaller angles.

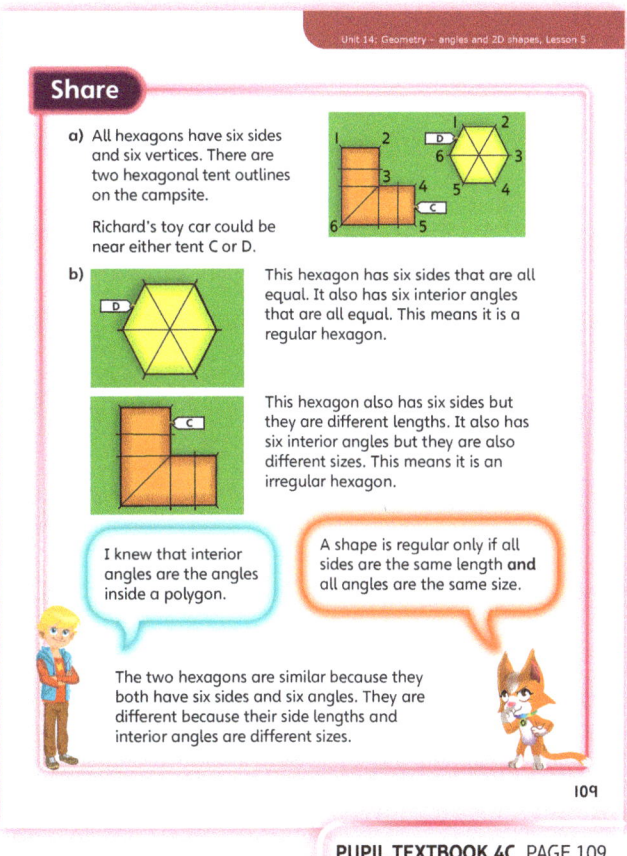

PUPIL TEXTBOOK 4C PAGE 109

143

Unit 14: Geometry – angles and 2D shapes, Lesson 5

Think together

WAYS OF WORKING Whole class teacher led (I do, We do, You do)

ASK

- Questions ❶ and ❷: *What properties will we need to look at when finding regular and irregular shapes?*
- Question ❸: *Can a shape be irregular if all the sides are the same?*

IN FOCUS Question ❶ gives an opportunity to recap how only one of the properties needs to change for a shape to be irregular. Focus on the rectangle, where only the property of side length is different, to help scaffold this understanding.

STRENGTHEN For children who are still confusing the interior and exterior angles in each shape, it may be beneficial to encourage them to draw the shapes they are looking at. Ask: *What angles can you spot inside the shape? Can you compare all the interior angles you have found?*

DEEPEN Question ❸ deepens children's reasoning by requiring them to interrogate each shape and work out where Alex has made a mistake. Encourage children's reasoning by asking: *What mistakes did Alex make? What advice would you give Alex to help her understand her mistake?*

ASSESSMENT CHECKPOINT At this point in the unit, children should be able to discuss what makes a shape regular or irregular. Question ❷ provides a good opportunity to check children's understanding. They should be more confident at identifying regular and irregular shapes and should be able to explain their ideas using the correct vocabulary.

ANSWERS

Question ❶: The irregular polygons are the isosceles triangle and the rectangle.

Question ❷: The triangles (all equilateral) and the hexagon are regular. The rectangle and parallelograms are irregular.

Question ❸: Alex has mistakenly put the isosceles triangle (not regular) and the rectangle (not regular) in the wrong places in the table. Other shapes that could go in each section:
A four-sided shape:
  Irregular: trapezoid
  Regular: square
Not a four-sided shape:
  Irregular: circle
  Regular: hexagon

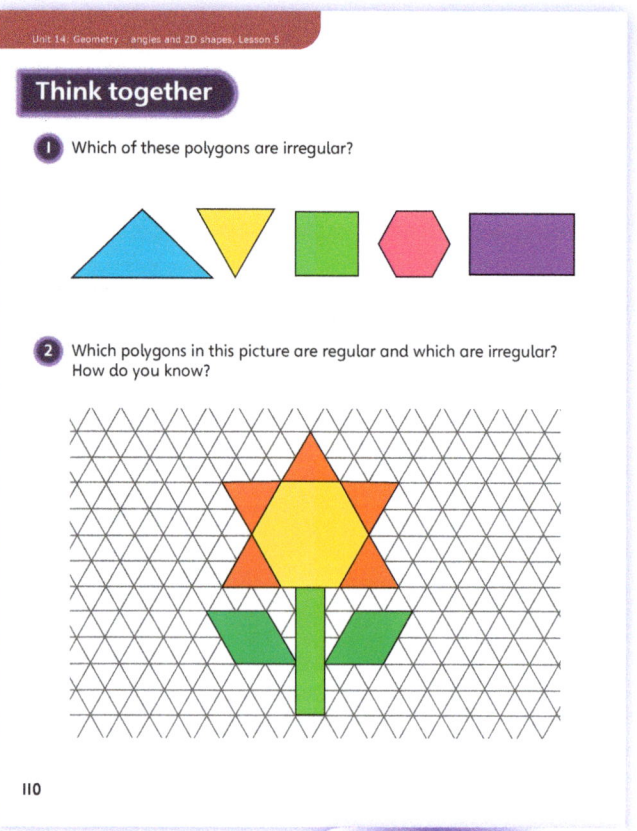

PUPIL TEXTBOOK 4C PAGE 110

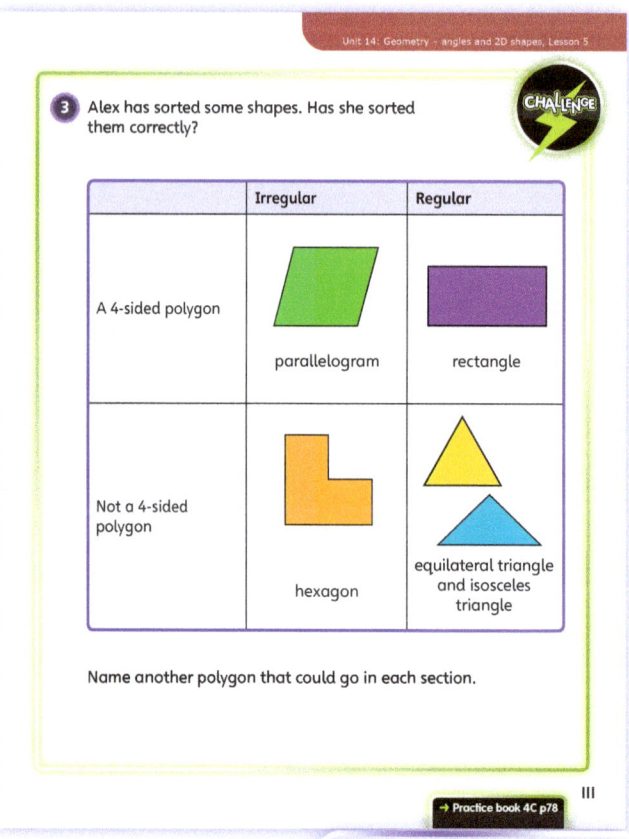

PUPIL TEXTBOOK 4C PAGE 111

Unit 14: Geometry – angles and 2D shapes, Lesson 5

Practice

WAYS OF WORKING Independent thinking

IN FOCUS For questions ❷ and ❸, ensure that children are aware that the pattern of dotted paper is different in each question. This could be highlighted to children by asking: *What is the same and what is different about these two questions? How will the dotted paper help you? What do you need to be careful of when drawing your shapes?*

STRENGTHEN In questions ❷ and ❸, it may be helpful to provide children with pictures of shapes or plastic 2D shapes for them to manipulate. Ask: *Which shape matches what you need to draw? Can you use the dots to help you draw that shape?*

DEEPEN When solving question ❺, deepen children's understanding and reasoning by asking them to provide proof of their findings. You could offer them pre-drawn, cut-out versions of the shapes in the question. Alternatively, children could be given isometric dotted paper to draw their own versions. Ask children how many solutions they can find and to prove that they have found all possibilities.

ASSESSMENT CHECKPOINT At this point in the unit, children should be able to confidently identify what makes a shape regular or irregular. Questions ❷ and ❸ are a good opportunity for children to demonstrate that they recognise that, for example, an irregular hexagon is still a hexagon. Question ❶ provides children with an opportunity to demonstrate that they are able to identify and sort shapes based on whether they are regular or irregular.

ANSWERS Answers for the **Practice** part of the lesson can be found in the *Power Maths* online subscription.

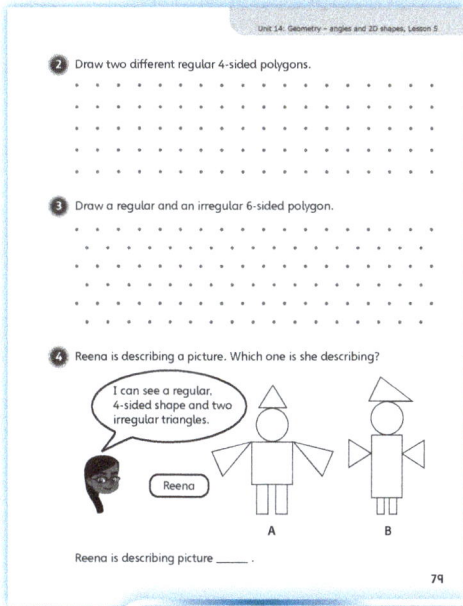

PUPIL PRACTICE BOOK 4C PAGE 78

PUPIL PRACTICE BOOK 4C PAGE 79

PUPIL PRACTICE BOOK 4C PAGE 80

Reflect

WAYS OF WORKING Independent thinking and pair work

IN FOCUS Children should formulate their ideas and summarise their understanding about irregular shapes. Children should then be given the opportunity to share their ideas with a partner and in a class discussion.

ASSESSMENT CHECKPOINT Children should be able to summarise clearly that it is important to remember that either the side lengths or angles should be different sizes if a shape is irregular. Look for children to point out that a shape is irregular if either both or only one of these things are not equal.

ANSWERS Answers for the **Reflect** part of the lesson can be found in the *Power Maths* online subscription.

After the lesson ⏸

- Are children confident at recognising what can vary in irregular shapes?
- Are children able to recognise and explain concisely how regular and irregular shapes are similar?

145

Unit 14: Geometry – angles and 2D shapes, Lesson 6

Reason about polygons

Learning focus

In this lesson, children will consolidate their learning about polygons and use it to help them solve shape problems and puzzles.

Before you teach

- Are there any types of shapes that children are less confident with?

NATIONAL CURRICULUM LINKS

Year 4 Geometry – properties of shapes

Compare and classify geometric shapes, including quadrilaterals and triangles, based on their properties and sizes.

ASSESSING MASTERY

Children can use the vocabulary and properties of 2D shapes and angles to understand and solve problems and puzzles with confidence. They can explain their ideas and reasoning fluently.

COMMON MISCONCEPTIONS

In this lesson, questions will focus on the polygons created when pieces of paper are overlapped. Some questions will focus on the complete shape made by the two pieces of paper, other questions will focus on the smaller shape made by the overlap. Children may confuse these two ideas. Ask:
- *Have you read the question carefully? What does it ask you to do? Can you point to the shape you're looking at?*

STRENGTHENING UNDERSTANDING

Before the lesson, play some games with children that recap their learning about polygons. For example, hold a polygon behind your back and describe it. Ask: *Can you guess the polygon?* Alternatively, children could play a similar game, but matching pairs. Each child should have a card with either a picture of a polygon or the name of a polygon on it. Children have to find their pair (the person with the card that matches theirs).

GOING DEEPER

Encourage children to create puzzles, similar to those in the lesson, for their partners. Ask: *Can you create an overlapping puzzle for your partner?*

KEY LANGUAGE

In lesson: polygon, deducing, facts, overlapping, regular, hexagon, largest, corners, sides, equal, angles, hexadecagon, quadrilateral, equilateral, triangle, edge, different, square, rectangle, rhombus, trapezium, kite, arrowhead, pentagon, isosceles, perimeter, length, polygon

Other language to be used by the teacher: irregular, scalene, heptagon, octagon, acute, obtuse, right angle, polygon

STRUCTURES AND REPRESENTATIONS

2D polygons

RESOURCES

Optional: 2D polygons made of plastic or card, paper squares, set of cards for pair games (half with pictures of different shapes, half with names of different shapes)

 In the eTextbook of this lesson, you will find interactive links to a selection of teaching tools.

Quick recap

Provide children with a list of 2D shape names. As a class, discuss the properties of each shape.

Unit 14: Geometry – angles and 2D shapes, Lesson 6

Discover

WAYS OF WORKING Pair work

ASK

- Question 1 a): *Why is Bella's polygon irregular?*
- Question 1 b): *Can you make a regular hexagon?*
- Question 1 b): *What other polygons can you make by overlapping two square pieces of paper?*
- Question 1 b): *Is it possible to make a polygon with an acute angle using the two square pieces of paper?*

IN FOCUS Be sure to point out how the hexagon has been created by the *outer* lines of the two overlapping shapes. Any edges of the original squares that are inside the composite shape (such as the top edge of the purple square) are not edges of the composite shape. Ask children if it is possible to make a polygon with an acute angle by overlapping the two squares. Discuss this as a class. (The answer is 'no'. Since both squares only contain right angles at the vertices, any composite shape made from the squares must have vertices that are at least as big as a right angle.)

PRACTICAL TIPS Make sure you give children an opportunity to copy the activity shown in the **Discover** picture. Children could investigate what other hexagons they can make or how many different shapes it is possible to make. It will be beneficial to give children square pieces of paper to use to recreate the polygon in this lesson. They could also use plain paper to draw the polygons they create as a way of recording them.

ANSWERS

Question 1 a): Bella's shape cannot be a regular hexagon as the angles and sides are unequal. Bella could make shapes such as a rectangle, an irregular heptagon and an irregular octagon.

Question 1 b): Bella could make a hexadecagon, which has 16 corners.

Share

WAYS OF WORKING Whole class teacher led

ASK

- Question 1 a): *What does it mean for a polygon to be regular?*
- Question 1 a): *What polygons did you find? Did you and your partner find similar shapes? Was it easier to create regular or irregular polygons?*
- Question 1 b): *What was the polygon with the fewest possible number of angles/sides?*
- Question 1 b): *How can you arrange the squares so that all the vertices in the purple square and all the vertices in the yellow square are vertices in the new shape?*

IN FOCUS Encourage children to consider why some shapes are impossible to create with the given squares of paper. For example, they could be encouraged to reason why it is impossible to make a triangle using what they learnt in **Discover** about not being able to form acute angles by overlapping two squares.

PUPIL TEXTBOOK 4C PAGE 112

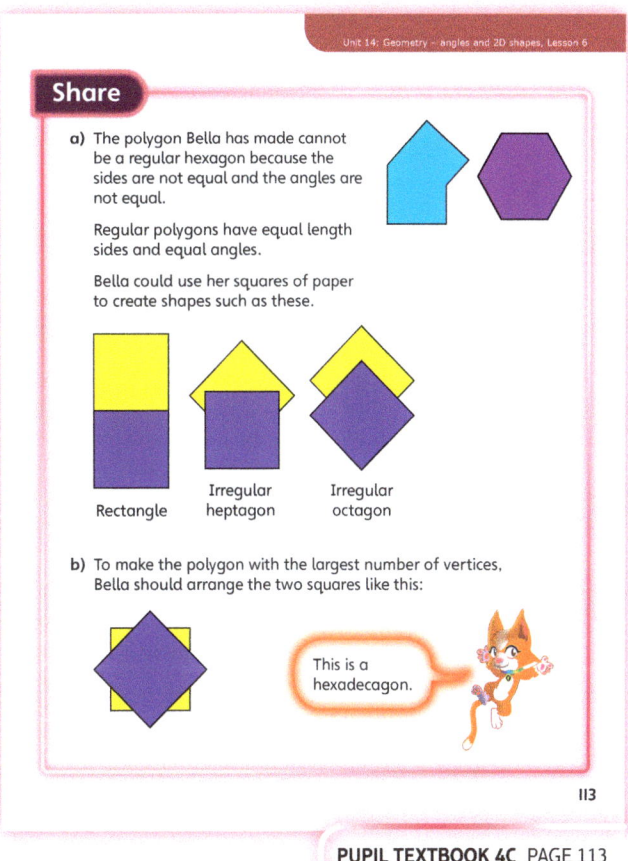

PUPIL TEXTBOOK 4C PAGE 113

147

Unit 14: Geometry – angles and 2D shapes, Lesson 6

Think together

WAYS OF WORKING Whole class teacher led (I do, We do, You do)

ASK
- Question ❶: *What quadrilaterals have you learnt about? What are their properties?*
- Question ❷: *Is it possible to make a square using equilateral triangles?*
- Question ❷: *How can you prove your ideas?*
- Question ❷: *How will you know you have found all the possibilities?*
- Question ❸: *What type of angles can you see in this shape?*

IN FOCUS For all the questions in this part of the lesson, offer children practical opportunities to investigate the solutions. Have cut-out shapes ready for children to manipulate. Question ❸ focuses on the shape made within the overlap of two squares of paper. It will be important for children to be aware of this to solve the problem successfully.

STRENGTHEN Have resources available for children to manipulate to visualise the shapes. These could include plastic 2D shapes or pictures of the shapes they have been studying. Ask: *Which shapes look like those in the Textbook? Can you combine the shapes to make the ones pictured?*

DEEPEN Question ❸ will deepen children's understanding that a single shape can be classed as multiple types of quadrilaterals. If children are insisting that a rhombus or a kite cannot be made, ask them about the rhombuses they made before: *Did they all look the same? Did some look like other shapes they know?*

ASSESSMENT CHECKPOINT Children should be showing confidence at using their knowledge and understanding to solve shape puzzles. They should be using the vocabulary they have learnt fluently to explain their reasoning.

ANSWERS

Question ❶: Different answers are possible, for example: Raj used a square and a parallelogram; Raj used a rectangle and a parallelogram.

Question ❷: Ruby could make: a rhombus, an equilateral triangle, a trapezium, an irregular heptagon, an irregular hexagon, a parallelogram or an irregular pentagon. Ask children to check their working by using physical 2D shapes.

Question ❸:

Quadrilateral	Can it be made?
Square	Yes
Rectangle	Yes
Rhombus	Yes (as a square)
Trapezium	No
Kite	Yes (as a square)
Arrowhead	No

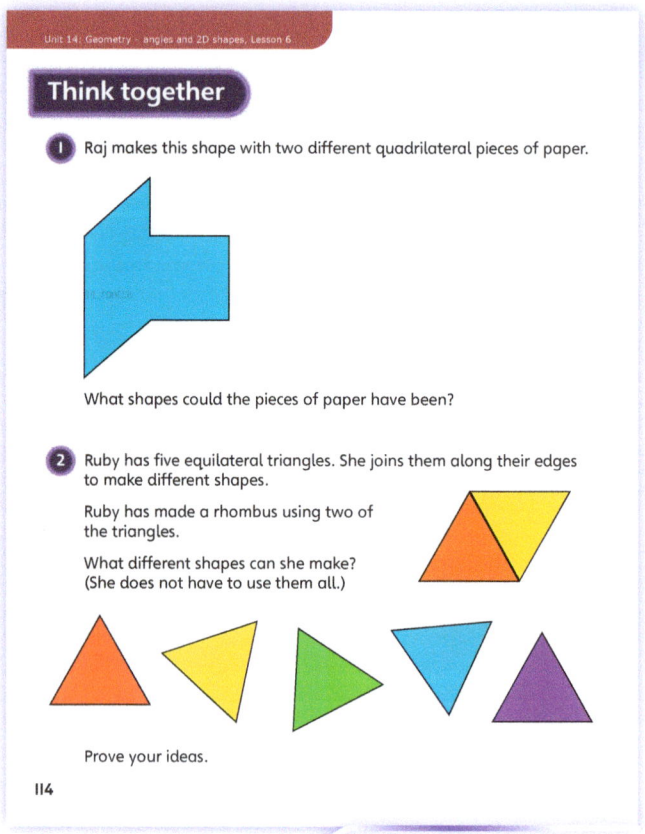

PUPIL TEXTBOOK 4C PAGE 114

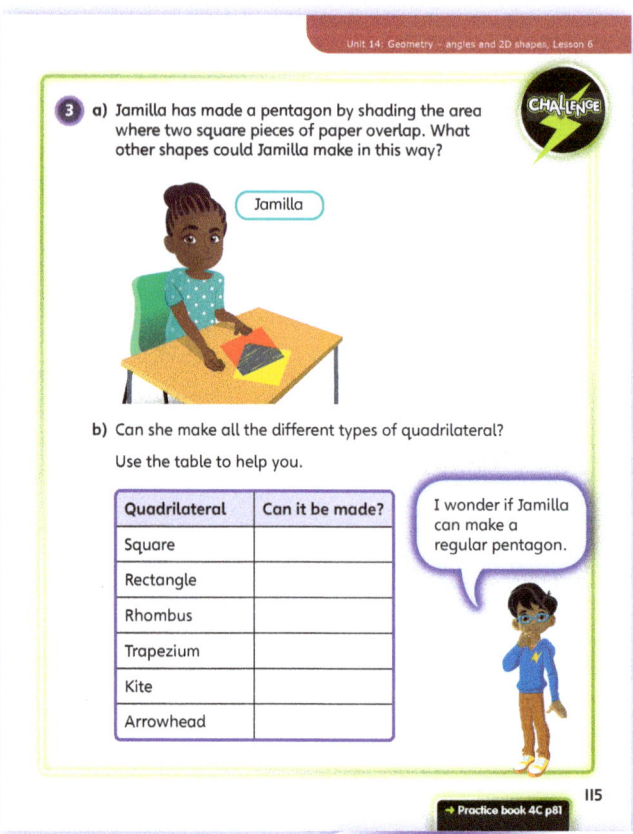

PUPIL TEXTBOOK 4C PAGE 115

Unit 14: Geometry – angles and 2D shapes, Lesson 6

Practice

WAYS OF WORKING Independent thinking

IN FOCUS Provide children with practical manipulatives to help them solve the puzzles in this part of the lesson.

STRENGTHEN To help children visualise quadrilaterals while solving question ③, ask them about the quadrilaterals they have learnt about. Ask: *What quadrilaterals do you know? Can you draw what they look like?* Get children to compare their drawings to the shapes on the page.

DEEPEN Extend question ④ by asking children to find another way of completing the headings for the table. Ask: *How many solutions are there? How do they know?*

THINK DIFFERENTLY When solving question ②, encourage children to investigate the different ways that they can orientate the two triangles in order to join them at each side. They should also consider how different polygons can be made by choosing different types of triangle: equilateral, isosceles or scalene; or right-angled or non-right-angled triangles.

ASSESSMENT CHECKPOINT Children should be confidently and fluently applying their knowledge and understanding, using appropriate vocabulary to describe the shapes and their properties, and sharing their reasoning concisely and clearly.

ANSWERS Answers for the **Practice** part of the lesson can be found in the *Power Maths* online subscription.

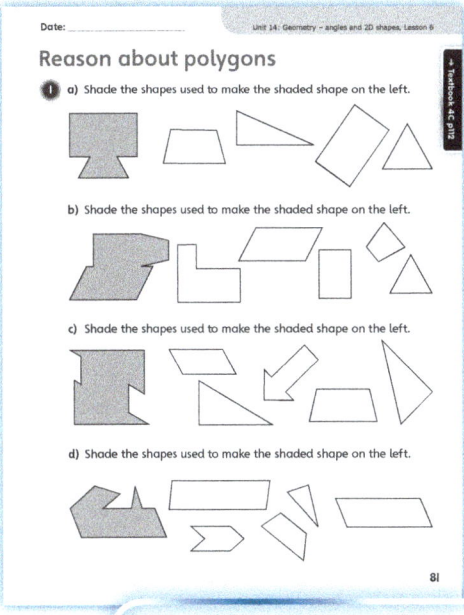

PUPIL PRACTICE BOOK 4C PAGE 81

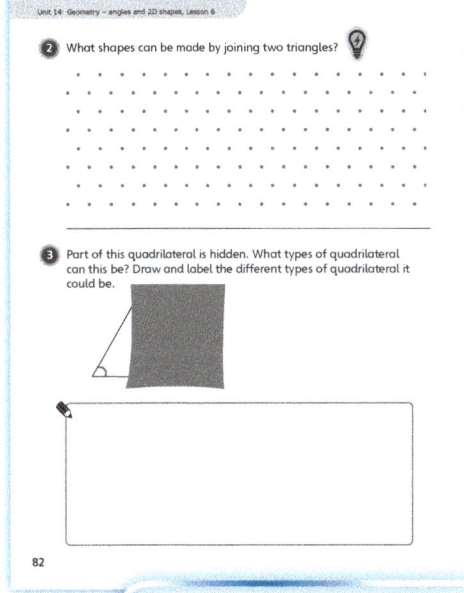

PUPIL PRACTICE BOOK 4C PAGE 82

Reflect

WAYS OF WORKING Independent thinking and pair work

IN FOCUS Give children time to formulate their own reasoning to finish the given sentence starter. Once they have written their ideas, they can share these with a partner and then with the class.

ASSESSMENT CHECKPOINT Children should be able to list all the properties they need to consider to identify a polygon.

ANSWERS Answers for the **Reflect** part of the lesson can be found in the *Power Maths* online subscription.

After the lesson ⏸

- Were children more confident with certain shapes than with others?
- How confident were children at applying their problem-solving skills in this lesson?

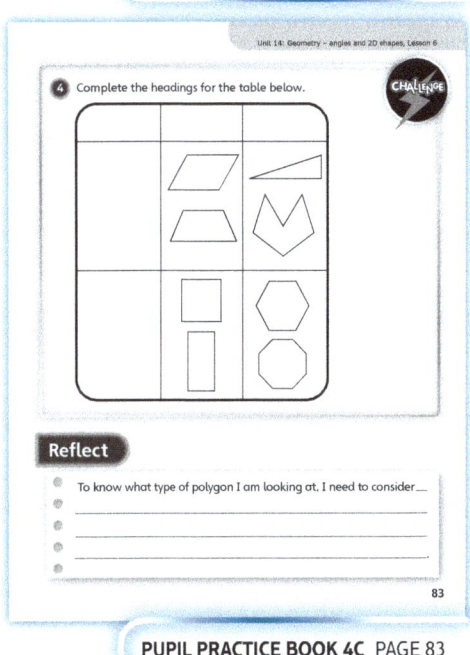

PUPIL PRACTICE BOOK 4C PAGE 83

149

Unit 14: Geometry – angles and 2D shapes, Lesson 7

Lines of symmetry

Learning focus
In this lesson, children will explore reflective symmetry. They will identify lines of symmetry within regular and irregular polygons.

Before you teach
- Do children have experience with symmetry?
- Are children secure identifying and describing a range of 2D shapes?

NATIONAL CURRICULUM LINKS

Year 4 Geometry – properties of shapes

Identify lines of symmetry in 2D shapes presented in different orientations.

ASSESSING MASTERY

Children can identify lines of symmetry in a range of 2D shapes. They can identify when a shape does not have reflective symmetry and explain why. They can identify when a shape has multiple lines of symmetry and explain what the concept of symmetry means.

COMMON MISCONCEPTIONS

Children may think that if a shape can be folded in half, then it has symmetry. For example, an oblong rectangle can be folded along the diagonal, producing two similar triangles. However, they are not mirror images of each other. Ask:
- *Would the whole shape be shown if you put a mirror against the line of symmetry? If not, then is it symmetrical?*

STRENGTHENING UNDERSTANDING

Encourage children to explore symmetry by folding shapes. Explain that the two halves need to match exactly when they are folded. You could also provide children with mirrors to identify lines of symmetry. This helps children understand that opposite sides of the line of symmetry are mirror images of each other.

GOING DEEPER

Ask children to work in pairs. Give children squared paper and ask them to draw a vertical line of symmetry down the centre. Ask one child to draw half a polygon on the right side of the line. The other child then has to complete the left side so that it is symmetrical. Children can make the shape as complex as they like. This challenge can be further extended by drawing both a vertical and horizontal line of symmetry. One child should then draw a quarter of a shape in the first quadrant.

KEY LANGUAGE

In lesson: reflective symmetry, symmetrical, lines of symmetry, square, equilateral, triangle, rectangle, hexagon, isosceles, regular, octagon, irregular, circle

Other language to be used by the teacher: isosceles, scalene, 2D, polygon

STRUCTURES AND REPRESENTATIONS

2D shapes

RESOURCES

Optional: range of 2D shapes, mirrors

 In the eTextbook of this lesson, you will find interactive links to a selection of teaching tools.

Quick recap

Ask children to draw an example of a symmetrical shape. They should then compare it with a partner's.

Unit 14: Geometry – angles and 2D shapes, Lesson 7

Discover

WAYS OF WORKING Pair work

ASK

- Question 1 a): *What do you think symmetry means?*
- Question 1 b): *What shapes do you know that are symmetrical?*
- Question 1 b): *How do you know if you have found a line of symmetry?*

IN FOCUS Question 1 b) requires children to visualise the triangle in order to identify the lines of symmetry. Children will have to draw on their knowledge of equilateral triangles from previous lessons in order to solve this problem.

PRACTICAL TIPS Provide children with paper squares and triangles for them to investigate the lines of symmetry. They could use mirrors to check if the lines they have found are lines of reflective symmetry.

ANSWERS

Question 1 a): The square has four lines of symmetry.

Question 1 b): There are three lines of symmetry in an equilateral triangle.

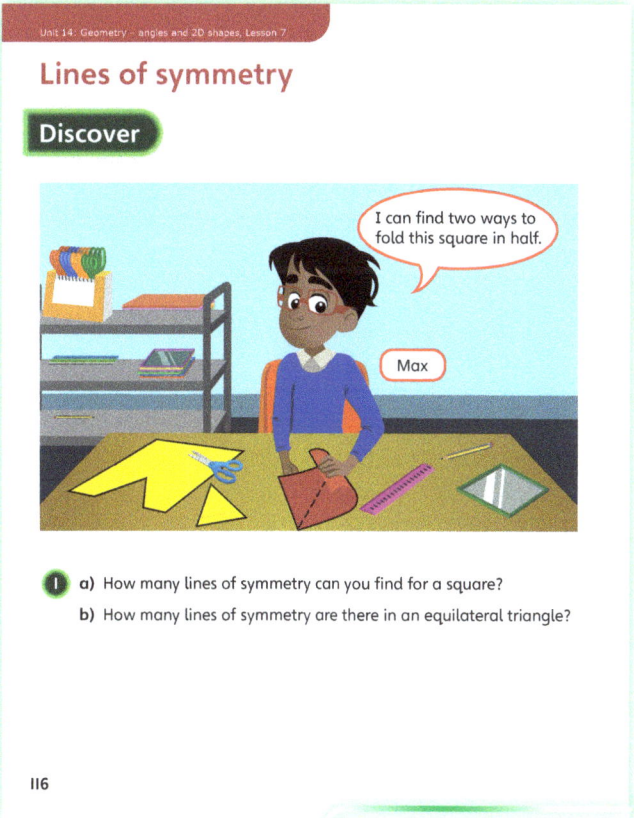

PUPIL TEXTBOOK 4C PAGE 116

Share

WAYS OF WORKING Whole class teacher led

ASK

- Question 1 a): *How can you prove that each line is a line of symmetry?*
- Question 1 a): *What do you notice about the number of lines of symmetry and the properties of the shape?*
- Question 1 b): *Does every triangle have a line of symmetry?*

IN FOCUS Ask children to think about symmetry in other types of triangles. This could lead to a discussion about symmetry in regular and irregular polygons. Ask children to think about symmetry in other types of quadrilaterals. Ensure children understand the term 'reflective symmetry'. Explain that the shape on one side of a line of symmetry should be a mirror image of the shape on the other side.

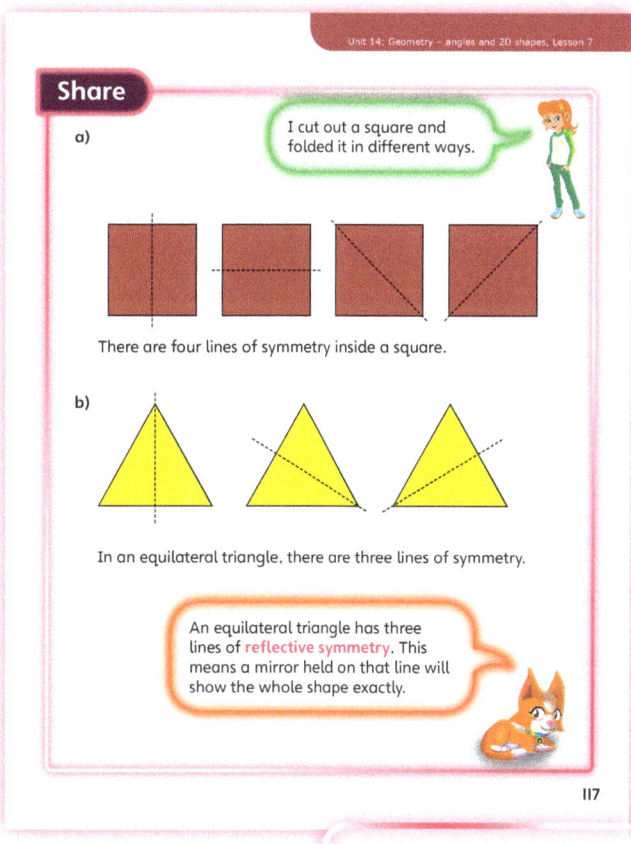

PUPIL TEXTBOOK 4C PAGE 117

Unit 14: Geometry – angles and 2D shapes, Lesson 7

Think together

WAYS OF WORKING Whole class teacher led (I do, We do, You do)

ASK
- Question ③: *How can you tell if a shape has symmetry?*
- Question ③: *Can you think of 2D shapes that do not have symmetry?*
- Question ③: *What shape do you think will have the most lines of symmetry?*

IN FOCUS Question ③ looks at symmetry within different types of quadrilaterals. The first parallelogram may raise the misconception that it has a line of symmetry between opposite corners as it produces two identical scalene triangles. Children need to understand that reflective symmetry means that one half is the mirror image of the other and not just the same shape rotated.

STRENGTHEN Give children the 2D shapes in the questions so that they can fold or explore them with mirrors. This will help children to identify any lines of symmetry.

DEEPEN Challenge children to find shapes with different numbers of lines of symmetry. Ask: *Can you find a shape that has one line of symmetry? Two lines? Three lines? Four lines? Five lines?*

ASSESSMENT CHECKPOINT Question ① will demonstrate whether children have an understanding of what symmetry means and question ③ will show whether children can identify symmetry in a range of quadrilaterals.

ANSWERS

Question ①: Dominic is not correct as the two halves are not mirror images of each other.

Question ②: Hexagon A has no lines of symmetry. Hexagon B has six lines of symmetry (because it is regular).

Question ③: The kite has one line of symmetry.

The parallelogram has no lines of symmetry.

The reflex kite has one line of symmetry.

The isosceles trapezium has one line of symmetry.

The rectangle has two lines of symmetry.

The rhombus has two lines of symmetry.

The square has four lines of symmetry.

The right-angled trapezium has no lines of symmetry.

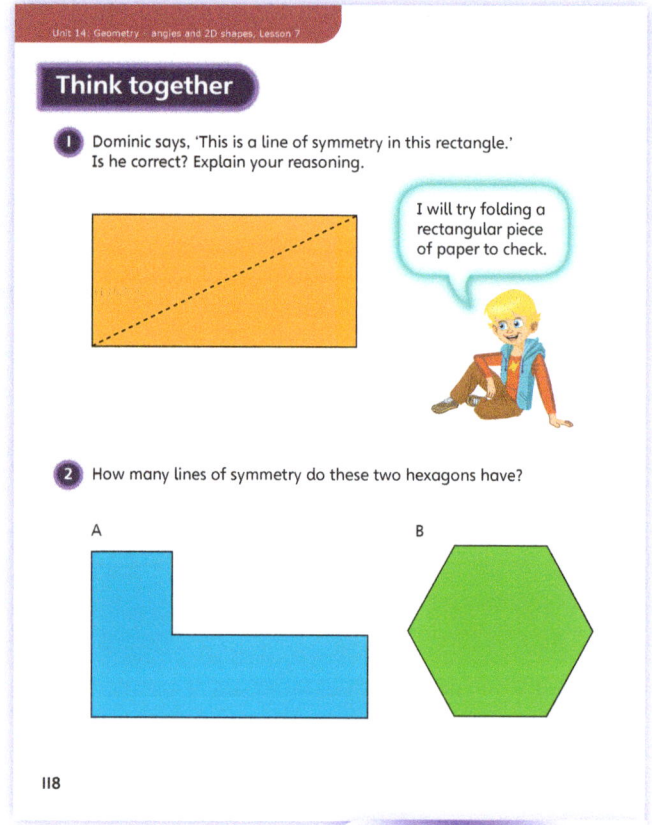

PUPIL TEXTBOOK 4C PAGE 118

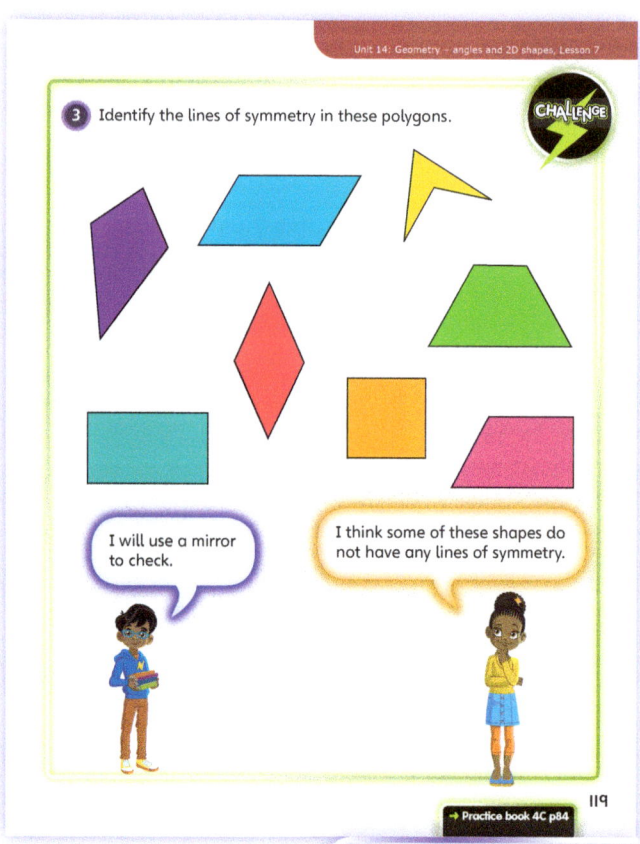

PUPIL TEXTBOOK 4C PAGE 119

Unit 14: Geometry – angles and 2D shapes, Lesson 7

Practice

WAYS OF WORKING Independent thinking

IN FOCUS Question ④ asks children to create a hexagon with two lines of symmetry. Children have to take care that there are only two lines of symmetry. Some children may start by drawing a random shape with six sides, while others may start with a regular hexagon. Children need to think about how to adapt a regular hexagon so that it becomes a shape with only two lines of symmetry.

STRENGTHEN Provide children with mirrors in order to investigate the symmetry of the shapes. For question ④, children could use a geoboard and an elastic band to try to solve the problem.

DEEPEN Challenge children to investigate the relationship between the number of lines of symmetry and the number of sides of regular 2D shapes. Ask: *What do you notice? Can you explain why?*

ASSESSMENT CHECKPOINT Question ③ will demonstrate whether children can sort shapes based on lines of symmetry and whether the shapes are regular or irregular, while question ⑤ will show whether children can create a shape with a given number of lines of symmetry.

ANSWERS Answers for the **Practice** part of the lesson can be found in the *Power Maths* online subscription.

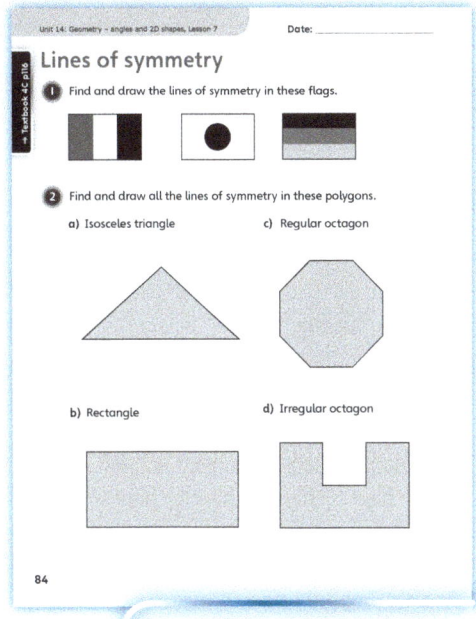

Reflect

WAYS OF WORKING Pair work

IN FOCUS This section requires children to think more deeply about symmetry in shapes. The closer a regular 2D shape gets to a circle, the more lines of symmetry it has.

ASSESSMENT CHECKPOINT This section will determine whether children understand symmetry and how to find symmetry in 2D shapes.

ANSWERS Answers for the **Reflect** part of the lesson can be found in the *Power Maths* online subscription.

After the lesson

- Did children identify all the lines of symmetry?
- Were children able to apply their knowledge from previous lessons on 2D shapes?
- Do children still need practical activities to support their understanding of symmetry?

153

Unit 14: Geometry – angles and 2D shapes, Lesson 8

Complete a symmetric figure

Learning focus

In this lesson, children will complete symmetric patterns when the lines of symmetry are given. They will reason about how shapes are affected by different lines of symmetry.

Before you teach

- What practical opportunities can you provide to strengthen children's understanding?
- How will you address misconceptions about how a shape's orientation changes when reflected?

NATIONAL CURRICULUM LINKS

Year 4 Geometry – properties of shapes

Complete a simple symmetric figure with respect to a specific line of symmetry.

ASSESSING MASTERY

Children can complete and add to symmetric patterns with two or more lines of symmetry. They can create their own symmetric patterns with increasing complexity. Children can describe how shapes will be affected by vertical, horizontal and diagonal lines of symmetry.

COMMON MISCONCEPTIONS

When children try to complete a pattern they may forget to change the orientation of the shape according to the line of symmetry or they may make errors in the position of the reflected shape. Ask:
- *How will the shape look if it is reflected vertically/horizontally/diagonally?*

STRENGTHENING UNDERSTANDING

Ask children to make their own symmetric patterns using a range of 2D shapes. In this way they can physically flip or rotate the shapes in order to create the mirror image.

GOING DEEPER

Challenge children to come up with their own versions of the problems in the lesson for their partner to complete. They can make the challenge more difficult by adding more shapes, more lines of symmetry or by using more complex shapes.

KEY LANGUAGE

In lesson: symmetric, symmetrical, vertical, symmetry, horizontal, diagonal, octagon, irregular, regular

Other language to be used by the teacher: polygon

STRUCTURES AND REPRESENTATIONS

2D shapes

RESOURCES

Optional: lolly sticks or straws, a range of 2D shapes, mirrors, geoboards, elastic bands

 In the eTextbook of this lesson, you will find interactive links to a selection of teaching tools.

Quick recap

Ask children to draw a square and then to mark all the lines of reflective symmetry on it. Ask: *How many lines of symmetry does a square have? Did you find them all?*

Unit 14: Geometry – angles and 2D shapes, Lesson 8

Discover

WAYS OF WORKING Pair work

ASK

- Question 1 a): *How do you know that Isla's chicken pen will not be a regular octagon?*
- Question 1 a): *Can you identify the lines of symmetry? How do you know?*
- Question 1 b): *What is the smallest number of pieces of fence that Isla would need, in total, to create an octagonal pen? What type of octagon would this be?*

IN FOCUS Question 1 a) requires children to first identify the lines of symmetry when the shape is still incomplete. They have to reason about what information they have in order to do this. This question should promote a high level of discussion. Ensure that children are prompted to justify their choices throughout.

PRACTICAL TIPS Provide children with sticks or straws that they can arrange to replicate the chicken pens. By having 'fence pieces' that they can move, they can try out their ideas, review and adapt if necessary.

ANSWERS

Question 1 a): Isla's chicken pen will look like this once it has been completed with five more pieces of fence. Isla's chicken pen is not an octagon because it has 10 sides.

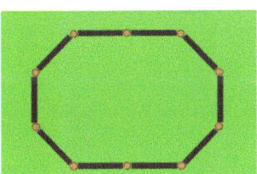

The pen will have two lines of symmetry.

Question 1 b): Isla can complete a symmetrical pattern using only three pieces of fence.

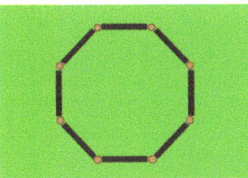

This regular octagon has 8 lines of symmetry.

Share

WAYS OF WORKING Whole class teacher led

ASK

- Question 1 a): *How do you know there are only two lines of symmetry?*
- Question 1 b): *What is the same and what is different about the octagon in question 1 a) and the octagon in question 1 b)?*

IN FOCUS Question 1 b) has a regular octagon which has more lines of symmetry than the irregular octagon in question 1 a). Discuss why this shape uses only 8 fence pieces and agree that it has 8 sides that are all equal length, and that this octagon is regular. Ask: *Could you complete a symmetric pattern with 7 sides? With 6 sides?*

PUPIL TEXTBOOK 4C PAGE 120

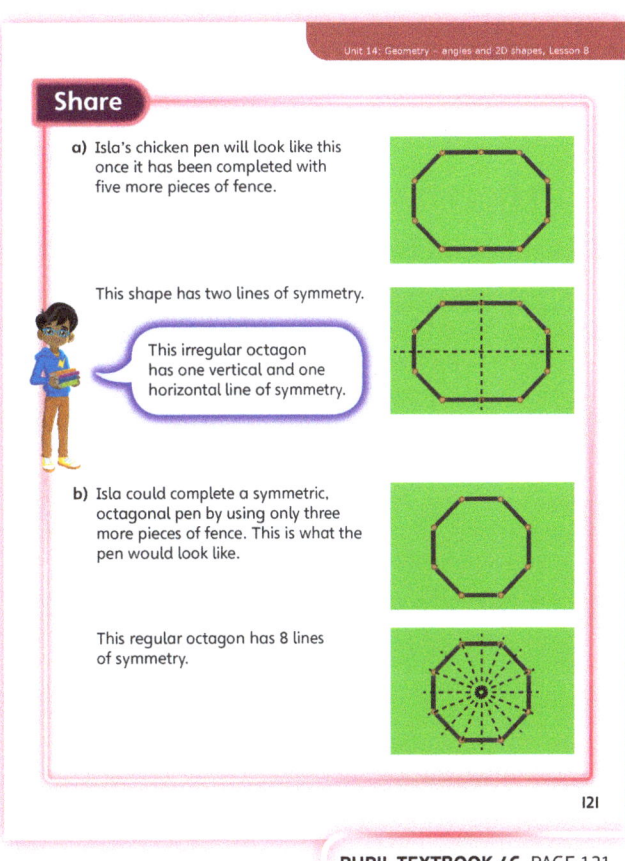

PUPIL TEXTBOOK 4C PAGE 121

Unit 14: Geometry – angles and 2D shapes, Lesson 8

Think together

WAYS OF WORKING Whole class (I do, We do, You do)

ASK

- Question ①: *How are the patterns here the same as the patterns in the **Discover** section? How are they different?*
- Question ②: *How will these shapes be different to those in question ①? How many sides will the completed shape have? How do you know?*
- Question ③: *What shape could you draw to check each statement?*

IN FOCUS Questions ① and ② ask children to complete symmetric shapes to make irregular polygons. In question ①, the lolly sticks meet the mirror line at right angles so will continue the other side of the mirror line to form a straight line. Children may mistakenly continue the lines in the same way in question ② a) to make a rectangle. Provide mirrors so that children can check why this is not correct.

STRENGTHEN Provide children with mirrors so that they can test their ideas. Giving children lolly sticks to manipulate allows them to test and adapt their ideas in a concrete way.

DEEPEN Challenge children to extend question ③ by writing their own true/false symmetry statement for a partner to prove or correct.

ASSESSMENT CHECKPOINT Questions ① and ② will demonstrate whether children are able to correctly complete a symmetric shape. Question ③ will assess how well children can reason about symmetry.

ANSWERS

Questions ① a) and b): Children should complete the shape correctly using 5 lolly sticks.

Questions ② a) and b): Children should complete the shape correctly using 6 lolly sticks.

Question ③: 1. True: you can draw a right-angled trapezium, for example.
2. False: it will depend on where the line of symmetry is.
3. False: it will depend on where the line of symmetry is.
If the line of symmetry meets a side of the shape at right angles, then the reflected side will form part of the same side. The shapes in question ① will not have double the number of sides when after reflection, but the shapes in question ② will have double the number of sides.

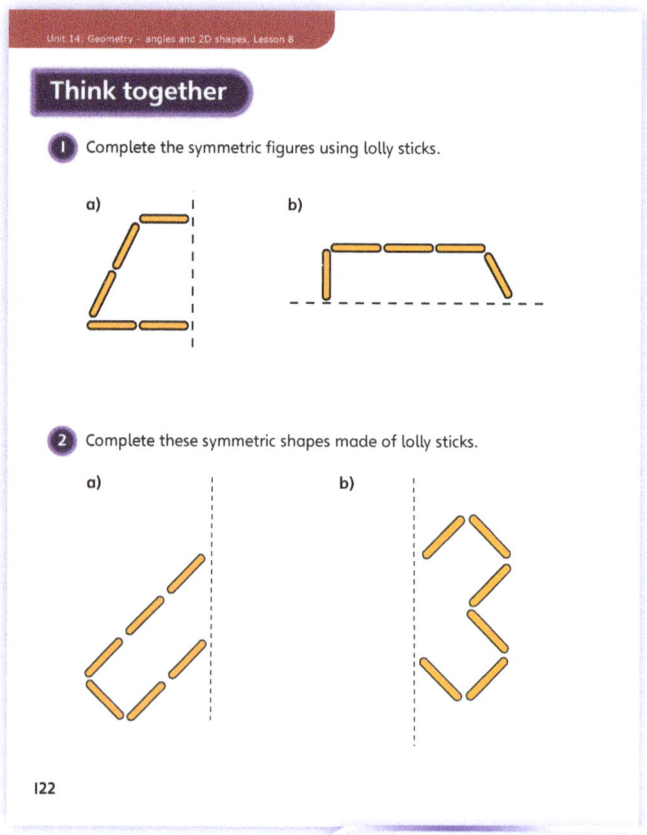

PUPIL TEXTBOOK 4C PAGE 122

PUPIL TEXTBOOK 4C PAGE 123

Unit 14: Geometry – angles and 2D shapes, Lesson 8

Practice

WAYS OF WORKING Independent thinking

IN FOCUS Question ③ requires children to reason about how the orientation of the shape changes with vertical, horizontal and diagonal lines of symmetry. Children need to visualise how the shape changes and describe the transformation. This question may expose misconceptions about how the orientations of shapes are changed by reflection. In question ④, children are given a quarter of a shape and complete it by reflecting the two given sides in the mirror lines. You might want to challenge children to explain how they know this shape will be regular before they even draw it. Look for explanations including both side lengths being equal and the interior angles will be equal after the reflection.

STRENGTHEN For questions ① and ②, provide children with mirrors so that they can see how the completed shape should look.

DEEPEN Challenge children to work in pairs to create a symmetric design. Each child has a blank grid with a vertical and horizontal line of symmetry. The first child draws a shape on the right side of their design. The second child then draws the reflected image on the left side of their design. Then the second child adds another shape on the left side and the first child draws the reflected shape on the right side of their design. Repeat for as long as required. The children then join their designs and check that between them they have created a design that has horizontal and vertical symmetry.

ASSESSMENT CHECKPOINT Question ③ will demonstrate whether children have secure understanding of how shapes are transformed when reflected along vertical, horizontal and diagonal lines.

ANSWERS Answers for the **Practice** part of the lesson can be found in the *Power Maths* online subscription.

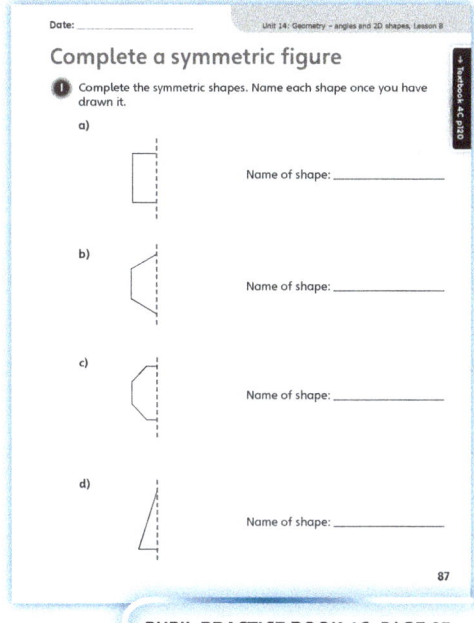

PUPIL PRACTICE BOOK 4C PAGE 87

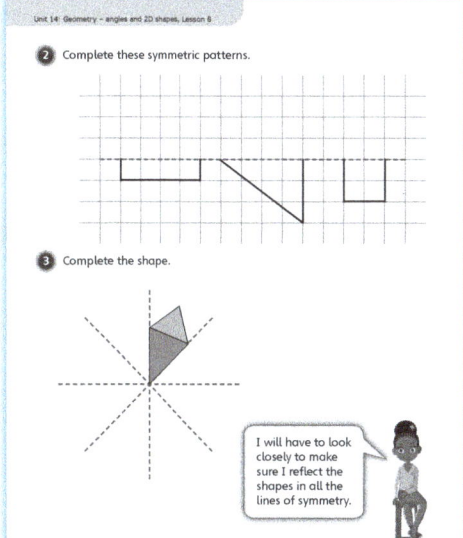

PUPIL PRACTICE BOOK 4C PAGE 88

Reflect

WAYS OF WORKING Pair work

IN FOCUS To explain how to complete a symmetric shape, children need to have a good understanding of symmetry and how symmetric shapes work. They should consider the orientation of the lines of symmetry and how this will affect the reflection when completing a symmetric shape.

ASSESSMENT CHECKPOINT This section will demonstrate whether children understand symmetry and how symmetric shapes work.

ANSWERS Answers for the **Reflect** part of the lesson can be found in the *Power Maths* online subscription.

After the lesson

- Do children understand what happens to a shape when it is reflected along vertical, horizontal and diagonal lines?
- Could children contribute to a class or school display that allows them to apply the skills learnt in this lesson?

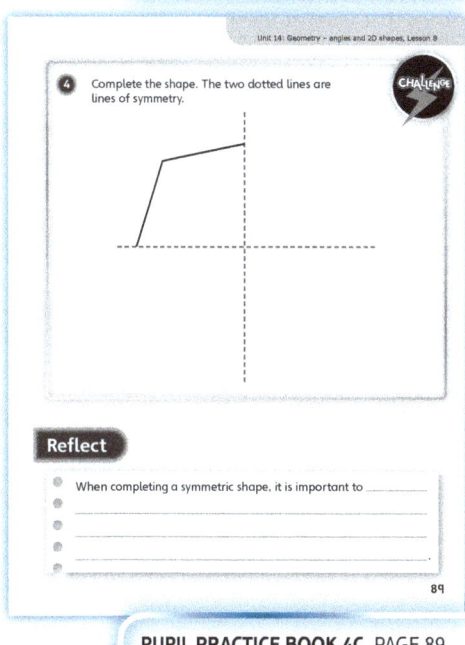

PUPIL PRACTICE BOOK 4C PAGE 89

Unit 14: Geometry – angles and 2D shapes

End of unit check

Don't forget the unit assessment grid in your *Power Maths* online subscription.

WAYS OF WORKING Independent work

IN FOCUS

This **End of unit check** will allow you to focus on children's understanding of angles and 2D shapes, including symmetry, and whether they can apply their knowledge to solve problems.

- In question ①, children should determine which of the four shapes are quadrilaterals and are irregular. Both B and D are irregular, but only B is a quadrilateral.
- Question ② assesses children's understanding of the the terminology of angles. Do they know that an obtuse angle is one that is greater than a right angle, and can they identify what an obtuse angle looks like?
- Question ③ assesses whether children understand that an isosceles triangle must have two equal sides and two equal angles.
- Question ④ assesses children's understanding of different types of angles inside polygons.
- Question ⑤ assesses children's ability to recognise lines of symmetry within 2D shapes. They should see that B is the only one with just 2 lines of symmetry (A has 4 lines of symmetry, C 3 and D 1).
- Question ⑥ is a SATs-style question and assesses children's recognition of angles and types of triangles.

ANSWERS AND COMMENTARY Children who have mastered the concepts in this unit will be able to recognise and order acute, obtuse and right angles with confidence, and explain how right angles can help them to do so. They will be able to name and describe the different types of triangles and quadrilaterals, and explain their similarities and differences. They will be able to point out how a quadrilateral may be classified in more than one way (for example, has two lines of symmetry *and* is a quadrilateral). Children will be able to complete shapes and patterns across lines of symmetry in different orientations and will be able to apply their knowledge and understanding to solve problems.

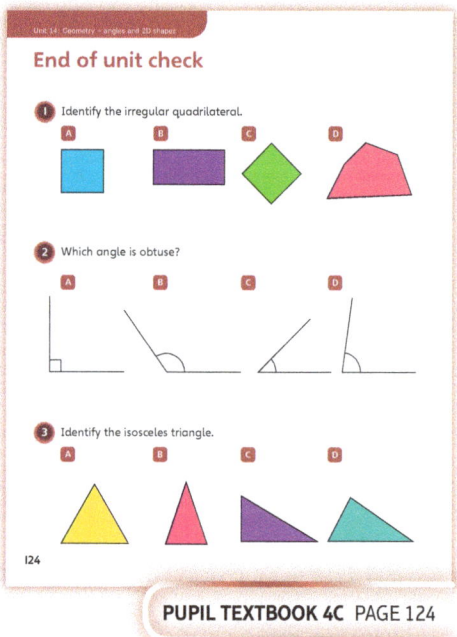

PUPIL TEXTBOOK 4C PAGE 124

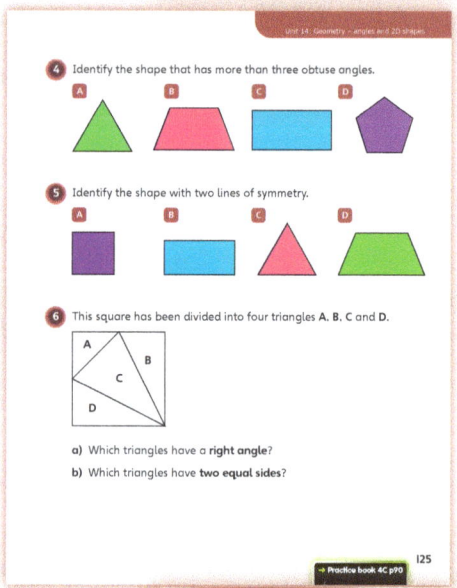

PUPIL TEXTBOOK 4C PAGE 125

Q	A	WRONG ANSWERS AND MISCONCEPTIONS	STRENGTHENING UNDERSTANDING
1	B	C indicates a lack of understanding about what irregular means, since this *is* regular but in a different orientation. D is irregular, but it has 5 sides so is a pentagon, not a quadrilateral.	**Symmetry:** Give children a mirror to help them check the lines of symmetry inside and outside of the shapes. **Angles:** Remind children about how they can use a right angle to help them judge whether an angle is acute or obtuse.
2	B	Choosing C or D suggests that children have mixed up acute and obtuse angles. Choosing A suggests that children do not recognise a right angle.	
3	B	A, C or D indicate children are unsure about types of triangles.	
4	D	A, B, or C indicate children are unsure about types of angles.	
5	B	A indicates children have neglected diagonal lines of symmetry. C or D indicates that children are unsure about lines of symmetry in 2D shapes.	
6 a)	A, B, D	Not identifying them all may suggest that children fail to identify right angles in unfamiliar orientations.	
6 b)	A, C	B and/or D suggests that children compared lengths of sides incorrectly.	

158

Unit 14: Geometry – angles and 2D shapes

My journal

WAYS OF WORKING Independent thinking

ANSWERS AND COMMENTARY Question ❶: For this question, look for children's ability to visualise the types of triangles and quadrilaterals that it may be possible to create using the interior of a regular hexagon. Ask:
- What types of quadrilaterals and triangles are there?
- Can you see how any of those shapes might fit into the hexagon? Can you make any of those shapes by drawing two lines across the hexagon?

Answer: There are two ways of dividing the hexagon. Children may represent these ways in a different orientation.

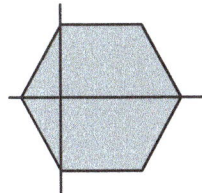 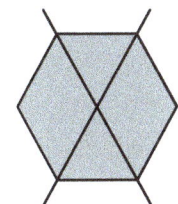

Question ❷: When solving this question, look for children to be experimenting and finding evidence. When solving the question and providing their ideas, encourage children to reason by asking:
- How have you proven your ideas?
- What is it about obtuse angles that means Greg cannot be correct?
- How many obtuse angles could he have? Why?

Answer: Greg cannot be correct. If you draw three lines connected by two obtuse angles, the outer pair of lines will never meet to form a triangle. Children may support their argument with a picture.

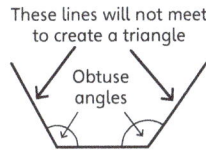

These lines will not meet to create a triangle

Obtuse angles

Power check

WAYS OF WORKING Independent thinking

ASK
- How confident are you at recognising acute and obtuse angles?
- Could you name and identify all types of triangles?
- Can you identify different quadrilaterals and their properties?
- Do you think you can complete any symmetrical shape or pattern now?

Power puzzle

WAYS OF WORKING Pair work

IN FOCUS Discuss with children the properties of the shapes they are making and ask them to justify how they know what shape they have made.

ANSWERS AND COMMENTARY

Folding a piece of A4 paper as shown will create a square.

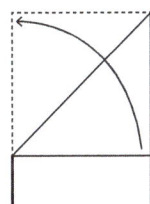

After the unit ⏸

- Can children find quadrilaterals and triangles in the classroom?
- How could you link the learning from this unit with the next?

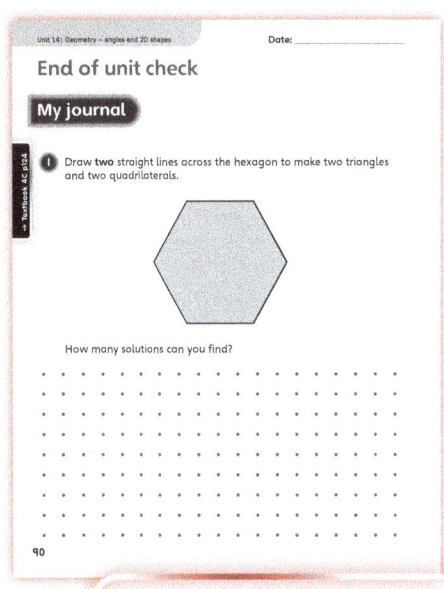

PUPIL PRACTICE BOOK 4C PAGE 90

PUPIL PRACTICE BOOK 4C PAGE 91

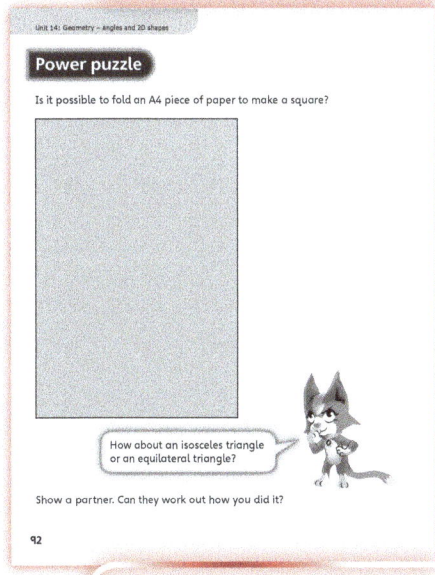

PUPIL PRACTICE BOOK 4C PAGE 92

Strengthen and **Deepen** activities for this unit can be found in the *Power Maths* online subscription.

159

Unit 15
Statistics

Mastery Expert tip! 'My class really enjoyed it when we made cross-curricular links to other subjects, collecting our own data to analyse. This helped them make real connections between the data and its presentation; it was particularly effective when introducing them to continuous data and line graphs for the first time.'

Don't forget to watch the Unit 15 video!

WHY THIS UNIT IS IMPORTANT

This unit exposes children to a range of ways in which information and data can be presented and interpreted. Children explore pictograms, bar charts and tables in more detail than they have before. Children begin exploring the use of a wider range of scales. They also begin interpreting quarter symbols in pictograms, as well as reading from bars which are a quarter of the way between two marked points on a bar chart. They are also exposed to a range of more complex, multi-step problems, which use information presented in a range of charts and tables.

Children are shown data presented in line graphs for the first time and are introduced to the distinction between continuous and discrete data. They also begin to draw their own line graphs to represent information given in tables.

WHERE THIS UNIT FITS

→ Unit 14: Geometry – angles and 2D shapes
→ **Unit 15: Statistics**
→ Unit 16: Geometry – position and direction

In this unit, children build on the work from Year 3 on statistics, when they were introduced to basic pictograms, bar charts and tables. Children are encouraged to explore the range of information that they can get from the data presented to them. Children will explore how the structure of line graphs, and the data presented within them, differs from bar charts.

Before they start this unit, it is expected that children:
- know how to interpret a basic pictogram and bar graph
- are confident in carrying out addition, subtraction, multiplication and division calculations
- can recall the 1–12 times-tables and related division facts.

ASSESSING MASTERY

Children who have mastered this unit can interpret data that is presented in a range of ways, including pictograms, bar charts, line graphs and tables. Children can use this data to answer a range of questions, including comparison, ordering and total questions. They can also make their own statements based on the data presented to them and will have begun to compare linked data presented across multiple sources. Children can answer more complex multi-step problems that use information presented in charts, tables or graphs. They can also present data on line graphs that they have drawn themselves.

COMMON MISCONCEPTIONS	STRENGTHENING UNDERSTANDING	GOING DEEPER
Children may miscount the number of pictogram symbols (and their value) or misread the value on the vertical axis when a point falls between two marked values on the axis.	Represent the pictogram and/or bar chart using counters, cubes or other objects. Encourage children to count each object, and to use the key in a pictogram, or scale on the vertical axis in a bar chart, to work out the total value. You can also link the vertical axis to a vertical number line.	Encourage children to make their own increasingly complex statements based on data, including data presented across multiple types of charts and tables. Ask: *What else can you tell me based on this data? How do you know? What questions could you ask someone else based on this data?*
Children may identify the incorrect operation when answering questions and carrying out calculations based on the data presented to them.	Ask: *What is the question asking you to do? What operation could this involve?* Encourage children to consider the different steps they need to take to solve multi-step problems.	Encourage children to think about whether a statement is true or false in relation to the data being presented.

Unit 15: Statistics

UNIT STARTER PAGES

Use these pages to introduce the unit focus to children. You can use the characters to explore how data can be presented.

STRUCTURES AND REPRESENTATIONS

Children are presented with a range of ways in which to represent data, including:

Pictograms:

Bar charts:

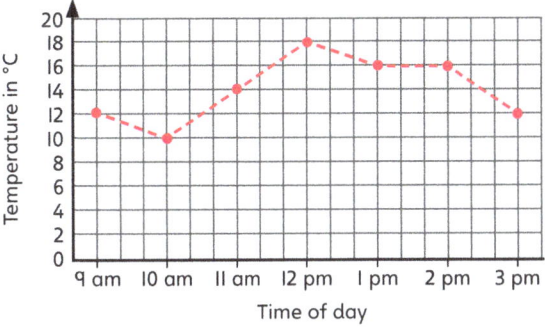

Line graphs:

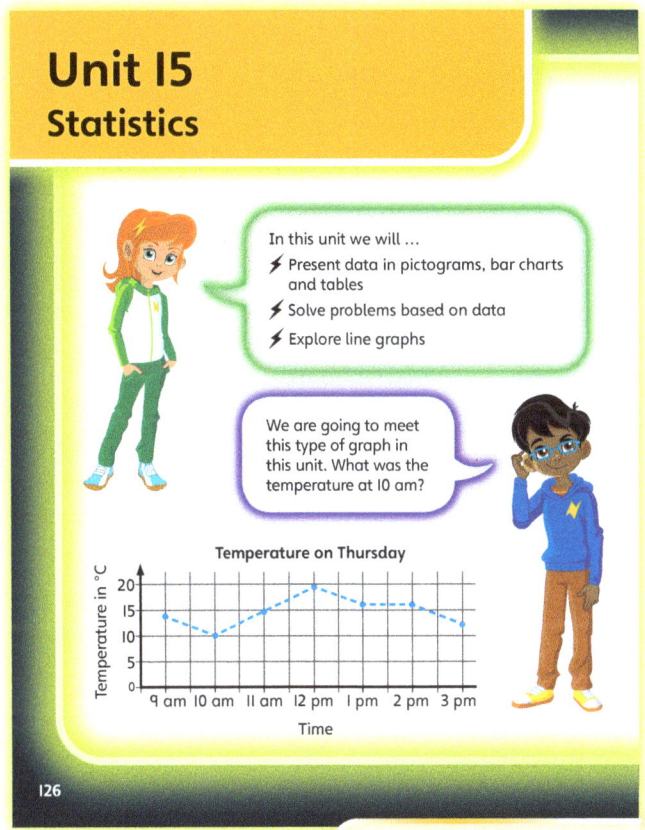

PUPIL TEXTBOOK 4C PAGE 126

Tables:

	Class 4T	Class 4A	Class 4S
Raisin	16	10	6
Chocolate	5	18	19
Rainbow	9	14	22

Children may also benefit from using the structures and representations introduced in Year 3 to support their calculations, including the number line.

KEY LANGUAGE

There is some key language that children will need to know as part of the learning in this unit:

- table, line graph, bar chart, pictogram
- data, discrete data, continuous data
- operation
- altogether, more than, greatest, smallest
- compare

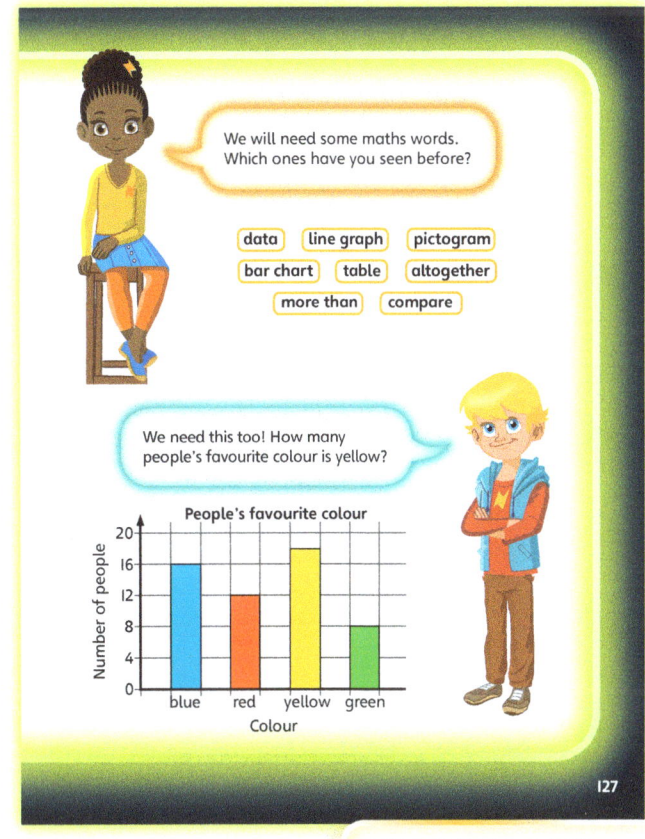

PUPIL TEXTBOOK 4C PAGE 127

Unit 15: Statistics, Lesson 1

Interpret charts

Learning focus
In this lesson, children will extend their knowledge of bar charts, tables and pictograms to interpret data with larger numbers and a wider range of scales.

Before you teach
- Are children confident finding numbers that lie half-way between two numbers?
- Can children interpret data given in tables?

NATIONAL CURRICULUM LINKS

Year 4 Statistics

Interpret and present discrete and continuous data using appropriate graphical methods, including bar charts and time graphs.

ASSESSING MASTERY

Children can read data and values from a range of bar charts and pictograms that have various scales and symbol values, including half and quarter values. Children can interpret data from tables and use this to complete charts and pictograms, as well as answering simple comparison questions.

COMMON MISCONCEPTIONS

Children may misread the scales on a bar chart, assuming that each square always stands for one. Ask:
- *What do you notice about the scale on the vertical axis of this chart? What steps does it increase in?*

Children may also assume that each symbol in a pictogram has a value of 1. Draw children's attention to the key on a pictogram and ask:
- *What can you look at to identify the value of each symbol? Is this always the same for every pictogram?*

STRENGTHENING UNDERSTANDING

Strengthen understanding of bar charts by asking children to recreate the bars using multilink cubes. This will help children compare the heights of each bar.

GOING DEEPER

Encourage children to make statements based on the data presented to them in different charts. For example, ask: *What can you tell me based on this bar chart/pictogram?*

KEY LANGUAGE

In lesson: bar chart, half, between, pictogram, symbol, table, row, column, vertical, horizontal

Other language used by the teacher: most, altogether, value

STRUCTURES AND REPRESENTATIONS

Number lines, bar chart, pictogram

RESOURCES

Mandatory: rulers

Optional: multilink cubes

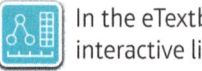 In the eTextbook of this lesson, you will find interactive links to a selection of teaching tools.

Quick recap

As a class, count on and back together in 2s, 5s and 10s.

Unit 15: Statistics, Lesson 1

Discover

WAYS OF WORKING Pair work

ASK

- Questions ① a) and b): *What types of chart are shown here?*
- Questions ① a) and b): *How you can you find the number of cupcakes from the pictogram? How can you find the number of cupcakes from the bar chart?*
- Question ① a): *What do you think half a symbol stands for?*

IN FOCUS This activity reintroduces children to pictograms and bar charts, which they last saw in Year 3. These charts are harder that the ones previously encountered, as one circle on the pictogram represents more than 1 item, and the scale on the vertical axis of the bar chart goes up in 10s. Children read a range of data, including data where half values are used, and make simple comparisons.

PRACTICAL TIPS Use multilink cubes to interpret data on the bar chart and pictogram to check children can make connections between the data that is being presented in different ways. Use a number line to help with the understanding of scales.

ANSWERS

Question ① a): Class 4T made 45 cookies. Class 4A made 55 cookies.

Question ① b): Class 4A made the most cupcakes. They made made 60 cupcakes.

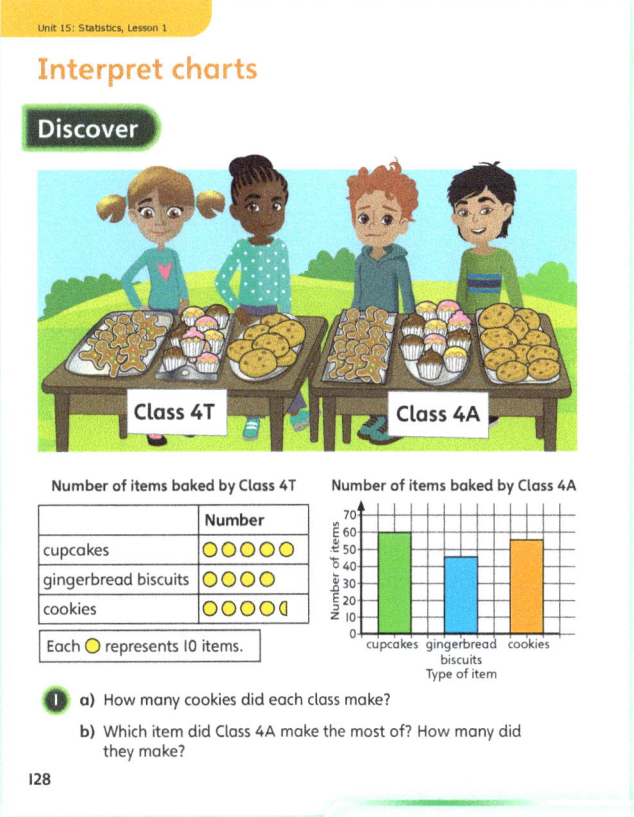

PUPIL TEXTBOOK 4C PAGE 128

Share

WAYS OF WORKING Whole class teacher led

ASK

- Question ① a): *How can you work out how many cookies Class 4T made from the pictogram?*
- Question ① a): *Look at the bar chart. How can you work out the value of a bar half-way between two marked values? How can you make sure you read the correct value on the vertical axis of the bar chart?*
- Question ① b): *Can you work out which item Class 4A made the most of without working out the value of each bar?*

IN FOCUS In this part of the lesson, children must interpret information from pictograms and bar charts, where there are half symbols in a pictogram and a bar is half-way between two marked values on a bar chart. When working out the total value of an item on a pictogram, draw children's attention to the two different ways of working (repeated addition and multiplication) and the link between the two.

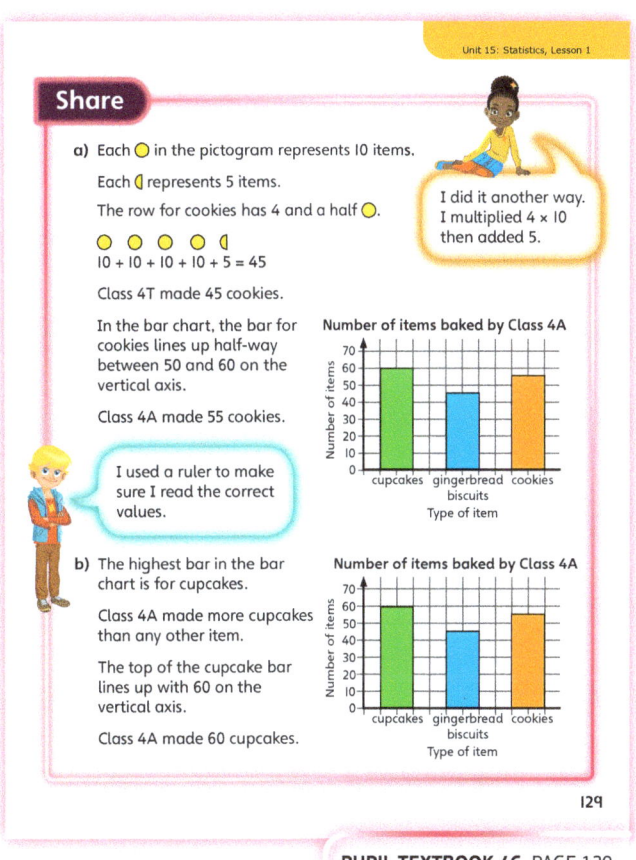

PUPIL TEXTBOOK 4C PAGE 129

163

Unit 15: Statistics, Lesson 1

Think together

WAYS OF WORKING Whole class teacher led (I do, We do, You do)

ASK
- Question 1 a): *How can you work out how many cupcakes each class has sold?*
- Question 1 b): *How can you work out the value of $\frac{1}{4}$ of a symbol?*
- Question 2: *How much money did Class 4B make from selling cupcakes? What multiplication do you need to do? How much did Class 4B make from selling gingerbread biscuits? How much did Class 4B make all together?*

IN FOCUS In question 1, children are introduced to $\frac{1}{4}$ pictogram symbols for the first time. They will need to extend their knowledge of how to calculate the value of $\frac{1}{2}$ symbols to calculating the value of $\frac{1}{4}$ symbols.

STRENGTHEN To strengthen understanding of the value of quarter symbols, represent a pictogram symbol using a set of 4 interconnecting cubes (in a 2 by 2 arrangement). You can then discuss what each quarter of the symbol would be worth, physically splitting up the symbol.

DEEPEN Deepen understanding by encouraging children to justify their responses to each question within question 3. As this is the first time children have come across quarters, ask: *How could you work out the value of the bar that is a $\frac{1}{4}$ of the way between two marked values?*

ASSESSMENT CHECKPOINT Use question 1 to assess whether children can independently read values from a bar chart and pictogram, including where the height of the bar falls between two marked numbers on the vertical axis on a bar chart, and when there are part symbols on a pictogram.

ANSWERS

Question 1 a): Class 5T sold 28 cupcakes.
Class 5A sold 45 cupcakes.

Question 1 b): Class 5T sold 36 gingerbread men.

Question 2: Class 4C raised the most money (£36).

Question 3 a): £650

Question 3 b): Olivia is wrong, it should be 3 quarters of the way up between £600 and £700.

Question 3 c): £650 (Year 3) + £525 (Year 4) + £350 (Year 5) + £675 (Year 6) = £2,200

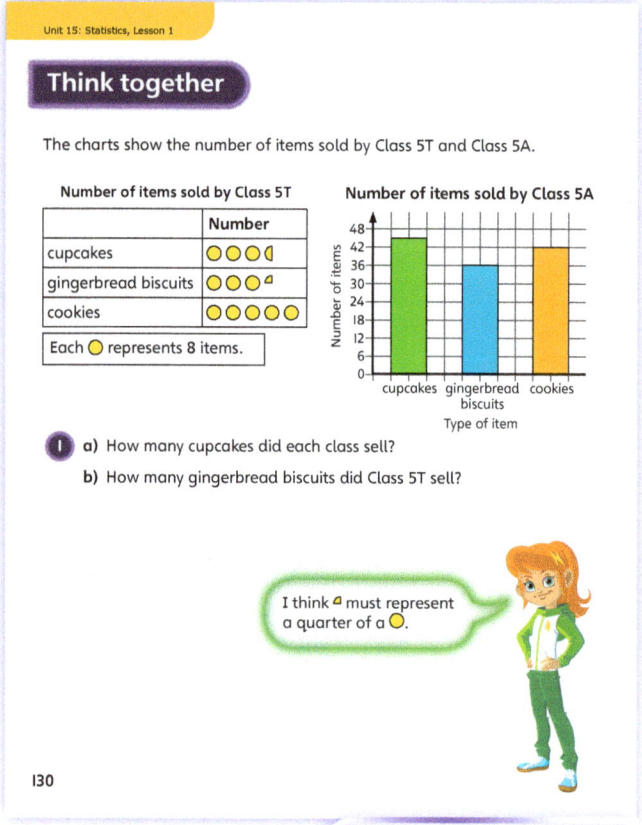

PUPIL TEXTBOOK 4C PAGE 130

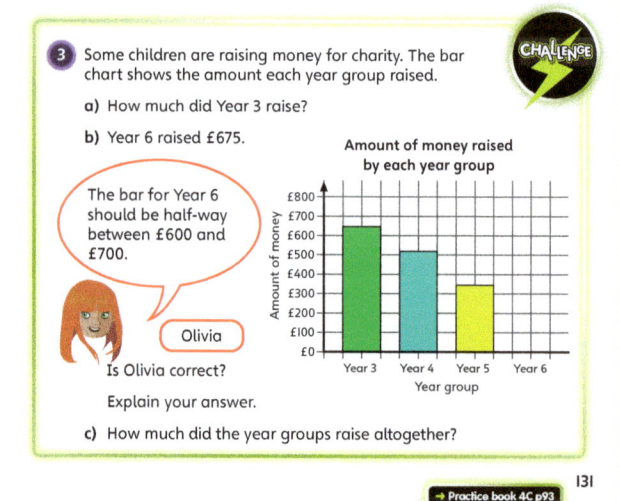

PUPIL TEXTBOOK 4C PAGE 131

Unit 15: Statistics, Lesson 1

Practice

WAYS OF WORKING Independent thinking

IN FOCUS In question ③, children must construct a pictogram using the information provided in the table and in the key.

STRENGTHEN To support children with question ①, encourage them to think carefully about the information provided in the key and how they can work out the value of a quarter symbol by halving and then halving again, or by dividing by 4.

DEEPEN Children should begin to solve more complex problems involving charts and tables including those where they need to compare different sources of data in order to complete a chart, and those where there are missing pieces of information. Question ⑤ encourages children to do this, and relies on children having a deep understanding of how each type of chart is constructed. Ask: *How can you work out what the scale on the vertical axis is? How can you work out what value each symbols has? What information can you use to help you?*

ASSESSMENT CHECKPOINT Use questions ② and ③ to assess whether children can correctly interpret data from a table and transfer this to another way of presenting data (in this case a pictogram).

ANSWERS Answers for the **Practice** part of the lesson can be found in the *Power Maths* online subscription.

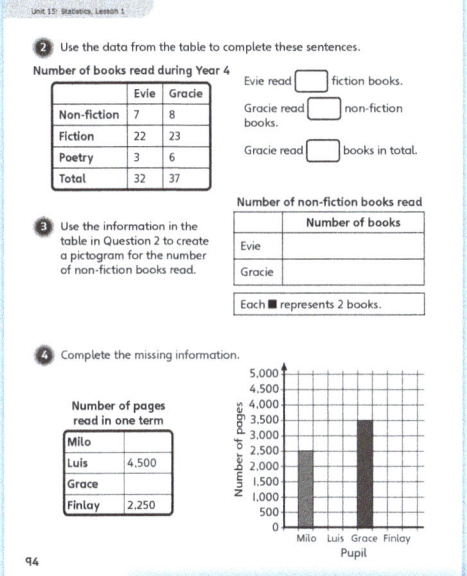

PUPIL PRACTICE BOOK 4C PAGE 93

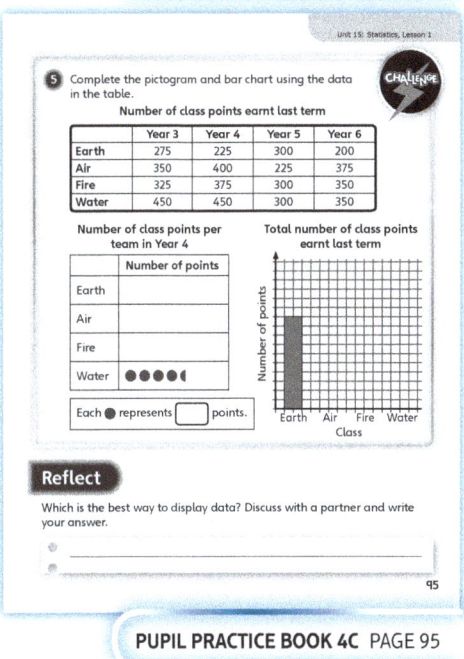

PUPIL PRACTICE BOOK 4C PAGE 94

Reflect

WAYS OF WORKING Pair work

IN FOCUS This **Reflect** question compares the benefits and similarities of each way of presenting data. Encourage children to discuss whether the type of data and the value of the data impact their choices.

ASSESSMENT CHECKPOINT Use this activity to assess whether children are able to identify the benefits of using each different type of representation.

ANSWERS Answers for the **Reflect** part of the lesson can be found in the *Power Maths* online subscription.

After the lesson

- Are children secure in reading data from bar charts, tables and pictograms?
- Can children confidently interpret $\frac{1}{2}$ and $\frac{1}{4}$ symbols in a pictogram?

PUPIL PRACTICE BOOK 4C PAGE 95

Unit 15: Statistics, Lesson 2

Solve problems with charts

Learning focus
In this lesson, children will use their knowledge of bar charts, tables and pictograms to answer increasingly complex problems, including those that involve differences and totals.

Before you teach
- Are children confident interpreting bar charts, pictograms and tables?
- Can children find $\frac{1}{4}$ and $\frac{1}{2}$ values on a number line?

NATIONAL CURRICULUM LINKS

Year 4 Statistics

Solve comparison, sum and difference problems using information presented in bar charts, pictograms, tables and other graphs.

ASSESSING MASTERY

Children can read data and values from different bar charts and pictograms that have a range of scales and symbol values, and use these to calculate sums and differences. Children can also make direct comparisons between data and draw conclusions from data presented in different ways.

COMMON MISCONCEPTIONS

Children may choose the wrong operation when finding totals or differences. Ask:
- *What is the question asking you to find? Is this an addition or subtraction question?*

STRENGTHENING UNDERSTANDING

Help children interpret the scales on a bar chart where the bar finishes part of the way between marked values. Link the scale on the vertical axis to a number line. Rotate the bar chart to help children see this connection. Ask: *What does this look like? How is it similar or different to a number line?* Help children identify the difference between each marked section, before writing what $\frac{1}{4}$, $\frac{1}{2}$ and $\frac{3}{4}$ of this difference is.

GOING DEEPER

Encourage children to draw their own conclusions based on the data that is presented to them. For example, ask: *Why do you think people spend more on chocolate in April than January?*

KEY LANGUAGE

In lesson: total, sum, difference, altogether, bar chart, half, between, pictogram, symbol, table, row, column, vertical, horizontal

Other language used by the teacher: most, quarter

STRUCTURES AND REPRESENTATIONS

Number lines, bar charts, pictograms

RESOURCES

Mandatory: rulers

Optional: multilink cubes

In the eTextbook of this lesson, you will find interactive links to a selection of teaching tools.

Quick recap

Ask children to draw a 0 to 100 number line with intervals marked in 10s, and then ask them to place different 2-digit numbers on the line as accurately as they can.

Discover

WAYS OF WORKING Pair work

ASK
- Question ❶: *What are these charts called?*
- Question ❶: *What operations do you need to use to solve these problems?*
- Question ❶ a): *How can you work out the difference in the number of tickets?*
- Question ❶ b): *What operation do you need to use to work out the total number of tickets sold?*

IN FOCUS This activity extends the learning from Lesson 1 and encourages children to find a difference and a total, using information drawn from two different representations of data.

PRACTICAL TIPS Use a number line or ruler to help find values along the vertical axis of the bar chart. Use multilink cubes to help children visualise multiples of 12 as well as half and quarter values of 12.

ANSWERS

Question ❶ a): The farm park sold 19 more child tickets on Saturday.

Question ❶ b): 55 + 60 = 115
The farm park sold 115 adult tickets altogether over the weekend.

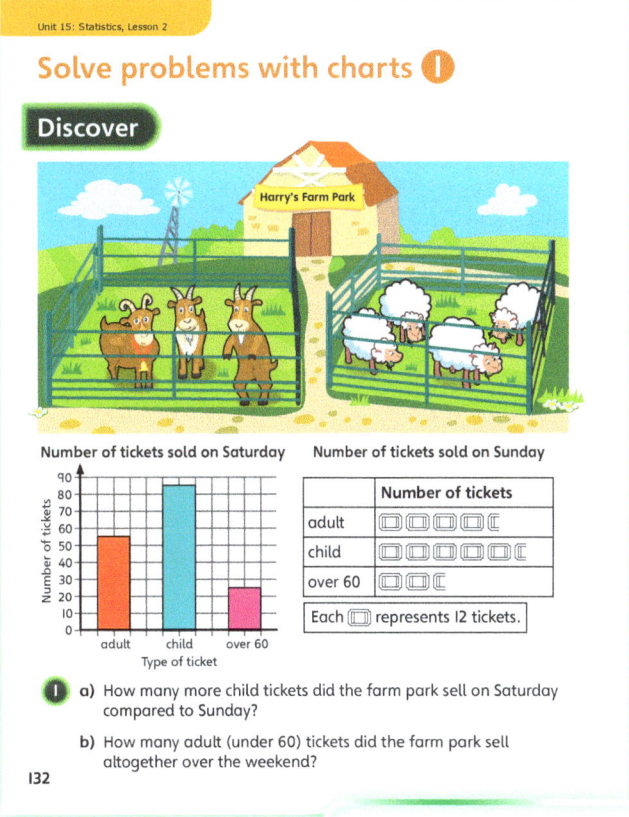

PUPIL TEXTBOOK 4C PAGE 132

Share

WAYS OF WORKING Whole class teacher led

ASK
- Question ❶: *How do you know how much each symbol represents on the pictogram?*
- Question ❶: *How can you make sure you read the correct value on the vertical axis of the bar chart?*
- Question ❶: *How can you work out the value of the bar if it is between two numbers on the vertical axis?*
- Question ❶: *Is there more than one way to work out the value of items on a pictogram?*

IN FOCUS In this part of the lesson, children identify the information they need from each chart and the operation they need to use to calculate the difference and total. Discuss the choice of operation with the children, encouraging them to justify and explain their decisions.

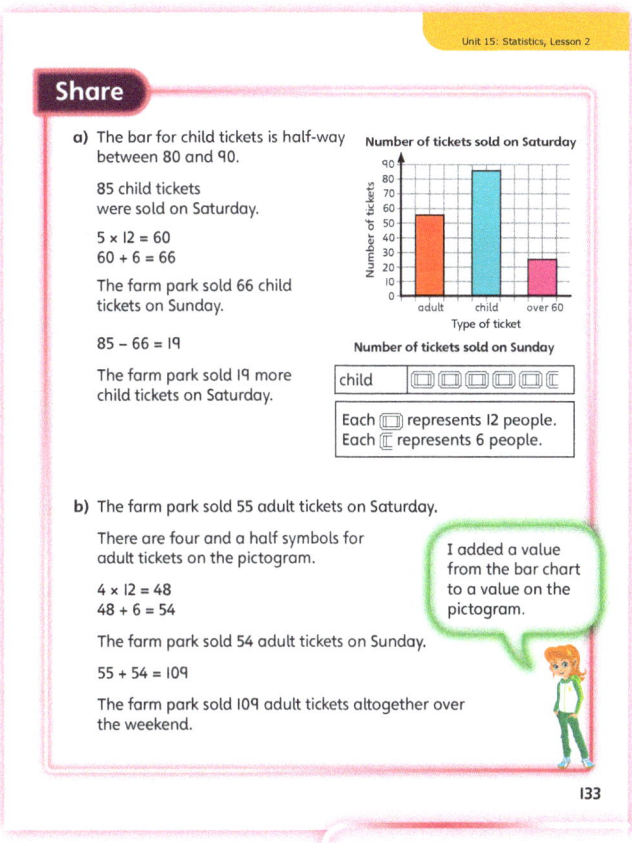

PUPIL TEXTBOOK 4C PAGE 133

Unit 15: Statistics, Lesson 2

Think together

WAYS OF WORKING Whole class teacher led (I do, We do, You do)

ASK
- Question ① a): *How can you work out if more children or adults fed the lambs?*
- Question ① b): *What operation do you need to use to find out how many people fed the foals altogether?*
- Question ②: *How do you know which row and column you need to look at to answer the question?*
- Question ③ a): *How can you use the information we have to find the answers?*

IN FOCUS In question ① a), children are asked to find the difference between two values, one of which is shown on a pictogram and one of which is shown on a bar chart. Ensure children realise that, as well as interpreting the charts to find each value, they will also need to carry out a subtraction to find the difference.

STRENGTHEN Use a bar model to represent the structure of both the sum and the difference problems. This will help children identify the correct operation to use in order to solve each problem.

DEEPEN Children should be able to extend their learning and begin to draw their own conclusions based on the data that is presented to them. For example, in question ③, children should be able to make a range of statements comparing single values, finding the totals and comparing sets of values. They can then be invited to draw conclusions from these statements. For example, ask: *Do people generally like their visit to the farm? How do you know?*

ASSESSMENT CHECKPOINT Use questions ① and ② to assess whether children can identify the correct operations needed to answer sum and difference questions.

ANSWERS

Question ① a): 16 more children than adults fed the lambs.

Question ① b): 75 people fed the foals altogether.

Question ② a): On Sunday, the café made £600 from hot meals.

Question ② b): The café made £75 more from cold children's meals on Saturday than Sunday.

Question ③ a): 33 more visitors rated the farm OK on Saturday (69) than Sunday (36).

Question ③ b): More people rated the farm on Saturday (148) than on Sunday (134).

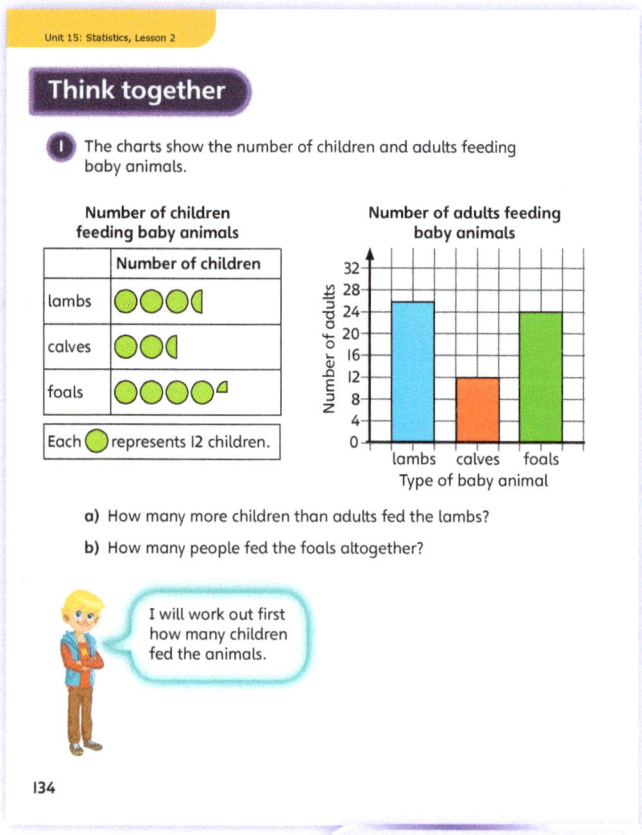

PUPIL TEXTBOOK 4C PAGE 134

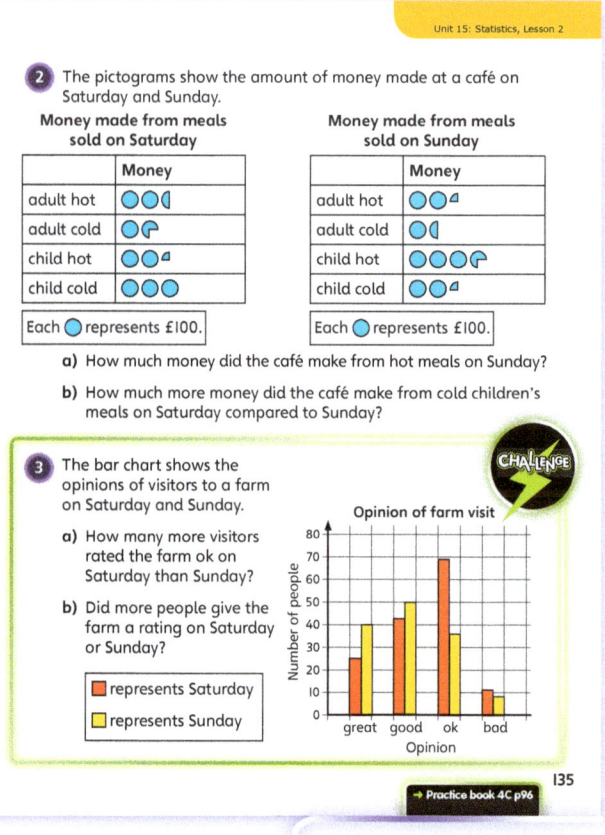

PUPIL TEXTBOOK 4C PAGE 135

Unit 15: Statistics, Lesson 2

Practice

WAYS OF WORKING Independent thinking

IN FOCUS In question ③, children's reasoning skills are developed further. They are asked to interpret the information given in order to calculate the missing pieces of information from a table and then to use this to populate a bar chart.

STRENGTHEN To support children with question ③, it may be useful to break down the task further. Encourage children to consider the relationships between the values in the table and the information given. For example, ask: *How many points did Max score on Vault Explorer? We know that Sarah scored 450 more than Max, so how do we work out Sarah's score?* Once children have correctly filled in the missing information from the table, look at the features of a bar chart. Review the scale provided, identifying what a half and a quarter of 100 are, before inviting children to mark the values on the chart.

DEEPEN Children should begin to solve more complex logic-style questions that involve charts, tables and pictograms. Question ④ provides children with the opportunity to develop these skills. Challenge children to create their own logic-style clues for other charts and tables, including those presented elsewhere in this lesson.

ASSESSMENT CHECKPOINT Question ② assesses whether children can use the relationship between individual pieces of data and the total; for example, can they work out the value of one piece of data if they know the total and the other data values?

ANSWERS Answers for the **Practice** part of the lesson can be found in the *Power Maths* online subscription.

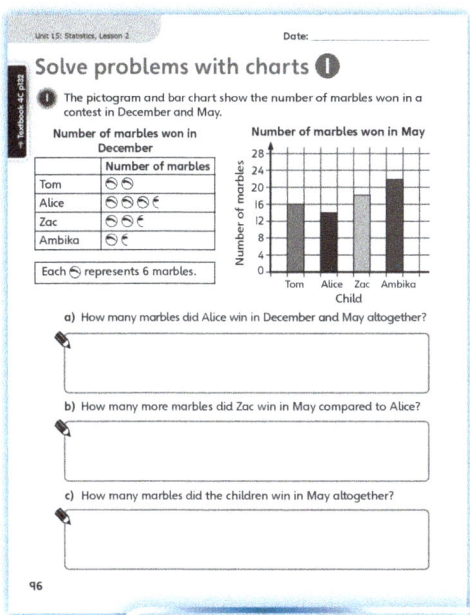

PUPIL PRACTICE BOOK 4C PAGE 96

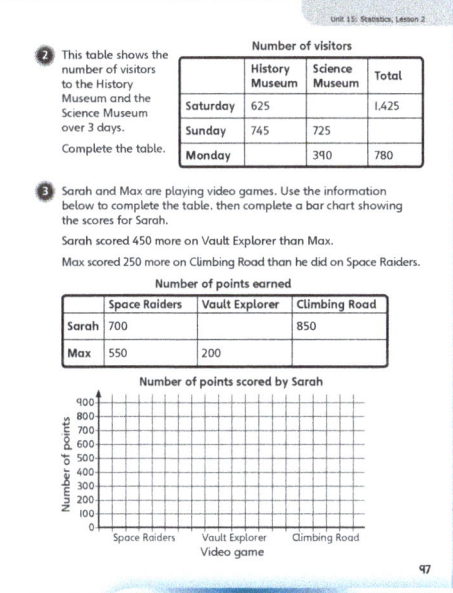

PUPIL PRACTICE BOOK 4C PAGE 97

Reflect

WAYS OF WORKING Independent thinking

IN FOCUS In this part of the lesson, children reflect on the different types of charts that they know.

ASSESSMENT CHECKPOINT Use this activity to assess whether children are able to describe different ways of presenting and identifying data and to provide coherent reasoning as to which method they prefer over others.

ANSWERS Answers for the **Reflect** part of the lesson can be found in the *Power Maths* online subscription.

After the lesson

- Are children secure at interpreting data from bar charts, tables and pictograms?
- How can you provide opportunities for children to further use and develop these skills during day-to-day school life?

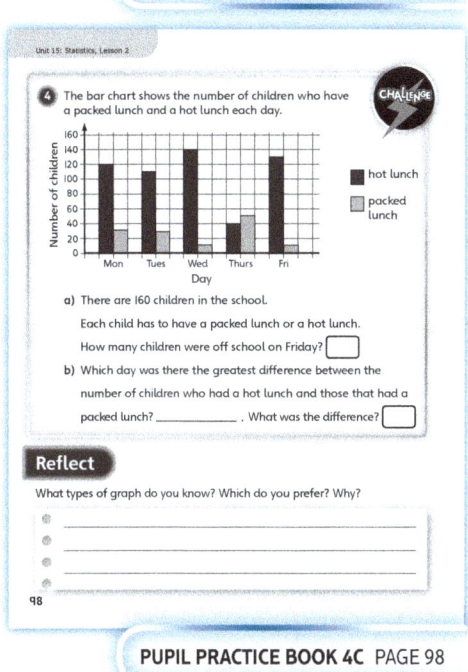

PUPIL PRACTICE BOOK 4C PAGE 98

Unit 15: Statistics, Lesson 3

Solve problems with charts ❷

Learning focus
In this lesson, children will apply their data interpretation and analysis skills to a range of increasingly challenging problems.

Before you teach ⏸
- Are children confident answering simple questions about data that is presented in different ways?
- Do children have any weaknesses in relation to calculation methods that need support?

NATIONAL CURRICULUM LINKS

Year 4 Statistics

Interpret and present discrete and continuous data using appropriate graphical methods, including bar charts and time graphs.

ASSESSING MASTERY

Children can read data from bar charts, pictograms and tables, and use this data to solve a range of complex problems involving multiple steps and different operations. Children can analyse what other information is available from the data. They can assess the benefits and drawbacks of how the data is presented.

COMMON MISCONCEPTIONS

Children may incorrectly identify the number of steps needed to solve a problem, and therefore leave a problem incomplete. Ask:
- *Can you answer this question just using information from the chart? What else do you need to do to the information in order to answer the question?*

STRENGTHENING UNDERSTANDING

To help children solve more complex problems, it can be helpful to break down a problem into steps. Steps could be provided in 'help envelopes' when children need support.

GOING DEEPER

Encourage children to create their own more complex questions for others. These should be based on data presented in a range of different ways.

KEY LANGUAGE

In lesson: bar chart, pictogram, table, axis, vertical, horizontal, comparison

Other language to be used by the teacher: operations, steps, addition, subtraction, multiplication, division

STRUCTURES AND REPRESENTATIONS

Tables, pictograms, bar charts

RESOURCES

Mandatory: rulers

Optional: number lines, squared paper, help envelopes

 In the eTextbook of this lesson, you will find interactive links to a selection of teaching tools.

Quick recap
As a class, count on and back from 0 to 20 in 2s.

Unit 15: Statistics, Lesson 3

Discover

WAYS OF WORKING Pair work

ASK
- Question 1 a): *How much money did Years 3 and 4 raise? How much money did Years 5 and 6 raise? What will be your next step?*
- Question 1 b): *How can you use the information you have to help you work out how many cards Year 4 sold? Is there more than one way to do this?*

IN FOCUS In this activity, children apply their knowledge of bar charts to answer more complex questions that involve comparisons across groups of data and carrying out further calculations. These skills will continue to be developed, using a range of data presentations, throughout this lesson.

PRACTICAL TIPS Remind children of the division method to find out how many cards Year 4 used. Use a number line to demonstrate the division method for numbers divisible by 2.

ANSWERS

Question 1 a): Years 3 and 4 raised £30 more than Years 5 and 6.

Question 1 b): Year 4 sold 60 cards in total.

PUPIL TEXTBOOK 4C PAGE 136

Share

WAYS OF WORKING Whole class teacher led

ASK
- Question 1 a): *How did you work out the difference between Years 3 and 4 compared to Years 5 and 6?*
- Question 1 a): *How many steps did you have to take in order to solve this problem? What operations did you have to use?*
- Question 1 b): *How did you work out how many cards Year 4 sold? What information did you use from the graph?*
- Question 1 b): *What operation did you need to use to help you work out how many cards were sold? How could you check your answer?*

IN FOCUS The focus in this part of the lesson is on children using the data presented in the bar chart to answer more complex, multi-step problems. The skill of reading from a bar chart is not covered in this section, as this should be a secure skill gained from work earlier in the unit. Instead, the focus is on how the data can be used to find out a wider range of information.

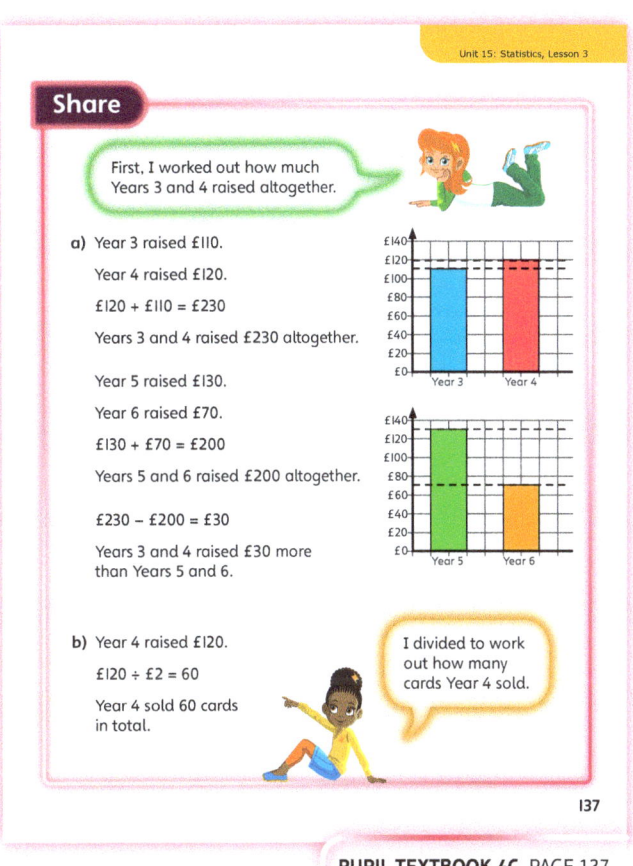

PUPIL TEXTBOOK 4C PAGE 137

171

Unit 15: Statistics, Lesson 3

Think together

WAYS OF WORKING Whole class teacher led (I do, We do, You do)

ASK

- Question ① a): *Will you need to use more than one operation?*
- Question ① b): *How can you work out the total amount raised?*
- Question ① c): *How can you use the fact that each child raised £5 to help you work out how many children there are?*
- Question ② a): *Is there more than one way to solve this problem?*
- Question ② b): *How many calculations do you need to carry out to solve this problem?*
- Question ③: *How can you use the clues to help you complete the table?*

IN FOCUS In this part of the lesson, children are provided with a further opportunity to develop their skills at answering more complex problems, using data presented in bar charts, tables and pictograms. Most questions require multiple steps, and the use of different operations to solve problems.

STRENGTHEN Help children identify the different operations needed to solve a multi-step problem. Ask: *What data do you need to read from the graph/pictogram/table? What do you need to do next to this information in order to solve the problem you've been given?*

DEEPEN Encourage children to create their own two-step problems. They should use a table or graph to set a question for their partner. This will help them consider how two parts of a question are related.

ASSESSMENT CHECKPOINT Use question ① to assess whether children are able to accurately answer total and comparison questions based on a bar chart.

ANSWERS

Question ①: Maple and Ash classes raised £60 more than Oak and Willow classes.

Question ① a): The classes raised £420 altogether.

Question ① b): There are 23 children in Oak class.

Question ② a): Lions and owls.

Question ② b): Lions and dogs made £100 for Year 3. (£70 + £30 or 20 × £5)

Question ③:

Maple	£24
Ash	£36
Oak	£42
Willow	£30

In total Year 5 raised £132.

PUPIL TEXTBOOK 4C PAGE 138

① This bar chart shows how much money was raised by different classes.

Amount of money raised by class

a) How much more money did Maple and Ash classes raise in total compared to Oak and Willow classes?

b) How much money did the four classes raise altogether?

c) Each child in Oak class raised £5. How many children are in Oak class?

I can use some of my working from part a) to help me work out part b).

---

② The pictogram shows the number of soft toys Year 3 sold at a summer fair.

a) Which soft toys did Year 3 sell more than 10 of?

b) Each soft toy sold for £5. How much money was made by selling lions and dogs?

Type of soft toy sold by Year 3

	Number
lions	⬤⬤⬤⬤⬤⬤⬤
dogs	⬤⬤⬤
cats	⬤◖
owls	⬤⬤⬤⬤⬤◖

Each ⬤ represents 2 soft toys.

③ Year 5 raised money by selling recordings of a class concert. Oak class sold 7 recordings. Each class sold recordings for the same amount.

Use the clues below to complete the table and work out how much money they raised in total.

Maple	£
Ash	£
Oak	£42
Willow	£

I am going to work out how much Oak charged for each recording first.

Willow collected £12 less than Oak.

Maple collected $\frac{8}{10}$ of the amount Willow collected.

Ash collected $\frac{1}{2}$ more than Maple's total amount.

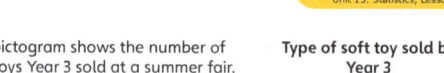

PUPIL TEXTBOOK 4C PAGE 139

Unit 15: Statistics, Lesson 3

Practice

WAYS OF WORKING Independent thinking

IN FOCUS Children are expected to solve problems based on all the ways of presenting data they have met so far: tables, pictograms and bar charts. Question ③ allows children to solve a series of more complex problems based on a bar chart. They will need to identify the relevant information in the bar chart and work out which operation or operations are needed to find each answer.

STRENGTHEN Provide scaffolding for children to complete that shows the operations needed for the different stages of a calculation. Children could then create their own frames, based on the operations that are needed to solve a problem.

DEEPEN Children should be able to make increasingly complex statements based on a chart. The charts in question ④ provide children with an opportunity to do this. Ask: *What other information can you tell from these charts?* Children could then be asked to create their own questions based on the information they have found.

ASSESSMENT CHECKPOINT Use question ③ to assess whether children can identify the multiple steps needed to solve a more complex problem. If children have not been successful with this question, ensure that you distinguish between calculation errors (where there is a complete method) and an incomplete method.

ANSWERS Answers for the **Practice** part of the lesson can be found in the *Power Maths* online subscription.

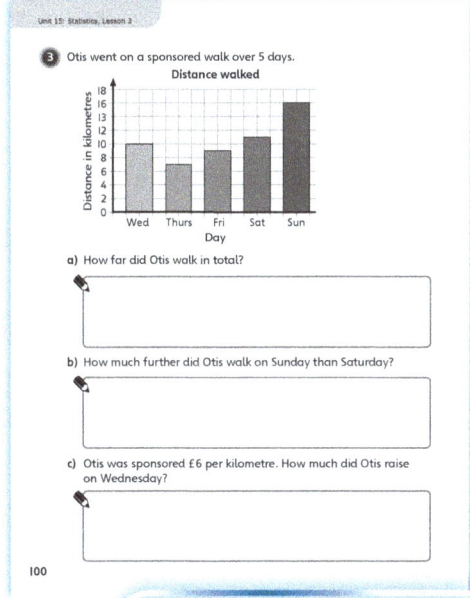

PUPIL PRACTICE BOOK 4C PAGE 99

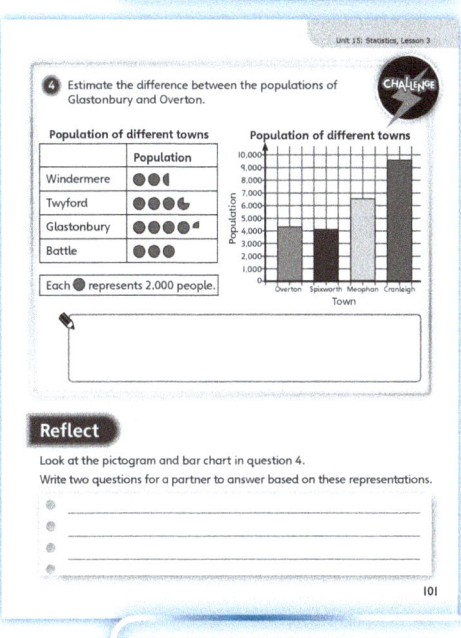

PUPIL PRACTICE BOOK 4C PAGE 100

Reflect

WAYS OF WORKING Independent thinking

IN FOCUS In this **Reflect** question, children must interpret the information given on a pictogram and a bar chart in order to devise two questions for a partner. These questions should be based on the data provided.

ASSESSMENT CHECKPOINT Do children refer to both the bar chart and the pictogram in their questions?

ANSWERS Answers for the **Reflect** part of the lesson can be found in the *Power Maths* online subscription.

After the lesson

- Are children secure in interpreting information and answering more complex questions based on different types of data presentations?
- Are children stronger or weaker at analysing a particular way of presenting data?

PUPIL PRACTICE BOOK 4C PAGE 101

Unit 15: Statistics, Lesson 4

Interpret line graphs ①

Learning focus
In this lesson, children will read values from a line graph.

Before you teach ⏸
- Are children confident at reading values from the vertical axis of a bar chart, including when the bar height is between two marked values?
- Have children been exposed to continuous data before in other subject areas?

NATIONAL CURRICULUM LINKS

Year 4 Statistics

Interpret and present discrete and continuous data using appropriate graphical methods, including bar charts and time graphs.

ASSESSING MASTERY

Children can read data from line graphs, including where values lie in between two marked points on an axis. Children can identify which axis to read the data from and read the value from any point on the line. They can make simple statements about the values.

COMMON MISCONCEPTIONS

Children may think they can only read data from the marked points on the x-axis. Draw children's attention to the type of data displayed. Discuss how this is continuous and that the line graphs help us to estimate values in between two marked points. Ask:
- *What do you notice about the type of data shown in this graph? How is it the same as or different from the types of data we were looking at in our last lesson?*

STRENGTHENING UNDERSTANDING

To help children interpret the continuous scales on a line graph, link the scales on both axes to a number line, rotating the chart so that the vertical axis is horizontal to help make the connection.

Children may also benefit from recording data and recreating a line graph so that they are able to understand the connection between the marked points and the continuous sets of data. Consider linking data collection to a real-life context. Discuss how the measurement is still changing when between marked values.

GOING DEEPER

Encourage children to begin to consider the benefits of a line graph over other ways of presenting data. Ask: *Why is the line graph better at presenting this data compared to a bar graph, pictogram or table?*

KEY LANGUAGE

In lesson: line graph, axis, vertical, horizontal

Other language to be used by teacher: most, least, longest, shortest, continuous data, bar chart, discrete data

STRUCTURES AND REPRESENTATIONS

Line graphs

RESOURCES

Mandatory: rulers

Optional: number lines, squared paper

 In the eTextbook of this lesson, you will find interactive links to a selection of teaching tools.

Quick recap

As a class, count on from 0 to 200 in 20s.

Unit 15: Statistics, Lesson 4

Discover

WAYS OF WORKING Pair work

ASK
- Question ①: *How is this chart the same as/different from the charts you have seen so far?*
- Question ① a): *How can you find out what the temperature was at a given time?*

IN FOCUS This is the first time children have been exposed to line graphs, so encourage them to explore the graph, including its title and axes. Discuss how this graph is different from other graphs they have explored in previous lessons.

PRACTICAL TIPS Use rulers to interpret continuous values on a line graph, reading from both the horizontal and vertical axes. Use a number line to help understanding of in-between values on a continuous scale.

ANSWERS

Question ① a): The temperature at 11 am was 14 °C.

Question ① b): The temperature decreased by 6 °C between 12:30 pm and 3 pm.

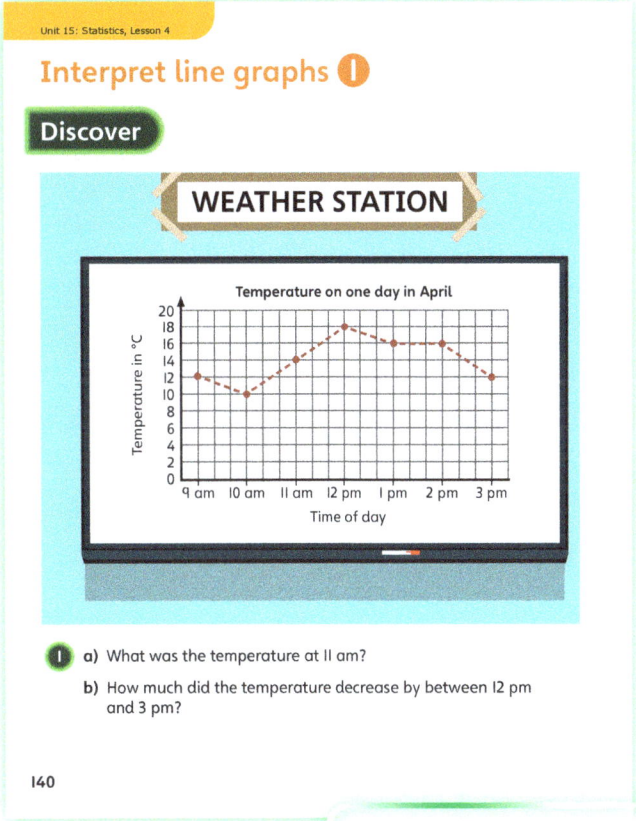

PUPIL TEXTBOOK 4C PAGE 140

Share

WAYS OF WORKING Whole class teacher led

ASK
- Question ①: *How is the data shown here different to the data shown on bar charts?*
- Question ① a): *Where can we find 11 am on the graph? How can you work out the temperature at 11 am?*
- Question ① a): *What could you use to help you read the times and temperatures accurately?*
- Question ① b): *Where is 12 pm marked on the horizontal axis? Where is 3 pm marked on the horizontal axis?*
- Question ① b): *What calculation do you need to do to find the difference?*

IN FOCUS In this part of the lesson, children read information from a line graph, starting from a given value on the horizontal axis and then reading the corresponding value from the vertical axis. Ensure children understand that a line graph shows continuous data, which means that they can read values that fall between marked values on the horizontal axis, and that they can use a line to find the approximate corresponding value on the vertical axis. In comparison, bar charts and pictograms show categorical, discrete data.

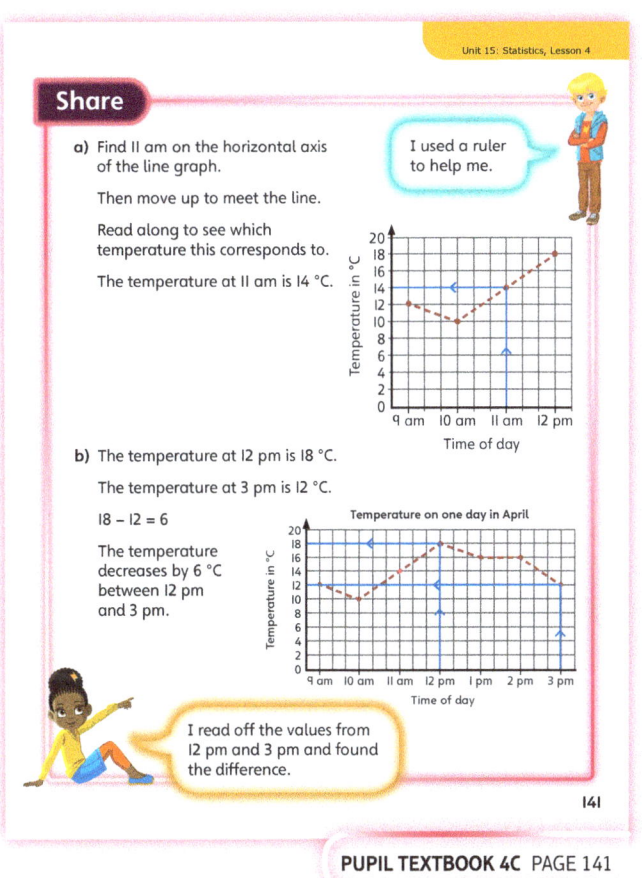

PUPIL TEXTBOOK 4C PAGE 141

175

Think together

WAYS OF WORKING Whole class teacher led (I do, We do, You do)

ASK
- Question 1 a): *How can you work out the temperature at a given time?*
- Question 1 c): *2:30 pm is not marked on the horizontal axis. How can you find the temperature at 2:30 pm?*
- Question 1 d): *How can you use the shape of the line to help you find out when it was warmest inside?*
- Question 3: *Which axis do you need to read from in order to answer each of these questions?*

IN FOCUS In this part of the lesson, children are introduced to reading values from a line graph from both the horizontal and vertical axes. Discuss how the continuous nature of the graph makes it possible to read values from either axis, including from points that lie in between marked values. In question 1 d), children determine the highest values by looking at the highest points of the line graph and begin to make statements based on the graph.

STRENGTHEN To help children read accurately from either the horizontal or vertical axis, encourage them to use a ruler to draw a horizontal or vertical line from a given point on each axis to the line. They can then draw a horizontal or vertical line from this point to the other axis and then read the required value.

DEEPEN Children should be able to extend their learning to interpret more complex line graphs, including those where multiple sets of data are plotted as two or more lines. Question 3 provides an opportunity for children to explore this. Ask children to explain why they think there are two lines on the same graph. They should begin to consider how they can use this to help them compare the two sets of data. Ask: *How can you use this line graph to help you compare the data for October and December?*

ASSESSMENT CHECKPOINT Use question 1 to assess whether children are able to accurately read values from a line graph, when they have to read values for a given point on the horizontal axis.

ANSWERS

Question 1 a): The temperature was 24 °C at 11 am.

Question 1 b): The temperature was 25 °C at 1 pm.

Question 1 c): The temperature was 25 °C at 2:30 pm.

Question 1 d): It was warmest at 2 pm.

Question 1 e): The temperature was 21 °C at 10:15 am.

Question 2: It is above 24 °C for approximately $2\frac{1}{4}$ hours (from 12:45 pm to 3 pm).

Question 3 a): The temperature was 11 °C.

Question 3 b): The difference is 2 °C.

Question 3 c): For example:
Same: It was warmest at 12 pm on both days.
Different: It was warmer at 8 am than it was at 2 pm on 1 October, but the opposite is true of 1 December (warmer at 2 pm than at 8 am).

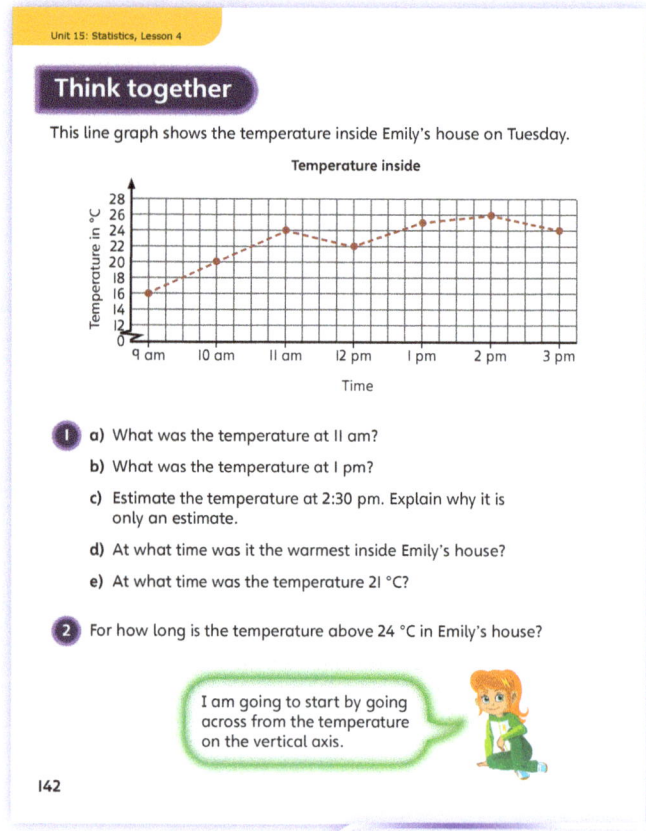

PUPIL TEXTBOOK 4C PAGE 142

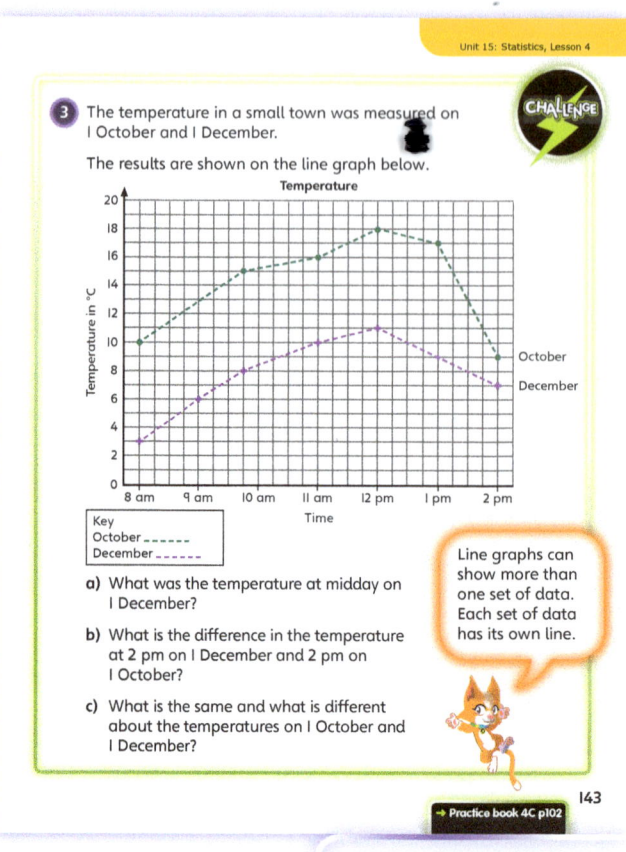

PUPIL TEXTBOOK 4C PAGE 143

Unit 15: Statistics, Lesson 4

Practice

WAYS OF WORKING Independent thinking

IN FOCUS Questions ❶ and ❷ help children practise reading from both the horizontal and vertical axes of a line graph. In question ❷ c), children make simple statements based on the line graph. For example, they must work out when the shadow is shortest and longest by looking at the height of the line at various points.

STRENGTHEN To support children in correctly identifying which axis to read from, ask children to consider which piece of information they 'know'. For example, in question ❷ c), ask: *Do you know the time or the length of the shadow?* Encourage children to ask themselves this question every time they are reading information from a line graph.

DEEPEN Children should begin to explore how line graphs can be developed and used to show more complex information. Question ❹ exposes children to line graphs where information that is not explicitly marked can be deduced – for example, that something caused the car to be temporarily stationary. Ask: *If the car was stuck in a traffic jam, would the distance it had travelled increase as time increased? Which part of the graph shows no increase in distance as time is increasing?*

THINK DIFFERENTLY Question ❸ requires children to consider the features of a line graph in order to decide if it would be a useful way to present the data provided in a table. They should identify that the information in the table is discrete data, and as such a line graph would not be an appropriate choice. Prompt them to identify that a bar graph or pictogram would be better.

ASSESSMENT CHECKPOINT Use question ❷ to assess whether children can correctly interpret data from a line graph and answer questions about what it shows.

ANSWERS Answers for the **Practice** part of the lesson can be found in the *Power Maths* online subscription.

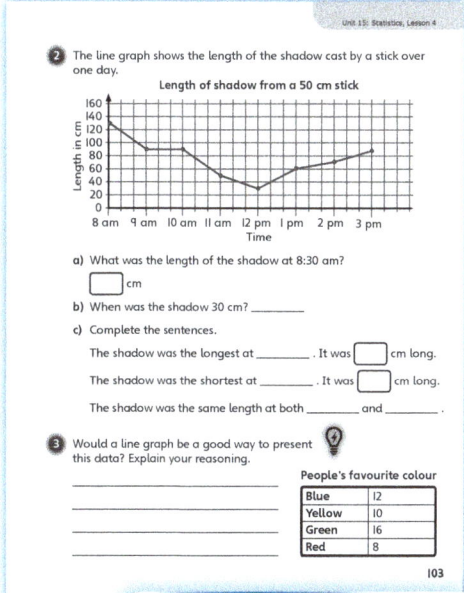

PUPIL PRACTICE BOOK 4C PAGE 102

Reflect

WAYS OF WORKING Independent thinking

IN FOCUS Children consider when it is appropriate to use a line graph.

ASSESSMENT CHECKPOINT Use this **Reflect** question to assess whether children are able to identify the key feature of a line graph, and realise when a bar chart would be the more efficient option.

ANSWERS Answers for the **Reflect** part of the lesson can be found in the *Power Maths* online subscription.

After the lesson

- Are all children secure in reading continuous data from a line graph?
- Are children able to make connections when looking at the same data presented differently? For example, if the same data were presented in both a table and a line graph (like in question ❹), could children work out where each data value in the table is represented on the line graph and vice versa?

Unit 15: Statistics, Lesson 5

Interpret line graphs ❷

Learning focus
In this lesson, children will continue to explore line graphs, and will make statements and comparisons based on data presented in line graphs.

Before you teach ⏸
- Are children confident reading line graphs?
- How could children collect data as part of your wider curriculum coverage?

NATIONAL CURRICULUM LINKS

Year 4 Statistics

Solve comparison, sum and difference problems using information presented in bar charts, pictograms, tables and other graphs.

ASSESSING MASTERY

Children can read and compare data from both axes on a line graph, including where values lie in between two marked points on an axis, and use this to make comparisons and find the difference between two points. They can also use the shape and structure of a line graph to make statements about the rate of change and the highest and lowest values.

COMMON MISCONCEPTIONS

Children may think that the highest and lowest values are always the first and last points of a graph. Ask:
- *Where would you find the highest and lowest value on the vertical axis? Which point of the graph is at the highest and lowest point?*

STRENGTHENING UNDERSTANDING

To help children make statements about the rate of change, encourage them to collect data and create their own graph. Ask: *What does the steepness of the line between each set of points say about the rate of change?*

GOING DEEPER

Encourage children to make deeper and more hypothetical statements based on data presented to them in line graphs. For example, if presented with the timings of a race, encourage children to consider which athlete they think is the best and why.

KEY LANGUAGE

In lesson: line graph, continuous data, axis, vertical, horizontal, comparison

Other language to be used by the teacher: most, least, longest, shortest

STRUCTURES AND REPRESENTATIONS

Line graph

RESOURCES

Mandatory: rulers

Optional: number lines, squared paper

 In the eTextbook of this lesson, you will find interactive links to a selection of teaching tools.

Quick recap

Ask children to draw a number line showing times from 6 o'clock to 9 o'clock and then to accurately place these times on the line:

06:30 08:45 07:15

Unit 15: Statistics, Lesson 5

Discover

WAYS OF WORKING Pair work

ASK

- Question 1 a): *How can you work out how far Sofia travelled between two different times?*
- Question 1 b): *How can you work out how long it took Sofia to travel a certain distance?*

IN FOCUS In this part of the lesson, children are expected to apply their knowledge of how to read information from line graphs, which they have developed in the previous lesson. They should use it to answer comparison questions based on information presented in a line graph.

PRACTICAL TIPS Use a ruler to draw lines up from the horizontal axis to the graph line to find the corresponding vertical axis value. Remind children of the subtraction method to find out the difference between two values.

ANSWERS

Question 1 a): Sofia cycled 25 km between 11 am and 12 pm.

Question 1 b): It took Sofia 1 hour and 15 minutes to travel the next 40 km.

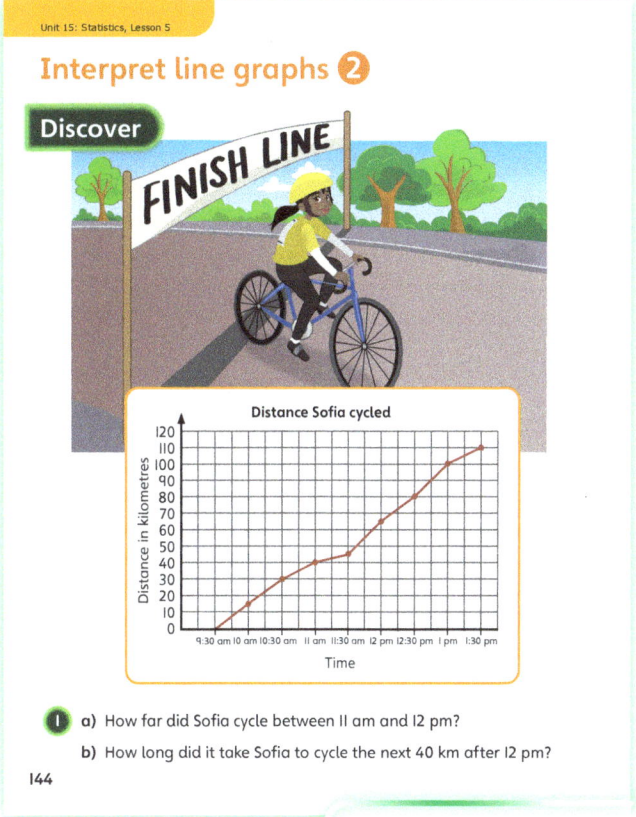

PUPIL TEXTBOOK 4C PAGE 144

Share

WAYS OF WORKING Whole class teacher led

ASK

Question 1 b): *Which axis should you look at first?*

IN FOCUS In question 1, children read first from the vertical axis and build on the skill of identifying which axis to read from, which was developed in the previous lesson.

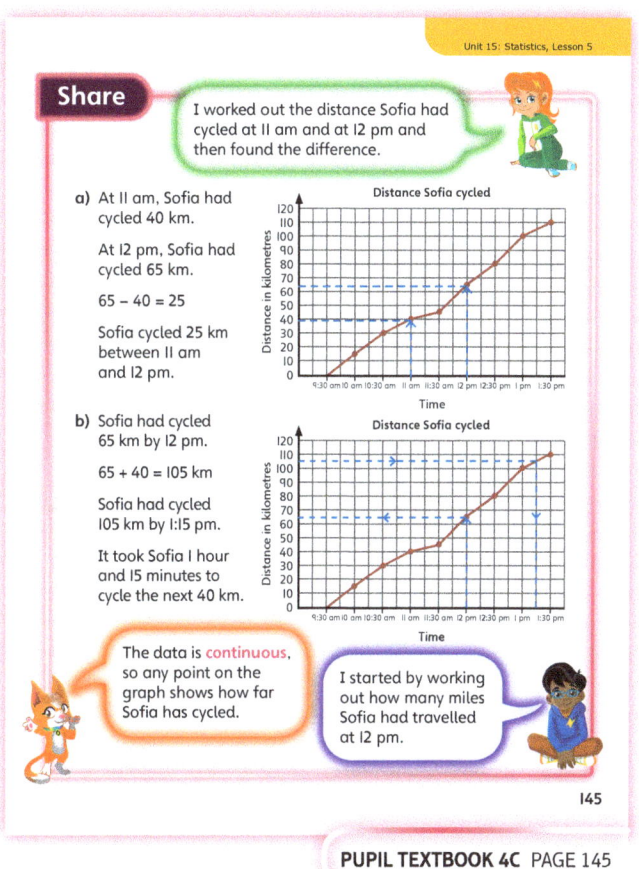

PUPIL TEXTBOOK 4C PAGE 145

Think together

WAYS OF WORKING Whole class teacher led (I do, We do, You do)

ASK
- Question ❶ b): *11:15 am is not marked on the horizontal axis. How can you work out the distance at 11:15 am?*
- Question ❷: *Which axis do you need to start to read from to solve this question?*
- Question ❸ a): *How can you use the two lines to help you make comparisons between the athletes? How does the shape of the two lines and their relationship to each other help you work out when both athletes had run the same distance?*

IN FOCUS In question ❷, children read first from the vertical axis, and build on the skill of identifying which axis to read from, which was developed in the previous lesson of this unit.

STRENGTHEN In question ❸, to help children differentiate between the two different sets of data shown on one graph, encourage them to focus on one set of data at a time. Break the question down into narrower ones based on each data set. For example, ask: *Which line shows how far Ian has run? How far has Ian run after 60 minutes?*

DEEPEN Children should be able to use line graphs in order to make their own statements. They should also be able to extend this to drawing more detailed conclusions or hypotheses, giving reasons to support their ideas. For example, in question ❸, ask: *Who do you think is the best athlete?* Suggest that children use the graph to help justify their answers.

ASSESSMENT CHECKPOINT Use question ❶ to assess whether children can accurately answer simple comparison questions based on information presented in a line graph. Question ❸ assesses whether children can make simple statements about data.

ANSWERS

Question ❶ a): Toshi travelled 25 km between 12:30 pm and 1:30 pm.

Question ❶ b): Toshi travelled 50 km between 11:15 am and 12:45 pm.

Question ❶ c): The race started at 9:30 am.

Question ❶ d): This could be the same race that Sofia took part in as they both cycled the same distance, and started and ended at the same times.

Question ❷: Toshi took $1\frac{1}{2}$ hours to travel between 20 km and 70 km.

Question ❸ a): After 60 minutes, Ian had run 16 km and Jo had run 14 km.
It took Jo 140 minutes and Ian 130 minutes to run 34 km.
Before the end of the race, Ian and Jo had both run exactly the same distance after 100 minutes.
The length of the running race was 42 km.

Question ❸ b): Children's answers will vary; look for clear comparisons involving the words listed.

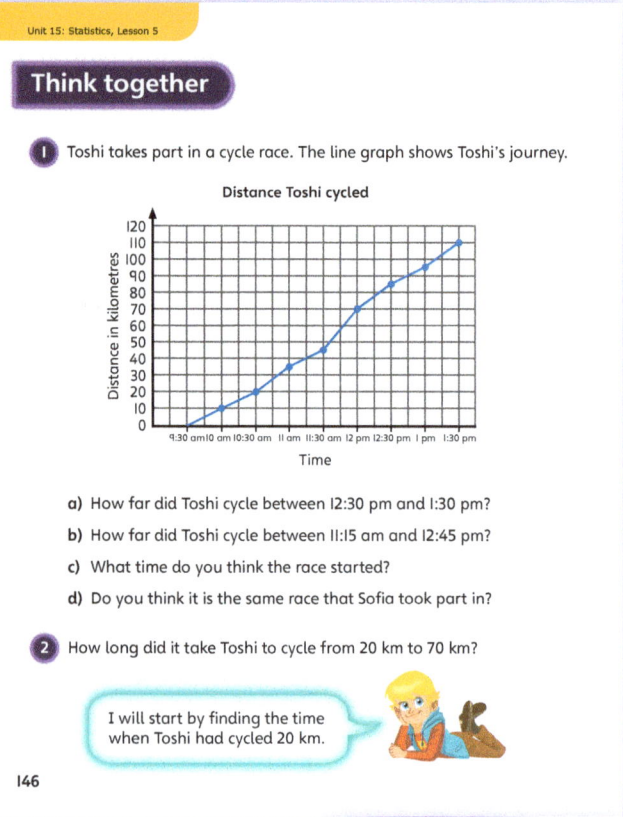

PUPIL TEXTBOOK 4C PAGE 146

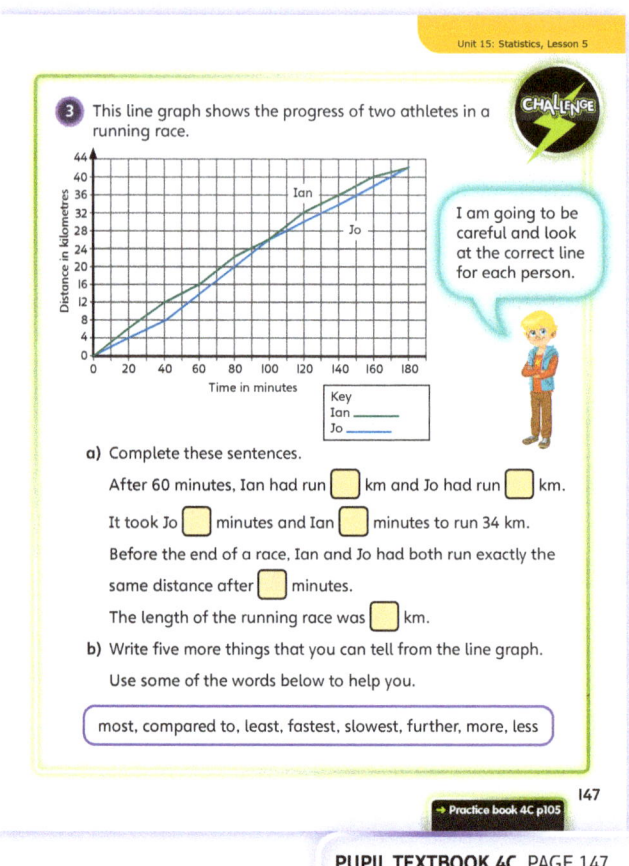

PUPIL TEXTBOOK 4C PAGE 147

Unit 15: Statistics, Lesson 5

Practice

WAYS OF WORKING Independent thinking

IN FOCUS For question 1 b), ensure children understand that the period when the depth of water in the container did not change is a period during which it did not rain at all so no water was added to the container. It is important for children to make the link between the horizontal line and no change in the data.

STRENGTHEN To support children in making their own statements as part of question 4, discuss the sentence structures as a group and ask questions together to decide on the information needed. For example, ask: *Between which two times does the temperature in July change the most? What about in December? Is the difference between the highest and lowest temperature in July greater than the difference between the highest and lowest temperature in December?*

DEEPEN Encourage children to make comparison statements between multiple sets of data presented on the same line graph. Question 4 provides the ideal stimulus for this; you could ask: *What statements could you make that compare the temperatures in July and December?* Challenge children to create stories around data to demonstrate a deeper understanding of what the data is telling them.

THINK DIFFERENTLY The line graph in question 3 is different to all the other graphs in this lesson because it is a smooth curve, whereas all the other graphs have straight lines connecting any two consecutive points (they are 'piecewise' linear). Discuss with children how the curve is a good way to represent the height of the golf ball: its height increases gradually to the highest point, and then falls gradually. Using a piecewise linear graph would suggest it travels up and down in a 'jerky' motion, which it does not. Can children understand that the highest point the ball reaches is shown by the apex of the curve, and can they successfully read the maximum height from the vertical axis at this point?

ASSESSMENT CHECKPOINT Use questions 1 and 2 to assess whether children understand the structure of a line graph and can use it to make statements about the data presented. Use question 4 to assess whether children can draw conclusions about two sets of data when plotted on the same set of axes.

ANSWERS Answers for the **Practice** part of the lesson can be found in the *Power Maths* online subscription.

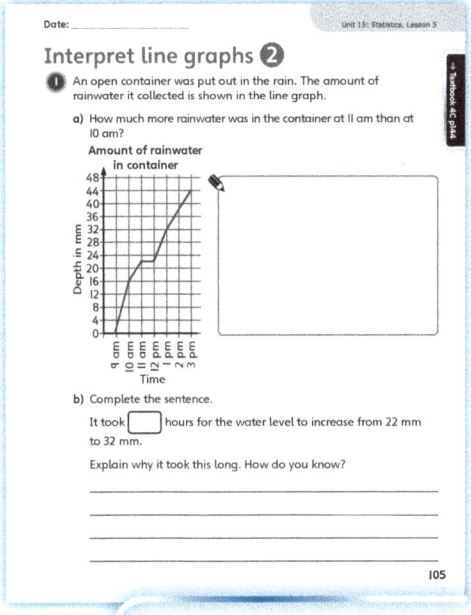

PUPIL PRACTICE BOOK 4C PAGE 105

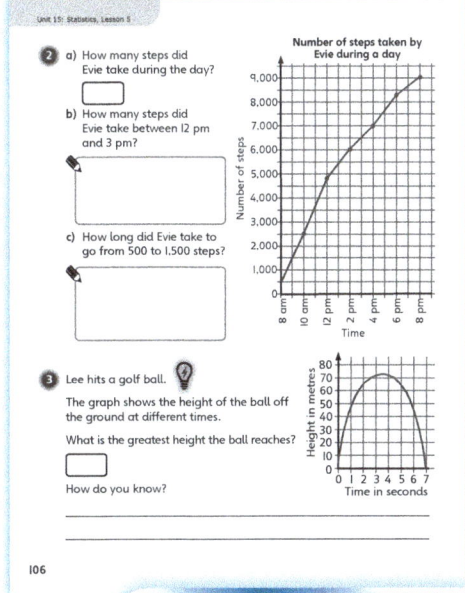

PUPIL PRACTICE BOOK 4C PAGE 106

Reflect

WAYS OF WORKING Independent thinking

IN FOCUS This **Reflect** question encourages children to consider the type of data that can be represented with a line graph. Prompt a discussion about the differences between line graphs and bar charts. This should lead children to think about discrete and continuous data.

ASSESSMENT CHECKPOINT Use this activity to assess if children are able to verbalise the importance of line graphs. Do they understand the concept of continuous data?

ANSWERS Answers for the **Reflect** part of the lesson can be found in the *Power Maths* online subscription.

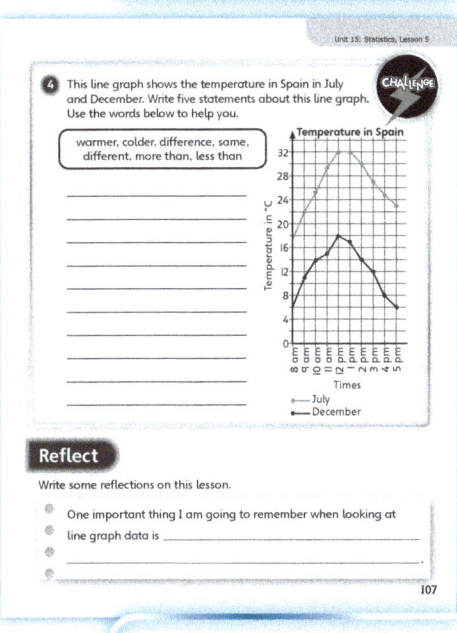

PUPIL PRACTICE BOOK 4C PAGE 107

After the lesson
- Are children secure in interpreting data and making comparisons from a line graph?
- Can children answer questions about data using inference and deduction?

Unit 15: Statistics, Lesson 6

Draw line graphs

Learning focus
In this lesson, children build on their understanding of statistics and interpreting data and draw their own line graphs from given information.

Before you teach
- Can children read a scale on a line graph when increments are in steps of 2, 5 or 10?
- Can children read data from a given line graph?

NATIONAL CURRICULUM LINKS

Year 4 Statistics

Interpret and present discrete and continuous data using appropriate graphical methods, including bar charts and time graphs.

ASSESSING MASTERY

Children can accurately plot and draw a line graph from a set of data provided in the form of a table.

COMMON MISCONCEPTIONS

Children may not remember how to plot a point based on two axes. Ask:
- What does the horizontal axis tell you? How does it change as you move across from left to right?
- What does the vertical axis tell you? How does it change as you move upwards?

STRENGTHENING UNDERSTANDING

Provide counters that children can place on a large axis grid to show how they are plotting the points on their line graph.

GOING DEEPER

Challenge children to explore the different line graphs that they can draw when plotting each of the times-tables. For example, if plotting the 6 times-table, values 1 to 10 could be plotted on the horizontal axis and the values 6, 12, 18 and so on could be plotted on the vertical axis.

KEY LANGUAGE

In lesson: axis, scale, interval, data

Other language to be used by the teacher: horizontal, vertical, value, trend, continuous data

STRUCTURES AND REPRESENTATIONS

Tables, axes for line graphs

RESOURCES

Optional: counters, large axis grid, large pieces of paper

 In the eTextbook of this lesson, you will find interactive links to a selection of teaching tools.

Quick recap

As a class, count on together in 100s to 1,000 and in 1,000s to 10,000. Then ask children to draw a number line from 0 to 10,000 with intervals marked in 1,000s and to accurately place these numbers on the line:

3,500   4,500   9,500

Unit 15: Statistics, Lesson 6

Discover

WAYS OF WORKING Pair work

ASK
- Question 1 a): *What does population mean?*
- Question 1 a): *What does the data in the table show? How does the table show this data?*
- Question 1 b): *What scale will you use on each axis?*

IN FOCUS Children will develop an understanding of how to turn data shown as entries in a table into a line graph. Start by discussing the information that can be found in the table, including any trends that are shown. Agree that the population increases over time and that a line graph would be a clear way to show this. In question 1 a), help children to see that the population should be plotted on the vertical axis so that the line graph will show how the population rises or falls over time. In question 1 b), have a class discussion about what scale to use on the vertical axis (showing population). Before looking at the **Share** page, you could ask children to work in groups and try out different scales to see which best fits on a single sheet of squared paper. To help them get started, you could ask: *Would the whole scale fit if it went up in 1s from zero? What about in 10s?*

PRACTICAL TIPS Provide children with large sheets of paper so that they can work together to sketch and complete the line graph as a group.

ANSWERS

Question 1 a): Time goes on the horizontal axis. It will go from 1930 to 2020. The population will go on the vertical axis.

Question 1 b):

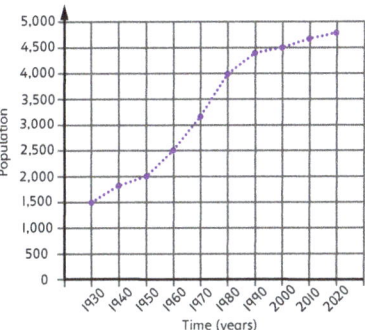

Share

WAYS OF WORKING Whole class teacher led

ASK
- Question 1 a): *How could you describe the increases between the values on the y-axis?*
- Question 1 b): *How would you describe the trend of population growth in Emma's village?*

IN FOCUS In question 1 b), children will need to start by constructing and labelling the axes, including identifying an appropriate scale for each axis. They can then plot points on the graph based on the information in the table. Agree that a line graph is a good choice for representing this information as it is continuous data, gradually increasing over time. Look together at Ash's comment and discuss why he has chosen to join the points using a dotted line. Agree that the dotted line between any two consecutive points should be a straight line.

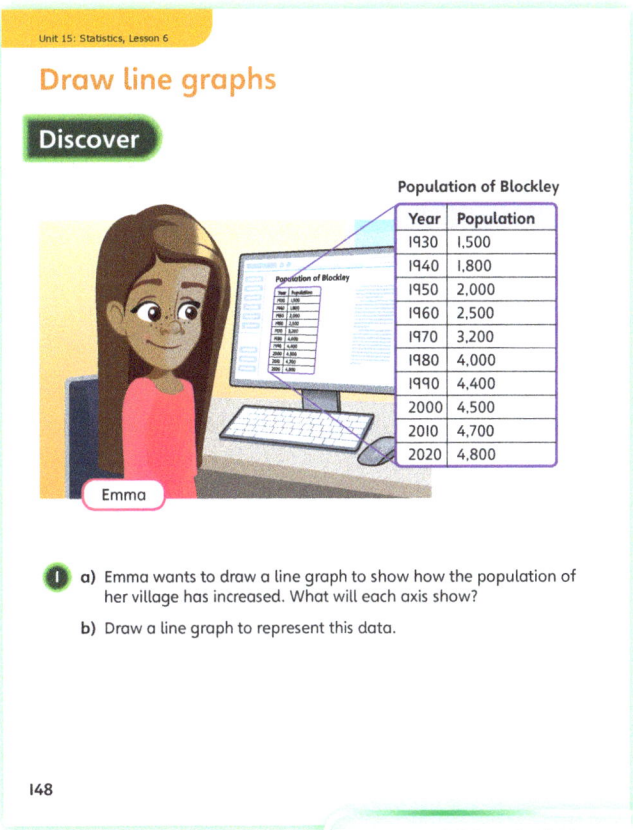

PUPIL TEXTBOOK 4C PAGE 148

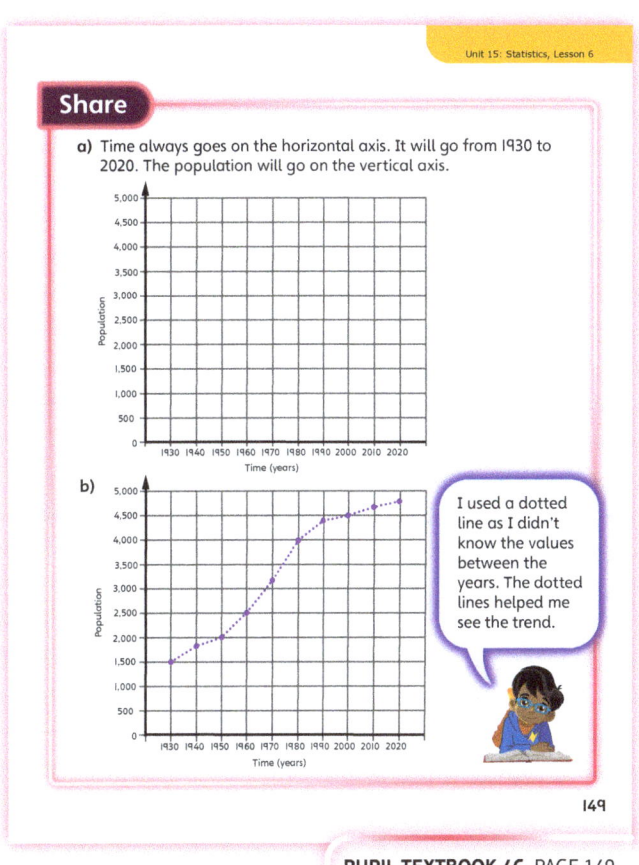

PUPIL TEXTBOOK 4C PAGE 149

183

Unit 15: Statistics, Lesson 6

Think together

WAYS OF WORKING Whole class teacher led (I do, We do, You do)

ASK
- Question ②: *How could you use a ruler to make your estimates as accurate as possible?*
- Question ③: *What do you think your line graph will look like?*

IN FOCUS In question ②, children will need to interpret which axis they are being given information about. Help children to understand the need to draw a vertical line with a ruler. For example, in question ② a), from 30 minutes on the horizontal axis to the line graph, and then a horizontal line from the graph to the vertical axis. In question ③, children will need to plot their own axes and decide on appropriate scales. The scale on the measuring jug might help with this. Or you could select measuring jugs with harder or easier scales depending on how secure children are with reading different types of scale. However, if the drip is slow and the measuring jug has not filled very much after 10 minutes, children may want to consider using a smaller scale for their graph than the one shown on the jug.

STRENGTHEN Encourage children to work on the process of plotting points on a line graph by reading along the x-axis, and then moving up to plot the correct data point by reading along the y-axis.

DEEPEN Ask children to discuss how intermediate values on line graphs can be used to make estimates about unknown values. Ask: *How does a line graph help us to make estimates? When might this be useful?*

ASSESSMENT CHECKPOINT Use question ① to assess whether children can plot given points accurately on a line graph.

ANSWERS

Question ①: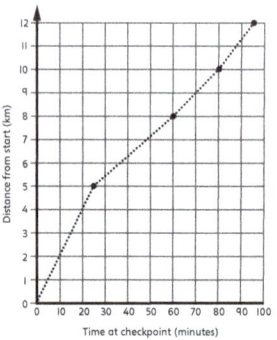

Question ② a): 5·5 km

Question ② b): 36 minutes (accept between 35 and 37 minutes)

Question ② c): The values are estimates because they are between the points on the graph.

Question ③: Children's answers will vary depending on the size of the hole in the yoghurt pot. Look for axes clearly and accurately labelled. For example: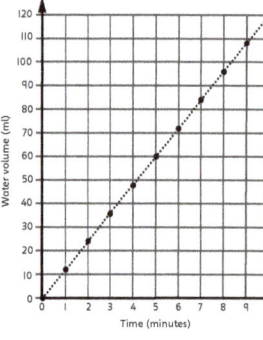

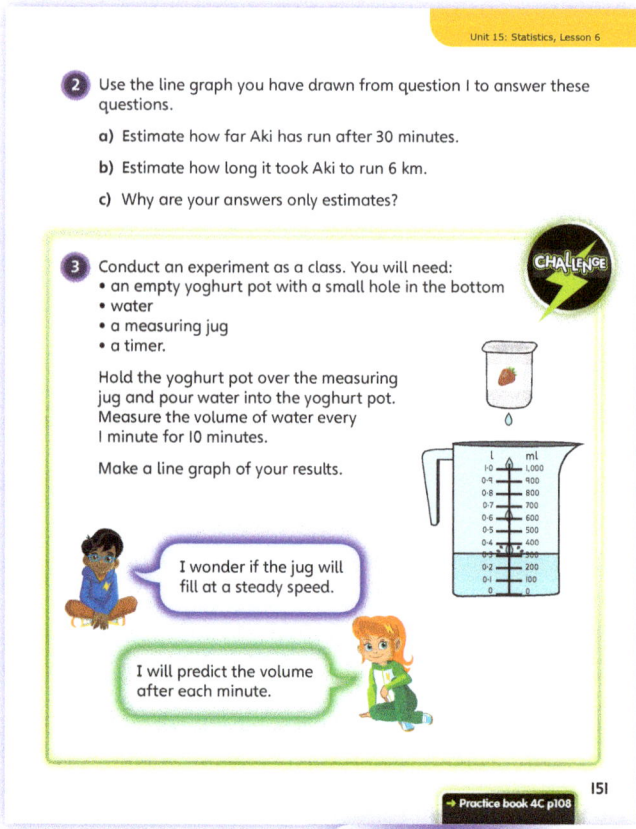

PUPIL TEXTBOOK 4C PAGE 150

PUPIL TEXTBOOK 4C PAGE 151

Unit 15: Statistics, Lesson 6

Practice

WAYS OF WORKING Independent thinking

IN FOCUS Questions 1 and 2 require children to plot line graphs on given axes. In question 1, the y-axis has a scale that counts up in 1s. In question 2, children will need to identify that the scale counts up in 2,000s and use this to plot points that fall a half or a quarter of the way between the labelled values. Question 3 prompts children to consider the appropriate use of line graphs, identifying that they can be used for continuous data such as population changes, but not discrete data such as items ordered in a shop.

STRENGTHEN Encourage children to work together as a group to plot the points on a line graph accurately. They should focus on developing the appropriate technique for sliding along to the required value on the x-axis, and then sliding up to plot their point at the correct 'height' according to the value on the y-axis.

DEEPEN Challenge children to plot points on their own line graphs, including making appropriate choices for the scales to be used on each axis.

ASSESSMENT CHECKPOINT Use question 1 to assess whether children can plot points on a basic line graph based on data provided in a table.

ANSWERS Answers for the **Practice** part of the lesson can be found in the *Power Maths* online subscription.

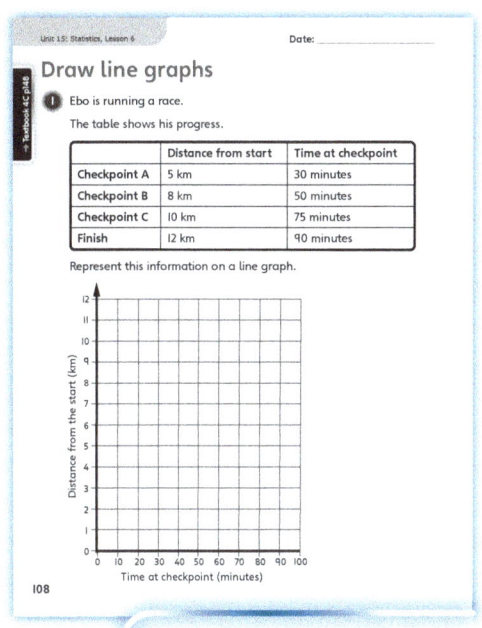

PUPIL PRACTICE BOOK 4C PAGE 108

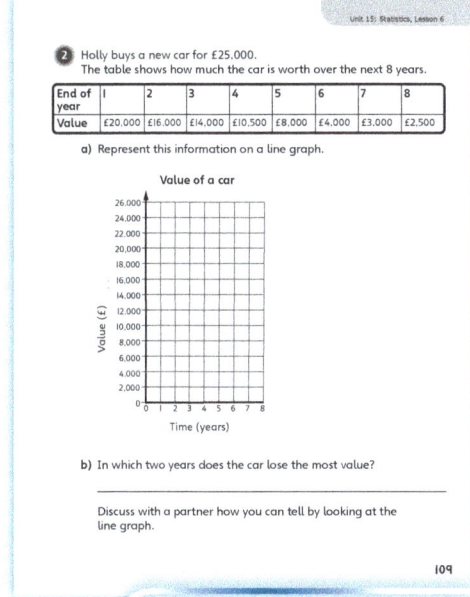

PUPIL PRACTICE BOOK 4C PAGE 109

Reflect

WAYS OF WORKING Pair work

IN FOCUS The **Reflect** part of the lesson prompts children to have a discussion comparing the features of line graphs and bar graphs. They should consider how each type of chart is drawn and what it can be used for. Draw out the distinction that bar graphs are used to plot discrete data, whilst line graphs show continuous data. Provide lots of examples of different types of data for children to classify as discrete or continuous so they become secure in telling the difference between the two.

ASSESSMENT CHECKPOINT Assess whether children can explain the differences between different types of charts using appropriate vocabulary such as continuous, discrete, trend, compare and difference.

ANSWERS Answers for the **Reflect** part of the lesson can be found in the *Power Maths* online subscription.

After the lesson

- Were children able to plot points on a line graph accurately?
- Were children confident when plotting points between the values labelled on the axes?
- Do children understand why the features of a line graph make it useful for tracking trends in continuous data?

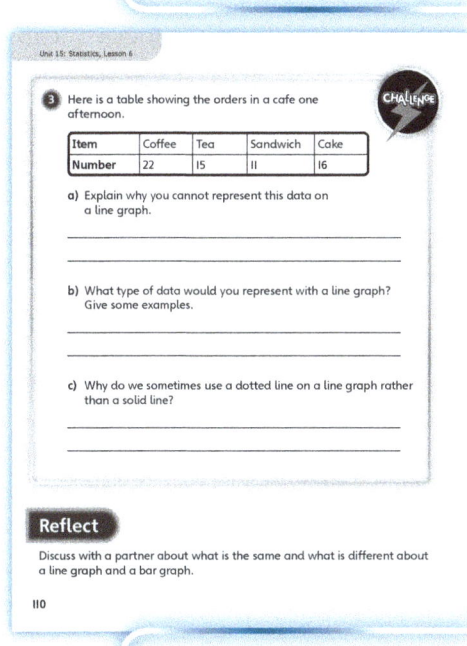

PUPIL PRACTICE BOOK 4C PAGE 110

Unit 15: Statistics

End of unit check

Don't forget the unit assessment grid in your *Power Maths* online subscription.

WAYS OF WORKING Group work adult led

IN FOCUS The questions in the **End of unit check** focus on data presented in pictograms, bar charts, line graphs and tables. Through this, children's ability to interpret data is also assessed: care needs to be taken to distinguish between a data interpretation error and a calculation error.

ANSWERS AND COMMENTARY

Children who have mastered this unit can interpret data that is presented in a range of ways, including pictograms, bar charts, line graphs and tables. Children can use this data to answer a range of questions, including comparison, ordering and total questions. They can also make their own statements based on the data presented to them. They should be beginning to compare linked data that is presented across multiple sources. For example, can they use linked data presented in a bar chart and table to answer and formulate their own questions. Children can answer more complex multi-step problems that use information presented in a chart, graph or table.

Children who have mastered this unit will also be able to draw their own line graphs from data presented in a table. They will be able to determine which variable should be plotted on which axis, select appropriate scales and plot the points accurately.

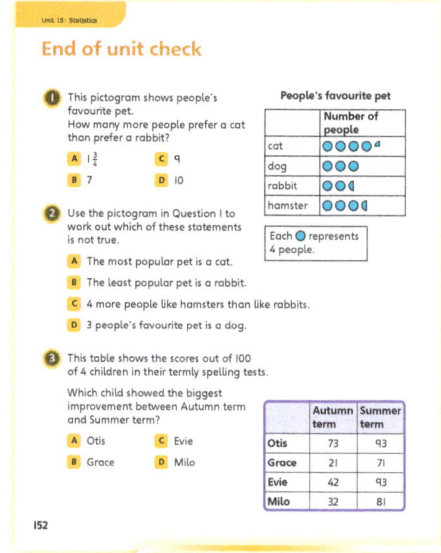

PUPIL TEXTBOOK 4C PAGE 152

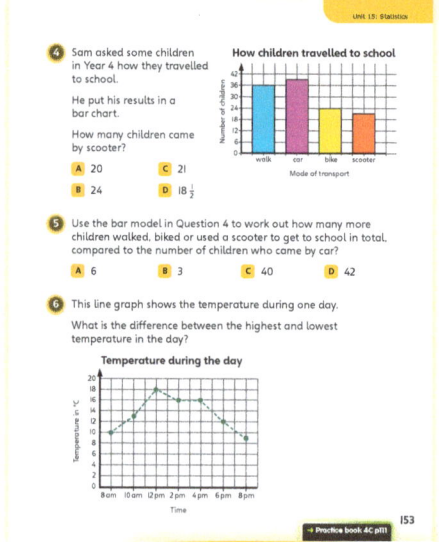

PUPIL TEXTBOOK 4C PAGE 153

Q	A	WRONG ANSWERS AND MISCONCEPTIONS	STRENGTHENING UNDERSTANDING
1	B	Choosing A suggests that the child is interpreting each symbol as representing 1 person.	Draw children's attention to the structure of each question and ask: • What is the question asking you to do? • What operation could this involve? In question ❶, encourage children to use the key in the pictogram. To help children to accurately read from the vertical axis, in questions ❹ and ❻, link the vertical axis to a number line. For multi-step problems, encourage children to consider the different steps they need to take to solve the problem before they start to solve it.
2	D	Choosing A and B indicates that the child is unfamiliar with the basic structure of a pictogram.	
3	C	An incorrect answer suggests the child has either carried out the wrong calculation or carried out the correct calculation but made a mistake.	
4	C	Choosing A, B or D indicates that the child is unsure of how to read a half value on the scale.	
5	D	A and B both suggest that children have not interpreted the steps needed to solve the problem.	
6	9 °C	Children must understand that a subtraction is required once the data has been read.	

Unit 15: Statistics

My journal

WAYS OF WORKING Independent thinking

IN FOCUS

Support children in creating their own statements by providing them with sentence structures to use. For example, you could provide them with the following structures:
- Between ☐ and ☐ the value of the car increased by ☐.
- The value of the car doubled between ☐ and ☐.
- The car increased in value by ☐ between ☐ and ☐.

ANSWERS AND COMMENTARY

Children's answers will vary. For example:
- The price at 6 pm was £2·00 more than the price at 4 pm.
- The total price was £5·50.
- The price at 12 pm was £1·50 less than the price at 3 pm.
- The final price was £4·00 more compared to the starting price of £1·50.

Power check

WAYS OF WORKING Independent thinking

ASK
- *What do you know now that you didn't know at the start of this unit?*
- *How confident do you feel about interpreting data in bar charts, pictograms, line graphs and tables?*

Power puzzle

WAYS OF WORKING Pair work

IN FOCUS Encourage children to work through the clues step by step, and first record the heights in a table similar to the one below, before completing the bar charts. If need be, ask specific questions about each clue. For example, ask: *We know Maisie was 130 cm tall in January. Which bar is Maisie? We know that Raj was 10 cm shorter than Finlay in December.*

When working through the clues, it is important to tell children that this is 1 January and 1 December of the same year – so the second bar chart records children's heights at a *later date* than the first. The clues on the left do not necessarily relate solely to the left-hand bar chart (likewise for the right-hand side). Encourage children to mark any clues where they need more information, and come back to them later.

ANSWERS AND COMMENTARY If children can complete this **Power puzzle**, it suggests they can logically follow clues to aid their interpretation of a chart.

	Height on 1 January	Height on 1 December
Finlay	115	125
Evie	120	135
Maisie	130	135
Raj	100	115

After the unit

- How can you continue to expose children to a range of statistical representations through your day-to-day classroom activities?
- What cross-curricular links can you make?

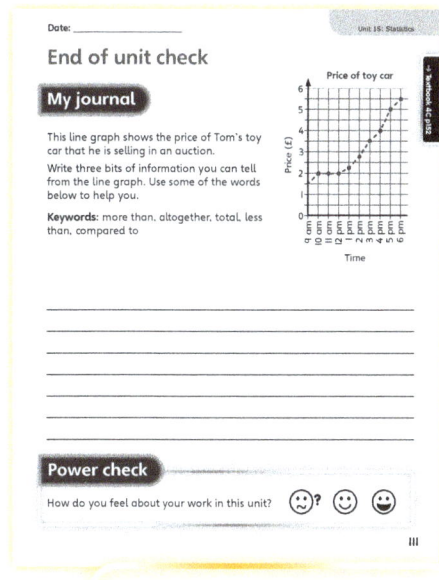

PUPIL PRACTICE BOOK 4C PAGE 111

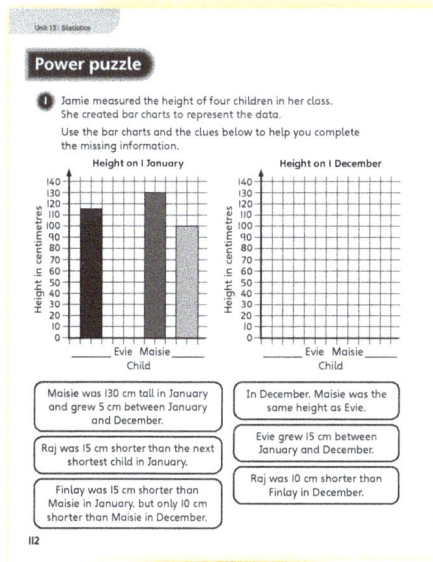

PUPIL PRACTICE BOOK 4C PAGE 112

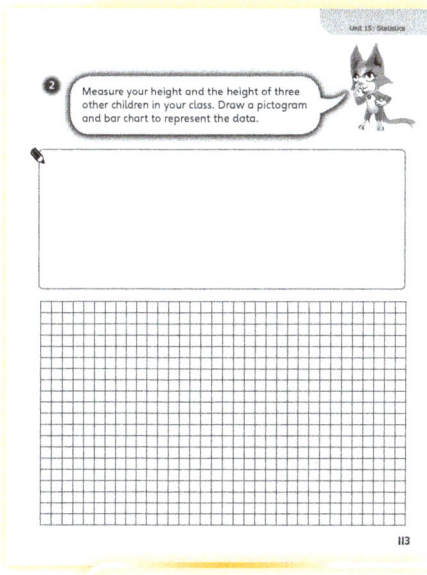

PUPIL PRACTICE BOOK 4C PAGE 113

Strengthen and **Deepen** activities for this unit can be found in the *Power Maths* online subscription.

Unit 16
Geometry – position and direction

Mastery Expert tip! 'Allowing the children to use computer geometry packages meant they could plot lots of points quickly and easily, without the complication of drawing grids and axes by hand. This provided great practice to reinforce the correct order of coordinates.'

Don't forget to watch the Unit 16 video!

WHY THIS UNIT IS IMPORTANT

Coordinate geometry is one of the most powerful ideas in basic mathematics. Coordinates use numbers to describe positions on a grid and connect the worlds of arithmetic and geometry. In later work, coordinates will be used with algebra to allow children to visualise the behaviour of mathematical rules, connections and conditions. This unit focuses on the use of coordinates to describe positions and movements, and provides a solid foundation for some key ideas that will be used to underpin a wide variety of more advanced concepts.

WHERE THIS UNIT FITS

→ Unit 15: Statistics

→ **Unit 16: Geometry – position and direction**

This unit introduces children to coordinate grids, using them to describe the positions of points and translations from one point to another. It builds on the knowledge developed in Unit 14 of the properties and symmetry of 2D shapes to identify and represent such shapes using coordinates.

Before they start this unit, it is expected that children:

- know how to read positions on a number line (to the nearest half unit)
- understand how maps and plans can be used to represent a real-life scene
- understand a range of simple ideas and vocabulary related to position and direction: for example, left/right and horizontal/vertical.

ASSESSING MASTERY

Children can read and write coordinates for positions in the first quadrant (points to the right of and above the origin (0,0)). They can plot points given a pair of coordinates and understand the convention that the first coordinate represents the horizontal distance to the right of the origin and the second coordinate represents the vertical distance above the origin. They understand translations as movements on the coordinate grid; they can describe the result of making a translation in words and they can find the translation required for the movement between given positions. They can use simple geometrical reasoning on a coordinate grid to draw patterns and complete shapes.

COMMON MISCONCEPTIONS	STRENGTHENING UNDERSTANDING	GOING DEEPER
Children may confuse the order of coordinates.	Explain that the order of coordinates is *conventional*, in the sense that it is a convention that everyone has agreed to follow.	Provide children with a variety of coordinates, including half units, and ask children to plot them on a grid.
Children may confuse the ideas of coordinates and translations.	Be clear that coordinates tell us where things are, and have a simple notation in the form (6,5); translations tell us how to move, and are written out in words.	At a deeper level, coordinates *are* translations – from the origin to the point we are interested in. Ask children to describe the translation to go from the origin to a point and to explain the pattern that they find between the translation and the coordinates of the point.

Unit 16: Geometry – position and direction

UNIT STARTER PAGES

Use these pages to introduce the unit focus to children. Use the characters to discuss the concepts and phrases that children have not heard before.

STRUCTURES AND REPRESENTATIONS

Coordinate grid: Children use coordinate grids throughout the unit to describe positions of points and translations from one point to another.

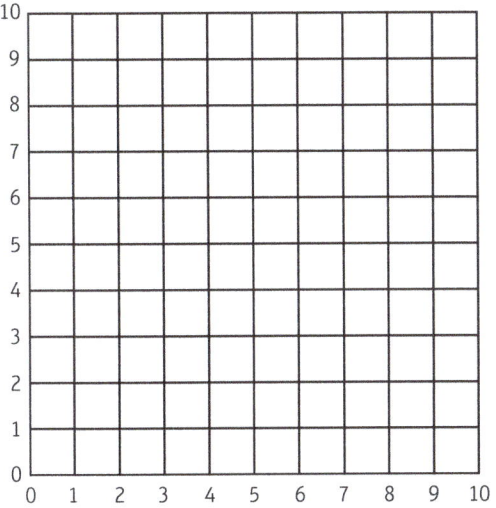

KEY LANGUAGE

There is some key language that children will need to know as part of the learning in this unit:

- coordinate
- position
- horizontal, vertical
- up, down
- left, right
- square, rectangle
- vertex, vertices
- plot, point, grid
- translate

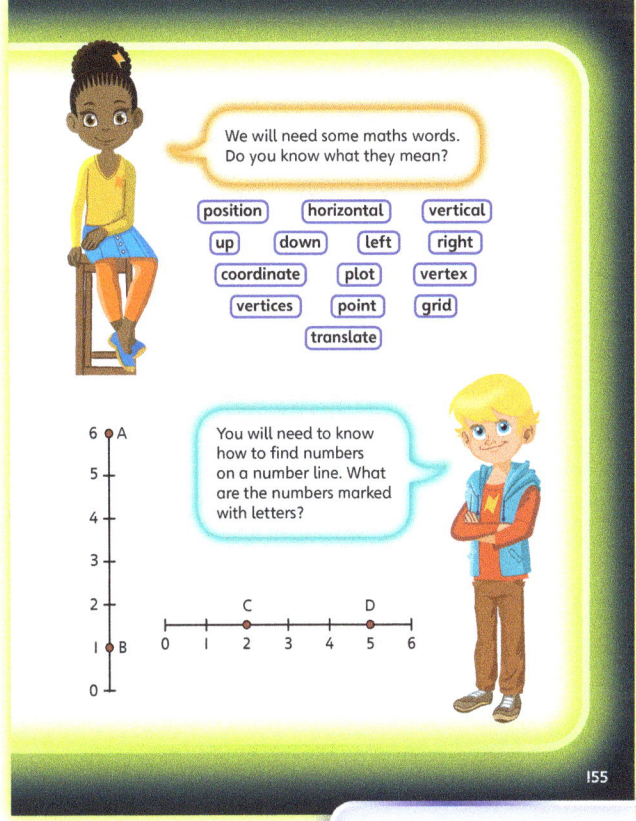

PUPIL TEXTBOOK 4C PAGE 154

PUPIL TEXTBOOK 4C PAGE 155

Unit 16: Geometry – position and direction, Lesson 1

Describe position

Learning focus

In this lesson, children will describe relative positions on a map, initially without a grid and then with a grid. They will develop the understanding and skills that will be needed when numbered axes and coordinates are introduced in the next lesson.

Before you teach

- Can children describe their position relative to other children or objects using the terminology of position, such as 'in front of', 'behind', 'left', 'right', 'above', 'below'?
- Have children met situations where they need to find places on maps?

NATIONAL CURRICULUM LINKS

Year 4 Geometry – position and direction

Describe positions on a 2D grid as coordinates in the first quadrant.

ASSESSING MASTERY

Children can describe the relative positions of objects using terms such as near, closest, centre, between, and half-way between. They can use a grid to describe the positions of objects in relation to other objects, counting squares as necessary.

COMMON MISCONCEPTIONS

Children may need support to identify when places are half-way between other places. Ask:
- *Describe the position of A relative to B and C. What can you tell me about the distance from A to B and from A to C? Are they the same? Complete this sentence: A is ☐ between B and C.*

STRENGTHENING UNDERSTANDING

To strengthen understanding of how to describe relative position, position children around the classroom or the playground and ask them to describe their position relative to other children. Encourage them to describe their position in a number of different ways.

GOING DEEPER

Ask children to find a map on the internet and to make up questions about the locations of places. A partner can then try to find the places from the information.

STRUCTURES AND REPRESENTATIONS

Gridlines

KEY LANGUAGE

In lesson: map, next to, near, closest, centre, between, half-way between, **grid**, left, right, up, down

Other language to be used by the teacher: horizontal, vertical

RESOURCES

Optional: access to the internet, simple maps

 In the eTextbook of this lesson, you will find interactive links to a selection of teaching tools.

Quick recap

Choose an object in the classroom and play a 'guess the object' game. Children should ask positional questions such as 'Is it next to *x*?', 'Is it between *y* and *z*?', 'Is it above *w*?' to try to guess the object.

Unit 16: Geometry – position and direction, Lesson 1

Discover

WAYS OF WORKING Pair work

ASK
- Question 1 a): *Say some places you can see on the map.*
- Question 1 a): *Which places are close to each other? Which places are far apart?*
- Question 1 a): *How many playgrounds are there?*

IN FOCUS This activity develops the ability to describe one place relative to another, encouraging children to use different ways to describe position.

PRACTICAL TIPS Use a real map (perhaps of the local area around your school) as an alternative or addition to the map shown in **Discover**.

ANSWERS

Question 1 a): Bella is looking for the roller coaster.

Question 1 b): The roller coaster is half-way between the log flume and the dropzone ride.

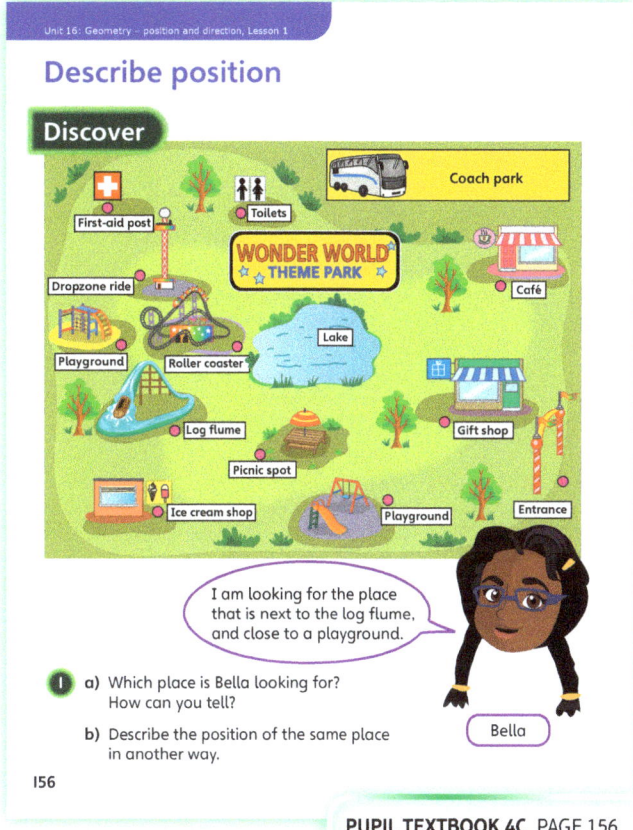

PUPIL TEXTBOOK 4C PAGE 156

Share

WAYS OF WORKING Whole class teacher led

ASK
- Question 1 a): *Why does Dexter say he needs to use both pieces of information?*
- Question 1 b): *Whose description gives a better idea of where the roller coaster is: Astrid's or Flo's?*
- Question 1 b): *Can you describe the position of the roller coaster in any other way?*

IN FOCUS This activity establishes that the location of one place can be described relative to other places in different ways. It introduces terms such as 'next to' and 'between'. Question 1 b) introduces the idea that descriptions can be made more precise by using words such as 'half-way'.

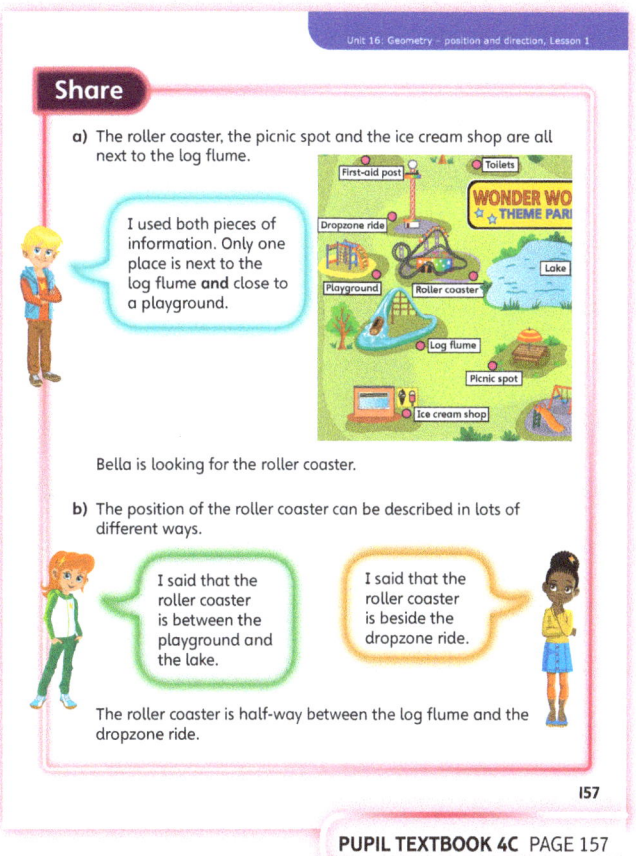

PUPIL TEXTBOOK 4C PAGE 157

191

Unit 16: Geometry – position and direction, Lesson 1

Think together

WAYS OF WORKING Whole class teacher led (I do, We do, You do)

ASK
- Question 2 a): *Which place is closest to the ice cream shop? Which place is furthest away?*
- Question 2 b): *Does your description only apply to the café, or could it be describing another place? Do you need to add to your description?*
- Question 3 a): *How many squares are there across the map? How many squares up and down?*
- Question 3 a): *How can you use the squares to find somewhere half-way between two points?*

IN FOCUS Question 3 introduces a grid of squares, which makes it easier to describe where places are. Emphasise that, since the squares are all the same size, locations can be given accurately by counting the number of squares. The grid uses horizontal and vertical lines – introduce this terminology, making sure that children understand which direction is which.

STRENGTHEN Give children additional practice at identifying locations from your descriptions before asking them to describe locations for themselves. Put children in pairs to describe locations to each other. This will help them to develop the idea that they need to be precise, so that only one location fits the description.

DEEPEN Challenge children to think about the most efficient way to describe locations. Before the grid is introduced, you could encourage them to use left/right and above/below as well as near/far and so on.

ASSESSMENT CHECKPOINT Use question 1 to assess whether children can find places given a description of their locations. Use question 2 to assess whether they can describe locations unambiguously.

ANSWERS

Question 1 a): Café (or toilets)

Question 1 b): Lake

Question 1 c): Gift shop

Question 1 d): Roller coaster

Question 2 a): Near the log flume; left of the picnic spot and playground.

Question 2 b): Near the coach park, above the gift shop.

Question 2 c): Between the first-aid post and the roller coaster.

Question 2 d): Near the top of the map, close to the dropzone ride.

Question 3 a): Log flume

Question 3 b): Toilets

Question 3 c): Gift shop

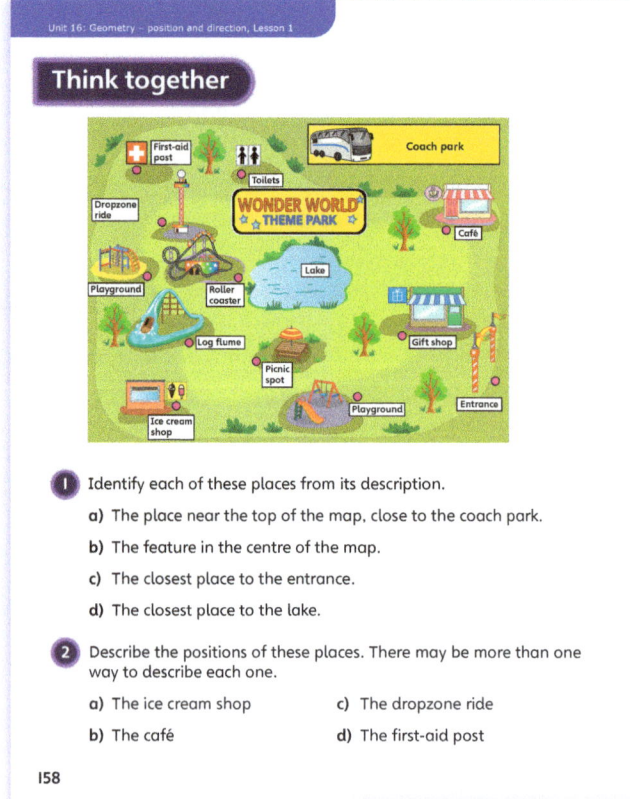

PUPIL TEXTBOOK 4C PAGE 158

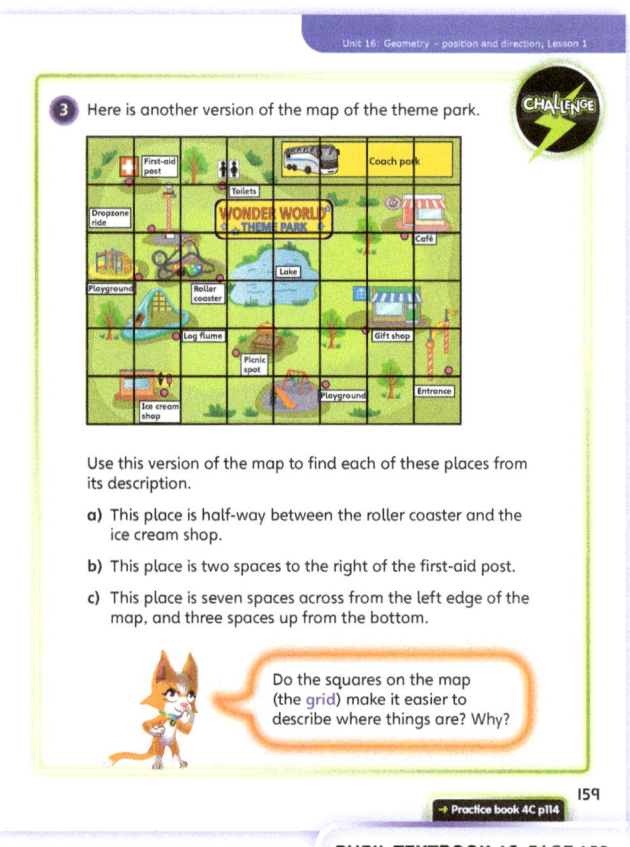

PUPIL TEXTBOOK 4C PAGE 159

Unit 16: Geometry – position and direction, Lesson 1

Practice

WAYS OF WORKING Independent work

IN FOCUS Question ② involves describing locations relative to other places on a map. Encourage children to use a variety of ways of describing locations, rather than using the same term (for example, 'next to') in all their descriptions.

STRENGTHEN In question ⑤, ask children questions about the grid. For example: *How many squares across … ? How many squares up … ?* Describe some locations for them to identify using the grid before they use it to describe locations to a partner.

DEEPEN Ask children to investigate how many places they need to reference to describe a location. For example, 'the moor is half-way between the woods and the cliff' references two locations – the woods and the cliff. When they have a grid (as in question ⑤), they do not need to reference any other locations to describe the position of the moor. By starting from the bottom left corner of the grid, they could simply state that the moor is '4 squares right and 2 squares up'.

THINK DIFFERENTLY Question ④ requires children to clarify that places located between two points are not necessarily situated exactly half-way between the two.

ASSESSMENT CHECKPOINT Use question ① to assess whether children can find places given a description of their locations. Use question ② to assess whether they can describe locations unambiguously. Use question ③ to check that they are confident at identifying positions that lie on a given straight line.

ANSWERS Answers for the **Practice** part of the lesson can be found in the *Power Maths* online subscription.

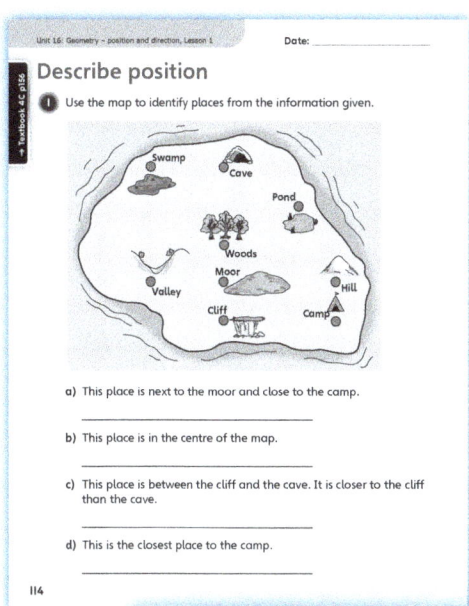

PUPIL PRACTICE BOOK 4C PAGE 114

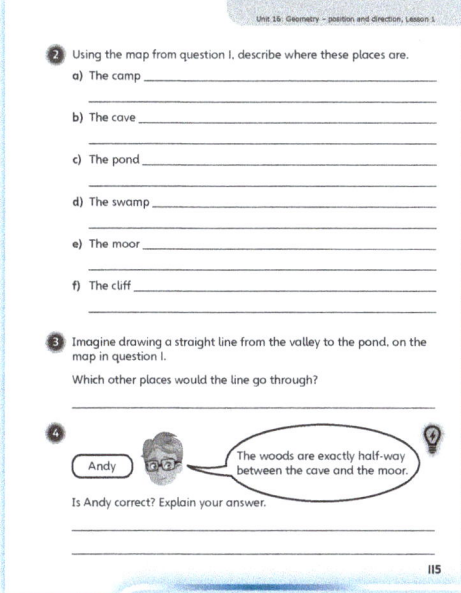

PUPIL PRACTICE BOOK 4C PAGE 115

Reflect

WAYS OF WORKING Independent thinking

IN FOCUS This activity provides an opportunity for children to reflect on the maps they have used, with and without grids, and on the different ways in which they have specified locations.

ASSESSMENT CHECKPOINT Check that children understand the importance of providing descriptions that identify only one possible location. They may realise that this is easier to do with a grid.

ANSWERS Answers for the **Reflect** part of the lesson can be found in the *Power Maths* online subscription.

After the lesson

- Can children describe positions relative to other locations?
- Were children confident in using directions left/right and up/down on a grid?
- Are children prepared for the introduction of a formal system of coordinates in the next lesson?

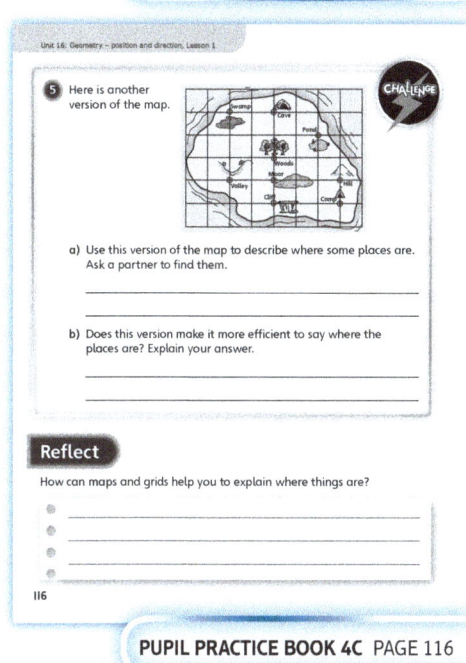

PUPIL PRACTICE BOOK 4C PAGE 116

Unit 16: Geometry – position and direction, Lesson 2

Describe position using coordinates

Learning focus
In this lesson, children will use coordinates in the first quadrant to describe positions on a grid, using the conventional order and notation.

Before you teach
- Are children confident when describing relative positions on an unnumbered grid?
- Do children appreciate the usefulness of measuring positions from a common reference point?

NATIONAL CURRICULUM LINKS

Year 4 Geometry – position and direction

Describe positions on a 2D grid as coordinates in the first quadrant.

ASSESSING MASTERY

Children can use coordinates to describe the positions of objects on a grid. They understand the importance of being consistent with the order in which the coordinates are given (horizontal then vertical), and they recognise and use the conventional notation for coordinates.

COMMON MISCONCEPTIONS

Children may write coordinates in the wrong order. Indicate point (4,2) and ask:
- *How many squares along is this point? How many squares up? Which do you put first when writing coordinates?*

STRENGTHENING UNDERSTANDING

It may be useful for some children to think about the coordinate axes as number lines. For example, you could ask: *How far along this number line [the horizontal axis] do you need to go? How far up this number line [the vertical axis] do you need to go?*

GOING DEEPER

More confident learners can be challenged to answer questions 'without the pictures'. For example, ask them which is closer to (4,4): (9,4) or (4,0), and encourage them to explain their answers.

KEY LANGUAGE

In lesson: coordinates, point, position

Other language to be used by the teacher: parentheses, horizontal, vertical, origin, grid

STRUCTURES AND REPRESENTATIONS

Coordinate grid

RESOURCES

Optional: computer geometry package

 In the eTextbook of this lesson, you will find interactive links to a selection of teaching tools.

Quick recap
Look together at a simple map and discuss the relative positions of different places on the map using the language of position.

Unit 16: Geometry – position and direction, Lesson 2

Discover

WAYS OF WORKING Pair work

ASK

- Question 1 a): *What is different about this map compared to the maps in the last lesson?*
- Question 1 a): *What do you think the numbers in (2,2) mean?*

IN FOCUS This activity introduces the coordinate grid and the concept that the location of objects on the map can be given by two numbers (the horizontal and vertical coordinates). Question 1 a) has been chosen so that the order of the coordinates does not matter and question 1 b) establishes that there needs to be an agreed order for the numbers.

PRACTICAL TIPS Do not explain the order of the coordinates at this stage. The most important idea to establish is that there needs to be *some* consistent order for the coordinates – the remainder of the lesson will be used to reinforce what the conventional order is.

ANSWERS

Question 1 a): The sword was found at position (2,2).

Question 1 b): The gold cup was found at position (2,1).

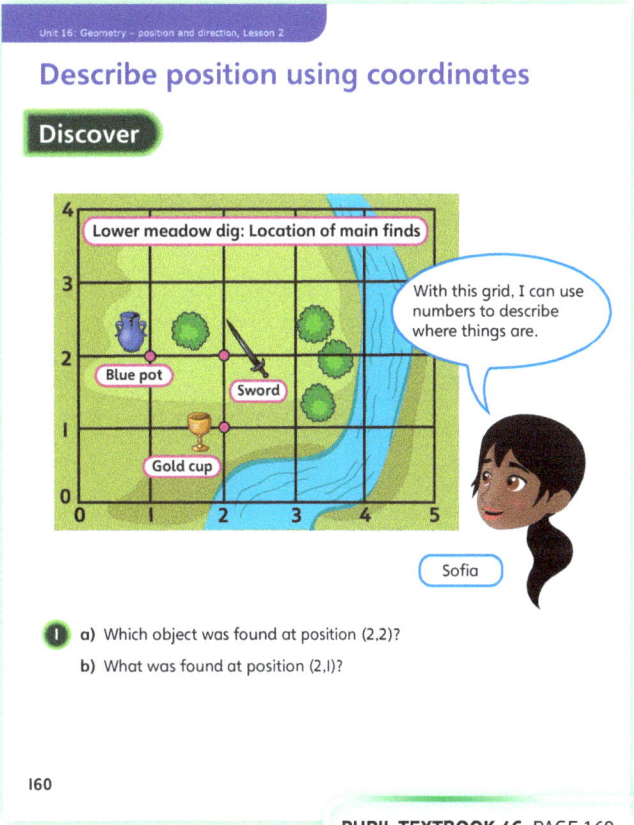

PUPIL TEXTBOOK 4C PAGE 160

Share

WAYS OF WORKING Whole class teacher led

ASK

- Question 1 a): *What do you notice about the two numbers? Does it matter whether you go across or up first?*
- Question 1 b): *Does it matter whether you use the first number to go across or up?*
- Question 1 b): *What is at (1,2)?*

IN FOCUS This introduces children to a number of important concepts:

- Always give the 'across' number first, followed by the 'up' number
- These numbers are called coordinates
- Coordinates are written as two numbers, separated by a comma and surrounded by parentheses – for example, (3,5) is 3 squares across and 5 squares up.

Also draw attention to the fact that the grid numbering starts from the bottom left corner, so that the horizontal coordinate is measured to the right, and the vertical coordinate is measured upwards.

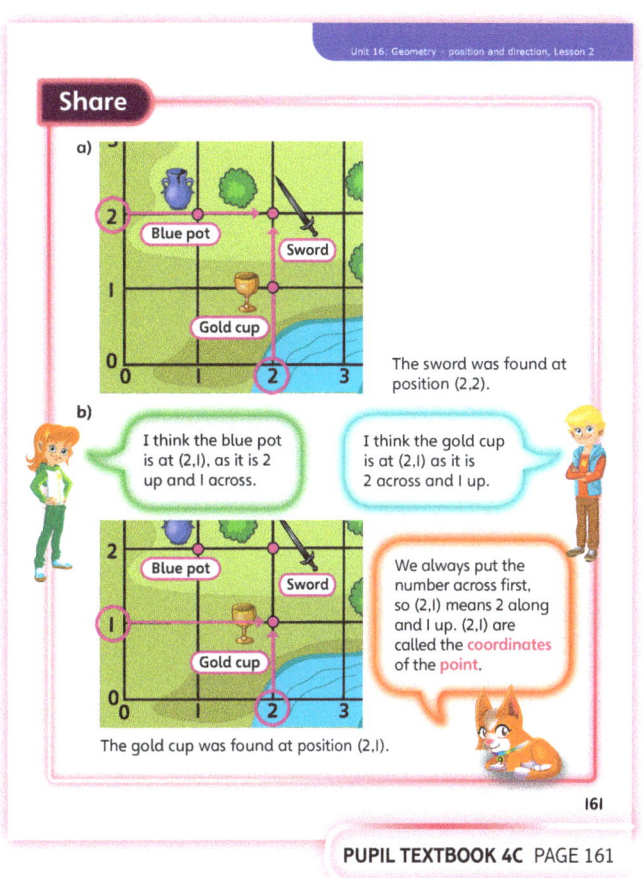

PUPIL TEXTBOOK 4C PAGE 161

195

Unit 16: Geometry – position and direction, Lesson 2

Think together

WAYS OF WORKING Whole class teacher led (I do, We do, You do)

ASK

- Question ❶: *Can you see that some other things have been found and marked on the map?*
- Question ❸: *Do you think coordinates are a good way of recording where things were found? Would it be easier to just say something like 'The silver pin was found near the trees'?*

IN FOCUS Question ❸ emphasises the advantage of coordinates over word descriptions to accurately describe the positions of things.

STRENGTHEN Reinforce children's understanding of the correct order of coordinates by asking questions such as: *Which position would be in the river: (4,1) or (1,4)?* Draw a grid on the board clearly showing going across then up.

DEEPEN Ask further questions based on the map of the dig, for example: *Imagine that another gold cup was found, one grid space from the first one: what could its coordinates be? A shield was found half-way between the spear and the red pot: what were its coordinates?*

ASSESSMENT CHECKPOINT Use question ❶ to assess whether children can find locations given by coordinates. Use question ❷ to check that children can give the coordinates of specified locations correctly.

ANSWERS

Question ❶ a): Blue pot

Question ❶ b): Statue

Question ❶ c): Spear

Question ❷ a): (1,1)

Question ❷ b) i): (0,3)

Question ❷ b) ii): (4,0)

Question ❷ b) iii): (5,1)

Question ❸: C (4,1) because this is in the river, not in the middle of trees.

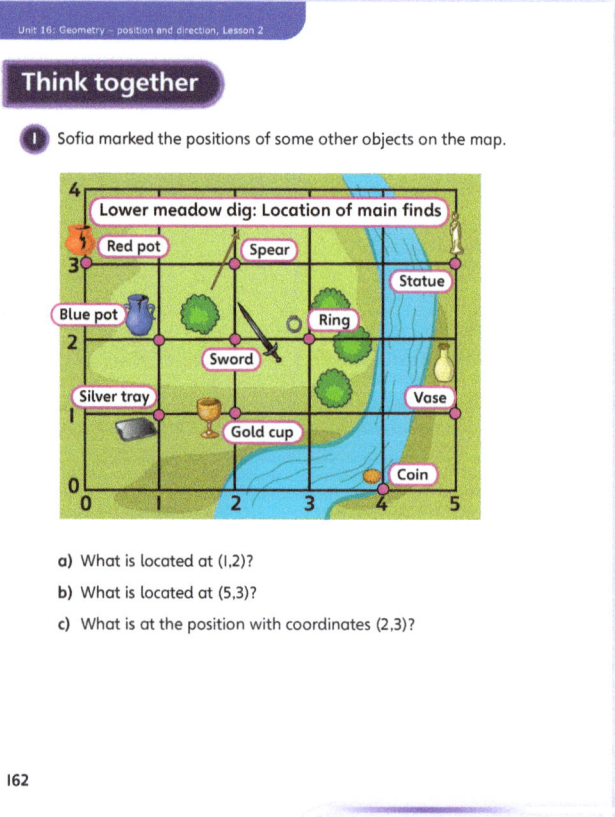

PUPIL TEXTBOOK 4C PAGE 162

PUPIL TEXTBOOK 4C PAGE 163

196

Unit 16: Geometry – position and direction, Lesson 2

Practice

WAYS OF WORKING Independent thinking

IN FOCUS Questions 4 and 7 require children to interpret the information given on the plan to decide where to plant. Question 5 introduces children to the origin of the grid – that is, the reference point from which all of the distances on the grid are measured. If necessary, discuss what makes this a sensible choice of origin: all measurements can be made to the right and up, and the location of any position in the diagram can be expressed by a pair of positive coordinates.

STRENGTHEN Children who are still finding it difficult to remember the correct order of coordinates may benefit from additional practice using a computer geometry package. Play a game where children can see a coordinate grid on the screen in front of them. Tell them that there is 'buried treasure' at (4,6), for example. Ask them firstly to point to where they think the buried treasure is on the grid. Then, instruct them to enter (4,6) into the geometry software and see where the plotted point pops up. Did children correctly identify the plotted point?

DEEPEN Ask children to mark a tree on the map of Jamie's garden and then write out the coordinates of that tree. Alternatively, ask children to work in pairs. One child describes the position of a new object in Jamie's garden and the other child has to plot the object on their grid. Then swap over.

THINK DIFFERENTLY Question 3 is more open-ended and gives children the opportunity to consider and describe the correct order of coordinates, namely that you always give the 'across' number first, and then the 'up' number. Ask: *What are the real coordinates of the gnome?*

ASSESSMENT CHECKPOINT Use questions 1 and 2 to assess whether children are writing coordinates correctly, giving the 'distance across' followed by 'distance up'.

ANSWERS Answers for the **Practice** part of the lesson can be found in the *Power Maths* online subscription.

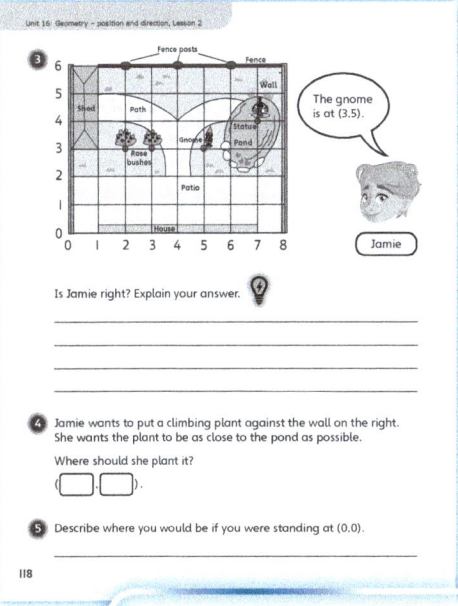

Reflect

WAYS OF WORKING Independent thinking

IN FOCUS This **Reflect** activity provides a final opportunity to revisit the key learning point for this lesson – the use of coordinates to specify positions in the first quadrant.

ASSESSMENT CHECKPOINT Check that children understand that the coordinates represent horizontal and vertical distances from the origin (in that order), and that this means that the example given is incorrect.

ANSWERS Answers for the **Reflect** part of the lesson can be found in the *Power Maths* online subscription.

After the lesson
- Are children using coordinates correctly?
- What opportunities can you provide for additional practice in plotting points?

Unit 16: Geometry – position and direction, Lesson 3

Plot coordinates

Learning focus
In this lesson, children will use coordinates to plot points in the first quadrant and to construct simple shapes by plotting their vertices. They will also plot points to complete shapes.

Before you teach
- Do children understand the conventional order of coordinates?
- What support will you provide for children who need additional practice?

NATIONAL CURRICULUM LINKS

Year 4 Geometry – position and direction

Plot specified points and draw sides to complete a given polygon.

Describe positions on a 2D grid as coordinates in the first quadrant.

ASSESSING MASTERY

Children can plot points in the first quadrant. They can continue simple patterns, determining and plotting the coordinates that are required, and they can draw simple geometric shapes when they are given a list of coordinates for the vertices.

COMMON MISCONCEPTIONS

Children may still interpret coordinates in the wrong order. Children need to know that the order matters (and that we therefore need to agree on one order). They also need to know what the conventional order is. Indicate point (4,2) and ask:
- *Does it matter whether you give the across coordinate first, or the up coordinate first? How will I know which one you are giving first?*

STRENGTHENING UNDERSTANDING

All of the plotting exercises in this lesson could usefully be carried out (or repeated) using a computer geometry package. Seeing the same coordinate system used in as many different contexts as possible should help to strengthen children's understanding of the system. In the previous lesson, children used coordinates on maps – this lesson introduces floor robots and more abstract grids as additional contexts in which the same rules apply.

GOING DEEPER

Challenge more confident children to research how computer game designers use coordinates to specify positions on the screen of a device.

KEY LANGUAGE

In lesson: plot, coordinates, point, vertices, horizontal, vertical, predict

Other language to be used by the teacher: rule, vertex, pattern, rectangle, square, triangle, pentagon

STRUCTURES AND REPRESENTATIONS

Coordinate grid

RESOURCES

Mandatory: squared paper

Optional: computer geometry package, squared paper, ruler

 In the eTextbook of this lesson, you will find interactive links to a selection of teaching tools.

Quick recap

As a class discuss the rule for reading and writing coordinates in the order (x,y): first across and then up.

Can children show how this works by tracking the path they would take with a finger?

Unit 16: Geometry – position and direction, Lesson 3

Discover

WAYS OF WORKING Pair work

ASK

- Question 1 a): *The robot is plotting a new point. How many points has it plotted before this one?*
- Question 1 a): *How do the numbers on the grid help you to see where the points will be plotted?*

IN FOCUS This activity provides further experience with coordinates, in a new context. The use of a 'robot' moves the emphasis from 'remembering what the correct order of coordinates is' to 'using the available clues to work out what the robot is doing'. Check that children understand the idea of 'plot a point' – it may be necessary to explain that this is simply the way that the robot is told where to draw the little circles on the grid. In question 1 b), see if children can spot a pattern in the way that the coordinates are changing as the robot moves from one point to the next. Can they see that the horizontal coordinate increases by 1 each time, whilst the vertical coordinate decreases by 1? Can they use this fact to predict further coordinates of points that lie on the line?

PRACTICAL TIPS If available, use a simple computer geometry package to demonstrate plotting different points.

ANSWERS

Question 1 a): Plot a point at (3,5).

Question 1 b): Reena should plot the points (4,4), (5,3), (6,2) and (7,1) to continue the dots in a straight line.

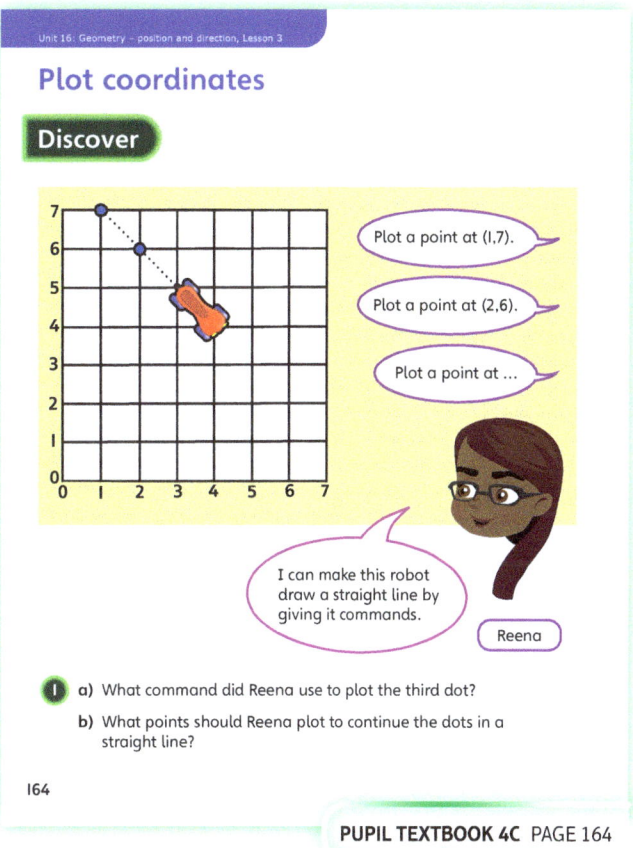

PUPIL TEXTBOOK 4C PAGE 164

Share

WAYS OF WORKING Whole class teacher led

ASK

- Question 1 a): *Why did Dexter choose to count from zero? Why does he count across and then up? Do you know the meaning of 'horizontal' and 'vertical'?*
- Question 1 b): *How does Flo find where the next points are? Could you find them without drawing the line?*
- Question 1 b): *If you say the numbers in the wrong order, where will the robot plot the points?*

IN FOCUS Remind children of the terms 'horizontal' and 'vertical' from their work in Unit 15 with graph axes. Make reference to the similarities to grids here and to the order in which coordinates are written and carried out.

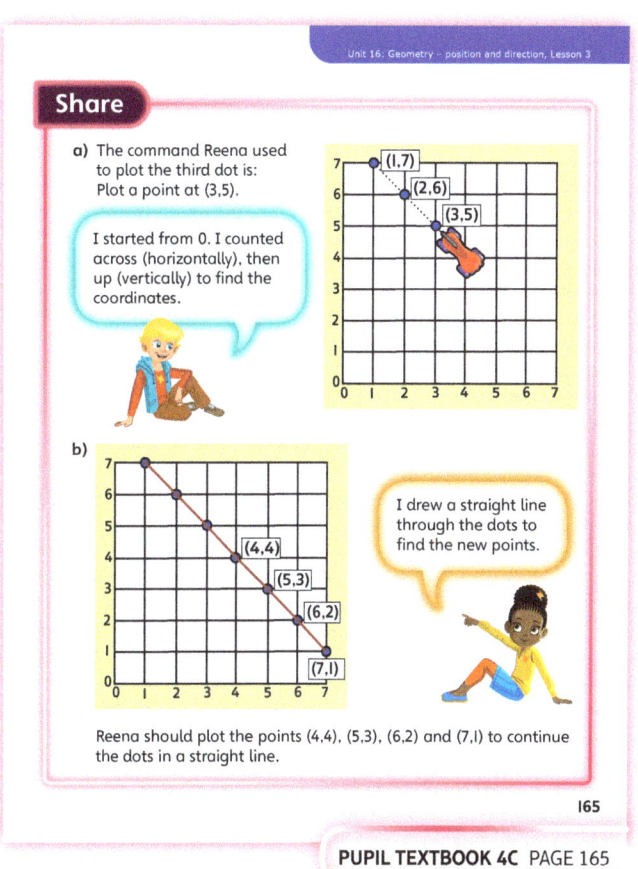

PUPIL TEXTBOOK 4C PAGE 165

Unit 16: Geometry – position and direction, Lesson 3

Think together

WAYS OF WORKING Whole class teacher led (I do, We do, You do)

ASK

- Question ❶: *How many squares do you need to go across for the point (0,2)? How will you plot that?*
- Question ❷: *Can you see a pattern in the coordinates? Can you predict the next point without drawing the line?*

IN FOCUS Question ❶ provides an opportunity to focus on the role of 0 on the axes. Children need to plot a point on the vertical axis and so the grid needs to have a properly labelled origin.

STRENGTHEN Children may need extra support when reading coordinates with 0, such as (0,4) or (3,0). Remind children that the bottom left corner of any grid is at (0,0). Point to one of the grids in the Textbook and ask them to give the coordinates of the top left corner and the bottom right corner.

DEEPEN Extend question ❷ by giving children the coordinate (10,10) and asking them to predict what the coordinates of the points on the line would be if they were to draw a straight diagonal line towards (0,0).

ASSESSMENT CHECKPOINT Use question ❶ to assess whether children can plot given points. Use question ❷ to assess whether they can work out the coordinates of points to complete shapes or continue lines. Use question ❸ to assess whether children know how to work out coordinates that are not whole-number values.

ANSWERS

Question ❶:

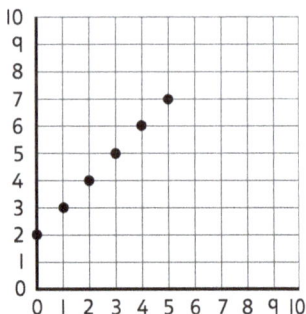

Question ❷ a): (8,2) (9,1), (10,0)

Question ❷ b):

(7,3), (6,4), (5,5), (4,6), (3,7), (2,8), (1,9), (0,10)

Question ❷ b): The first part of the coordinate decreases by 1 and the second part increases by 1 each time.

Question ❸: (3,3), (1,3), (1,2$\frac{1}{2}$), (2,2$\frac{1}{2}$), (2,1$\frac{1}{2}$), (1,1$\frac{1}{2}$), (1,1), (3,1), (3,0), (0,0)

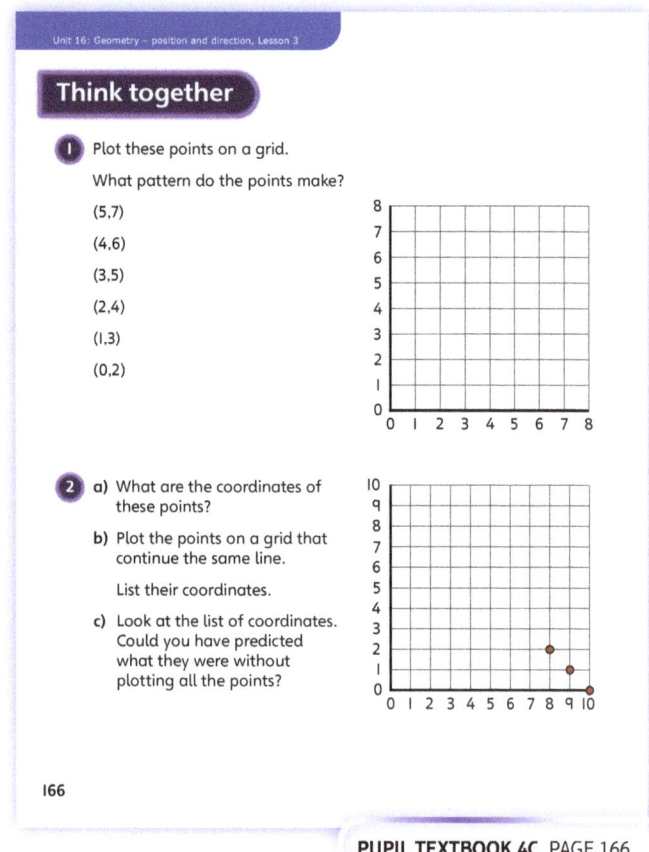

PUPIL TEXTBOOK 4C PAGE 166

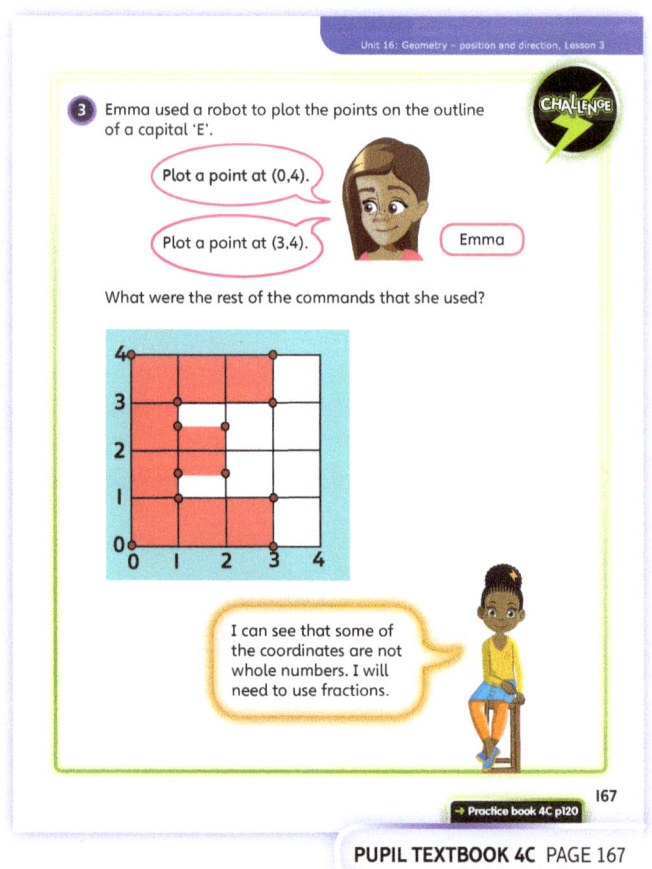

PUPIL TEXTBOOK 4C PAGE 167

Unit 16: Geometry – position and direction, Lesson 3

Practice

WAYS OF WORKING Independent thinking

IN FOCUS Question ➋ links this lesson's work on coordinates with children's existing knowledge of shapes. It also provides further practice in plotting coordinates. Make sure that children understand the term 'vertices', as well as 'triangle', 'rectangle' and 'pentagon'.

STRENGTHEN Question ➊ provides an opportunity to reinforce children's understanding of the coordinate system. All of the required points could fit on the grid, even if plotted in the wrong order. Where children find this difficult, refer back to the examples used earlier in the lesson.

DEEPEN Encourage more confident children to think more deeply about the properties of shapes and their relationships to coordinates. For example, you could use question ➌ to ask: *Do three points always make a triangle, and five points a pentagon, and so on?* The answer is no – where three consecutive points are in a straight line, the 'middle' one would not be a vertex of a polygon.

ASSESSMENT CHECKPOINT Use questions ➊ and ➋ to assess whether children can plot given points. Use question ➌ to check children's familiarity with the conventional order of coordinates. Children who understand that the first coordinate is measured horizontally should be able to spot that line 1 will be horizontal, because the distance 'across' changes but the distance 'up' is constant. Similarly, line 2 must be vertical because the points are all the same distance 'across' the grid.

ANSWERS Answers for the **Practice** part of the lesson can be found in the *Power Maths* online subscription.

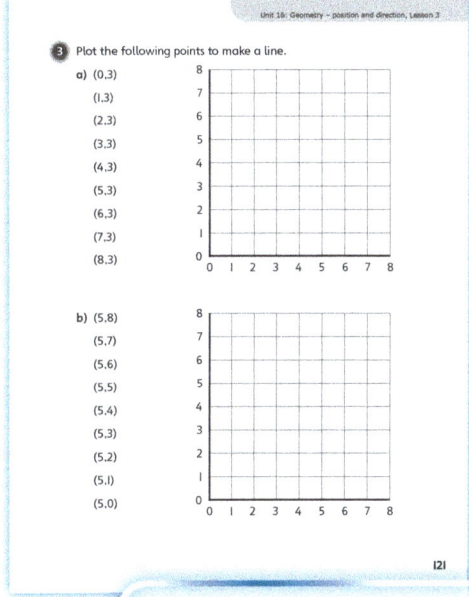

PUPIL PRACTICE BOOK 4C PAGE 120

PUPIL PRACTICE BOOK 4C PAGE 121

Reflect

WAYS OF WORKING Independent thinking

IN FOCUS This question provides a simple check on the main learning from this lesson, ensuring once again that children are using the order of coordinates properly, and that they can visualise vertical and horizontal straight lines, given a sequence of coordinates.

ASSESSMENT CHECKPOINT Assess whether children can explain why the line is vertical. Explanations should include the idea that both points are three units across from (0,0), but at different heights.

ANSWERS Answers for the **Reflect** part of the lesson can be found in the *Power Maths* online subscription.

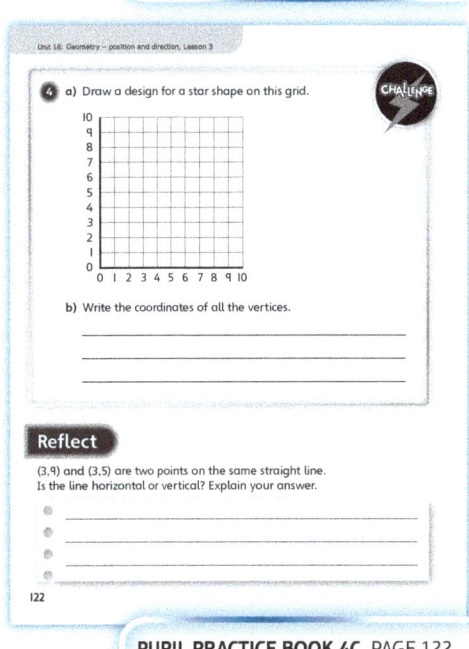

PUPIL PRACTICE BOOK 4C PAGE 122

After the lesson

- Children should now be familiar with the idea that coordinates can be used to draw a variety of shapes, as well as for plotting simple points. Can you provide examples of how this is used – for example, in computer graphics?

201

Unit 16: Geometry – position and direction, Lesson 4

Draw 2D shapes on a grid

Learning focus
In this lesson, children will use the properties of shapes and points to help them make constructions on the coordinate grid.

Before you teach
- Are children confident in working with properties of simple shapes – for example, finding the area of a square, or understanding that the opposite sides of a rectangle have equal lengths?

NATIONAL CURRICULUM LINKS

Year 4 Geometry – position and direction

Plot specified points and draw sides to complete a given polygon.

ASSESSING MASTERY

Children can use simple properties of shapes to plot missing points and complete geometrical diagrams.

COMMON MISCONCEPTIONS

Children may need support to link their developing understanding of coordinates with their existing knowledge of the properties of shapes. Ask:
- *What do you know about the sides of a square? How can you use that to work out where the next vertex will be plotted?*

STRENGTHENING UNDERSTANDING

Use a computer geometry package to provide additional practice with the material covered in this lesson and to check solutions to the exercises. Some children may need to re-visit the properties of squares and rectangles before covering this lesson. It is especially helpful for them to see that the opposite sides of a rectangle are of equal length. For example, in **Think together** question ❶, children should use this fact to see that the missing vertex is 4 units above (7,1) as the opposite side is 4 units long.

GOING DEEPER

Ask children to explore more complex problems, perhaps using a computer geometry package. For example, they could try to identify the remaining two vertices of squares where (5,4) and (9,4) are opposite vertices; or where (3,5) and (9,6) are adjacent vertices. In both these cases, the square will not align with the gridlines of the coordinate grid, so they will need to think very carefully about where the coordinate points should be placed.

KEY LANGUAGE

In lesson: grid, coordinates, symmetry, vertices, vertex, line, square, rectangle, horizontal, vertical, plotted

STRUCTURES AND REPRESENTATIONS

Coordinate grid

RESOURCES

Optional: computer geometry package, squared paper, chalk, tape

 In the eTextbook of this lesson, you will find interactive links to a selection of teaching tools.

Quick recap

Give children simple coordinates to plot on a small coordinates grid.

Unit 16: Geometry – position and direction, Lesson 4

Discover

WAYS OF WORKING Pair work

ASK

- Question 1 a): *Where did the robot start drawing?*
- Question 1 a): *How many lines will it have to draw in total? How long will they be?*

IN FOCUS This activity provides a simple example of using geometrical knowledge (the fact that the sides of a square are of equal length) to complete a construction using coordinates. The robot is again used here to take the focus away from trying to remember the correct order of coordinates – instead, children can simply look at the robot and see how it responded to the commands that were already given. However, children should be encouraged to use the information in the question to check that the robot has plotted the coordinates in the correct position. Before asking children to find the coordinates of the third vertex of the square, encourage them to use the partially completed square to determine what the side length of the square is. Establish that the side length is 3 squares. Then ask: *If the robot is going to travel 3 squares up from (4,1), which coordinate will go up by 3? Is it 4 or 1?*

PRACTICAL TIPS Create a simple grid on the floor (using tape) or outside in the playground (using chalk). Children can alternate being the 'robot'. Ask children to plot specific coordinates, so together they create different shapes.

ANSWERS

Question 1 a): Draw a line to (4,4).

Question 1 b): Draw a line to (1,4).

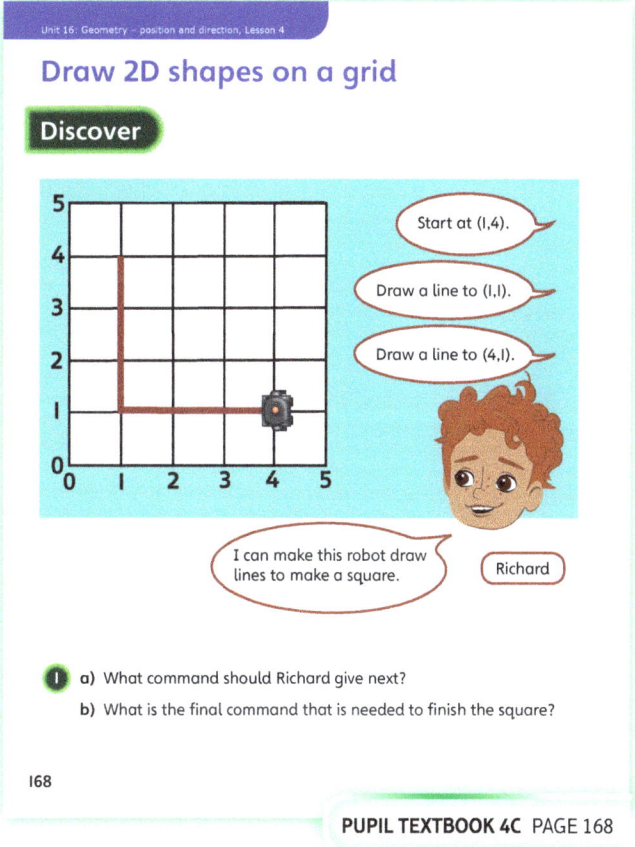

PUPIL TEXTBOOK 4C PAGE 168

Share

WAYS OF WORKING Whole class teacher led

ASK

- Question 1 a): *How has Dexter worked out where the square will be?*
- Question 1 b): *It took five commands to draw the square – but a square has only got four sides. Why is there an extra command?*

IN FOCUS Ensure children understand that the idea of shading the square is simply to help locate the final corner. In this question, children need to focus on the lengths and directions of lines rather than the area of the square.

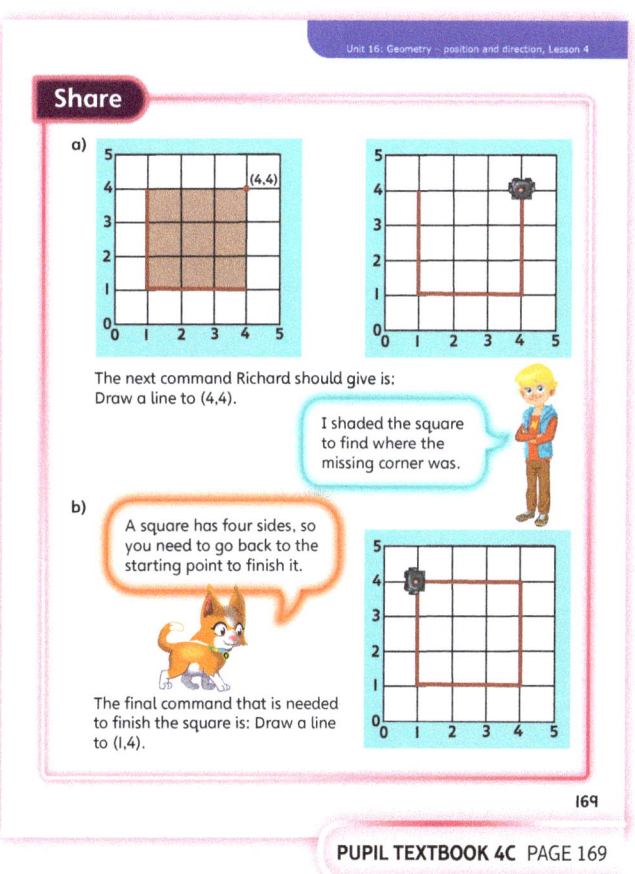

PUPIL TEXTBOOK 4C PAGE 169

Unit 16: Geometry – position and direction, Lesson 4

Think together

WAYS OF WORKING Whole class teacher led

ASK

- Question ❶: *There are no angles marked on the diagram. What should the angles be? Have you got enough information to draw the shape accurately?*
- Question ❷: *What shape are you trying to draw? What do you know about the sides of that shape?*

IN FOCUS Question ❷ is a two-step problem: children need to work out the length of the side of the square from the given points and then use this knowledge to work out the other two coordinates. Question ❸ has a number of possible answers, depending on whether the given points are taken as adjacent or opposite corners of the square. In question ❹, provide children with printed copies of this grid that they can draw on. Encourage them to start by drawing the reflection of the turquoise shape in the line of symmetry. They can use a mirror to help them with this if need be. Then, ask them to identify and write the coordinates of the vertices of their reflected shape on their diagram.

STRENGTHEN Children who need additional practice could use a computer geometry package to reproduce the diagram from question ❶.

DEEPEN Use question ❹ to encourage children to look for patterns in the coordinates for the original and reflected shapes. They should notice that the horizontal coordinates do not change, and they should be able to relate this to the fact that the reflected points move directly downwards.

ASSESSMENT CHECKPOINT Use questions ❶ to ❸ to assess whether children can use their knowledge of the properties of squares and rectangles to find missing coordinates. Use question ❹ to assess whether they can apply reflecting a shape in a mirror line to a coordinate grid.

ANSWERS

Question ❶: (7,5)

Question ❷: (2,7) and (8,7)

Question ❸: (4,9) and (8,9) or (4,1) and (8,1)

Question ❹: (1,2), (2,1), (5,2), (6,1)

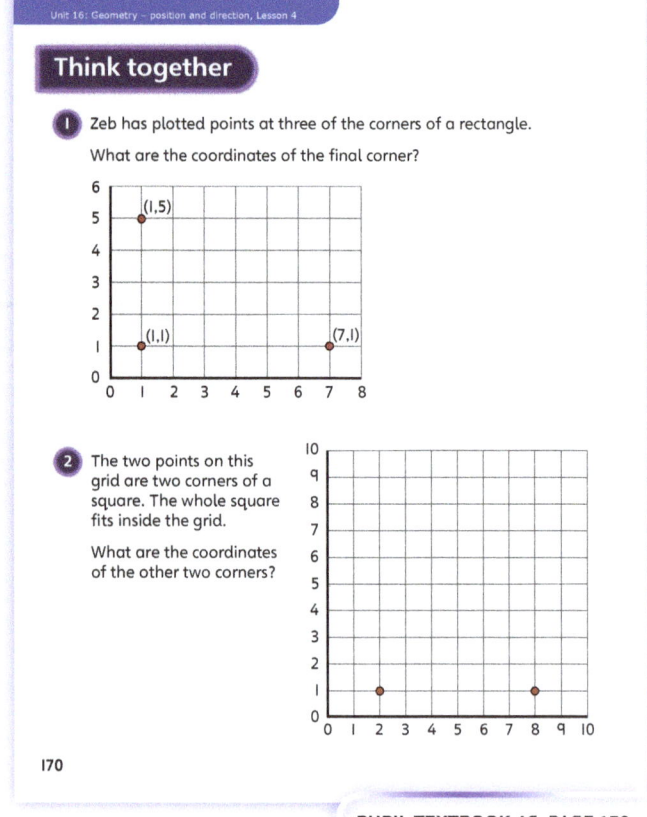

PUPIL TEXTBOOK 4C PAGE 170

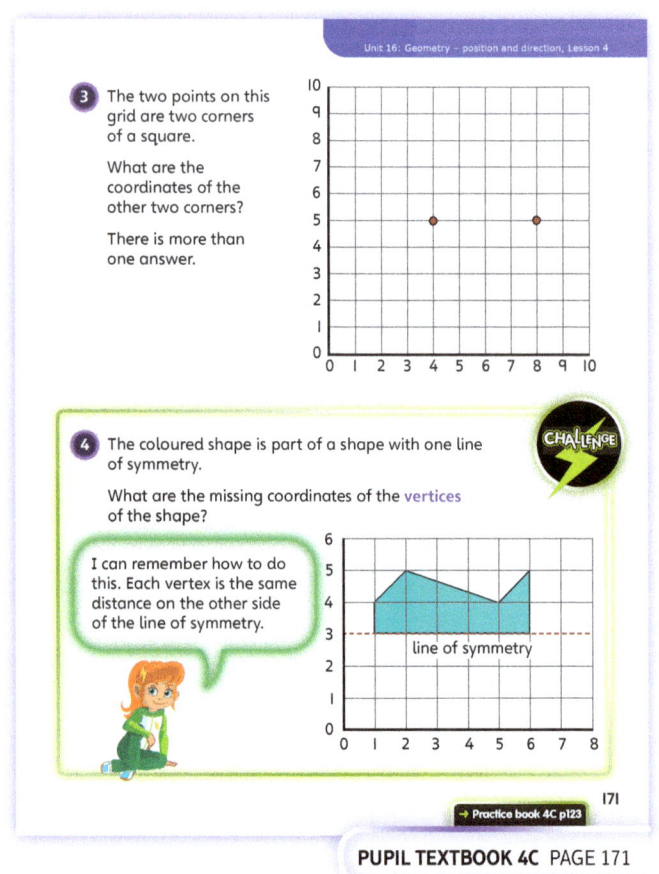

PUPIL TEXTBOOK 4C PAGE 171

Unit 16: Geometry – position and direction, Lesson 4

Practice

WAYS OF WORKING Independent thinking

IN FOCUS Question ❷ provides a further opportunity to combine the properties of shapes with the context of drawing on a coordinate grid. Use opportunities like this to explain that, although mathematics is taught as a series of separate topics, in reality there are many links and connections. Focusing on mathematical connections is a good means of changing the emphasis of learning – away from memorising, and towards understanding.

Question ❹ requires some deeper thinking. Children will need to consider the possible orientations of the rectangle in part b). Since these are not specified in the question, the width could be taken as 5 units and the height as 7, or vice versa.

STRENGTHEN Ask children to visualise what the completed rectangle in question ❶ will look like. If children find it difficult to picture the completed shape, cut out a small piece of paper that they can fit in the required space.

DEEPEN Give children practice questions in which they are given, for example, three vertices of a parallelogram and then need to find the fourth vertex. Ask them to explain how they found the fourth vertex.

THINK DIFFERENTLY Question ❸ is a more open-ended task – there are many different possible locations for the rectangle as the question does not indicate the orientation of the rectangle.

ASSESSMENT CHECKPOINT Use question ❷ to assess whether children can work accurately with coordinates and that they can make effective use of their understanding of the properties of shapes.

ANSWERS Answers for the **Practice** part of the lesson can be found in the *Power Maths* online subscription.

Reflect

WAYS OF WORKING Independent thinking

IN FOCUS This activity asks children to think about the other mathematical ideas that were needed in this lesson and is a further opportunity to establish connections between topics.

ASSESSMENT CHECKPOINT Check that children appreciate that many of the geometrical ideas that they already know (such as symmetry and reflection, and the side and angle properties of squares and rectangles) can be usefully applied on a coordinate grid.

ANSWERS Answers for the **Reflect** part of the lesson can be found in the *Power Maths* online subscription.

After the lesson

- Are children readily making connections between mathematical ideas?
- What further opportunities can you provide for making this kind of connection?

PUPIL PRACTICE BOOK 4C PAGE 123

PUPIL PRACTICE BOOK 4C PAGE 124

PUPIL PRACTICE BOOK 4C PAGE 125

Unit 16: Geometry – position and direction, Lesson 5

Translate on a grid

Learning focus
In this lesson, children will carry out simple translations on a coordinate grid, following instructions given in the form 'left/right, up/down'.

Before you teach
- Are children confident in using coordinates?
- Do you have a suitable space inside or outside the classroom where you could model translations using spoken instructions to move a child to a destination?

NATIONAL CURRICULUM LINKS

Year 4 Geometry – position and direction

Describe movements between positions as translations of a given unit to the left/right and up/down.

ASSESSING MASTERY

Children can carry out simple translations – they can explain the effect of moving an arbitrary distance to the left/right and up/down. (The terminology of translations will be fully introduced in Year 5.) They can find the coordinates of a destination point, given the coordinates of the starting point and the translation. They know the conventional order in which translations will be given (horizontal movement, vertical movement). They can combine a succession of translations to produce a 'journey' with multiple stages.

COMMON MISCONCEPTIONS

Children may confuse the horizontal and vertical components of a translation with the corresponding coordinates of a point. For example, they may confuse 'move 2 right and 3 up' with (2,3). Ask:
- *What is your starting point? How many squares are you moving to the right/left/up/down? What is your end point?*

Some children count gridlines instead of squares, incorrectly starting the count at 1 at the starting point, rather than counting 1 at a distance of one unit from the starting point. Ask:
- *What is your starting point? What is 1 right or 1 up from your starting point? How do you know?*

STRENGTHENING UNDERSTANDING

To strengthen understanding of translations, children could use a computer geometry package to give instructions to move right/left and up/down. Alternatively, use a grid on the ground and ask children to carry out the translation by moving on the grid.

GOING DEEPER

Encourage more confident children to see a translation as a single (diagonal) movement from the starting point to the end point. Ask why it is convenient to describe each journey using two components (horizontal and vertical), even though it might make more sense to carry out the journey as a single (diagonal) movement.

KEY LANGUAGE

In lesson: across, right, left, up, down

Other language to be used by the teacher: horizontal, vertical, coordinates

STRUCTURES AND REPRESENTATIONS

Coordinate grid

RESOURCES

Optional: computer geometry package

 In the eTextbook of this lesson, you will find interactive links to a selection of teaching tools.

Quick recap

Look together at a simple map and discuss possible routes from one place to another.

Unit 16: Geometry – position and direction, Lesson 5

Discover

WAYS OF WORKING Pair work

ASK

- Question 1 a): *Can you see where the position of the drone is marked on the screen?*
- Question 1 a): *What are the coordinates of the drone? How does Sofia want it to move?*

IN FOCUS This activity provides a simple practical context in which the importance of being able to give instructions for movements should be clear. Notice that, although this has returned to the context of a map, there is no scale given and the drone would need to be using the same set of coordinates as Sofia.

PRACTICAL TIPS You could use a practical activity to introduce the idea of translations: ask a child to move around the classroom (or other suitable space) following simple instructions such as 'Move 2 paces left, then 3 paces back'. This will help children to establish that they can move from any point on a grid to any other point on the grid by giving just two pieces of information: the distance to move left or right, and the distance to move up or down.

You may want to reinforce the difference between coordinate points on the grid – such as (4,2) – and translations, such as 'go 3 squares right and 1 square up'. The point (4,2) is a fixed point that is always 4 across and 2 up from the origin, and this never changes. The instruction 'go 3 squares right and 1 square up' is a *movement* that children must make, and where they finish depends on where they started.

ANSWERS

Question 1 a): Sofia wants to look at the jetty.

Question 1 b): Sofia sent the drone to the castle.

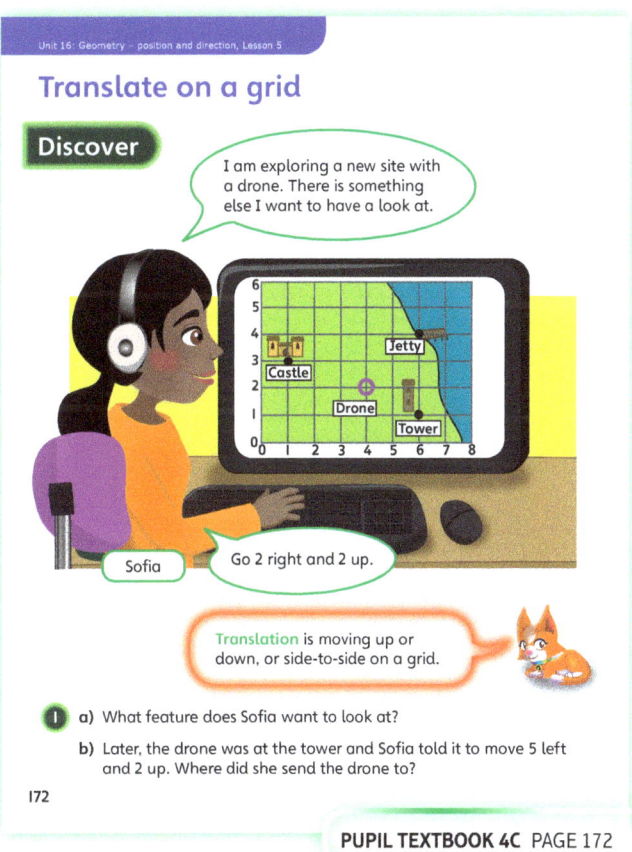

PUPIL TEXTBOOK 4C PAGE 172

Share

WAYS OF WORKING Whole class teacher led

ASK

- Question 1 a): *How did Astrid mark the starting point for the drone?*
- Question 1 b): *Can you see how you could work out where the drone went without drawing?*

IN FOCUS Working out the final position of the drone without drawing is an important step. State that in question 1 b), the drone is at (6,1), and moves 5 left. Ask which number will change, the 6 or the 1. Ask children to explain how they know this.

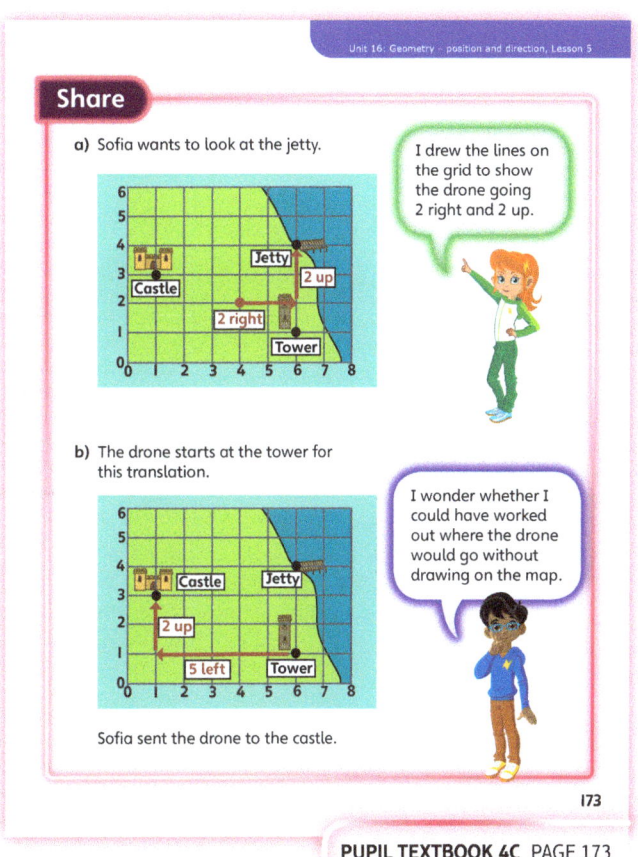

PUPIL TEXTBOOK 4C PAGE 173

Unit 16: Geometry – position and direction, Lesson 5

Think together

WAYS OF WORKING Whole class teacher led (I do, We do, You do)

ASK

• Question ❶: *This drone is going to do all of these journeys, one after the other. What is the first place it will go to? Where will it go after that?*

IN FOCUS Question ❷ can be tackled in a variety of ways. You could suggest trial and error – for each translation, children should try each of P, Q, and R as potential starting points until they find the one that works. A better approach is to think about what each of the translations means. For example, if 3 right, 1 up finishes on one of the marked locations it cannot start at R (which is already the rightmost point), and it also cannot start at Q (which is already further 'up' than the other two points).

STRENGTHEN Provide further practice by asking other questions based on the diagram in question ❶. For example, ask: *I am at A and I go 6 right and 1 down. Where do I finish?*

DEEPEN In question ❷, ask children if they can see a link between, for example, the journey from P to Q and the journey from Q to P. Ask them to investigate whether this pattern is the same for the other journeys. They should explain their findings.

ASSESSMENT CHECKPOINT Use questions ❶ and ❷ to assess whether children can carry out simple translations. Check that they understand translations with a single component, such as '4 down' in question ❶, and that this could be written as '0 right, 4 down'.

ANSWERS

Question ❶: B, D, C, E, A

Question ❷:
3 left, 1 down: Q to P
4 right, 3 down: P to R
4 left, 3 up: R to P
1 left, 4 up: R to Q
1 right, 4 down: Q to R

Question ❸: B: (7,7), C: (11,7), D: (11,4)

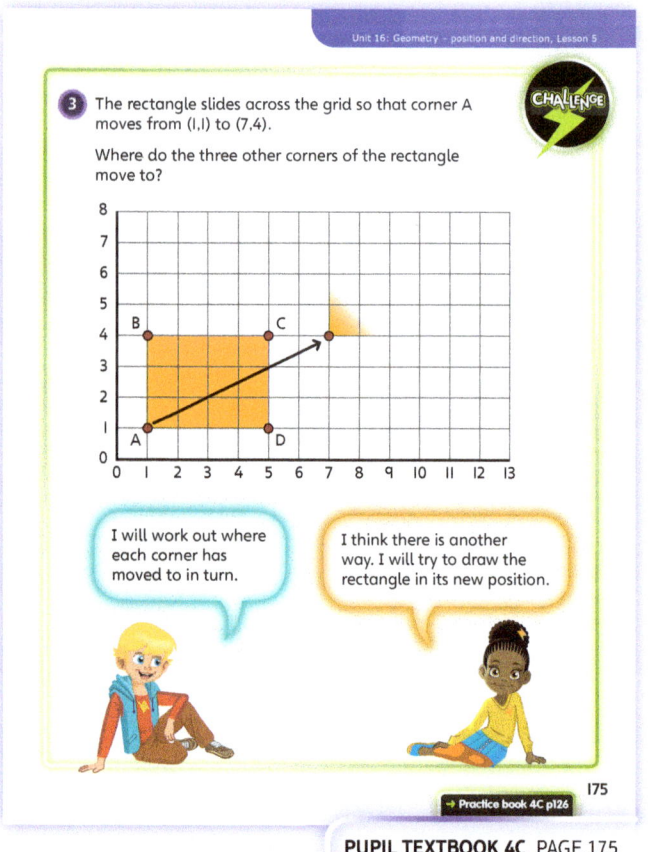

PUPIL TEXTBOOK 4C PAGE 174

PUPIL TEXTBOOK 4C PAGE 175

Unit 16: Geometry – position and direction, Lesson 5

Practice

WAYS OF WORKING Independent thinking

IN FOCUS Question ❶ provides further practice at working out the effects of translations on the coordinate grid. Make sure that children understand that these movements all start from the marked position of the boat – they are not intended to be carried out in succession.

STRENGTHEN Use question ❷ to check that children can follow a series of instructions to move to a succession of points on the coordinate grid. To give children additional practice, ask further questions based on this diagram, for example: *I am at (3,7), and I move 6 right and 3 down. Where am I positioned now?*

DEEPEN Ask children questions similar to question ❺, where the required translation will move the shape off the grid provided: for example, move 10 right and 8 up. Children will need to use reasoning to work out the coordinates of the translated shape.

THINK DIFFERENTLY Question ❹ requires children to use reasoning without the support of a grid showing the translation. In question ❹ b), they need to 'think backwards' – they are given the end point and a translation, and have to work out the start point.

ASSESSMENT CHECKPOINT Use questions ❶ and ❸ to assess whether children can carry out simple translations. Use question ❷ to check whether they can follow a series of translations around the coordinate grid.

ANSWERS Answers for the **Practice** part of the lesson can be found in the *Power Maths* online subscription.

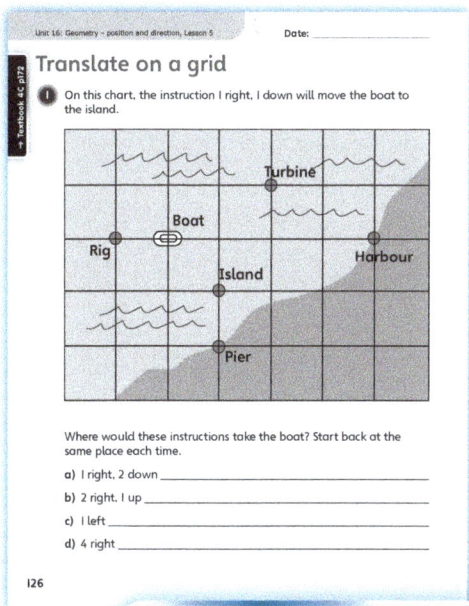

PUPIL PRACTICE BOOK 4C PAGE 126

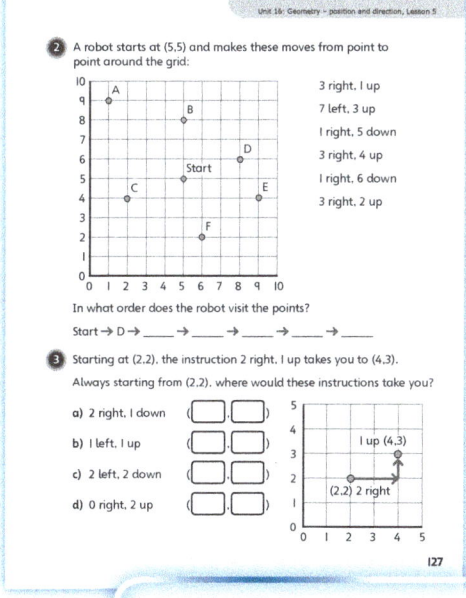

PUPIL PRACTICE BOOK 4C PAGE 127

Reflect

WAYS OF WORKING Independent thinking

IN FOCUS This question provides an opportunity to reflect on the effect of a translation on the coordinates of a point.

ASSESSMENT CHECKPOINT Check that children understand that the first coordinate will increase after a translation to the right and decrease after a translation to the left; and that the second coordinate will increase after a translation upwards and decrease after a translation downwards.

ANSWERS Answers for the **Reflect** part of the lesson can be found in the *Power Maths* online subscription.

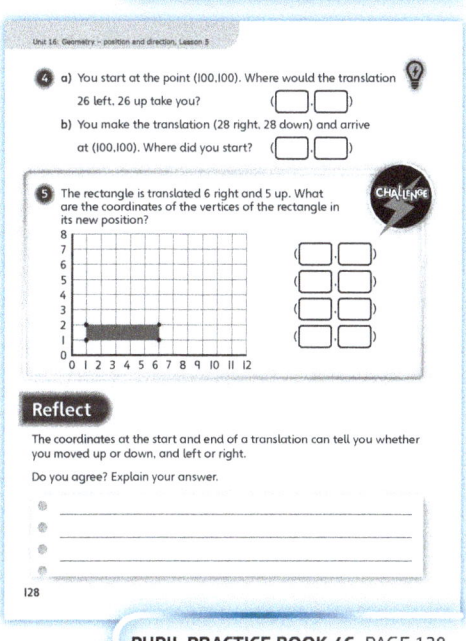

PUPIL PRACTICE BOOK 4C PAGE 128

After the lesson

- Are children able to determine the coordinates of the image of a point following a translation?

209

Unit 16: Geometry – position and direction, Lesson 6

Describe translation on a grid

Learning focus
In this lesson, children will work out the translations (expressed in the form 'right/left, up/down') that are needed to move from one position on the coordinate grid to another.

Before you teach
- Are children able to use coordinates to describe positions on a coordinate grid?
- Can they describe movements on the grid using translations (in words)?

NATIONAL CURRICULUM LINKS

Year 4 Geometry – position and direction

Describe movements between positions as translations of a given unit to the left/right and up/down.

ASSESSING MASTERY

Children can state the translation that is required to move between any two points on a coordinate grid, giving their answer in the form '3 left, 2 up'. They can apply their understanding to a range of grid systems (including maps, scale diagrams and abstract coordinate grids).

COMMON MISCONCEPTIONS

Children may not immediately see that the type of translation that they met in the previous lesson can be used in a range of real-life situations, such as describing the route between houses or other landmarks. Ask:
- *Does this grid look like the coordinate grids you used to translate shapes on in the previous lesson? What is the same? What is different?*

STRENGTHENING UNDERSTANDING

Make sure that children understand the change in emphasis between this lesson and the previous one. In the previous lesson they were working out the effect of a given translation, while in this lesson they find the translation that is needed to produce a certain movement. You may find it helpful to 'personalise' some of the questions in order to prompt children to think about the translations as an active and dynamic process of moving from one point to another. Ask: *If you were at this point A, and you wanted to move to this point B, what move would you need to make?*

GOING DEEPER

Challenge children who are more confident with the material in this lesson to investigate games where movements can be described using translations: for example chess, draughts or peg/Chinese solitaire. Ask them to find examples of cities laid out on a grid system, where translations might be a sensible way of describing journeys.

KEY LANGUAGE

In lesson: grid, move, journey, left, right, up, down

Other language to be used by the teacher: horizontal, vertical

STRUCTURES AND REPRESENTATIONS

Coordinate grid

RESOURCES

Optional: computer geometry package, chess board

 In the eTextbook of this lesson, you will find interactive links to a selection of teaching tools.

Quick recap

Look together at a simple map. Draw a small coordinate grid over the map and discuss possible translations to move from one place on the map to another.

Unit 16: Geometry – position and direction, Lesson 6

Discover

WAYS OF WORKING Pair work

ASK

- Question 1 a): *Have you ever seen a city with a grid of streets like this? Why would you design a city like this?*
- Question 1 a): *Suppose instead that Luis stays where he is and Jamilla travels to Luis instead. If Luis travels 2 squares right to Jamilla, how many squares left does Jamilla need to go to Luis? If Luis goes 1 square down to Jamilla, how many squares does Jamilla need to go up to Luis?*

IN FOCUS This question provides another example of a situation where a grid system might be used and where it would be important to be able to describe movements in a consistent way.

PRACTICAL TIPS It may be necessary to acknowledge that the system of crossroads used here will only provide approximate locations in a real-life context. For example, Luis's position at the crossroads of Second Street and First Avenue does not mean that he is standing in the middle of either of those roads. Despite this lack of complete precision, the grid system is useful and will enable the convenient location of places or (as in this example) people.

ANSWERS

Question 1 a): Jamilla could write her journey as '2 left, 1 up'.

Question 1 b): The journeys are the same: both are correct.

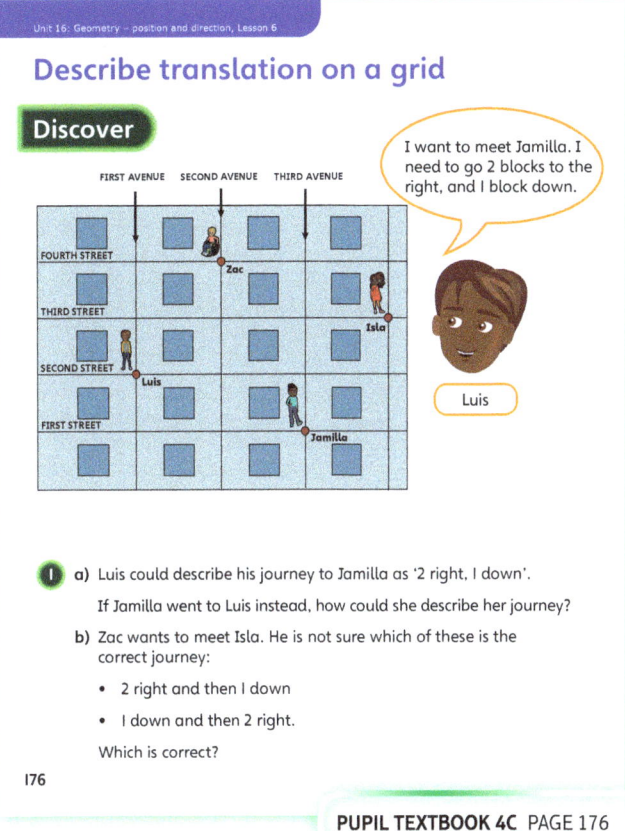

PUPIL TEXTBOOK 4C PAGE 176

Share

WAYS OF WORKING Whole class teacher led

ASK

- Question 1 a): *Why does Flo say that Jamilla's journey is the opposite of Luis's?*
- Question 1 b): *Can you explain why the two journeys are the same?*

IN FOCUS This activity encourages children to look at journeys as translations – that is, a movement of a particular distance in a particular direction, rather than between two specific points.

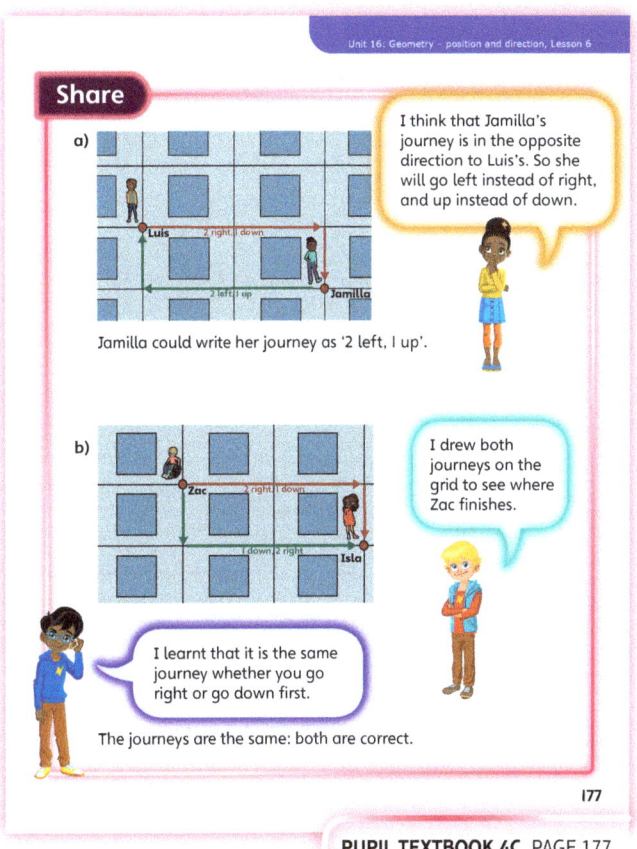

PUPIL TEXTBOOK 4C PAGE 177

211

Unit 16: Geometry – position and direction, Lesson 6

Think together

WAYS OF WORKING Whole class teacher led (I do, We do, You do)

ASK

- Question ① c): *Could Luis go down first and then across? Could he go across first and then down? Is there any other way he could travel to the cafe? Can you describe each route?*
- Question ③: *Where does this corner [point to one] of the rectangle move to? Do all the corners move by the same amount?*

IN FOCUS Question ① starts with translations that have both horizontal and vertical components, as in the **Share** activity. However, questions ① c) and d) are examples where one of the components is zero. Discuss whether children need to write 0 up/right, or whether they can omit this component. It is possible to leave the 'missing' component out completely (so, for example, a translation of 5 units right could simply be written as '5 right'), or include it with a zero value (for example, '5 right, 0 up'). Although the second option is slightly longer, it is more consistent and makes it clear than the missing component has not just been forgotten. In question ②, opposite journeys have been arranged side by side to encourage children to spot the pattern. Tell children to lay the answers out like this in their exercise books when answering the question.

STRENGTHEN Use question ② to reinforce the idea that a translation should be described in the order: distance left/right, then distance up/down. If children write the components in the 'wrong' order, the translation will, of course, still work – '2 up then 1 right' is equivalent to '1 right then 2 up'. However, it is sensible to be consistent and give the components in the same order as is used with coordinates; this will reinforce the idea of 'horizontal first'.

DEEPEN Challenge children to generalise the process for finding the 'opposite' of a journey (finding the translation B to A, given the translation A to B).

ASSESSMENT CHECKPOINT Use questions ① and ② to assess whether children can find the horizontal and vertical components of any translation on a grid. Check that children know what to do if one component is zero.

ANSWERS

Question ① a): 1 right, 2 down

Question ① b): The journeys are the same: both are correct.

Question ① c): 2 right, 1 down or 1 down, 2 right

Question ① d): 1 up

Question ②: A to B: 5 left, 2 up   B to A: 5 right, 2 down
A to C: 3 left, 3 down   C to A: 3 right, 3 up
B to C: 2 right, 5 down   C to B: 2 left, 5 up

Question ③: A: 2 right, 3 up
B: 4 right
C: 1 left, 2 down

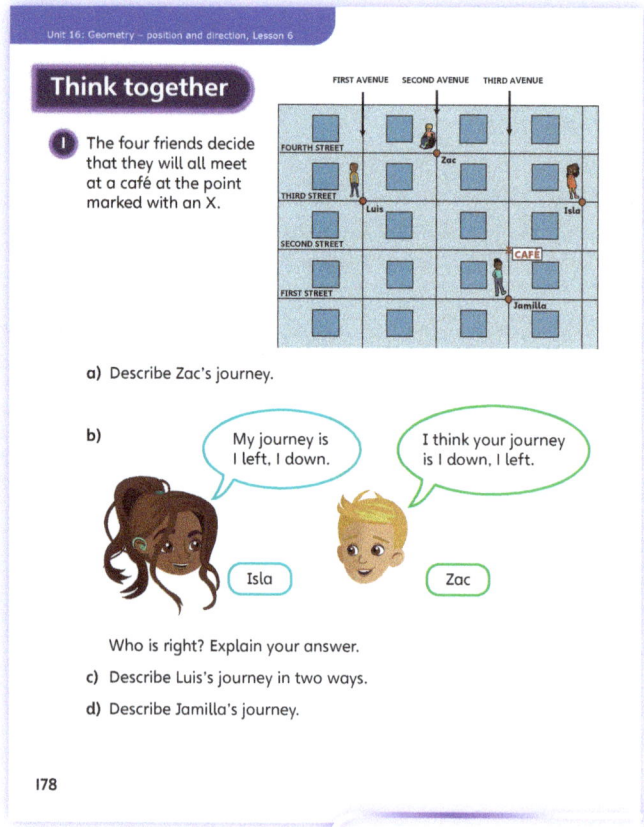

PUPIL TEXTBOOK 4C PAGE 178

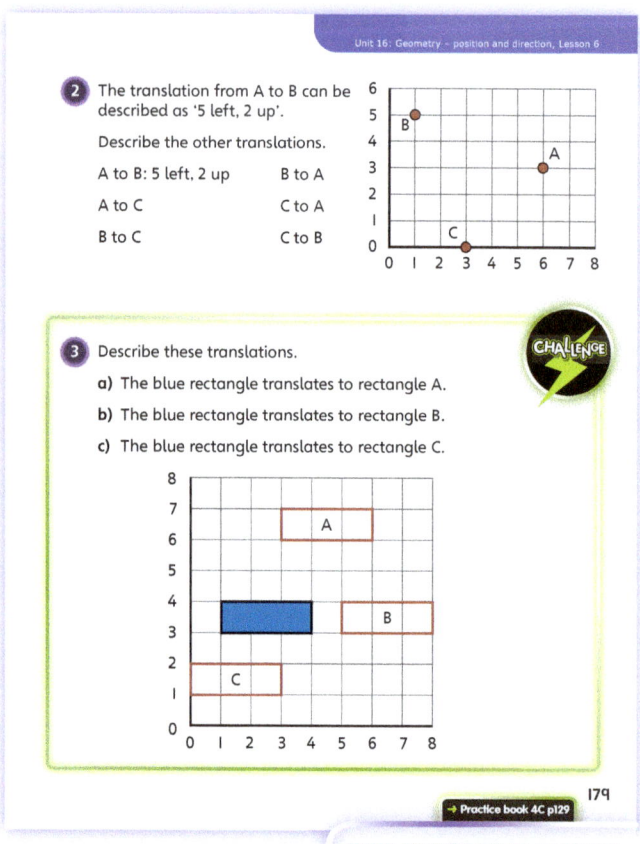

PUPIL TEXTBOOK 4C PAGE 179

Unit 16: Geometry – position and direction, Lesson 6

Practice

WAYS OF WORKING Independent thinking

IN FOCUS Question ❶ uses the same grid scenario that was introduced in the **Discover** exercise, but this time applies it in a different context: counting shelving blocks in a library. This helps to emphasise the idea that the same mathematical techniques can be applied to a variety of practical situations. Question ❹ makes the point that a translation can be described using numbers, even without knowing the coordinates of any of the points.

STRENGTHEN Draw a grid on the board and mark two points. Ask a child to trace the distance across and then up/down, describing what they are doing as they do so. Repeat for different pairs of points until children can confidently state the journey.

DEEPEN In question ❷, tell children to write down the coordinates of A, B and C. Ask them to look for patterns connecting the translation and the coordinates. If necessary, suggest that they look at the horizontal coordinates and translation components together, and do the same for the vertical coordinates and translation components.

ASSESSMENT CHECKPOINT Use question ❶ to assess whether children can describe translations on a grid system. Use question ❷ to check that they can apply this knowledge to a coordinate grid.

ANSWERS Answers for the **Practice** part of the lesson can be found in the *Power Maths* online subscription.

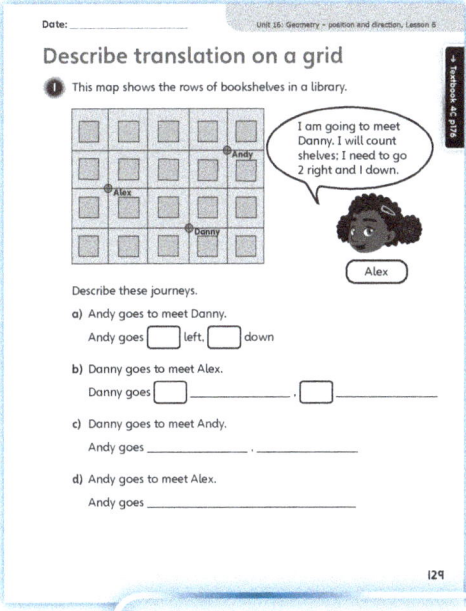

PUPIL PRACTICE BOOK 4C PAGE 129

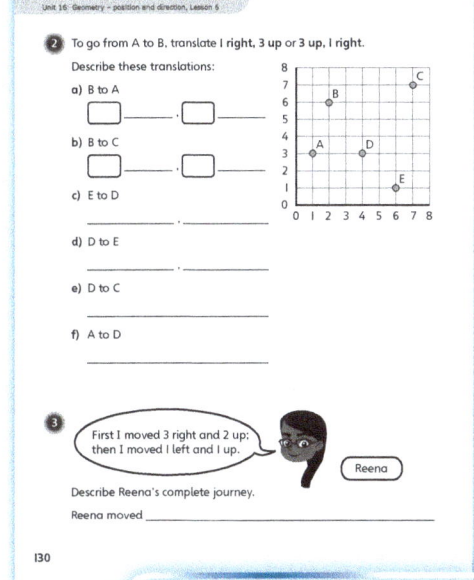

PUPIL PRACTICE BOOK 4C PAGE 130

Reflect

WAYS OF WORKING Independent thinking

IN FOCUS This question looks at the idea of finding the opposite of a translation – that is, the translation that takes us back to the starting point. This provides an opportunity to think about translations in a more abstract way, finding the opposite of any translation, rather than that of a particular case.

ASSESSMENT CHECKPOINT Check that children can describe the process of finding the opposite of a particular translation (using an example of their choice). A more complete explanation should describe a more general process (for example: *If it says 'up', change it to 'down'*).

ANSWERS Answers for the **Reflect** part of the lesson can be found in the *Power Maths* online subscription.

After the lesson ⏸

- Can children confidently find translations on a coordinate grid?

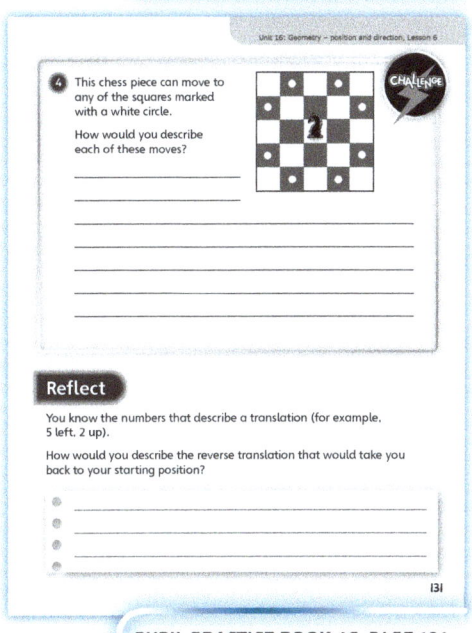

PUPIL PRACTICE BOOK 4C PAGE 131

Unit 16: Geometry – position and direction

End of unit check

Don't forget the unit assessment grid in your *Power Maths* online subscription.

WAYS OF WORKING Group work adult led

IN FOCUS

- Question ❶ provides an opportunity to check that children understand the order of coordinates when identifying and plotting points.
- Question ❷ allows children to show their understanding of how shapes can be plotted on a coordinate grid.
- Questions ❸ to ❺ enable children to demonstrate that they understand translations and the convention of right/left and up/down on a coordinate grid.
- Question ❻ is a SATs style question that provides children with an opportunity to give reasoning with their answer.

ANSWERS AND COMMENTARY

Children who have mastered the concepts in this unit can read, write and plot coordinates. They can use simple geometrical reasoning on a coordinate grid to draw patterns and complete shapes. They understand translations as movements on the coordinate grid; they can describe the result of making a translation in words, and they can find the translation required for the movement between given positions.

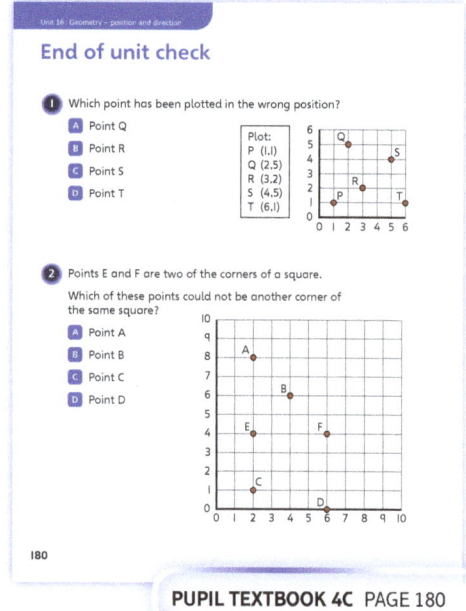

PUPIL TEXTBOOK 4C PAGE 180

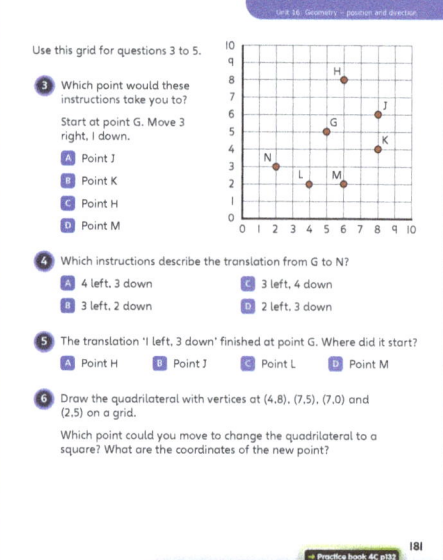

PUPIL TEXTBOOK 4C PAGE 181

Q	A	WRONG ANSWERS AND MISCONCEPTIONS	STRENGTHENING UNDERSTANDING
1	C	A, B or D suggest that the child has not fully grasped the correct order of coordinates.	Children who need further practice may benefit from using a computer graph plotting package. These packages are very easy to use and children could use them to check their answers.
2	C	B suggests that the child has not understood that E and F could be opposite corners. Answering D suggests that they think E and F must form the base of the square.	
3	B	A suggests that the child does not understand the direction of the components of a translation.	
4	B	A or C suggest the child has wrongly counted the number of squares in one or both directions. D suggests that they have identified the magnitude of the two movements, but mixed the vertical translation with the horizontal translation.	
5	A	C suggests that they have started at G instead of finishing there.	
6	(4,8) to (2,0)	Some children may plot the coordinates on the wrong axes.	

Unit 16: Geometry – position and direction

My journal

WAYS OF WORKING Independent thinking

ANSWERS AND COMMENTARY

Cards A and D will combine to give a translation of 5 right, 5 up, which represents the movement from (5,5) to (10,10).

There are several stages involved in this solution – children will first need to identify the required translation, and then use their number sense and understanding of relative movement to identify the required pair of cards.

Question 2 uses a game children may have played before, where they must place four counters in a row without being intercepted. This could also be used in the classroom, where children must announce the position of each counter as they play.

Kim should place her counter in position (4,5) to win the game.

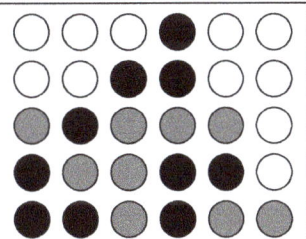

Power check

WAYS OF WORKING Independent thinking

ASK

- Had you seen maps and plans used to show where things are before you started this unit?
- Do you think you are better able to describe positions and movements after doing the unit?
- Can you explain how to write a coordinate?

Power play

WAYS OF WORKING Pair work

IN FOCUS Use the game of battleships to provide a further example of the use of coordinates in a practical context.

ANSWERS AND COMMENTARY In this **Power play**, children extend the idea of a set of coordinates to include naming positions on a game board using the conventions that have been developed in this unit – first give the direction across to the right, then the distance up. Model placing the battleships on a grid to emphasise that ships must not occupy adjacent points, including diagonally.

After the unit

- How will the work in this unit prepare children for more advanced work, where directed numbers are used to describe translations and coordinates in other quadrants?
- The order of coordinates is a good example of a mathematical convention – we could use any order, but we all need to agree on the same one. You may want to point out that, as children progress in mathematics, they will meet other conventions – such as using letters like *x* or *y* to represent an unknown number.

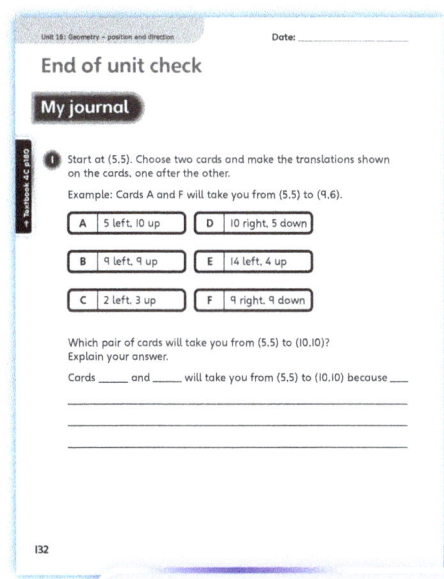

PUPIL PRACTICE BOOK 4C PAGE 132

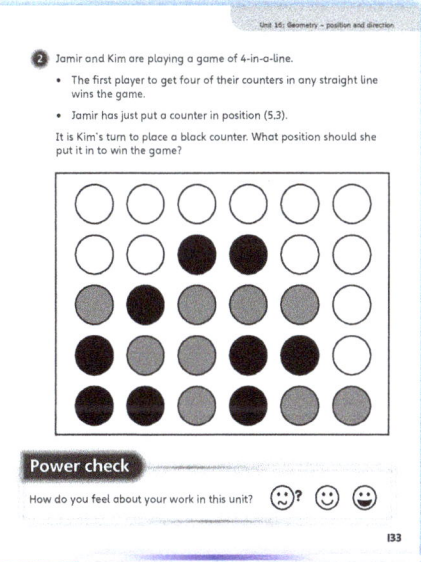

PUPIL PRACTICE BOOK 4C PAGE 133

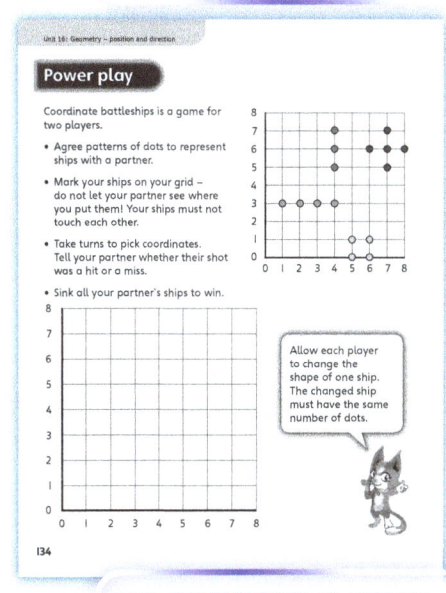

PUPIL PRACTICE BOOK 4C PAGE 134

Strengthen and **Deepen** activities for this unit can be found in the *Power Maths* online subscription.

Published by Pearson Education Limited, 80 Strand, London, WC2R 0RL.

www.pearsonschools.co.uk

Text © Pearson Education Limited 2018, 2023
Edited by Pearson and Florence Production Ltd
First edition edited by Pearson, Little Grey Cells Publishing Services and Haremi Ltd
Designed and typeset by Pearson and PDQ Digital Media Solutions Ltd
First edition designed and typeset by Kamae Design
Original illustrations © Pearson Education Limited 2018, 2023
Illustrated by Laura Arias, John Batten, Fran and David Brylewski, Diego Diaz, Nigel Dobbyn, Virginia Fontanabona, Adam Linley and Nadene Naude at Beehive Illustration; and Emily Skinner at Graham-Cameron Illustration
Images: The Royal Mint, 1971, 1982, 1990, 1992, 1997, 1998, 2017: 73, 75–77, 79–81, 83–85, 87–89, 91–93, 95–98; Bank of England: 73, 75–77, 79–81, 83–85, 87–89, 91–93, 95–98
Cover design by Pearson Education Ltd
Back cover illustration © Diego Diaz and Nadene Naude at Beehive Illustration

Series editor: Tony Staneff; Lead author: Josh Lury
Authors (first edition): Tony Staneff, Josh Lury, Neil Jarrett, Stephen Monaghan, Beth Smith and Paul Wrangle
Consultants (first edition): Professor Liu Jian and Professor Zhang Dan

The rights of Tony Staneff and Josh Lury to be identified as authors of this work have been asserted by them in accordance with the Copyright, Designs and Patents Act 1988.

This publication is protected by copyright, and permission should be obtained from the publisher prior to any prohibited reproduction, storage in a retrieval system, or transmission in any form or by any means, electronic, mechanical, photocopying, recording, or otherwise. For information regarding permissions, request forms and the appropriate contacts, please visit https://www.pearson.com/us/contact-us/permissions.html Pearson Education Limited Rights and Permissions Department.

First published 2018
This edition first published 2023

27 26 25 24 23
10 9 8 7 6 5 4 3 2 1

British Library Cataloguing in Publication Data
A catalogue record for this book is available from the British Library

ISBN 978 1 292 45058 2

Copyright notice
All rights reserved. No part of this publication may be reproduced in any form or by any means (including photocopying or storing it in any medium by electronic means and whether or not transiently or incidentally to some other use of this publication) without the written permission of the copyright owner, except in accordance with the provisions of the Copyright, Designs and Patents Act 1988 or under the terms of a licence issued by the Copyright Licensing Agency, Barnards Inn, 86 Fetter Lane, London EC4A 1EN (http://www.cla.co.uk). Applications for the copyright owner's written permission should be addressed to the publisher.

Printed in the UK by Ashford Press Ltd

For Power Maths online resources, go to:
www.activelearnprimary.co.uk

Note from the publisher
Pearson has robust editorial processes, including answer and fact checks, to ensure the accuracy of the content in this publication, and every effort is made to ensure this publication is free of errors. We are, however, only human, and occasionally errors do occur. Pearson is not liable for any misunderstandings that arise as a result of errors in this publication, but it is our priority to ensure that the content is accurate. If you spot an error, please do contact us at resourcescorrections@pearson.com so we can make sure it is corrected.